CONTESTI

JAN-WERNER MÜLLER is Professor of Politics at Princeton University, where he also directs the Project in the History of Political Thought at the Center for Human Values. His previous books include *A Dangerous Mind: Carl Schmitt in Post-War European Thought* (2003) and *Another Country: German Intellectuals, Unification and National Identity* (2000), both published by Yale.

CONTESTING DEMOCRACY

POLITICAL IDEAS IN
TWENTIETH-CENTURY EUROPE

JAN-WERNER MÜLLER

YALE UNIVERSITY PRESS
NEW HAVEN AND LONDON

For information about this and other Yale University Press publications, please contact:
U.S. Office: sales.press@yale.edu   www.yalebooks.com
Europe Office: sales@yaleup.co.uk   www.yalebooks.co.uk

Set in Minion Pro by IDSUK (DataConnection) Ltd
Printed in The United States of America

Library of Congress Cataloging-in-Publication Data

Müller, Jan-Werner, 1970-
    Contesting democracy : political thought in twentieth-century Europe /Jan-Werner Müller.
        p. cm.
    Includes bibliographical references and index.
    ISBN 978-0-300-11321-1 (cloth : alk. paper)
    1.   Democracy—Philosophy—History—20th century. 2.   Democracy—Europe—
History—20th century. 3.   Ideology—Europe—History—20th century. 4.   Political
science—Europe—History—20th century.   I. Title.
    JC421.M88 2011
    321.8—dc22

                                                                                2011011273

A catalogue record for this book is available from the British Library.

ISBN 978-0-300-19412-8 (pbk)

For Erika

Contents

List of Illustrations   *ix*

Introduction   1

1   The Molten Mass   7

2   Interwar Experiments: Making Peoples, Remaking Souls   49

3   Fascist Subjects: The Total State and *Volksgemeinschaft*   91

4   Reconstruction Thought: Self-Disciplined Democracies,
    'People's Democracies'   125

5   The New Time of Contestation: Towards a Fatherless Society   171

6   Antipolitics, and the Sense of an Ending   202

Notes   243

Index   273

Acknowledgements   279

Illustrations

1 Max Weber and Ernst Toller at a conference in Burg Lauenstein, Thuringia, 1917. bpk–images, Berlin.
2 Karl Ehn's, Karl-Marx-Hof (1927–30), Heiligenstädter Strasse, Vienna. © Österreichische Nationalbibliothek, Vienna, 116.926-B/C.
3 'Commissar Lukács thanks the proletariat for its help in overcoming the counter-revolution.' Still from a newsreel by Red Reportage Films. Hungarian Film Institute.
4 'Soviet Constitution. Article 1: The Union of Soviet Socialist Republics is a Socialist State of Workers and Peasants' by El Lissitzky and Sophie Küppers, fold-out poster from *USSR in Construction*, nos 9–12 (September–December 1937). Getty Research Institute, Los Angeles (87-S197).
5 Giovanni Treccani, Benito Mussolini, Calogero Tumminelli, Giovanni Gentile and Ugo Spirito at the inauguration of the Italian Encyclopaedia of Science, Letters, and Arts (*Enciclopedia Treccani*), 1933. Centro Documentale Lampi Neri.
6 Pope Paul VI consults with Jacques Maritain about the Second Vatican Council, 1964. Archives du Cercle d'Etudes, J. et R. Maritain, Kolbsheim, France.
7 'Nous sommes tous des juifs et des allemandes', poster by Atelier Populaire, Paris (1988 reprint of 1968 original). International Institute of Social History, Amsterdam.
8 Herbert Marcuse at an event at the Freie Universität Berlin, 1967. Ullstein Bild, Berlin.
9 Jean-Paul Sartre, André Glucksmann and Raymond Aron, Palais de l'Elysée, 26 June 1979. © Richard Melloul/Sygma/CORBIS.
10 Jean-Paul Sartre and Michel Foucault at a demonstration in the Goutte d'Or quartier, Paris, 1971. Photograph by Gerard Aimé/Rapho/Gamma, Camera Press, London.

Introduction

. . . it is less the facts that I am looking for than the traces of the movement of ideas and sentiments. It is that above all that I want to paint. . . . the difficulties are immense. The one that most troubles my mind comes from the mixture of history properly so called with historical philosophy. I still do not see how to mix these two things and yet, they must be mixed, for one could say that the first is the canvas and the second the color, and that it is necessary to have both at the same time in order to do the picture.

Alexis de Tocqueville

Have you forgotten the other bankruptcies? What was Christianity doing in the various catastrophes of society? What became of Liberalism? What has Conservatism produced, in either its enlightened or its reactionary form? . . . If we are indeed honestly to weigh out the bankruptcies of ideology, we shall have a long task ahead of us.

Victor Serge

Democracy has developed wherever the abstract appeal of the ideologue and the concrete experimentation of the practical man have worked together.

A. D. Lindsay

THE HISTORIAN of ideas Isaiah Berlin once observed: 'I have lived through most of the twentieth century without, I must add, suffering personal hardship. I remember it only as the most terrible century in Western history.'[1] The century was also one in which political ideas seemed to play an exceptionally important role – so much so that contemporaries connected them directly to the catastrophes and cataclysms through which they were living. This belief in the vast influence of ideas did not depend on political allegiance: the Polish poet (and anti-Communist) Czesław Miłosz pointed out that during the mid-twentieth century 'the inhabitants of many European countries came, in general unpleasantly, to the realization that their fate could be influenced directly by intricate and abstruse books of philosophy'.[2] Around the same time the Soviet leader Nikita Khrushchev remarked matter-of-factly of the uprising against the Soviets in socialist Hungary: 'None of this would have happened if a couple of writers had been shot in time.'

Consequently, the twentieth century is often interpreted as, above all, an 'age of ideologies'. From such a perspective, ideologies are understood as forms of passionate, even fanatical belief in ideas and blueprints for the betterment of society.[3] The story then tends to go like this: Europeans were more or less inexplicably seized by an ideological fever in or about 1917, the date of the Russian Revolution, an affliction from which they were cured only in 1991 or so, with the fall of the Soviet empire and the apparent triumph of liberal democracy over both fascism and Communism.

Yet seeing the twentieth century simply as an age of irrational extremes or even as an 'age of hatred' means failing to understand that ordinary men and women – and not just intellectuals and political leaders – saw many of the ideologies contained in abstruse books (and the institutions that were justified with their help) as real answers to their problems. True, ideologies were also expected to provide meaning, even redemption, so calling some of them 'political religions' or, with Churchill, 'non-God religions' is justified. But many of the institutions created in their name made a further promise to function much better than those of liberalism, which in the eyes of many Europeans seemed like a hopelessly outdated relic of the nineteenth century. In retrospect, a sentence such as 'Fascism came into being to meet serious problems of politics in post-war Italy' – uttered by the Fascist philosopher Giovanni Gentile in the American magazine *Foreign Affairs* in 1927 – seems banal (and, at the same time, a repulsive understatement).[4] But any account which completely leaves out the dimension of ideologies as making claims to problem-solving and successful institutional experimentation misses one of their essential aspects.[5] We need to restore a sense of why and how ideologies could have been attractive in this way – without thereby making any excuses, of course. Few clichés have done more harm to the serious study of the history of ideas than *tout comprendre c'est tout pardonner*.[6]

To gain this kind of understanding, we cannot rest content with existing accounts of the development of high political philosophy during the European twentieth century. Rather, we ought to be concerned with what happens *in between* more or less academic political thought on the one hand and, on the other, the creation (and destruction) of political institutions. In short, we must grasp the political thought that mattered politically, the areas where, as the British scholar A. D. Lindsay once put it, the work of the 'abstract ideologue' and practical experimentation come together.[7]

Consequently, this essay will take a particularly close look at what one might call 'in-between figures': statesmen-philosophers, public lawyers, constitutional advisers, the curious and at first sight contradictory phenomenon of 'bureaucrats with visions', philosophers close to political parties and movements, as well as what Friedrich von Hayek once referred to as 'second-hand dealers in ideas'.[8] Describing them in this way was no sign of contempt: Hayek thought they were often much more important than many original producers of ideas. And in fact, there was a particular need for such dealers during an era when 'mass democracy' came into its own, because mass democracy, among other things, imposed the need for what we might call mass justification (or mass legitimation) – the need, that is, to justify forms of rule and institutions, but also, less obviously, the creation of entirely new political subjects, such as a 'purified nation' or a people putting its trust in a single socialist 'vanguard party'.[9] Once traditional conceptions of legitimacy as well as the principles of dynastic descent had become widely discredited – as they had been after the First World War at the latest – the justifications for political rule had to become different.

The point is not that there was no need for public justification before 1919 or so – of course there was. But in the twentieth century it had to become both more extensive and more explicit. This was even the case when legitimacy was supposed to be grounded in the personal charisma of a leader, or rely on a functioning state bureaucracy capable of delivering what citizens desired: neither charisma nor welfare provision speaks for or explains itself. The new pressure for public justification was especially evident with right-wing regimes which sought to rule in the name of tradition, as well as with the royal dictatorships which flourished in interwar Europe in particular: tradition and monarchical legitimacy were no longer understood to be self-evident or habitually accepted – they had to be articulated and actively promoted. There was simply no way back from the demands for mass political justification.

The sense that the twentieth century was different, that it was an age of compulsive doctrine production (and doctrine consumption) was acutely shared by those who lived through it. The British philosopher Michael Oakeshott, surveying *The Social and Political Doctrines of Contemporary Europe* in the late 1930s, observed:

> We live in an age of self-conscious communities. Even the crudest of the regimes of contemporary Europe, the regime which, admittedly, owes least to

a systematically thought-out doctrine, the Fascist regime in Italy, appears to value self-righteousness enough to join with the others in claiming a doctrine of its own. Opportunism has suffered the emasculation of being converted into a principle; we have lost not only the candour of Machiavelli but also even the candour of the *Anti-Machiavel*.[10]

In a very specific sense, then, the European twentieth century, after the First World War, was an age of democracy. Not all European states had become democratic. On the contrary, many of the newly established democracies were destroyed during the 1920s and 1930s, in the eyes of many Europeans making forms of dictatorship seem the obvious way for the future. But even the political experiments that stridently defined themselves against liberal parliamentary democracy – state socialism as it actually existed and the fully Communist society it promised on the one hand, and fascism on the other – played on the register of democratic values. And sometimes they claimed that they were the real thing: Gentile, for instance, explained to his American readers that 'the Fascist State . . . is a people's state, and, as such, the democratic state *par excellence*'.[11]

To be sure, they were not democracies by any stretch – though, as we will see later on, many defenders of these regimes did engage in strenuous conceptual stretching precisely to make that claim plausible. But both promised fully to realize values commonly associated with democracy: equality, especially a form of equality more substantive than formal equality before the law; genuine inclusion in a political community; and real, ongoing participation in politics, not least to create a collective political subject – a purified nation, or a socialist people – capable of mastering a common fate.[12] This might sound rather abstract. But passion for such values played an important role in animating the major departures from liberal democracy. Not to recognize this is historically naive; it also constitutes a form of liberal complacency which we – which is primarily to say we in the West – can ill afford.

Making this point is not to malign democracy. It actually underlines the power of democratic ideas. As the Austrian jurist Hans Kelsen, commenting on the employment by Communist theorists of democratic vocabularies, put it at mid-century: 'it seems that the symbol of democracy has assumed such a generally recognized value that the substance of democracy cannot be abandoned without maintaining the symbol'.[13] Though few people, to put it mildly, would nowadays defend the Nazis' 'Germanic democracy' or the post-war Eastern European 'people's democracies', it is not superfluous to say that most of the 'democratic promises' of the extreme anti-liberal regimes were disingenuous (or, at the very least, dysfunctional in practice). But it is also important to ask why these regimes felt compelled to make these promises in the first place. Their rhetoric points to the larger constraints in an age when demands for participation could simply no longer be ignored, when claims to rule had to employ a political vocabulary that was at least partly shared with liberal democracy: an age, in short, when political argument was crucially about contesting the meaning of democracy.

More important still for the present: we can make sense of the particular character of the democracies erected in Western Europe after 1945 only if we understand that they were constructed with an eye both to the immediate fascist past and to the claims their Eastern rivals were making to embody true democracy. These post-war democracies were defined not just in stark contrast with state terror or aggressive nationalism, but in opposition to the totalitarian notion of unconstrained historical action by collective political subjects, such as the Nazi *Volksgemeinschaft*.

It is not wrong, but historically far too unspecific, to argue that the second half of the twentieth century saw 'the return of democracy' or 'the return of liberalism', first in most of Western Europe and then in Southern and Eastern Europe. Rather, Europeans created something new, a democracy that was highly constrained (mostly by unelected institutions, such as constitutional courts). The constitutionalist ethos that came with such democracies was positively hostile to ideals of unlimited popular sovereignty, as well as the 'people's democracies' and later 'socialist democracies' in the East, which in theory remained based on the notion of a collective (socialist) subject mastering history. It is often forgotten that this new set of institutions was not justified by the inherited political languages of liberalism – because liberalism was widely seen as having paved the way for the totalitarian nightmares of the century in the first place. Two particularly important post-war innovations – the democratic welfare state and the European Community – have to be understood in the same light: the former was intended to prevent a return to fascism (competition with the East was an important but ultimately secondary concern) by providing citizens with security or even, as the British Labour politician Nye Bevan once put it, with 'serenity'.[15] European integration, on the other hand, was meant to place further constraints on nation-state democracies through unelected institutions.

This account questions that there ever was a golden age for democracy, and for Social Democracy in particular, in the years after the Second World War. Outside Britain (and Scandinavia, a special case, as I will argue in Chapter 2), the Western European post-war settlement was the work, if anything, of moderate conservative forces, primarily Christian Democracy. If one had to choose one movement in ideas and party politics that has created the political world in which Europeans still live today, the answer has to be Christian Democracy. This may come as a surprise to all those who see Europe as the blessed (or, as the case may be, benighted) island of secularism in our world. Clearly, it helped that Christian Democracy could present itself simultaneously as the party of anti-Communism par excellence and as a movement that retained connections to a real religion – as opposed to the fake political religion of fascism.

The new post-war form of democracy was eventually confronted with two major challenges: the rebellion that is often abbreviated as '1968' and the calls to scale back the state and free up both the market and the individual, which are now commonly summed up as 'neoliberalism'. As has often been pointed out, the supposed revolution of 1968 might have been rooted in a profound crisis of representation (of youth, of women, of gays), but it left political institutions largely unchanged. Consequently, one may well wonder if '68 deserves a prominent place in accounts of twentieth-century European political thought. It does, because it posed a radical challenge to the post-war constitutional settlement, and to its core principles of a constrained democracy. In the long run, the aftermath of '68 proved that the constitutional settlement was compatible with profound social, moral and ultimately also political changes: the end of cultures of deference and hierarchy, whether in families or universities; and, above all, women (and gays) acquiring power over their own bodies.

Neoliberalism offered a plausible response to what was often called the 'crisis of governability' in the 1970s. It undoubtedly had a major impact on Margaret Thatcher's Britain. But its original political – and moral – programme had been about much more than weakening trade unions and deregulating markets (something that Thatcher herself openly acknowledged when she explained in 1983 that 'economics are the method; the object is to change the heart and soul').[16] A thinker like Hayek would have liked to see a radically new constitutional settlement – and that did not happen either.

This is no reason to be triumphant about the West European post-war constitutional settlement (which was essentially extended eastwards after 1989) and the ideas that animated it. Rather, historical awareness of how Europeans got there might help at least a little in dispelling the comforting illusion that liberal democracy is necessarily the default position of Europe, or of the West more broadly.

CHAPTER 1

The Molten Mass

The whole state of society is more or less molten and you can stamp upon that molten mass almost anything as long as you do it with firmness and determination.

David Lloyd George, 1917

Today, the state enjoys its beatification. We turn to it almost blindly in sure faith that its way spells salvation.

Harold Laski, 1917

Today the relation between the state and violence is an especially intimate one.

Max Weber, 1919

Nowadays, a sure sign of the power of democratic ideology is the fact that so many people pretend to accept it. A sure sign of the decadence of aristocratic ideology is that it has no hypocritical defenders at all.

Vilfredo Pareto, 1920

The only meaning I can see in the word 'people' is 'mixture'; if you substitute for the word 'people' the words 'number' and 'mixture', you will get some very odd terms . . . 'the sovereign mixture', 'the will of the mixture', etc.

Paul Valéry

A T Christmas 1918 Max Weber had recently returned from Berlin to Munich, only to find himself in the midst of a 'bloody carnival'. In the capital he had played a prominent role in deliberations about a new German constitution. This was somewhat surprising: for almost twenty years, the Heidelberg professor had suffered from various illnesses and was hardly seen in public. In the last two years of the First World War, however, he had written a series of polemical articles and tried desperately to act as a political educator of the German nation. He had also hoped to stand for the constitutional assembly and, eventually, parliament. But it was clear now that the liberal party with which he had associated himself would always nominate more professional politicians, and not someone widely considered an irascible academic. Weber could not have had high hopes either that the constitution drafters would follow any of his recommendations.

A few months earlier, Weber had been asked by a student society at Munich University whether he would deliver a lecture on 'Politics as a Vocation' for them, in a series where he had already given one talk on 'Academia as a Vocation' in 1917. Weber had been reluctant, but apparently, when he learnt that the students were considering Kurt Eisner as an alternative, he agreed. Eisner, a freelance journalist and life-long socialist, had declared a republic in Bavaria on 8 November 1918, even before the German Kaiser had abdicated in Berlin – and thereby precipitated what Weber was to call the 'bloody carnival' of revolution. He had only contempt for a character like Eisner: in Weber's estimation the man was a littérateur dabbling in politics, a demagogue in love with his own rhetoric, but also the victim of his very short-term success – which, in Weber's view, the head of the Bavarian council republic mistook for genuinely political success when it was merely literary: rather than Eisner actually projecting authority (or just power), romantic hopes for redemption through politics were projected on to a man who, after all, was just a hack.

Weber held that there were three bases of legitimating rule: there was tradition, where men and women obeyed on the basis of precedent; there were formal legal procedures, so that law was judged to be legitimate if it had passed through the correct channels and could be executed by bureaucrats *sine ira et studio*; and, finally, there was personal charisma, which had an affinity with revolutionary politics.[1] The latter term had originated in the sphere of religion and initially designated the qualities of prophets: 'it is written . . . but I say unto you'. According to Weber, it could be applied generally to leaders who seemed to have been graced with special gifts and who therefore inspired fervent devotion and deep trust among their followers. Eisner, Weber thought, was this last type, and a dangerous variety. And so rather than have the self-declared head of the new Bavarian *Volksstaat* seduce the students with his high-flying socialist dreams, he would offer some hard-won lessons in political realism.

On 28 January 1919 Weber began what would turn out to be the most famous single lecture in the history of political thought: 'Politik als Beruf', with 'Beruf' referring to both profession and a sense of personal calling. Weber did not exactly start off on a high note:

This lecture ... will necessarily disappoint you ... You will instinctively expect me to take a position on problems of the moment. But that will be the case only in a purely formal way ... when I shall raise certain questions concerning the significance of political activity in the whole conduct of life. In today's lecture, all questions that refer to *which* policy ... one should adopt must be eliminated. For such questions have nothing to do with our general question ...[2]

What was this 'general question'? In Weber's lecture it was: what is politics as a profession or a vocation? But, more broadly speaking, the question was how possible were responsible political action and stable liberal regimes in what Weber called a disenchanted world, a world in which religion, metaphysics and other sources of meaning – especially collective meaning – seemed all to have been placed in doubt. Weber was convinced that traditional legitimacy – based on precedent and prescription – was disappearing, and that Europeans had entered the democratic age for good. The charisma of monarchs – not so much a personal quality as what Weber called 'the charisma of blood', passed down from one generation to the next, but also attaching to the institution itself – had been dispelled by the disasters of a war during which monarchs had generally revealed themselves as incompetent. What had also disappeared was the belief that members of different nationalities and religions could live peacefully together in one political association like the Habsburg Empire, watched over by a revered Kaiser in whom his subjects felt some genuine trust. Weber was sure that democracy could be realized only within homogeneous nation-states. And there was no way back from democracy now. In Weber's mind, disenchantment and democracy went together; they were both peculiar to the path of development that the West had taken. Dealing with them responsibly posed the greatest political challenge to Europeans in the first decades of the twentieth century.

The Age of Security (for Some)

To understand how European political thought developed in the twentieth century, it helps to understand how it had developed in the nineteenth – and which of its underlying assumptions no longer seemed credible in the period after the First World War. Weber had been shaped by the high tide of nineteenth-century liberalism, and what the Austrian writer Stefan Zweig in retrospect called 'the golden Age of Security' (which, he added, had also been the golden age of insurance policies). Writing from the vantage point of exile in Brazil in 1942 (and about to take his own life), Zweig remembered that in those pre-war years 'everything radical, everything violent seemed impossible in an age of reason'. People of his generation, those who had been young before the First World War, had felt an incomparable optimism and trust in the world, a world which they thought was well on the way to ever more freedom as well as 'true cosmopolitanism'.[3]

This age of reason and security had rested on three central ideas (or sometimes just moral intuitions) which had solidified in particular political and economic institutions. Security had meant, to begin with, the absence of war and other kinds of large-scale violence (at least when seen from Vienna or somewhere else safely removed from the Balkans, to say nothing of the world outside Europe). Fewer Europeans died in combat in the nineteenth century than in the eighteenth; and the period 1871 to 1914 proved to be the longest stretch of intra-European peace up to that point in history (the most obvious exception, when the rest of the globe is taken into account, was Great Britain – which was almost always at war somewhere).[4]

Security in the sense of international peace was not thought to be just a lucky break for Europeans; it seemed to be connected to the increasing inter-dependence of European states and empires through the circulation of money, goods – and people. The decades before the First World War saw what has sometimes been called a 'first wave of globalization'. The *Manchester Guardian* announced that 'space has been eliminated' and that 'frontiers no longer exist'.[5] It was a golden age of internationalism in the sense of free trade, international co-operation in setting standards and pooling sovereignty for economic benefits: there was, for instance, the European Postal Union, the Scandinavian and Latin monetary unions; above all, there was the gold standard linking all major currencies. But there was also a sense – and a reality – of freedom of movement and consequently large waves of migration. As Zweig's contemporary Felix Somary, a banker born in fin-de-siècle Vienna, pointed out: 'all barriers, as well as the words "hostage" and "exile", seemed to us to belong to a distant age which had long been overcome'.[6] Travel seemed easy; in fact, in the late nineteenth century, only Turkey and Russia had passport controls, and they regulated internal movement only (in the eyes of many observers, it was not an accident that, along with Montenegro, these were the only countries which, by 1900, still had no parliaments). The German industrialist and politician Walther Rathenau observed in 1912 that never before had the European peoples been so close to each other, visited each other so much and known each other so well.

Freedom of movement was just one aspect of a general liberal belief in increasing liberty for everyone, especially if that term primarily meant 'freedom from the state'. As the British historian A. J. P. Taylor was to put it, until August 1914 'a sensible, law-abiding Englishman could pass through life and hardly notice the existence of the state, beyond the post office and the policeman'. Citizens could live where they liked; they needed neither identity cards nor passports; and, not least, they could buy foreign currency (and goods) to their hearts' content.[7] John Maynard Keynes added that the Englishman 'regarded this state of affairs as normal, certain, and permanent, and any deviation from it as aberrant, scandalous and avoidable'. And he went on: 'The projects and politics of militarism and imperialism, of racial and cultural rivalries . . . were little more than the amusements of his daily newspaper, and appeared to exercise almost no influence at all on the daily course of social and economic life, the internationalization of which was nearly complete in practice.'[8]

The freedom for things and people to move across borders and the self-determination of societies were not seen by European liberals as incompatible. As has often been pointed out, up until the First World War there existed a by and large unbroken belief in progress, especially scientific progress; what has been less noticed was an equally firm and fundamental belief among liberals that individual and collective self-determination could go together harmoniously.

But 'collective self-determination' had a very limited meaning: the state, if it played any major role at all, was to be at the service of society; and society in turn could best express what it needed and wanted in parliaments run by gentlemen with a sense of the common good: the Age of Security was also the Age of Parliamentarism. To be sure, only those parts of society could express themselves which actually had the vote – and, in most European countries, suffrage remained heavily restricted. Liberals assumed that over time more and more people would qualify for it through education and property; those without either could not be trusted with choosing governments, as they were likely to destroy the very foundations on which the Age of Security rested.[9] Full democratization thus always remained a *theoretical* possibility for liberals, though one likely to be far off in the future.

But not everybody wanted to wait until liberals deemed the people to be rich or well read enough to participate in politics. Across Europe the late nineteenth century and the early twentieth century saw a series of struggles over the franchise and the nature of political representation. Women demanded the vote, first with peaceful demonstrations, then with attacks on property, then with attacks on themselves, that is to say hunger strikes. The vote was to be uncoupled from income; an officially unequal power distribution like Prussia's three-tier system – which made political power depend on the capacity to pay taxes – seemed increasingly scandalous. Ethnic groups wanted their say in the large multinational empires. And ruling elites with hereditary political privileges came under attack – as in the epic battles over the role of the House of Lords in Britain, which resulted in the aristocrats' disempowerment in 1911.

Both liberal and conservative elites thought they could master what increasingly looked like a comprehensive crisis in representation – in terms both of who was represented and of what kinds of political claims could be made and reconciled within the political system as it was.[10] Italy proved a paradigmatic example: the liberals there gambled that they could slowly extend the franchise and yet contain social conflict through the strategy of *trasformismo*: drawing ever more groups into the system by making them share some power – while, more importantly, rewarding them with spoils (and inducing them to moderate their claims). So they gave the vote to peasants by removing literacy requirements, betting that the peasants would stay politically quiescent or at least controllable. As Giovanni Giolitti, a liberal and past-master of *trasformismo* (and in fact originator of the word), explained in 1901: 'No one should deceive himself into thinking that the lower classes can be prevented from acquiring their share of economic and political influence. The friends of existing institutions have one duty above all: it is persuading these lower classes, with facts, that they have more to hope from existing institutions than from any dreams of the future.'[11] This kind of transformation by co-optation had little to do with anything like responsible cabinet government through a cohesive Liberal Party in the way it became consolidated in Britain, for example – in fact, there was no Italian liberal party, just a collection of soi-disant liberal notables, until the early 1920s.

In practice, extending the franchise and empowering parliaments did not proceed in a neat parallel.[12] And neither did the professionalization of parliaments. While legislatures in general were becoming more effective in controlling executives, they were not necessarily populated by ever more specialized politicians. Indeed countries on the European periphery were nominally governed by liberal legislatures, but de facto controlled by notables and gentlemen-administrators who built ad hoc coalitions to get themselves elected – and, as in Italy, used their local power to keep newly enfranchised groups under control. Nonetheless, while discontent with the kind of democracy on offer in even the most advanced European countries simmered, there remained a sense that claims for participation would be addressed in an orderly and peaceful way; they did not fundamentally seem to threaten the Age of Security.

In addition to hopes for continuing peace and progress, there was a third intuition underlying the age: what one might call a belief in the eventual Europeanization of the world, in the sense of European dominance of the world and global acceptance of Europe's civilization as a model.[13] Europeans, or so it was assumed, ruled other parts of the world for their own good, not for the benefit of the 'old continent'. As the French writer Paul Valéry put it: 'Wherever that [European] Mind prevails, there we witness . . . the maximum of *labor*, *capital*, and *production*, the maximum of *ambition* and *power*, the maximum *transformation* of *external Nature*, and the maximum of *relations* and *exchanges*.'[14] This unashamed superiority complex of what Valéry called *Homo europaeus* could persist not least because others were always ready to acknowledge Europe's pre-eminence. As William James lamented, 'it seems the natural thing for us to listen whilst the Europeans talk. The contrary habit, of talking while the European listens, we have not yet acquired.'[15]

Thus, whatever particular political challenges the Age of Security were throwing up, it seemed they could be contained in a Europe understood as a secure order built on nation-states, all liberalizing and even democratizing (though at different speeds). There were no dictators in pre-war Europe. Leonard Woolf remarked: 'It seemed as though human beings might really be on the brink of becoming civilized.'

However, there was also a quite different, not quite so liberal (let alone democratic) way of understanding the age. In fact, Woolf, a sentence after commenting on the almost complete process of civilization, conceded that 'the forces of barbarism and reaction were still there' (although clearly in 'retreat').[16] And indeed an impartial observer in 1911 (the year Woolf was writing about) might easily have concluded that the most likely future scenario was not liberal nation-states in a secure international order: it was great, rival empires which were the most obvious feature of the world scene at the beginning of the century. In fact, empire could appear as the dominant, perhaps even the obvious way in which human beings organized themselves. There were the powerful Russian and German empires; and the less powerful Habsburg and Ottoman ones; further afield, there was China, which was under the sway of European powers, but could still count as an empire in its own right. Then there were the large colonial empires of France and Great Britain, not to forget the colonial empires of the smaller West European countries such as Belgium, Portugal and the Netherlands. Belgium, for instance, had an empire eighty times its own size (Britain's by 1914 was 140 times its own size). Some countries, it seemed, could only see themselves in this imperial form: the Germans spoke of themselves as a *Reichsvolk* with a universal calling as a *Weltvolk*; Count Sergei Witte, prime minister under Nicholas II, claimed that there was no such thing as Russia, just a Russian empire.[17]

An impartial observer might also have concluded that rather than empires and nation-states being the two obvious rival political forms, in reality two types of empire were competing for pre-eminence: on the one hand, what appeared like old, established nation-states with vast colonial overseas ventures (and attendant 'civilizing missions'); on the other, continental – that is to say, large land-mass – empires. The difference can be summed up as having an empire as opposed to being an empire.[18] The latter type was almost always highly authoritarian and featured strong religious overtones in its self-presentation: the Ottoman Empire obviously contained the Caliphate, but there was also the conception of Holy Russia as the 'Third Rome', or the notion of the newly unified Germans as inheritors of the Holy Roman Empire.[19] In all these continental empires strong movements were pushing for expansion: the Pan-Slavic movement, the All-German movement and the Pan-Turanians in the Ottoman Empire – again, with all of them employing religious languages to justify monarchy and empire. This fact did not go unnoticed by the enemies of empire. Tomáš Masaryk, philosopher, politician and eventually first president of Czechoslovakia, pointed out that 'aristocracy (oligarchy-monarchism), as it developed historically, is based on theocracy, on religion and church'.[20]

The competition between the nation-state as a political form and the two different types of empires was played out most obviously in the very heart of Europe: Germany's unification in 1871 had at least partially been justified on nationalist principles. Yet Germany was a state that called itself an empire, and not without reason: it had been unified in a quasi-imperial manner by Prussia and contained substantial ethnic minorities; like all empires, it seemed to have fuzzy frontiers (especially in the east with Poland), rather than clearly demarcated borders. Most importantly, it was acting simultaneously like a continental empire and like a nation-state with colonialist ambitions. Imperialist policies seemed to be pursued precisely in order to achieve full nationhood domestically: *Weltpolitik* served *Innenpolitik* in a polity that was more powerful than its neighbours and yet not powerful enough to dominate them. These German peculiarities increasingly became a source of instability. In fact, Germany was to remain a 'problem' – in many ways, *the* geopolitical and ideological problem – for most of the twentieth century.

Apart from the endurance, even flourishing, of empire, another European commonality could not have failed to strike the observer in 1911 or so: the apparently persistent legitimacy of monarchy and the old feudal and aristocratic regimes. When Queen Victoria died, just a few days after the beginning of the new century, her funeral was attended by two emperors, three other sovereigns, nine crown princes and heirs apparent, and forty princes and grand dukes.[21] The personal qualities of such people mattered little; what mattered was, in Weber's words, the 'charisma of blood' they had inherited and would pass on to their children – barring some catastrophic political failure.

True, in increasingly complex polities it was actually bureaucracies which really ruled, not royals – except that the most powerful members of bureaucracies and armies were drawn from the landed aristocracy whose legitimacy was in turn bolstered by monarchy. Even in Britain the first government with a majority of non-aristocrats in the cabinet was formed only as late as 1906.[22]

Not only did Europe still have an international society of royal families (which in turn was shadowed by a kind of international society of conspirators and assassins), the obvious way of organizing and legitimating rule in emerging polities still appeared to be monarchy. When in 1913 the great powers agreed to set up an independent Albania, they decided as a matter of course to give it a (German) prince. These monarchs were drafted from what one might call a whole reserve army of unemployed or underemployed princes (very often German), who were all too happy to head Greece, Romania or Bulgaria.

In one way, the dominance of monarchy as a form of legitimacy might have contributed to a sense of stability and security. In the words of the journalist Walter Bagehot, as a 'transcendent element' alongside 'religious sanction', monarchy seemed to confirm and perpetuate the existing political order; in the case of Britain, according to the *Economist*'s editor and leading commentator on the British constitution, it also served to fool the masses into thinking that one man (or even, sometimes, one woman) was reliably in charge. As Bagehot observed:

> The best reason why Monarchy is a strong government is, that it is an intelligible government. The mass of mankind understand it, and they hardly anywhere in the world understand any other. It is often said that men are ruled by their imaginations; but it would be truer to say that they are governed by the weakness of their imaginations.[23]

As with empire, however, there were really two types of monarchy: on the one hand, parliamentary monarchies that took their distance from the doctrines of divine right which had been propagated most fervently by monarchist thinkers after the French Revolution.[24] Such monarchs – for instance all those on the British throne since Queen Victoria (who had still viewed her powers as a 'gift from God') – presented themselves ever more self-consciously as servants of their people, and as symbols of national unity. Thus, while obviously not being democratic in any electoral sense, they became increasingly conscious of the question of how best to appeal to their people. In the decades before the First World War, 'royal tradition' was often reinvented or at least refined with a view to what impression it would make on the public. For the first time, monarchy became 'mass-produced' and personal charisma manufactured.[25]

To be sure, kings had always been supposed to awe and enchant. But now they tried to do so by means of modern public relations. And thinkers who supported them did so not by invoking divine right or specific political achievements, but by appealing to (often invented) tradition and the peculiar needs of a country.[26] Legitimacy, in short, was based on monarchy's usefulness for keeping together the nation or the empire.

The popularity which constitutional monarchs sought (and often acquired) was not a sign of increased power, then, but a consequence of diminishing political influence.[27] As Bagehot had predicted, 'the more democratic we get, the more we shall get to like state and show, which have ever pleased the vulgar'.[28] And indeed, the pioneer of pursuing popularity for royalty, the British monarchy, eventually reached what the historian David Cannadine has called an 'Olympus of decorative, integrative impotence'.[29]

On the other hand there were monarchs – in particular those in charge of continental empires – who still did believe in divine right; they considered constitutions, where they existed at all, to be nothing but 'pieces of paper' (in the infamous words of the Prussian king Friedrich Wilhelm IV). Here pageantry and pomp were not employed to gain domestic popularity, but as symbolic weapons in the international competition of emperors. More importantly still, these monarchs thought of their states and empires as essentially their personal possessions, as 'agglomerations of lands belonging to a family'.[30] In Russia in particular, this perception reinforced a style of government based on the assumption that subjects were the natural enemies of the rulers.[31] Tsar Nicholas II had claimed, 'I regard Russia as one big estate, with the czar as its owner, the nobility as overseers and the working people as its farmers,' and it was only logical that in the 1897 census he would register as 'landowner'.[32] The 'Emperor and Autocrat of all Russians' also repeatedly rebuffed and even ridiculed what he called 'senseless dreams of participation' by the people.[33]

Goodbye to Most of That

The First World War put into question every single institutional arrangement and every single political idea (or even just moral intuition) on which the Age of Security had rested. The optimistic liberal view of the world could never be the same again. But its authoritarian alternative suffered an even greater loss of credibility: dynasticism and divine right effectively disappeared as plausible means of legitimating political rule. And the war swept away all four great continental empires: the German, the Habsburg, the Russian and the Ottoman.

The continental empires had not only been more or less authoritarian; they had also all been multinational. And as such they conspicuously failed to inspire the ongoing loyalty of their various peoples during the war. The most striking example was the Habsburg Empire. There the potential rivalries of different nationalities had long been held in check not so much by a supranational, Reich patriotism – although such an ideology was promoted from above – as by depoliticizing ethnic relations (and, occasionally, by playing ethnic groups off against each other). Kaiser Franz Josef, who always spoke of his 'peoples', claimed to be loyal primarily to his family – and expected everyone else to do the same. During peacetime that seemed just about enough; if nothing else, inertia (and a well-functioning bureaucracy) kept things together. As Robert Musil put it, 'Kakania' (that is, the Habsburg Empire) was 'the state that somehow just went along with itself, one was negatively free in it, always with the feeling of insufficient reasons for one's own existence'.[34] The war revealed that the empire as a whole, in the eyes of its constituent peoples, had insufficient reasons for existence, economic benefits notwithstanding. Imperial patriotism turned out to be even more of a fiction than its supporters had feared.

The international family of royalty itself was exposed as largely dysfunctional in the face of the imperatives of great-power politics. Kaiser 'Willy' and Tsar 'Nicky' had not been able to prevent the war, although they had tried to do so in direct communication (and George V of England refused to grant 'Cousin Nicky' asylum, after the Tsar was deposed in 1917). Towards the end of the war, the not-so-constitutional monarchs were losing whatever aura might have remained; they were visibly dominated by their own politicians and military men. War leaders like General Ludendorff in Germany acted like dictators – not just in the Kaiser's presence, where Ludendorff shouted 'the German people are more important for me than the emperor', but increasingly in the public eye.[35] Monarchs had not really led their own armies since the eighteenth century, but where they actually did so now, the outcome proved disastrous – the obvious example being Tsar Nicholas II, who had dismissed the Duma and taken over military leadership, thereby becoming directly associated with defeat on the battlefield.[36] Thus where monarchs did not act, they were seen as ineffective; where they acted, they revealed themselves as incompetent.

Even the various abdications had nothing dignified, let alone heroic, about them. Wilhelm II had his imperial possessions brought to his Dutch exile in ninety-five freight cars, pulled by five locomotives – he seemed less a sovereign royal than a petty-bourgeois clinging to his bric-a-brac. Nicholas II abdicated in favour of his brother Michael (who refused), instead of his son – and this violation of the law of succession just seemed to prove once more how much the Tsar had perceived the throne as his private possession rather than as an impersonal office with objective duties.[37]

Charisma, as Weber claimed at the time, had to keep proving itself – and many monarchs had plainly come up short.[38] However, it was not just state forms that suffered a tremendous loss of legitimacy. A whole European order of deference and clearly defined feudal or quasi-feudal hierarchies was destroyed, or at least profoundly shaken. It was not just the monarchs who had lost legitimacy; it was also aristocrats, who had by and large had a rather good nineteenth century, clinging to power and privileges, and to an honour code which clearly distinguished them from ordinary people. One thinks of the memorable depiction of the aristocrats von Rauffenstein and de Boeldieu fighting on different sides in the war in Jean Renoir's *The Grand Illusion*; they recognize and honour each other across enemy lines, but also realize that their kind of war – an individualist's war of sorts – is disappearing.[39]

Certainly, there were still monarchists after 1919. But there were to be no more major theorists of monarchy, in the way that Friedrich von Stahl or Charles Maurras had been sophisticated defenders of rule by royals. In the remaining monarchies their role had to be even more strongly justified as ensuring national unity. In Britain (the only monarchy in a major state after the war, apart from Italy), George V was celebrated above all as a proper 'People's King', who toured London in an open car.

Just one of the Central and Eastern European successor states turned out to be a monarchy: Yugoslavia. And only one monarchy was established in the period between the wars: Albania, which featured King Zog, a self-made president-turned-monarch with no credible lineage at all. This somewhat bizarre figure would only eat meals which had been prepared by his mother and would not venture out on to the streets of Tirana without her.

Thus, for the first time in European history, republics became the rule rather than the exception. Consequently, as the British political thinkers G. D. H. and Margaret Cole put it, Europeans had to plunge 'into an orgy of constitution-making'.[40] Many of the constitution drafters perceived one of their main challenges to be how to stabilize states without the 'transcendent element' of monarchy. In fact, it was far from obvious which positive principles constitution-making should proceed upon. In particular, the liberal story in its nineteenth-century laissez-faire version had hardly emerged triumphant. Far from it: the war marked the end of that era of freedom from the state; it had demanded an unprecedented mobilization of populations – never before had there been such large armies in Europe – and an unprecedented growth in state power. What Ludendorff had been the first to call 'total war' had meant, above all, total mobilization, of men and of money, and also, as the war dragged on, of civilians. To quote Taylor again:

The mass of people became, for the first time, active citizens. Their lives were shaped by orders from above: they were required to serve the state instead of pursuing exclusively their own affairs. Five million men entered the armed forces, many of them (though a minority) under compulsion. The Englishman's food was limited, and its quality changed, by government order. His freedom of movement was restricted; his conditions of work prescribed ... The publication of views was fettered. Street lights were dimmed, the sacred freedom of drinking was tampered with; licensed hours were cut down, and the beer watered by order. The very time on the clocks was changed ... The state established a hold over its citizens which, though relaxed in peacetime, was never to be removed ... The history of the English people and of the English state merged for the first time.[41]

The state also merged with the economy in a way it had never done before. Especially in Germany, industrial production became highly concentrated – de facto leading to cartels – and co-ordinated by ministries. Labour representatives were asked to take part in comprehensive planning. Negotiations between capital and labour became publicly institutionalized and sometimes supervised by the state.[42] Observers began to speak of 'organized capitalism'. Others thought that what they were looking at had ceased to be capitalism altogether. The Austrian Marxist Karl Renner enthused 'socialism wherever our eyes can see'.[43] 'War socialism' was hardly the real thing. But there was no doubt that social and economic life inside states had become much more tightly regulated, as was the case with life between states: after 1918, all European countries required their citizens to carry passports.

Yet increased state power was not just feared as restricting the freedom of individuals. With state power had grown a sense of social and political possibility. A strict line separating state and society had always been a fiction, but whatever separations there had been now became increasingly blurred. Rather than the educated and 'responsible' parts of society reasonably articulating their interests through parliaments based on a very limited franchise, the idea gained ground that the state could be harnessed by society as a whole in order fundamentally to transform itself. This was particularly the case in countries where the establishment of a strong bureaucratic state had preceded any attempts at democratization and the extension of citizenship – that is, practically all of continental Europe, in contrast with Britain (and the United States), where the basics of electoral democracy had been established before modern state-building.

Now most of these countries saw a significant widening of the franchise; it was not just the male masses who were let in, but sometimes also the other half of humanity (or at least some of its older and more educated members). Before the war, women had been allowed to vote only in Finland and Norway; in 1918, Britain introduced universal manhood suffrage and the vote for women over thirty (thereby excluding the women who had worked hardest for military victory). In 1919 the first woman was elected to a European parliament – Lady Astor to the House of Commons. Five years later the Danish Social Democratic politician Nina Bang became the first female cabinet minister in Europe (in charge of education).

And the liberals, who had always feared a hasty extension of the franchise? They largely failed in their attempts to create a new form of statecraft for what the German liberal Friedrich Naumann had called the impending age of 'mass life'. Instead, they often fell back on simply lamenting the rise of 'the masses'. What became a commonplace in interwar cultural criticism was given its most elegant and influential expression by a Spanish liberal philosopher. In 1930 José Ortega y Gasset observed that:

> towns are full of people, houses full of tenants, hotels full of guests, trains full of travellers, cafés full of customers, parks full of promenaders, consulting-rooms of famous doctors full of patients, theatres full of specta-tors, and beaches full of bathers. What previously was, in general, no problem, now begins to be an everyday one, namely, to find room.[44]

The anxiety about 'the masses' was a qualitative, not a quantitative problem. 'Mass man' was characterized primarily by what he lacked: the supposed qualities of the good nineteenth-century liberal self, above all rationality and self-restraint. Even worse, 'mass man' was getting hold of the levers of the state and modern technology, which in turn further homogenized 'the masses'. The state, 'the machine' and 'the masses' almost inevitably appeared together as a single threat. Ortega warned that 'statism is the higher form taken by violence and direct action when these are set up as standards. Through and by means of the State, the anonymous machine, the masses act for themselves.'[45] Through such pronouncements, liberalism seemed to reveal itself as a quasi-aristocratic approach to politics, one that simply could not cope with mass democracy, or what Ortega called the spectre of 'hyper-democracy'.

However, aesthetic contempt for ordinary people apart, it was a fact that in many parts of the continent entire new groups and classes had entered politics. In Central and Eastern Europe, the peasantry had become politically active for the first time, and with their mobilization appeared an explicit ideology of 'agrarianism'. In Bulgaria, a peasant leader, Alexander Stamboliski, even came to head the government; he carried out large land redistributions and tried to form a 'Green International'. Prejudices against peasants persisted and were stoked by the prospects of agrarianism becoming more powerful. The Romanian writer Emile Ciroan complained about the crowds in Bucharest – 'peasants will be peasants even when in the capital city' – and made no secret of what he thought of the country's 'timeless peasants enamoured of their own torpor and almost bursting with hebetude'.[46] Stamboliski was assassinated in 1923, his hands and ears were cut off and his severed head sent to Sofia. In the end, no country except Czechoslovakia – which was in any case highly industrialized – proved able to integrate the peasants into a functioning democracy.

New groups thus demanded their say in national politics, as well as their share of national resources (or, for that matter, rejected their share of the costs of the war). For many observers it seemed plausible that, with new kinds of people in politics, states should more actively mould their peoples into one. And there was even a theoretical principle that could justify such an approach, at least indirectly: the norm of national self-determination.

Liberal Revolutions without Liberals

William James had called war 'the gory nurse that trained societies to cohesiveness'. The ideal of national unity across class lines – whether in the form of the French *union sacrée* or the German *Burgfrieden* – had encouraged claims for democracy and, ultimately, had also helped these demands to succeed. But nationalism did not neatly map on to existing states or newly created states. In theory, the post-war period – after the destruction of the great continental-religious empires – saw the triumph of the principle of national self-determination. In practice this was to translate into the deliberate establishment of states with supposedly homogeneous populations, based on ethnic and linguistic criteria – all in the name of democracy. As Masaryk argued: 'On the whole, great multinational empires are an institution of the past, of a time when material force was held high and the principle of nationality had not yet been recognized, because democracy had not been recognized.'[47] President Woodrow Wilson's Fourteen Points had unleashed a revolution in the way of organizing states that was as important as the Russian Revolution. The norms of national self-determination and statehood based on homogeneous populations, supported by the new League of Nations, was explicitly to serve as an alternative to the idea of a 'concert of Europe'; and it was 'urged on hard-nosed European politicos by President Wilson with all the liberal fervour of a Princeton political scientist'.[48] Max Weber could not hide his surprise, remarking on the 'strange fate of the world that the first real world ruler' had turned out to be a professor.[49]

So there was one advance for liberalism in the nineteenth-century sense after all – except that Wilson's supposed liberal revolution also seemed to call for what Lord Curzon had carelessly dubbed the 'unmixing of peoples'. In practical terms, this often translated into invitations to physical or, at least, psychological violence: threats, bullying, forced deportations and even killing. As the Russian writer Nadezhda Mandelstam was to observe: 'Mass deportation is something quite new, for which we have the twentieth century to thank.' She also explained what it meant in practice: 'every mass deportation – whether of whole classes or ethnic groups – was accompanied by waves of voluntary migration. Children and old people died like flies.'[50]

Even the 'unmixing' of individual people was not a straightforward matter. What, after all, was one to do with men like the writer Ödon von Horvath, who, when asked what his native country was, replied, 'I answer: I was born in Fiume, grew up in Belgrade, Budapest, Pressburg, Vienna and Munich, and I have a Hungarian passport; but I have no fatherland: at once Magyar, Croatian, German and Czech; my country is Hungary, my mother tongue is German.'[51] De facto, then, Europe was reorganized as a series of ostensible republican nation-states with very large minorities within them. A third of Poland's population did not speak Polish, a newly enlarged Romania contained a million Hungarians, and some states were based on what Eric Hobsbawm has called 'political shotgun marriages' – in particular Czechoslovakia and what soon came to be known as Yugoslavia. All in all, the Treaties of Paris gave sixty million people a state of their own, but at the same time it turned twenty-five million into minorities. Neither minorities nor majorities believed in the idea of assimilation or even compromise, which, according to Masaryk, for instance, was the very essence of democracy.[52] In theory, minorities should have been protected through collective rights. But such rights protection had not been part of the general settlement in the Paris Treaties. Rather, at the insistence of the British who were concerned about the legal implications for their empire, it had been enshrined in bilateral treaties – thereby making minorities particularly vulnerable to the vagaries of great-power politics.[53] The victors also denied minorities any kind of corporate status, leaving it fatally vague whether protection really extended to collectives or to individuals. On the other hand, from the perspective of majorities, alternatives to having permanent, grumbling minorities appeared increasingly attractive: the 1923 Treaty of Lausanne had set a precedent in legitimizing 'population exchanges'. As a result, about a million Christians were forced to leave Turkey for Greece; about 350,000 Muslims went from Greece to Turkey. 'Exchanges' or, to use a less polite word, deportations seemed to be a straightforward way fully to implement the norm of national self-determination or, as Wilson had put it to Congress, the 'imperative principle of action'.

There was one country on Europe's periphery which set a striking example of what this imperative principle could mean in practice, creating cultural consensus from above and carrying out a cultural revolution without a social revolution. That country was Turkey, which tried to harness the power of the state to bring about a homogeneous national population, and it did so at least in the name of some ostensibly liberal values like progress and reason. But the outcome was hardly liberal-democratic.

Kemal Atatürk had read Rousseau and the nineteenth-century French philosopher Auguste Comte; he concluded that the prowess of the Western Europeans could be explained by their supposedly clear separation of state and church.[54] Consequently, he assembled a group of advisers and bureaucrats he called the 'men of the future'; they embarked on a cultural revolution that took its inspiration from anti-clerical French Republicanism: men had to take off the fez, which, as Atatürk put it in 1927, had sat 'on the head of our nation as an emblem of ignorance, negligence, fanaticism, and hatred of progress and civilization';[55] in addition, all expressions of popular Islam were suppressed, dervishes arrested and sometimes executed. Atatürk affirmed that 'there are different countries, but only one civilization. The precondition of progress of the nation is to participate in this civilization'; the newly created Turkish Republic had to 'prove its civilization'.[56] In this spirit, Italian criminal law and Swiss civil law were introduced wholesale to replace sharia. The Latin alphabet replaced the Arabic.

To make sense of all these measures, Atatürk eventually proclaimed as principles of the state nationalism, laicism, republicanism, populism, revolutionism and, not least, etatism (which actually turned into a Turkish word). They were symbolized by six arrows and watched over by Atatürk himself – literally the 'father of the Turks', a title with which parliament had honoured him. He was widely admired in the West; books poured forth about 'the grey wolf' and the 'incredible Atatürk', revealing a fascination with a ruthless reshaping of society from above, in part because it contrasted so markedly with the notion of the negotiating – and hence, it seemed to many people, weak – state in Western Europe. The Turkish experiment seemed not simply about belated nation-building, or a form of enlightened absolutism transposed to the twentieth century; rather, it was something new, and its novelty lay in fully harnessing a modern bureaucratic state to bring about a desirable kind of people – a thought that we shall examine more closely in Chapter 2.

In theory, Turkey's legitimacy conformed to the Wilsonian precept of a state based on a self-determining homogeneous national population. The new

Turkish parliament was adorned with the maxim: 'All public power derives from the people.' But the abstract idea of the 'people' had little to do with actual people: despite the proclaimed principles of nationalism and populism, most Kemalists could only perceive Anatolian peasants and folk Islam as a threat. Echoing Ortega y Gasset, the governor of Istanbul, Fahrettin Kerim Gökay, lamented: 'The people are flooding the beaches, the citizen can no longer bathe.'

Thus a secular elite, mostly in the army and the bureaucracy, developed the *devlet baba* – the increasingly authoritarian father-state. In 1931 Turkey proclaimed itself a one-party polity. After his death, Atatürk's heirs instigated a vast personality cult around him: in terms of Weber's categories, Turkey's legitimacy was to be propped up both by charisma – now transferred from the real father to the father-state – and by a well-functioning bureaucracy. But, above all, it was based on an unconditional affirmation of nation-state sovereignty.[57] This yet again proved Weber's point that traditional, and in particular monarchical, legitimacy had disappeared for good – but that the result would not be anything obviously resembling liberal democracy.

Clearly, then, ostensibly liberal principles of action did not automatically come with the kind of political actors suited to implementing them. To be sure, there were some high-minded bureaucrats and intellectuals of international standing who wanted European nation-states to co-operate in the name of peace and shared prosperity – John Maynard Keynes, for instance, or Felix Somary or the German Harry Count Kessler. They were men who volunteered their time, and often risked their reputations, to explore the possibilities of reasonable compromise.[58] Apart from the 'world-ruler professor' Wilson, a whole range of academics and experts had been present in Versailles – Max Weber, not least – who kept submitting memoranda (a jointly authored 'professors' memorandum', in Weber's case) and plans transcending nationalist passions. Yet attempts to have bureaucracies and free-floating cosmopolitan intellectuals work together across borders mostly failed. This confirmed some of them in the belief that if even men of the best will could not overcome deep-seated antagonisms, then perhaps the post-war order was flawed in its very foundations. Keynes derided the 'Wilsonian dogma', which according to the English economist 'exalts and dignifies the divisions of race and nation-ality above the bonds of trade and culture, and guarantees frontiers but not happiness.'[59]

This failure also reinforced a growing general crisis of confidence among European elites after the war. Europe was exhausted, not just physically, but also morally. Keynes captured the general retreat from universalism, too, when he wrote: 'Our power of feeling or caring beyond the immediate questions of our material wellbeing is temporarily eclipsed ... We have moved already beyond endurance, and need rest. Never in the lifetime of men now living has the universal element in the soul of man burnt so dimly.'[60] Many were looking to the United States for political and moral leadership; Emil Müller-Sturmheim argued in a book entitled *Without America It Doesn't Work* (*Ohne Amerika geht es nicht*) that it was 'the great fortune of humanity that a nation like America has the leadership role of the world'.[61] And Masaryk professed: 'I see no harm in our becoming Americanized; we've been Europeanizing America for centuries.'[62] But those who had really hoped for some sustained American commitment to putting the European house in order were to be disappointed by the United States' post-war isolationism. 'Americanization' of the economy and, above all, of culture did proceed nonetheless; and, in the eyes of many European cultural critics, it hastened the descent into 'mass society'.

There could also be no more simple faith in the eventual Europeanization of the world. As Valéry observed in 1919, in what was to become a much repeated passage:

> We later civilizations ... we too know now that we are mortal.
>
> We had long heard tell of whole worlds that had vanished, of empires sunk without a trace, gone down with all their men and all their machines into the unexplorable depths of the centuries, with their gods and their laws, their academies and their sciences pure and applied ... We were aware that the visible earth is made of ashes, and that ashes signify something. Through the obscure depths of history we could make out the phantoms of great ships laden with riches and intellect ... But the disasters that had sent them down were, after all, none of our affair.[63]

But even now that disaster had become a European affair, very few Europeans realized that Europe might have lost its global pre-eminence for good. Nineteen-seventeen had marked the point when for the first time since the Ottoman attacks of the sixteenth century Europe depended on non-European powers to settle its fate.

Loss of confidence and cultural pessimism were not the only results of the war, though. The war had levelled and homogenized: the democracy of the trenches at the front and Lloyd George's 'molten mass' at home. But it had also created a new kind of elite consciousness. Where Wilfred Owen had denounced 'the old Lie: Dulce et decorum est Pro patria mori', the German writer Ernst Jünger celebrated the mystique of a new male brotherhood among the social groups that had suffered the greatest losses – junior officers and unskilled workers, the real 'princes of the trenches'.[64] He was awed by a 'new and commanding breed rising up' in 'old Europe' and hailed them as 'fearless and fabulous, unsparing of blood and sparing of pity – a race that builds machines and trusts to machines, to whom machines are not soulless iron, but engines of might which it controls with cold reason and hot blood. This puts a new face on the world.'[65]

The war seemed to have left a legacy of two political imaginaries: on the one hand, a politics of compromise among state, labour and capital, or, to put it differently, a politics of the pursuit of rational interests; on the other hand, a militarized politics of the will concentrated on saving the nation. Both were denials of classical nineteenth-century liberalism, and both were in their own ways attempts to face the challenge of what was often referred to as 'the entry of the masses into politics'.

Weber's Questions

Max Weber had been steeped in the assumptions of nineteenth-century liberalism, but he was keenly alert to what he often referred to as 'the demands of the day' – that is, the political challenges thrown up by new historical constellations. Redefining the role of the state and its relation to democracy, and asking what form of political action individuals could be expected to engage in under these circumstances, were clearly such demands.

Weber, who had been trained as a lawyer, was in certain regards a symptom, rather than a diagnostician, of what was widely perceived as a crisis of traditional conceptions of the state. Like many of his German contemporaries, he was a legal formalist and sought to demystify the state, arguing that it was not any kind of 'organism', and that it could not be identified by particular goals. He simply defined the state through the means it used, and arrived at one of the most quoted sentences in political science: 'the state is a human community that (successfully) claims the monopoly of the legitimate use of physical force within a given territory'.

The emphasis on force fitted well with Weber's image of politics as perpetual conflict, of social life as never-ending struggle (which, however, in Weber's view, also put a premium on the capacity for compromise). But the more important point concerned the legitimacy of force. With the modern state legitimacy was gained through legality, not through the promise of pursuing particular purposes. It was a result of following the correct procedures in law-making, leaving execution to an administrative staff who were clearly separated from the means of administration – unlike in feudalism and other systems where offices could be owned like private property. What Weber called the modern 'mass state' thus necessarily came with bureaucracy.

Like other legal positivists, Weber divorced law from any distinctively moral foundations. He thought that belief in natural law or objective universal values had irreversibly declined: thus law was valid if it was enacted as prescribed in the constitution and then obeyed, even if for most people obedience was just a matter of habit, and belief in the state's legitimacy only half conscious or 'darkly felt'.[66] Politically, legal positivists were mostly liberals – but there was no real moral basis in their theory for liberalism.

While not being a particularly original thinker in relation to the state, Weber did make a number of highly influential observations on the changing nature of law in the 'mass state'; these were later taken up by, among others, Carl Schmitt and Friedrich von Hayek. In particular, Weber was concerned that the liberal rule of law was being eroded with the emergence of the welfare state and demands for material 'justice'. Rule by general statute – which was transparent and for which politicians could be held accountable – was becoming conflated with measures and decrees aimed at particular situations or specific citizens. Ideals like justice, Weber felt, might well be symbolically endorsed by parliaments. But they would not translate into general and predictable law; rather, they might give rise to a new patrimonialism or feudalism, where unaccountable administrators turned into lords dispensing favours to select groups.

Bureaucratization posed a challenge not just to a modern state which Weber viewed as a distinctive achievement of the Occident; it also called into question notions of free individuality. Of course, anxieties about free individuality had long predated the war and been expressed in many pseudo-scientific treatises about 'mass society' and 'crowd behaviour'; most of these alleged, with the French 'crowd psychologist' Gustave Le Bon, that the divine right of kings was being replaced by the divine right of the masses. Weber was deeply concerned about the prospects for the kind of individual autonomy which the Enlightenment had promised. But he saw the dangers less in the supposedly inferior nature of 'the masses' than in social phenomena like ever-growing bureaucracy and demagogy, both of which he thought inevitable in the democratic 'mass state'.

Weber, in short, saw two crises – of liberal statehood and mass democracy on the one hand, and of the individual self on the other. They were clearly related. Understanding them required an accurate view of where modern individuality had originated and what had come to endanger it.

In 1904–5, in what turned out to be his most famous work, *The Protestant Ethic and the Spirit of Capitalism*, Weber had argued that in the early modern period the Calvinist doctrine of predestination had led individuals to experience a sense of tremendous inner loneliness; they simply could never know for sure whether they were among the elect or not, though naturally they wanted to know at any price. Priests told them simply to believe that they were. A practical way, however, to reduce religious anxiety was unceasing work – not just because, as Weber suggested, work took one's minds off religious doubts, but because in work the believer could see himself as an instrument of God's power.

Calvinism thus drove believers to prove themselves as graced in the coming world by engaging in successful economic activity in this world. Weber did not put too fine a point on it when it came to explaining the basic idea: God will help you if you help yourself.[67] Calvinists thus developed a specific form of life conduct, characterized by systematic self-control and devoted to a particular 'calling'.[68] According to Weber, this life conduct had become *rationalized* in the sense of being disciplined, methodical and strenuously specialized; it was also 'rational' in having broken with tradition, whether religious or economic.

The new ethos demanded the pursuit of ever more money, while strictly avoiding all pleasure. The concrete conduct it inspired, Weber held, 'is so entirely removed from all . . . hedonist aspects, so purely conceived as an end in itself that it appears as something . . . completely irrational from the point of view of individual "happiness" . . '. In short, 'man is subordinated to gain as his life's goal; gain is no longer subordinated to man as the means to the end of satisfying his material needs'.[69] It might have been irrational, but it was the precondition to, or, in Weber's own words, 'an adequate condition' (though not, strictly speaking, the cause) of, the emergence of the 'spirit of capitalism'.

The Protestant Ethic was above all a story of unintended consequences: the Calvinists set in motion a historical development which might end with the greatest form of collective enslavement the world had ever known – what Weber called the 'steel-hard casing' (*stahlhartes Gehäuse*, commonly mistranslated as 'iron cage') of universal rationalization and bureaucratization. As he put it,

> as asceticism was carried out of the monastic cells into vocational life, and began to dominate this-worldly ethics and conduct, it did its part in building the powerful cosmos of the modern . . . economic order, which today determines the way of life of all individuals who are born into this mechanism – not just those who are gainfully employed – with overwhelming force. Perhaps it will so determine them until the last ton of fuel has burnt itself out. The care for external goods should only lie on the shoulders of the saint like 'a light cloak which can be thrown off at any moment' . . . But fate let it happen that the cloak became a steel-hard casing.[70]

The idea of systematically devoting oneself to a specialized line of work had become universalized. But in the form of a 'job' it had lost its inner meaning;

the original spirit of capitalism had disappeared from the steely casing. As Weber put it, 'the Puritan *wanted* to be a *Berufsmensch* [a man devoted to work]; we are *forced* to be one'.[71] Modern capitalism had been a highly specific Western development, but, in Weber's eyes, it had no particular affinity with freedom or democracy. In fact, remorseless rationalization threatened to make the heirs of the Puritans into nothing more than petty utility maximizers: in Weber's words, 'specialists without spirit, hedonists without a heart'.

This was not the only peculiarity of Western modernity: science had proved that there was no objective meaning in the natural order and had thereby undermined traditional and theological certainties. Science could destroy beliefs, but it could not itself create new values. Weber claimed that 'the fate of an epoch which has eaten of the tree of knowledge is that it must know that we cannot learn the meaning of the world from the results of its analysis, be it ever so perfect; it must rather be in a position to create this meaning itself'. All science could deliver was the prediction of consequences, the means required for mastery of the external world.

There was one further feature peculiar to the Occident. The modern West had seen the emergence of a number of different 'value spheres', or 'orders of life', as Weber called them, each with its own leading values, its own inner laws, and each subject to its own form of 'rationalization': the economy, for instance, but also aesthetics, religion and, of course, politics. These value spheres, according to Weber, had become more systematic and specialized – hence 'rationalized'. But they were also, for the most part, incompatible in the claims they made on individuals: the fully committed religious believer in pacifism was unlikely to succeed in politics, where power and violence counted. Weber held: 'it is like in the world of the ancients when it was not yet disenchanted of its gods and demons, only in a different sense . . . Fate, and certainly not "science", holds sway over these gods and their struggle'.[72]

Since God was dead, many secular gods had appeared, and no overarching ethical system could integrate all their conflicting demands. Thus value pluralism – if one wanted to lead a serious life at all – ultimately required a basically irrational decision and existential commitment by individuals. As Weber put it:

> the fruit of the tree of knowledge, which is distasteful to the complacent but which is, nonetheless, inescapable, consists in the insight that . . . ultimately life as a whole, if it is not to be permitted to run on as an event in nature but is instead to be consciously guided, is a series of ultimate decisions through which the soul . . . chooses its own fate, that is, the meaning of its . . . existence.

Every man or woman – unless they wanted their lives to be no more than an 'event in nature' – had to make his or her own choice as to which god to serve, knowing that they would automatically enter into conflict with the servants of other gods.

The necessity of choice placed a tremendous burden on modern individuals. According to Weber, it took a great deal of maturity to realize that this experience could also prove liberating, as long as the modern condition was faced up to with dignity and determination. After all, as Weber once pointed out, 'we will never be asked whether we want a given historical development'. Weber thus favoured an ethical stance that affirmed the fragmented world as it was, in a spirit of self-conscious realism.[73]

It was not that he could not see the temptation of fleeing from choice: one escape route was aestheticism, another an ethics of 'brotherliness', that is, a political utopianism where all human beings (and all values) would become reconciled. Such temptations increased, as the means–ends rationality suggested by science for dominating nature invaded other spheres of life – leading to the domination not just of nature, but also of human beings. In particular, according to Weber, together with modern business, bureaucracy was busy fabricating a kind of bondage that might make the moderns one day as powerless as 'the fellahs of ancient Egypt'.

The modern self, then, might become entrapped in a structure of its own making, and myth – long, it seemed, discredited by the Enlightenment – might return in secular fashion, as the impersonal, dehumanizing forces that regimented individuals. The insight of the Italian seventeenth-century philosopher Giambattista Vico that human beings could understand what he called 'artificial nature', because human beings had themselves created the world they inhabited, would no longer hold true. At the same time, the dominance of technology and the imperatives of work reinforced the temptations of what Weber called modern 'subjectivist culture', where individuals were primarily concerned with cultivating their inner life and chasing after 'experiences'.[74] One consequence was that what Weber termed the 'ultimate and most sublime values' had retreated from public life.[75] Impersonal, seemingly uncontrollable and in fact plain incomprehensible forces on the one hand, and, on the other, a flight into over-stimulated subjectivity (what Weber, following Simmel, called 'sterile excitation') – such was the fateful split of the modern age that Weber diagnosed.

The notion that history – and modern life in particular – was a matter of unintended consequences or even tragedy was widespread among German social theorists during the early twentieth century. Georg Simmel, who was heavily promoted by Weber to become a fellow professor in Heidelberg, lamented what he called the 'tragedy of culture'. According to Simmel, human beings created objective cultural 'forms' and structures which accumulated and weighed ever more heavily on succeeding generations. On the one hand, Simmel insisted that the soul could 'find itself' only through these 'cultural crystallizations'.[76] On the other hand, the individual born into the modern order confronted these forms without really being able to understand more than a fraction of them, and necessarily had to perceive them as oppressive. Life, to reassert itself, would have to tear these forms apart, and yet culture could not really be created without them – hence the tragedy.

This sense was acutely shared by many contemporaries of Weber and Simmel. Robert Musil, in his *Man without Qualities*, observed: 'The thing has us in its hand. One moves day and night in it and does everything else in it; one shaves, one eats, one loves, one reads books, one engages in one's profession, as if all four walls stood still, and the uncanny matter is just that the walls are moving, without one noticing it.'[77] In less interesting prose: one did not live; one was being lived.

Still, both Simmel's assessment of the tragedy of culture and Weber's view of rationalization were highly ambiguous. All modern institutions had two sides: bureaucracy could be highly oppressive – but, as the most rational form of authority, it was also a genuine achievement. What Weber called the modern impersonal *Menschenmaschine* of bureaucracy could be dismantled only at the price of reinstating more arbitrary forms of rule (which is also why it made no sense to try to dissociate mass democracy completely from bureaucracy).[78] There was no exit from Musil's 'thing'; in particular, the path back to *Gemeinschaft* – organic communities promising a simpler and yet more holistic life, for which so many of Weber's German contemporaries yearned – was neither available nor for that matter desirable.

Except when it seemed to be. Both Weber and Simmel appeared ready to shed their scepticism about national *Gemeinschaft* in 1914, welcoming what Weber called a 'great' and 'wonderful' war. The reserve lieutenant Weber, by then fifty, was too old to serve at the front; instead he was charged with outfitting Heidelberg military hospitals (after which he was promoted to captain of the reserve). His attitude towards the war was not simple chauvinism, though. He thought that an ultimate aim of politics – and of war-making as one aspect of politics – was to create or sustain particular forms of culture. These forms of culture were in turn justified by the individual qualities of character different cultures encouraged. He sometimes went so far as to claim that he actually 'did not give a damn' about the state form, as long as Germany emerged with 'more honour' and a more desirable form of culture. He had also made it clear that only some were called to act as *Herrenvölker*: 'small states' like Switzerland could afford a more moral kind of politics, but they were unable to generate cultures of any larger consequence. In this vein, Weber justified the First World War as ultimately being about the culture of the future, and, more particularly, about preventing the world being divided up between 'Russian bureaucracy' and 'Anglo-Saxon conventions of society'.[79]

This quest for cultural significance and collective meaning – the 'sublime and ultimate values' which Weber felt were disappearing from public life – also explained why politics had to be kept apart from other spheres of modern life, such as the economy. Politics should never merely be about negotiating on the basis of material interests or ensuring the smooth functioning of the market: the state and the public realm, according to Weber, had their own special dignity.[80] Power politics as such was pointless; it could be justified only as a way of achieving something more meaningful. Thus Weber also held that the state should be preoccupied not so much with the well-being of people in the future as with the 'quality' of future people's character.[81] The 'fatherland' was the land not of the fathers, but of the descendants.

The Great Experiment

Apart from the war, there was another violent theatre of political action where the character of future people, in fact the very possibility of entirely 'New Men', was being fought over. Weber had long been a keen observer of developments in Russia; he had even learnt Russian so as to be able to read first-hand accounts of the 1905 uprising. He had hoped for the emergence of a credible form of Russian liberalism (even though he did not consider Russia to be part of the Occident), but felt that the various reforms undertaken after 1905 amounted merely to a kind of 'pseudo-constitutionalism'. De facto, autocracy – with its systematic *Volksentmannung*, literally a 'castration of the people' – persisted. Thus in 1917 the fall of Nicholas II and the end of Tsarism were celebrated in Heidelberg.

Weber was sceptical, however, about Alexander Kerensky, prime minister of the post-Tsarist provisional government, and what he saw as the triumph of a 'Duma plutocracy' designed to keep the peasants down. He was even more sceptical about the Bolsheviks who came to power in October 1917. He could not know that his very own government had subsidized Lenin's enterprise with substantial sums of money, in addition to sending him to St Petersburg in a sealed train. Of course, German bureaucrats got what initially seemed a great return on their investment: the Bolsheviks concluded a humiliating peace treaty with the Reich in March 1918. Lenin had long advocated 'revolutionary defeatism' – calling on the workers to bring down their belligerent governments and turning an 'imperialist war into a series of national civil wars'. Weber's pupil Georg Lukács thought Lenin had thereby single-handedly rescued the honour of international socialism – virtually every other socialist party had supported their respective national governments, as opposed to workers of the world uniting across national frontiers.[82]

Weber could also not have suspected that the October Revolution was in fact not so much a revolution or even a putsch as a seizure of power when nobody else seemed to want it. In the end, only a few cadets and a women's battalion were left in the Winter Palace to defend Kerensky's government. Lenin had been absolutely determined to bring down legal authority before the planned constituent assembly (in which the Bolsheviks commanded only about a quarter of the vote) could meet; he bludgeoned his Central Committee colleagues with threats and promises, and even risked the leadership of his own party, to push through his plan of immediate insurrection.

Success seemed to vindicate Lenin's larger political theory: at least since the turn of the century he had argued that those who were truly serious about revolution should put their faith in a vanguard consisting of utterly committed revolutionaries, with specialized skills and a highly developed socialist consciousness. Without such professionals in revolution-making, according to Lenin, the working class, no matter how oppressed, could only ever develop 'trade union consciousness'. Along the same lines, he had derided 'economism', that is, attempts to obtain material improvements for the workers short of real socialism, just as much as he had dismissed 'spontaneity' – that is, political action by the working masses not guided by a sophisticated theory as formulated by the vanguard party.[83]

For his 'party of a new type', then, Lenin preferred a handful of fully committed revolutionaries to a mass membership – in fact, 'new people', just as the subtitle of Lenin's favourite novel, *What is to be Done?*, had suggested: in it, Nikolai Chernyshevsky had celebrated the 'new person' who was strong-willed, supremely rational, fully in control of his mind and body.[84] Lenin himself certainly sought to embody the ideal of the single-minded revolutionary specialist, though he did not follow the practical prescriptions of Chernyshevsky's heroes who ate only half-cooked meat and slept on a bed of nails. But as one moderate socialist observed about Lenin: 'there's no such person who is so preoccupied twenty-four hours a day with revolution, who thinks no other thoughts except those about revolution and who even dreams in his sleep about revolution'.[85]

Commitment was not enough, however. Party members had to be guided by the correct revolutionary theory, or what Lenin called 'the most advanced theory', which would furnish a 'granite foundation' for Bolshevism.[86] Theoretical – as opposed to temporary and tactical – compromise with less radical forces was the surest way to fail at the revolutionary task. Lenin had made the point with a striking image:

> We are marching in a compact group along a precipitous and difficult path, firmly holding each other by the hand. We are surrounded on all sides by enemies, and we have to advance almost constantly under their fire. We have combined, by a freely adopted decision, for the purpose of fighting the enemy, and not of retreating into the neighbouring marsh, the inhabitants of which, from the very outset, have reproached us with having separated ourselves into an exclusive group and with having chosen the path of struggle instead of the path of conciliation.[87]

Thus Lenin managed to create one of the most innovative and powerful political instruments of twentieth-century Europe. It was a combination, as Eric Hobsbawm put it – speaking from within the Communist movement – of 'discipline, business efficiency, utter emotional identification and a sense of *total* dedication'.[88] One may wonder about 'business efficiency' (though it is true that Lenin had always wanted the party to be rigidly centralized 'like a large factory').[89] But there is no doubt that what Lenin called a 'party of iron' was not for romantics, as Hobsbawm also observed.

However, the party did offer something to those looking for a charismatic institution, as opposed to a charismatic person.[90] Party members would exhibit intense devotion and a willingness to sacrifice, in a way that Weber thought individual leaders, and especially prophets, could inspire.[91] As the historian Raphael Samuel put it when describing life in (and for) the British Communist Party:

> The ambitions of the Communist Party – and the self-perception of members – were unmistakably theocratic. Organizationally, we conceived ourselves to be a communion of the elect, covenanted to a sacred cause ... Authority in the Party was theocratic too, an institutionalized form of charisma which operated at every level of Party life.[92]

To be sure, it was not the case that *personal* charisma played no role at all in what critics called 'Lenin's sect'. Lenin himself inspired exceptional levels of trust; when he was only thirty-three, his followers already called him *starik*, the old and wise one, just like one of the ancient prophets that Weber took as prime examples of charismatic leadership. And many Bolsheviks would recount how they effectively fell in love with their leader.[93]

Yet, according to Lenin himself, it had not been the charisma of the *vozhd* (or 'supreme leader', as Lenin was called after the Revolution), but correct organization which had made the difference in October. Correct organization in turn meant correct theory, and vice versa: as Lenin had argued, 'it is impossible to differentiate a political question from an organizational one'. Lenin constantly split his own (and other) parties, imposing the utmost discipline and going with equal ferocity after outright opponents and those willing to compromise for the sake of organizational unity.[94] One consequence was that theory always had to be fashioned for concrete challenges; even though he had given his pre-revolutionary occupation as 'writer', Lenin was never interested in abstract theorizing divorced from immediate practical questions.[95]

In the end, then, the party with a proper theory, not the leader, was the real 'hero'; and a true revolutionary followed the correct line of the party, not a person. This vision also addressed the awkward problem that orthodox Marxism had not reserved any space for heroic individuals making a difference in history. And it was wholly consistent that upon the first signs of a personality cult around himself, Lenin would complain that 'all our lives we have carried on an ideological struggle against the glorification of personality . . . We long ago solved the question of heroes, and now we are again witnessing the glorification of personality. This is no good at all.'[96]

However, what really helped the Bolsheviks consolidate their power was not so much correct theory or charisma – whether collective or individual – as two policies: the decision to redistribute land to the peasants, or ratify the land seizures that had already occurred spontaneously; and, more importantly still, the decision to sue immediately for peace with Germany or what Lenin later called the 'imperialist bandits'.

Lenin countered the obvious objection that a socialist revolution was supposed to break out in advanced capitalist countries like Britain and Germany with the argument that war had made Russia ready for an immediate transition to socialism. Faithful to the tradition of 'Russian Jacobinism', he claimed that a party like his, having seized power, could bypass a bourgeois stage and start creating the 'dictatorship of the proletariat and the peasantry' right away. But he also insisted that revolutions in Western Europe were indispensable to completing the Russian Revolution, thereby making it a genuine world revolution.

Of course this did not mean that the Bolsheviks should somehow bide their time until, as Lenin put it, 'the flame of our revolution' would set light to Europe. In the months before the October seizure of power Lenin had outlined an ambitious programme of reorganizing the economy, doing away with the 'parasite' state and establishing 'a truly complete democracy'. He lauded – of all things – the postal service as 'a model for the socialist economic system'. True, for the moment it was still a state-capitalist monopoly. But:

> we have only to overthrow the capitalists, to crush the resistance of these exploiters with the iron hand of the armed workers, to smash the bureau-cratic machine of the modern state – and we shall have a well-equipped mechanism of a high technical quality, freed from the 'parasite', a mechanism which can very easily be set in motion by the united workers themselves, who will hire technicians, foremen and bookkeepers and pay them all, and indeed all state officials in general, a workman's wage.[97]

The 'parasite' state, with its bureaucracy and standing army serving the inter-ests of capitalism, would be abolished – and with it not just 'bourgeois parlia-mentarism', whose 'real essence', according to Lenin, was in any case 'to decide once every few years which member of the ruling class is to repress and crush the people in parliament'. Also gone would be democracy, at least in its tradi-tional understanding as a political form legitimating (temporary) rule of some over others. In its bourgeois definition, democracy, Lenin explained, is also 'a state which recognizes the subordination of the minority to the majority, i.e. it is an organization for the systematic use of violence by one class against another'. Instead, the Bolsheviks set themselves the ultimate aim of:

> abolishing the state . . . We do not expect the advent of a social order wherein the principle of the subordination of the minority to the majority will not be observed. But, in striving for socialism, we are convinced that it will develop into communism and that, in connection with this, the need for violence against people in general, for the subordination of one person to another . . . will vanish altogether since people will become accustomed to observing the elementary conditions of social life without violence and without subordination.[98]

Thus, with Communism fully realized, there would no longer be a need for a separate public power monopolizing the means of legitimate violence, as Weber had defined the state. Political representation would not disappear, however; Lenin insisted that 'we cannot imagine democracy, even proletarian democracy, without representative institutions, but we can and must imagine democracy without parliamentarism if our criticisms of bourgeois society are not mere empty words for us'. He even admitted that 'there can be no talk of eradicating the bureaucracy at once, everywhere and completely. That is utopia.' But he immediately insisted that 'to *smash* the old bureaucratic machine at once and to begin immediately to construct a new one that facilitates the gradual eradication of all bureaucracy: this is *not* utopia . . .'.[99]

These statements from *The State and Revolution* must not be taken too seriously. Lenin penned them hastily, when he temporarily had to flee Russia in the summer of 1917 and put everything into firing up the Bolsheviks back home with a socialist and, ultimately, Communist vision; it is hard to think that he himself meant his claim that in the end a cook could run whatever remained by way of administration.

Yet some of the most utopian-sounding claims in *State and Revolution* directly took up Marx's writings on the 1871 Paris Commune, when workers had begun to manage their own affairs, officials, including policemen, were elected and traditional state structures dismantled in favour of a fusion of legislation and administration (an ideal whose practical contours never became very clear, given how quickly the Commune was crushed by the French government). To be sure, the brief moment of the Commune had actually been led (and been inspired) more by anarchists than by Marxists, and Marxs' own comments remained ambiguous on the question whether a proper Communist society would be quite like this. Nonetheless, Lenin was eager to invoke the ideal of the 'commune state'. And immediately after the Revolution he actually did support the soviets – in the form of workers' control of production – and soldiers electing their own officers in the army.

But then he decided that 'soviet democracy' of this kind was utopian after all, or at least that it was incompatible with the survival of the new regime. He announced 'a retreat from the principles of the Paris Commune'.[100] And he admitted that 'the whole difficulty of the Russian Revolution is that it was much easier for the Russian revolutionary working class to start than it is for the West European classes, but it is much more difficult for us to continue'. By now he had also made another discovery: that the Russian worker was in fact 'a bad worker compared with people in advanced countries' – and could thus not be trusted with workers' democracy.[101] Apparently only French anarchists could be.

There had been some vague suggestions in Marx and Engels' writings that the proletariat, once it has seized power, should aim at a great industrialization push. Lenin now agreed with this; he claimed that 'the war has taught us much . . . that those who have the best technology, organization, discipline and the best machines emerge on top . . . It is necessary to master the highest technology or be crushed.'[102] So the actual model became – of all things – 'German state capitalism'. Russian socialism should be run just as the Germans had run the war. And 'bad' Russian workers had to be turned into good German ones. This also meant that a new culture – especially a new culture of work, with people devoting themselves to a calling – was not an add-on for true socialism. It was a precondition.

Max Weber had thought that successful revolutionaries would have to bring their own bureaucrats; otherwise they were likely to be dominated by the existing state administration, or what in Russia soon came to be known as 'the former people'. Lenin and the other leaders of the October Revolution would never have accepted this officially. But they had to realize that running something like 'German state capitalism' did require 'specialists' – who simply could not be found among the members of the 'party of a new type'. Thus Leon Trotsky, as head of the Red Army, dissolved soldiers' committees and banned the election of officers. He also returned 'military experts' to their positions. In other words, he reinstated the old officers.

An idea later often attributed to Stalin – that the state had to gain strength before it could 'wither away' – was announced by Trotsky very soon after the Revolution: 'Just as a lamp, before going out, shoots up in a brilliant flame, so the state, before disappearing, assumes the form of the dictatorship of the proletariat, i.e. the most ruthless form of the state, which embraces the life of its citizens authoritatively in every direction.'[103] 'The most ruthless form of the state' was justified by the fact that the regime needed to do whatever it took to survive in a civil war, faced with a hostile outside world. It soon mandated systematic 'mass terror' – explicitly authorized by Lenin and promoted by Trotsky as being 'very efficient against a reactionary class which does not want to leave the scene of operations'.[104] The 'most ruthless state' was animated by an ethics of revolutionary violence, where the ultimate ends unambiguously justified the means. As Trotsky infamously put it in rejecting the criticisms of Bolshevik terrorism by a leading German Social Democrat:

> we were never concerned with the Kantian-priestly and vegetarian-Quaker prattle about the 'sacredness of human life'. We were revolutionaries in opposition, and have remained revolutionaries in power. To make the individual sacred we must destroy the social order which crucifies him. And this problem can only be solved by blood and iron.[105]

'War Communism' also seemed to mandate the complete centralization of the party – not just 'like a factory', as Lenin had said, but like an army under strict command. Trotsky, before rallying to the Bolsheviks, had predicted the consequences: 'these methods lead, as we shall yet see, to this: the party organization is substituted for the party, the Central Committee is substituted for the party organization, and finally a "dictator" is substituted for the Central Committee'.[106]

This potential dynamic and especially the dangers of 'German state capitalism' did not entirely escape the revolutionaries. One problem was bureaucratization. Another, less obvious one was that successful state capitalism did not really need a charismatic force alongside it (which in fact led to some suggestions to abolish the party altogether after the Revolution). What emerged, however, was not what Lenin had called a 'flexible amalgamation' of party and government. Rather, a fateful duality was established: an ever expanding state with 'experts' and 'specialists' on the one side, and, on the other, a party of professional revolutionaries and trained ideologues whose role was to inject all institutions – and especially state institutions – with *partiinost*, or party spirit.[107] Thus state (and, increasingly, society) became wholly bureaucratized, while the party – not officially an administrative organ at all – kept acting, at least in its more charismatic moments, like a radical sect.[108]

And democracy? Lenin did not officially abandon the commune state as a goal. The Bolsheviks kept repeating the slogan of 'involving the masses' directly in state administration and the economy. The default option, though, was to claim that for now *demokratiia* had to mean the dictatorship of the proletariat (the peasantry was already dropping out of the picture) – which implied, among other things, that only those considered 'productive' should be involved in politics at all, starting with the vote.[109] Rights accrued exclusively to 'the working and exploited people'; 'former people' – that is, anybody considered bourgeois – at the very least had to be disfranchised, if not worse.

Those within the party who felt that progress towards the commune state and a complete merger of state and people was too slow regularly complained of 'bureaucratism'.[110] But those who thought it was not 'progressing' at all and instead wanted to return to soviet democracy as it had briefly existed in 1917–18 – that is to say, elections and worker control over production – were brutally suppressed. When, in 1921, workers and sailors in Kronstadt near Petrograd demanded 'Soviets without Bolsheviks', Lenin sent in the troops. Even internal criticism within the party was now severely curtailed: 'factions' were officially forbidden and there was of course no such thing as freedom of the press. All such measures were routinely justified on the ground that the building of 'socialism in one country' (Lenin's phrase, not Stalin's) remained threatened by mighty enemies, outside and inside.

It's not that Lenin entirely failed to see signs of 'bureaucratism'. But, as with the Russian worker and his supposed deficiencies, he sometimes seemed to think it would take nothing less than a change of national character:

> We are indeed in a position, and it must be said that it is a very absurd
> position, of people sitting endlessly at meetings, setting up commissions and

drawing up plans without end. There was a character who typified Russian
life – Oblomov. He was always lolling on his bed and mentally drawing up
schemes. That was a long time ago. Russia has experienced three revolutions,
but . . . [i]t is enough to watch us at our meetings, at our work on commissions, to be able to say that *old Oblomov still lives; and it will be necessary to
give him a good washing and cleaning, a good rubbing and scouring to make a
man of him.*[111]

In the end, however, the only practical solution Lenin – like Weber a lawyer by
training, with a taste for formalism – could imagine to counter paralysing
bureaucratization was more supervision: that is to say, more bureaucracy.[112]

And this dynamic was the very reason why Max Weber rejected socialism:
he held that socialism – as an unintended consequence – would produce
the nightmare of universal bureaucratization. It would fuse what at least in the
West remained separate: economic and state bureaucracy, resulting in the
'the dictatorship of the bureaucrat'.[113] And in fact he watched what he called
the 'great experiment' of Bolshevism with increasing horror. In 1918 he
met Felix Somary as well as the economist Joseph Schumpeter in the Café
Landmann in Vienna. The conversation had turned to the Russian Revolution
and Schumpeter gleefully declared that socialism had finally ceased to be a
'paper discussion', but now had to prove its viability.[114] Weber vehemently
countered that trying socialism in Russia, given the country's level of development, was basically a crime and would end in catastrophe. Somary reports that
Schumpeter coolly replied that this might well be, but that Russia would
constitute a 'nice laboratory'. Weber exploded: 'A laboratory with heaps of
human corpses.' Schumpeter pointed out: 'That's what every anatomy lab is.'
The exchange grew even more heated, Weber became louder, Schumpeter
more sarcastic, until Weber finally jumped up, exclaiming, 'This is unbearable!' and stormed out into the Ring. Schumpeter wondered aloud how
'anyone could yell like this in a coffeehouse'.

Weber's Answers (For Some)

What, though, did Weber propose as a preferable or at least bearable political
ethics instead, and which institutions were to embody or at least protect liberal
intuitions in the new era of 'mass life'? Weber had hidden an allegory of German
society during his own time in the *Protestant Ethic*: pointing to the kind of
autonomous and responsible personality he admired and attacking Lutheranism
for having made the Germans submissive, he admonished the bourgeoisie to
invigorate itself through struggle and finally become self-determining.[115] In

general, Weber thought monarchy the best state form. But the political system of
the German empire had perpetuated political immaturity: it had falsely
suggested that the monarch could actually govern, when in fact unaccountable
civil servants made all the decisions. The bumbling, almost childish Wilhelm II
had merely acted the charismatic leader, although sometimes he had also tried
truly to exercise power – and, to boot, engaged in loud political advertising for
himself. Given his obvious lack of political judgement, Wilhelm's dilettantism
led to mildly ridiculous faux pas at best, or, at worst, imposed heavy political
costs on the nation. Modern monarchy, Weber held, meant rule by bureaucracy,
unless by chance one happened to have an exceptionally talented king or
emperor. The real question was whether this bureaucracy was going to be supervised. In Wilhelmine Germany it had not been; moreover, governments had
been composed of characters who had never had to prove their mettle in party
politics or parliament.

Weber's prescription was clear: parliaments with real power were crucial in
neutralizing untalented monarchs, in constraining bureaucracies and in
providing a training ground for political judgement. Ideally, they would also
help select charismatic leaders through competition. Such leaders would
provide political direction and inject dynamism into political life, thereby also
countering the dangers of bureaucratic rule. For all of this, however, a price
was to be paid: charismatic leaders had to be supported by undemocratic, soulless and of course bureaucratic political machines, which mobilized the vote
for them. As it happened, parliamentarians became dependent on both what
Weber called 'the plebiscitary dictator in parliament' and the party machine
supporting him; they were reduced to 'well-disciplined lobby fodder'.

Weber was unambiguously in favour of widening the franchise. After all,
the recognition of equal status was part and parcel of the modern order; a
nineteenth-century system of notables running politics for themselves was
simply no longer viable. He also found it unbearable to think that the soldiers
returning from the front should end up with fewer political rights than the
propertied who had comfortably stayed at home. Weber vehemently dismissed
the fashionable idea of giving more votes to those with higher degrees; he also
held that education, especially in the humanities, more often than not led to a
lack of political judgement (as with Eisner, who had been a philosopher before
turning to journalism and party politics and who had now become the
'hostage of his own demagogic success').

Political inclusion, Weber thought, was the best way to foster political responsibility. But he never entertained the thought that the people could actually
themselves exercise power. 'Direct democracy', Weber argued emphatically, was
only possible in very small settings, where everyone knew everybody else, such

as certain Swiss cantons (and there the government would still be run by quasi-aristocracies of people with enough time and money not to have a regular *Beruf*). Anywhere else, democracy necessarily had to mean delegation – and therefore rule by some over others. It also necessarily implied bureaucratization, and, again, the real question was not whether to have it but how to contain it.

Quite apart from practical considerations about the size of states, however, Weber could never quite see most citizens as anything other than passive and incapable of understanding the complexities of modern social life. All they could – and all they should – do was cast a vote. Hence he dismissed the notion of a coherent popular will or mandate that could be translated into government programmes: as he wrote in a letter, 'concepts such as the "will of the people", the "*true* will of the people", etc., ceased to exist for me long ago. They are *fictions*.'[116] At best, elections established a kind of popular feedback rewarding leaders who had better political skills and at least some concern for the wishes of the populace. Struggling for the vote ensured that only those politicians rose to the top who were, unlike bureaucrats, decisive and, unlike pure demagogues, politically responsible. In that sense, the argument that inclusion bred responsibility was complemented by an argument that an infusion of struggle increased the quality of political leadership.[117]

So, in terms of Weber's categorization of legitimacy as traditional, charismatic or legal-rational, he advocated a combination of the last two: merging the rationalization of law and bureaucracy with the supposed personal heroism of the leader. Weber was adamant that the only alternative to 'leadership democracy' supported by a party political machine was 'leaderless democracy', with party bureaucrats and notables vying for influence behind the scenes. Any polity would be worse off with the latter.

But leadership democracy placed great burdens – or perhaps false hopes – on leaders. Clearly Weber owed his audience an account of how leaders were supposed to behave, what ethical limits and guidelines they ought to observe, especially if politics was somehow also a source of collective meaning. His 1919 lecture was to be that missing account.

Every politician, according to Weber, needed three decisive qualities: passion, a feeling of responsibility and a sense of proportion. Passion, however, did not denote a romantic cult of experience; rather, it meant devotion to a chosen cause. But such a passion was blind without a feeling of proportion and a sense of reality – in short, a capacity for keeping one's distance from things and from men, and, above all, from one's own feelings. Conversely, a lack of objectivity – and a mindless worship of power – was a deadly sin for the politician.

For the students listening to Weber's lecture on 'Politics as a Vocation', it must have seemed initially that he was drawing a clear distinction here:

between what he called an 'ethics of conviction' or pure intentions and an ethics of responsibility; and that he distinctly favoured the latter. The ethics of conviction was unconditional; it made the practitioner responsible only to his conscience. Politicians of conviction, such as radical pacifists and utopian socialists, were most concerned about preserving the purity of their intentions. In Weber's eyes, they stuck to a naive belief that only good would follow from good and only evil come of evil. They simply could not understand the autonomy of the political sphere and bear the seeming ethical irrationality of a world full of unintended consequences. But while being in denial, they could not escape the inner logic of politics – that is, the inevitable presence of violence. Tellingly, such men of conviction never accepted responsibility for any consequences, as long as their intentions had been pure. Weber chided them: 'If an action undertaken with purely good intentions has evil conse-quences, then, in the actor's eyes, not he but the world or the stupidity of other people is responsible – or God's will who made them thus.'[118]

An ethics of responsibility, on the other hand, meant that the politician would take account of the consequences of his actions, would compromise and would accept the ethical dangers involved in letting himself become the plaything of the paradoxical, even demonic forces at work in politics. But what was to be the measure for estimating consequences and deciding which consequences were and were not acceptable? Weber did not wish to portray the politician adhering to an ethics of responsibility as a pure pragmatist, or even opportunist. He also had to adopt an ultimate worldview, the choice of which lacked any rational foundations; in addition, he would in all likelihood at one point reach a situation where, unable to justify his stance rationally, he would be forced to declare: 'Here I stand; I can do no other.'

However, with such an irrational *cri de coeur*, it seemed that the ethics of responsibility would collapse into the ethics of conviction. This, Weber insisted, was not an ethical problem, but 'something genuinely human and moving'. He continued:

> Every one of us who is not dead on the inside must realize that this situation
> *could* happen. In that sense, an ethics of conviction and an ethics of respon-
> sibility are not absolute opposites but rather complement each other
> in constituting the genuine man – a man who *can* have the 'calling for
> politics'.[119]

A genuine ethics of responsibility therefore steered the course between a self-centred flight from the political world on the one hand and a ruthless opportunism on the other.

How was this intuition to be translated into any kind of liberal political practice? Weber was acutely, anxiously, aware that the social basis of liberalism had been eroded and that many of its ideals – progress and individual rights, above all – had been discredited in the eyes of many contemporaries. True, he thought the casual or, for that matter, sincere dismissal of Enlightenment ideas completely irresponsible: he warned reactionaries of all stripes that 'it is a gross self-deception to believe that without the achievements of the Age of the Rights of Man any of us, including the most conservative, can go on living his life'. But the belief in natural law, or any other metaphysical under-pinning of rights, could not credibly be sustained in a disenchanted world. If anything, Weber was eager to historicize and relativize liberal achievements. And of course he could not resort to justifying liberalism with utilitarian 'happiness' – which for him would have seemed like the happiness of the herd.

What, then, could possibly carry liberalism in the age of mass democracy? The most plausible theoretical answer, given the positions Weber had staked out in politics and sociology, was this: liberalism should generate a new account of culture (which, for Weber, necessarily had to mean national culture) and its tasks. And these could be achieved only with politics: the public realm, affirmed in its dignity (and thus transcending mere power poli-tics and haggling over material advantages), might thereby regain some of the 'most sublime values' which had retreated from it.[120] In addition liberals might appeal to value pluralism itself. Given the right circumstances, and above all, the human will to freedom, value pluralism could justify liberalism – not because it provided a secure philosophical foundation, but in a pragmatic manner: once the plurality of values and the human need to create meaning through choosing among them had been recognized, then individualism (and toleration) might at least appear as attractive propositions.[121] Each individual had to be given room to choose their values (and also to live with the painful consequences which could follow from these choices). And each individual's choice should in some sense be recognized, not because it was objectively right, but because one should, in Weber's words, 'regard as objectively valuable those innermost elements of the "personality", those highest and most ultimate value-judgements which determine our conduct and give meaning . . . to our life'.

But such general considerations were always one thing, respecting actual political choices in actual circumstances another. Weber's judgements in the tragic circumstances of 1919 were harsh. Soon after Weber's lecture, Kurt Eisner lost the first elections in the Bavarian republic. The very day he had planned to resign, Eisner was shot by a young right-wing aristocrat. In the ensuing revolutionary turmoil a soviet republic was declared, replacing what the Communists derided as Eisner's 'pseudo council republic'. As we saw, Weber did not for a minute believe in direct democracy, in councils as means of political self-administration or in 'people's delegates' who had no room for individual judgement and could be recalled at any time. This was not because ordinary people were always out of their depth – in Heidelberg Weber had actually served on a council, and he later expressed his regard for the sheer decency, discipline and *Sachlichkeit*, or realism, of simple workers and soldiers (as well as his satisfaction that the Germans were a *Disziplinvolk* after all).[122]

But something like the Bavarian experiment, Weber felt, was fundamentally not serious. After the soviet republic had been crushed, he appeared as a witness for the writer Ernst Toller. Toller was a poet and a socialist who had turned into a fervent pacifist after fighting on the western front. Toller had frequented Weber's Sunday gatherings for students and intellectuals in Heidelberg; probably he had also sat in the audience of 'Politics as a Vocation'. In spring 1919, he had briefly commanded the Bavarian 'Red Army'. Now he was tried for high treason, punishable by death. In Weber's eyes, Toller had been another littérateur who had become lost in politics, even a pure *Gesinnungsethiker* (a politician of conviction). Weber's wife reported her husband as saying of Toller: 'God in his anger has made him a politician'. But Weber spoke up for Toller in court and might well have saved his life, although Toller's attorney thought Weber's emphasis on his client's political inexperience had actually made things worse. At the same time, Weber lauded the chivalrous behaviour of Eisner's assassin in court, though regretting that the man had not been shot once convicted. Instead he was turned into a 'coffee house celebrity', whereas Eisner was worshipped as a political martyr.[123]

Embittered by his failure to succeed in the Democratic Party (which he left in April 1920), Weber continued to attack soulless party politicians. But he did exert some influence on the new German constitution. In general, it gave much more power to parliament than he would have liked, but majorities' and minorities' right of 'enquête' (to supervise the bureaucracy) was incorporated, as was Weber's proposal for a strong, directly elected president as a counterweight to parliament – a position which should ideally be filled by what Weber did not hesitate to call 'heroes'. But then again, the constitution had something for everyone: a liberal parliament with proportional representation, popular referendums, a quasi-monarch in the form of the president. As the legal theorist Franz Neumann was to point out, it seemed less a coherent framework for politics than 'a set of treaties among the powerful social and political forces of Germany', in particular between labour and capital, and between the army and the state.[124]

Max Weber died in 1920, after witnessing the ill-fated beginnings of the Weimar Republic. The end of the monarchy and the entrenchment of a liberal democracy had confirmed him in his belief that the state – in the form of the bureaucracy – would serve anyone, as long as the new rulers guaranteed the existence of the bureaucracy itself. It had also reinforced his belief that genuine revolutions were feasible only if the revolutionaries provided their own staff. The latter would have to create a counter-state (or else revolution-aries would be more like a board of management, trying to control a staff of specialists doing what they had always been doing – which is what Weber thought might be happening in Russia). Ultimately, even revolutionaries had the same incentives as bourgeois politicians: just as the latter would always try to live off politics, the former would try to live off the revolution. Hence the Bolsheviks, according to Weber, were likely to engage in something like permanent revolution.

Given his peculiar liberalism, no one can predict what Weber would have said had he lived to see the deep crisis of the Weimar Republic in the early 1930s. His friends and followers were eager to promote the idea that he would have played a central political role; his wife could already see him as chan-cellor.[125] But Weber himself ruefully noted that he was excitable and lacked the 'calm nerves' required for politics. He had always been an academic trouble-maker, who could hate with unparalleled passion. He was not at all given to compromise (but then why should a scholar be given to compromise?). While calling for realism in politics, he never wavered in seeing national prestige and honour as supreme political values. Yet willingness to compromise as well as some tempering of nationalist passions seemed precisely what were required for the new democratic age – a fact Weber himself saw clearly.

The war had left new norms, but no obviously workable institutions to implement or enforce them; newly created constitutions framed a fragile balance of social forces, rather than providing a shared moral basis for politics, let alone leading to a lasting constitutional settlement; and the ideal of national self-determination by homogeneous states seemed to call for further acts of 'national purification', rather than lead to harmonious relations between self-governing polities. The new international order which had been envisaged by that 'philosopher' Woodrow Wilson trying to 'to bind the princes of the world', as Keynes had put it, was beset with tensions from the very begin-ning. In particular, while the international and the domestic had always been connected, they were now even more closely tied together for the weak states that had been created in 1919. This meant that failures of collective security – and the system of protection for minority groups that had been established by the League of Nations – almost always immediately caused drastic deterioration in the quality of whatever there might have been by way of liberal democracy. Keynes observed as early as 1922 'the paradox that the first experiment in international government should exert its influence in the direction of intensifying nationalism'.[126]

Had he lived, Weber would have been deeply disappointed, particularly in the fate of the institutions which were to make up leadership democracy: parliaments kept losing power to state bureaucracies, and to business and labour representatives working out compromises under the tutelage of the state (which further undermined any remaining distinctions between public political and private economic power).[127] This in turn shook any remaining faith in parliamentarism. As early as 1923 the German right-wing legal thinker Carl Schmitt – a one-time participant in Weber's special seminar for young lecturers in Munich – issued an intellectual death certificate for parliament and its supposed core principles of openness and discussion:

> The situation of parliamentarism is critical today because the development of modern mass democracy has made public discussion an empty formality. Many norms of contemporary parliamentary law, above all provisions concerning the independence of representatives and the openness of sessions, as a result function like a superfluous decoration, useless and even embarrassing, as though someone had painted the radiator of a modern central-heating system with red flames in order to give the appearance of a blazing fire.[128]

Parliament had become a façade; real power rested with powerful social groups. Other justifications of parliament, according to Schmitt, also no longer applied. He explicitly rejected the other role Weber had assigned to legislative assemblies:

> If someone still believes in parliamentarism, he will at least have to offer new arguments for it. A reference to Friedrich Naumann, Hugo Preuss, and Max Weber is no longer sufficient. With all respect for these men, no one today would share their hope that parliament alone guarantees the education of a political elite.[129]

Other liberal institutions came under pressure as well. The anxiety that the rule of law was being eroded – already voiced in Weber's diagnosis of an increasing deformalization of law – was exacerbated by the vision of a state called to many new tasks, which in the eyes of liberals meant the delegation of ever more power to essentially unaccountable bureaucracies. In 1929 Lord Hewart, Lord Chief Justice of England, alarmed his fellow citizens with the assertion that the rise of the administrative state was producing 'a despotic power which at one and the same time places Government departments above the Sovereignty of Parliament and beyond the jurisdiction of the Courts'.[130] Rule by the 'departmental despot', the expert bureaucrat 'at once scientific and benevolent', was destroying 'self-government' and creating 'administrative lawlessness'.

It would be tempting to contrast a new politics of will – which came in a Leninist and a nationalist version after the First World War – with a liberal Weberian one that prized reasonable compromise. But Weber's image of modern mass politics also concentrated on the necessity of faith in leaders, and his vision of a new liberal statecraft that could integrate the nation as a whole seemed to require a nationalistic foreign policy. Clearly, no liberal answers for the democratic age had emerged by the mid-1920s, when the trend towards democracy creation began to go into reverse and, as Paul Valéry observed, dictatorship was becoming 'contagious'. In the absence of any kind of stable constitutional settlement, Europeans would keep on experimenting with political forms and principles.

CHAPTER 2

Interwar Experiments
Making Peoples, Remaking Souls

The crisis consists precisely in the fact that the old is dying and that the new cannot be born. In this interregnum the most varied phenomena appear.

Antonio Gramsci

Everywhere, people are awaiting a messiah, and the air is laden with the promises of large and small prophets . . . we all share the same fate: we carry within us more love, and above all more longing than today's society is able to satisfy. We have all ripened for something, and there is no one to harvest the fruit . . .

Karl Mannheim

We are now striving to expand the party further . . . into a true, great people's party, that with the support of the majority of the people can realize the dream of the . . . people's home [folkhemmet]. The precondition for such a gathering is a politics that takes into consideration the need of different groups and without prejudice experiments with different ways of satisfying legitimate demands from wherever such demands may come.

Per Albin Hansson

To attempt, in practice, today, to anticipate this future result of a fully developed, fully stabilised and constituted, fully comprehensive and mature communism would be like trying to teach higher mathematics to a child of four . . . We can (and must) begin to build socialism, not with abstract human material, or with human material specially prepared for us, but with the human material bequeathed to us by capitalism. True, that is no easy matter . . .

V. I. Lenin

' A PERIOD of experimentation of all types' – with these terms the French philosopher Paul Ricoeur once described the interwar years through which he had lived as a young man.[1] Tomáš Masaryk, just installed as first president of the new Czechoslovak state, thought post-1918 Europe a 'laboratory built over the great graveyard of the World War.'[2] Europeans were partly forced to experiment because both tradition and dynastic legitimacy had ceased to provide principles for public order, but new ones had hardly become entrenched. A liberal restoration proved impossible – there were too many new people in politics, too many new claims being made – but so did a socialist revolution as theorized by Lenin. Not just Communists were deeply disappointed that what the British socialist Margaret Cole called an 'enormously inflated power of organized labour' after the war[3] had not been used to bring about fundamental political changes. In particular, they were frustrated by the foundering of one institution which, in the eyes of socialists critical of the Russian Revolution, seemed a promising instrument for achieving revolution without an authoritarian vanguard party: the councils of workers and soldiers which had not only played a role in the immediate period before and after the October Revolution, but had also sprung up all over Western Europe. By 1920 they had been either dismantled or absorbed into parliamentary pluralism.

Thus socialist and Communist political thought after 1919 has to be understood against the background of failure: left-wing intellectuals almost everywhere felt they confronted a stalemate of political forces and had to decide whether to work within the structures of parliamentary democracy, or whether they should somehow keep trying for revolution. Many started searching for ways to bring about fundamental change short of violent insurrection on the Soviet model. In particular, they sought to theorize the notion of first capturing the culture of a country and in a sense 're-educating' large parts of the population to share the same values before using political institutions to transform the economy. The socialist jurist Otto Kirchheimer, for instance, argued that majority rule was justified only if citizens shared moral values and simply used the mechanism of voting to decide about the best ways to implement them.[4] In the absence of value consensus, in other words, seemingly democratic procedures meant oppression of the minority; consequently, a true socialist democracy was dependent on first having patiently created such a consensus. And such consensus-building seemed necessarily to be of both a moral and a *cultural* character.

The Promise of Pluralism

When Mussolini declared, 'This is the collective century and therefore the century of the state', he was not saying anything that would have been recognized as specifically fascist at the time. As we saw in the last chapter, the First World War gave the idea of socialism, understood as central, state-directed economic development, a great push in Western Europe. Further east, Lenin had very quickly abandoned the ideal of the decentralized commune state and instead sought to emulate German war socialism. But what if that trend was resisted and a transformation of society sought not through harnessing the state but through completely disaggregating it? This thought seemed to go against the direction in which everything in twentieth-century Europe was moving; it might at best still be suitable for Southern Europe, where anarchism remained traditionally strong. But the most sophisticated version of that intuition came in fact from a number of English gentlemen-scholars: the pluralists.

Pluralism was not an exclusively left-wing phenomenon: the British church historian J. N. Figgis – not a socialist by any stretch of the imagination, but an important inspiration for pluralist thought – insisted that, under modern conditions of ever more powerful states, group pluralism was the only means of saving liberal aspirations for autonomy. He claimed in 1913 that 'the battle for freedom in this century is the battle of small societies to maintain their inherent life against the all-devouring Leviathan of the whole'.[5] The individual on his own had already lost that battle, but for groups there might be some hope.

Pluralist thinkers had been deeply impressed by Germany's *Kulturkampf*; in their eyes, the conflict between Bismarck and Catholics – which the Iron Chancellor was widely perceived as having lost – had proved that seemingly all-powerful state sovereignty was an illusion. States, it appeared, could function in the absence of overall cultural homogeneity, while giving groups such as unions and churches much more leeway than had been thought possible in state-centred traditions of political thought.

Older forms of legal community were excavated to bolster this anti-statist vision. In the late nineteenth century the German legal historian Otto von Gierke had drawn a distinction between 'unity-in-plurality' as the 'antique-modern' conception of political association and 'plurality-in-unity' as the medieval one.[6] A similar contrast was drawn between *Herrschaft*, or legal rule, and *Gemeinschaft*, or community and fellowship. The ancient Germanic ideal of fellowship was to serve as a model for group life and counter the modern tendency for uniform legal regulation from above, based on Roman law.

The English pluralists took their name from the American philosopher William James, not from Gierke. But they shared Gierke's ambition to disaggregate statehood and counter conceptions of unitary sovereignty. And they thought that England was a much better place for that project.[7] They argued that their country had never really subscribed to the continental tradition of the state as a unified public power. In 1915 Ernest Barker, in an article tellingly entitled 'The Discredited State', held that the English state had long been 'accustomed to discredit' and that 'to tell the truth it has never sought to take great credit to itself. It has not magnified its own office, or exalted its own dignity.'[8] English life, Barker claimed, had been particularly hospitable to creating porous groups with overlapping memberships. He argued that 'England is not unlike the University of Oxford – or for that matter any other amoeba. She can throw off by a ready process of fission colleges and delegacies.'[9] For obvious reasons such notions of England as a particularly 'clubbable country' and contrasts with a 'Prussian philosophy' of state worship proved attractive during the First World War. The war in turn exacerbated fears that the state would turn into what the socialist thinker G. D. H. Cole termed a 'tyrannical master'.

The pluralists sought decentralization and democracy within and among as many groups as possible. In this they were inspired not least by the example of the United States, which appeared to prosper and even project power abroad, all without a strong state tradition. Political science professor and Labour Party politician Harold Laski had spent parts of the war studying federalism at Harvard; there he began to advocate abandoning a Germanic conception of the state with its 'mystical monism' and any idea of the state as a 'kind of modern Baal, to which the citizen must, unheeding, bow a willing knee'. The state, Laski insisted, could not command automatic obedience; rather, it had to prove itself.[10] He stressed the resistance to the 1916 Military Service Act by conscientious objectors as yet another example of how fictitious the notion of all-powerful state sovereignty turned out to be in practice.[11] Laski admitted that pluralism had a radical, even anarchist streak, and he himself actually got into serious trouble when he supported the 1919 Boston Police Strike and advocated police unionization. Accused of being a 'boudoir Bolshevist' by colleagues in the Government Department, he left Harvard, although the university had backed him in the face of public criticism and alumni requests for his removal (the president later estimated that the British socialist had cost the university about 300,000 dollars in lost donations).[12]

The most radical (and the most consistent) proposal for pluralism in practice, however, came from Cole, an academic first in London, later in Oxford. Like Laski, Cole saw the state not just as a means of class oppression, but also as inherently incapable of realizing genuine democracy. He argued that 'the omnicompetent State, with its omnicompetent Parliament is . . . utterly unsuitable to any really democratic community, and must be destroyed or painlessly extinguished.'[13] Cole advocated 'guild socialism' instead: workers should organize themselves in guilds and assume control of industry. Direct control was best, but delegation of larger tasks (and therefore representation) was also acceptable, if absolutely necessary. Here Cole called for a new principle of representation, based on function rather than territory: this essentially meant dividing up people according to profession or other shared interests, as opposed to where they happened to live (or, as Laski explained, 'anyone can see that the railways are as real as Lancashire')[14] Cole also demanded multiple votes: 'man should have as many distinct, and separately exercised, votes, as he has distinct social purposes or interests'.[15] In short, only if all one's interests and purposes in different associations, as both a producer and consumer, could be represented would there be real democracy and what Cole termed 'a community which is self-governing in this complete sense, over the whole length and breadth of its activities'.[16] Thus guild socialism and pluralism more broadly were conceived as alternatives both to state-centred models of socialism and to liberal individualism.

However, it became increasingly clear that group pluralism suffered from a fair number of theoretical problems, and that it was very difficult in practice to compete with the politics of mass party systems that had been boosted by the First World War. At the level of theory, the supposedly discredited state always seemed to sneak in again through the back door: Cole claimed that the state should no longer coerce, but merely 'co-ordinate' the activities of self-regulating groups. But for certain national tasks, he conceded, central authorities, or what he called a national 'Commune', might be necessary. Critics pointed out that the civil servants running such authorities would probably 'chuckle *l'état c'est moi*'.[17] In other words, it seemed that a modern, complex society could not do with anything less than a centralized, bureaucratic state along Weberian lines. This fact might be disguised with medieval-sounding talk of guilds and such. But it did not change it.

Carl Schmitt, on the other hand, attacked Laski and Cole by claiming that, when the chips were down, there always *was* a sovereign, that the state did not simply constitute one association or group among others: even if it failed practically to get its way in every instance, there remained the brutal truth that it alone could call on the lives of its citizens (and authoritatively decide who was a friend and who an enemy of the state). According to Schmitt, 'the pluralist theory of the state is in itself pluralistic, that is, it has no center but draws its thoughts from rather different intellectual circles (religion, economics, liberalism, socialism, etc.)'. Ultimately, though, it was said to be just another version of liberal individualism: the state and whatever associations had been formed were supposed to be 'a revocable service' for individuals.[18]

Less harsh critics – and, in particular, those less invested in the idea that political institutions had to be understood and defined from the perspective of the extreme life-and-death situation – pointed out that pluralism seemed possible only against the background of an overarching moral consensus about the limits of politics, as well as a great deal of mutual tolerance. Put differently, it might be fine for England (or just Oxford, for that matter), where even amid bitter conflicts a certain civility could be taken for granted. But it was not able to solve the fundamental problems of an age where states had become much stronger, where groups with conflicting goals had been permanently mobilized, and precisely where consensus about politics as a whole was absent. No wonder some thinkers – Ernest Barker, for instance – later abandoned pluralism and instead started asking how best to preserve Britain's particular 'traditions of civility'.

Eventually Laski and Cole came to agree with the criticism of their statist opponents. Both started moving away from pluralist ideas in the mid-1920s. By that time, the post-war economic boom was decidedly over, the Great Strike of the miners in 1926 had failed and whatever might have passed as plausible initiatives for industrial democracy had been beaten back.[19] Laski seemed to repudiate the whole way of high-minded intellectual living from which pluralism had emanated in the first place. As he put it at one point: 'It is easier to think [this way] amid the dreaming spires of Oxford or in the loveliness of the Cambridge backs in June than if one is a blacklisted miner in a Welsh coalfield or a share-cropper trying to fix a decent price on his puny holding in Alabama.'[20]

The former pluralists now bet on the 'parliamentary method' – that is, support for the Labour Party gaining a majority – as the most promising tool for bringing about socialism. It was a return to the state as the primary means for politics, but also to the centralization of reform efforts associated with the Fabians, which G. K. Chesterton had ridiculed as Beatrice Webb 'settling things by the simple process of ordering about the citizens of the state, as she might the servants in a kitchen'.[21]

Cole and his wife Margaret had been – in Margaret's words – 'romantics about trade unions'. Cured of their romanticism, they now joined Laski in thinking that if the Labour Party won enough seats there could be a 'revolution by consent'.[22] But numbers in parliament were only one thing. For such a revolution to come about and last, something else was urgently needed: education. Consequently, Cole and Laski now put enormous effort into adult and, in particular, worker education. It seemed like the slow road to socialism – as opposed to the seeming shortcut to industrial democracy after 1918 – but they were still sure it would lead there.

The Politics of Pedagogy

The idea of the socialist mass party gaining state power through parliament as the royal road to radical change was hardly new in the 1920s: since the late nineteenth century it had provided the main alternative to the anarchist ideal of mass insurrection on the one hand (with the Paris Commune as the prime historical example) and, on the other, the Leninist vanguard party, which precisely did not want a mass membership. Also since that time, however, the notion of the socialist mass party had been afflicted by an ever more keenly felt ambiguity: was its point to reform from within liberal bourgeois institutions, such as parliament, or did its ultimate goal always have to be overthrowing these institutions altogether?

Marx and Engels had provided no clear answers. Sometimes they seemed to suggest that there was a legal road to revolution – Laski's 'revolution by consent' – in a country like Britain, with well-established liberal institutions and a seemingly ever more numerous working class; at other times they appeared to endorse the insurrectionary strategy of the Commune. In 1891 Engels still insisted that the German Social Democrats – the largest and electorally most successful party of its kind in continental Europe – commit themselves officially to Marxist doctrine, that is, to revolution.

But, as it turned out, committing to revolution was not quite the same as committing to making the revolution. According to the orthodox interpretation of Marxism as a science of historical laws – codified by Engels, who had claimed that 'just as Darwin discovered the law of development of organic nature, so Marx discovered the law of development of human history' – Social Democrats could simply wait for capitalism to go under (and meanwhile do their bit in parliament to make the workers' fate a little less unpleasant). The Social Democratic leader Karl Kautsky famously claimed: 'It is not our task to organize the revolution, but to organize ourselves for the revolution.'[23] Thus Marxism actually seemed to justify what came to be known as 'passive radicalism', a perhaps rather comfortable stance of being a revolutionary but not a revolution-making party (which was another of Kautsky's favourite – and ever so slightly contradictory – formulas).

But not everyone was comfortable or, for that matter, confident that waiting for the inner contradictions of capitalism to work themselves out was the right strategy. Another SPD leader, Eduard Bernstein, dared to point out that numerous predictions deducible from the supposed Marxist science were in fact turning out to be false: the British proletariat, for instance, was becoming more bourgeois; the bourgeoisie itself appeared to engage in serious social reform; society as a whole was not ever more polarized; and Marxist economics was unable to explain how wages could rise exactly in those industries where profits were also the highest. Eventually Bernstein decided to revise his conception of Marxism so that it incorporated a full endorsement of parliamentary democracy – not as a stepping stone to revolution, but as a building block of the final socialist edifice itself. Even more scandalously for orthodox Marxists, he claimed that Social Democracy was actually about fully realizing *liberal* values, such as individual autonomy. As he expressed it, 'democracy is . . . both means and end. It is a weapon in the struggle for socialism, and it is the form in which socialism will be realized.'[24] Bernstein held that democracy, as a 'school of compromise', transformed those participating in it morally: 'the right to vote in a democracy makes its members virtual partners in the community', 'and this virtual partnership must in the end lead to real partnership'. He dismissed 'class dictatorship' as a 'political atavism' and instead argued that 'there is no liberal thought that is not also part of the intellectual equipment of socialism'.[25]

This really was scandalous; and Bernstein did not emerge victorious in the great controversy over revisionism (and what Masaryk diagnosed as a general 'crisis of Marxism'). Opponents like Rosa Luxemburg insisted that abandoning revolution in favour of reform – essentially the same as saving capitalism from itself – meant abandoning socialism altogether. The Second International persisted in a policy of non-participation in bourgeois governments. As one socialist leader put it in 1900, 'a socialist who enters a bourgeois ministry either deserts to the enemy, or he surrenders to the enemy'.[26]

The question of reform or revolution – and the question whether revolution could be achieved through consent and education – also haunted Social Democrats after the First World War, when it seemed that their mass parties were the obvious contenders to dominate European politics. Debates and practical dilemmas associated with the choice between reform and revolution were nowhere more clearly articulated than among the so-called Austro-Marxists.[27] Who precisely were the Austro-Marxists? A short but entirely correct answer would be: a group of students who came together in the intellectual powerhouse of Vienna at the beginning of the century and decided to meet regularly at the Café Central. As Günter Nenning was to remark, 'in the Vienna of that period the move to a new café was a clear indication that a new era was beginning'.[28]

The Austro-Marxists were not just theorists; they shouldered political responsibility as party and eventually even as state leaders. Karl Renner was to be president of the first Austrian Republic, and then again the first president of the Second Austrian Republic after the Second World War; Otto Bauer was not just the most original Marxist theorist of nationalism, he was also leader of the Austrian Social Democratic Party and, for a short time, foreign minister.

Bauer in particular had systematically engaged with the challenge of inflamed national sentiments, especially acute in the Habsburg Empire, which for socialists constituted a little International all by itself. He boldly declared that socialism was not at all antithetical to nationalism; it would not obliterate national differences but in fact accentuate them, since it would for the first time integrate 'the masses' into a national cultural community from which they necessarily remained excluded in a class society. He asked: 'What do our workers know about Kant? Our peasants about Goethe?'[29] Only socialized production would free up the time required to read Kant and Goethe; and only socialism would create a comprehensive national education and eventually a new people where the creators and the consumers of culture were identical – for the first time in human history. He claimed that 'socialism makes the nation autonomous, so that its fate is determined by its own conscious will; this has the effect that in socialist society nations will be increasingly differentiated, their qualities more sharply defined and their characters more sharply distinct from one another.'[30] On the other hand, excessive nationalism was actually a form of class hatred in disguise; it would – conveniently – disappear with the end of capitalism.

Bauer firmly believed that a great diversity of nations was to be cherished and preserved. This, however, did not translate into a claim for self-determination in the form of one state per homogeneous national population. On the contrary, such demands, Bauer held, were actually one more symptom of class oppression – and of pernicious bureaucratic centralization. In multinational empires dominated by a capitalist class, revolutionary energies would be diverted into a struggle among nationalities to gain centralized power. Under socialism, however, nationalities would be able to live together in one federal state, content with cultural autonomy. Specifically, Bauer advocated the personal rather than the territorial principle of nationality. Since the Austro-Hungarian Empire was so mixed ethnically, every citizen should choose their national status themselves. Local minorities were to be constituted as public corporate bodies and administer their own affairs.

This irenic picture fitted with the Austro-Marxists' general view of Marxism: it was a science, but even more it was a language of universal moral values which potentially appealed to all 'rational minds', not just to angry proletarians.[31] The sense that violent revolution was not at all the best way to realize these human values was reinforced by the theories of Rudolf Hilferding, a paediatrician by training but to be known eventually as the twentieth century's most influential Marxist economist. Under conditions of what Hilferding called 'finance capitalism', monopolies and cartels in alliance with banks were already engaged in economic planning on a national scale – which allowed the state a much larger role in guiding and planning the economy. Given that the state, according to Hilferding, actually possessed a fair amount of autonomy, and given that it was itself already planning, the Austro-Marxists argued that the revolutionaries should seize the state and then use state power to bring planning to full fruition. Thus what Hilferding was the first to call 'organized capitalism' might allow for a relatively smooth transition to socialism.

All this had been theory, and the theory had flourished primarily in the period before the First World War. After the war, with the Habsburg monarchy and the empire destroyed, the socialists were called to praxis. Bauer's proposed nationalities policy could have been implemented in some of the new states that contained sizeable minorities. Yet, to put it mildly, there was little demand for experimenting with Bauer's ideas. Equally problematic was the question of how to implement socialism. On the one hand, the Austro-Marxists seemed to occupy a unique position of strength: they had at their disposal what was widely seen as a model left-wing party in the interwar years, a party with a huge membership and – unlike the German Social Democrats – not threatened by a Communist Party on its left. As their theories evolved, these intellectuals constantly had to make decisions about whether mainly to defend the socialist gains they had achieved under parliamentary democracy or to take the revolutionary offensive (to which their theoretical positions still committed them). So they were really looking for something like revolution through reforms. Typically, they founded a kind of compromise organization at the end of the war which came to be known as the Two-and-a-Half International (and which was soon dissolved). As it turned out, it was partly (but only partly) unresolved theoretical issues which made their overall strategy fail.

In the 1920s Bauer argued that a kind of democratic stalemate had been reached between Vienna, which was in the hands of the socialists, and the rest of the country, which remained agricultural, Catholic and politically conservative. He elaborated the theory of an 'equilibrium between class forces', whereby power would be shared between progressives and conservatives, neither of whom could hope to get a clear majority. However, he also thought that with education, and by building an attractive socialist culture in the Austrian capital, the party might gradually win over white-collar workers and the middle class. He now spoke of 'slow revolution'.

Yet the idea of a balance of class forces had only been plausible at the very beginning of the republic, as the jurist Hans Kelsen pointed out at the time and as Bauer himself was to recognize later on. After 1922 or so, the conservatives were hardly interested in power sharing. The socialists, on the other hand, began to concentrate their energies almost exclusively on making Vienna into a showcase of proletarian culture – through welfare and education, which were to serve the development of the individual worker, or what Bauer at one point called 'a revolution of souls'. Most of life became organized through the party, from the Workers' Symphony Orchestra to workers' sports (which were always team sports, thus avoiding competitive individualism) to the Proletarian

Nudists' Club and the Worker Rabbit Breeders.[32] This culture was to prefigure a generalized ideal of healthy and rational living, based on values of fellowship and mutuality. But what historians were to term 'anticipatory socialism' or the 'politics of prefiguration' eventually came to substitute for the actual exercise of power: the revolution of souls was never quite advanced enough for the revolution of political institutions.[33] Red Vienna turned into a kind of fortress surrounded by peasant conservatism; and the socialists developed a more and more defensive, if not outright defeatist, attitude. This mentality found its concrete expression in the Karl Marx Hof. The Hof was a set of modern buildings with cheap apartments for workers. But it also looked like a fortress.

The leaders never resolved the tension between their desire to abide by the rules of parliamentary democracy and the possibility of a violent upset of the equilibrium of class forces – which might necessitate deploying the Schutzbund, the socialist paramilitary. True, not all tactical and strategic mistakes could be blamed on the deficiencies in Austro-Marxist theory. But arguably they had something to do with the fact that philosophically the leaders never quite decided whether they should conceive of socialism as a matter of political will, as a matter of universal, rational morality or as a matter of historical laws.

In due course, Trotsky accused them of being 'conservative' and opportunistic, while Lenin ridiculed them as 'petty bourgeois democrats' who believed that new human beings had first to be created rather than proceeding as quickly as possible with revolution – which would then take care of creating new humans. Victor Serge, an ardent socialist during the 1920s (and, later, a sharp analyst of Communist failings), observed:

> Austro-Marxism organized and influenced over a million proletarians, it was master of Vienna . . . it could mobilize, in a few hours, 50,000 *Schutzbundler* on the Ring, uniformed in sports-tunics and (as everyone knew) tolerably well armed, it was led by the most able theoreticians in the working-class world; and yet . . . through its sobriety, prudence, and bourgeois moderation, it failed its destiny.[34]

This failure became final with 12 February 1934, when the Austrian state – by then already a 'post-liberal' polity under the Christian Socialist chancellor Engelbert Dollfuss, with parliament de facto abolished – confronted the last remnants of the Schutzbund (which had already been declared illegal). To the very end Bauer had believed that he could co-operate even with an authoritarian like Dollfuss, all in the name of preserving the parliamentary republic. Yet the socialists' nominal strength and what remained of the Schutzbund did not save them, although there were fierce battles around the Karl Marx Hof and other socialist fortresses. Hundreds died, some labour leaders were lynched and the 'most able theoreticians of the working-class world' almost all went into exile. Serge recounts how in Paris more than a decade later he was 'unable to recognize Otto Bauer, so cruelly had defeat shrivelled his solid, regular features, stamped not so long ago with a noble certainty. He was to die suddenly, from a heart attack, but actually from the defeat of working-class Austria.'[35]

The defeat of socialism in one city reverberated everywhere in Europe (with Laski, for instance, sending a 'Salute to the Vienna Martyrs'). It gave rise to the myth that a determined proletarian class consciousness had been betrayed by incompetent leaders. Many observers also concluded that while the socialists had tried to avoid a civil war at almost all costs, they had had to face it in the end anyway – and had lost it, partly because they had tried to do everything to avoid it. In fact, however, the lessons of Red Vienna were more ambiguous: on the one hand it seemed to reinforce the insight that in countries with deep political divisions a successful transformation towards socialism required putting together broad coalitions held together by beliefs which could not be reduced to working-class solidarity. For others, however, it simply confirmed the Leninist imperative to form militant vanguard parties prepared to break decisively with bourgeois democracy.

Some of the most innovative Marxist political thinkers of twentieth-century Europe accepted both lessons and worked out theories concentrating on conquering 'culture' and not just the means of production – but without abandoning that seemingly supremely effective political instrument, the charismatic party. The most important thinker of this kind was Antonio Gramsci, although Gramsci was not just a theorist: like Bauer, he combined the roles of innovative intellectual and leader of a mass party.

Gramsci had grown up in Sardinia, then a land of miners' unrest and banditry. His father, a civil servant, had been accused of embezzlement; his imprisonment and financial ruin meant that Gramsci had to spend several years working in the local tax office instead of attending school. Like his successor in the leadership of the Italian Communist Party, Palmiro Togliatti, Gramsci won a scholarship to the University of Turin, where he was to become particularly interested in linguistics – all the while also working as a journalist for socialist papers. The first encounters with the Italian mainland (and industrial society) turned out to be a shock for someone 'so very, so extremely provincial'. Gramsci reported in his first letter home that 'a short walk reduces me to fear and trembling, after just avoiding being run down by innumerable cars and trams.'[36]

Gramsci's first response to the oppression and exploitation he had witnessed on his native island had been a form of Sardinian nationalism. As he came to understand the mainland better, however, he embraced Marxism, without ever forgetting the national and cultural divisions with which he had grown up. In fact, throughout his life he retained an acute sense that Italy's national unification had been incomplete; a wide chasm still opened up not just between a prosperous industrial North and a poor agrarian South, but also between what Gramsci often called the 'legal Italy' of state institutions and the 'real Italy' of social and cultural fragmentation.

In the second decade of the twentieth century, Gramsci turned into a leading socialist intellectual, inspiring and being inspired by the *biennio rosso* of 1919–20, when trade unions increased their membership from a quarter of a million to two million, strikes swept over the North of Italy, and the socialists became the largest party in parliament. Most important for Gramsci was the emergence of workers' councils in the factories of the North. As in other European countries during the First World War, bodies had been formed within industry to involve not just management but also labour in planning; in Italy these were called 'Internal Commissions'. In June 1919 Gramsci claimed that:

> today the Internal Commissions limit the power of the capitalist in the factory and settle matters pertaining to workshop arbitration and discipline. Developed and enriched, tomorrow they must function as the organs of proletarian power capable of substituting the capitalist in his present useful functions of direction and administration.[37]

The young Sardinian was instrumental in organizing factory councils in Turin, the supposed 'Petrograd of the Italian Revolution'. In Gramsci's mind, these councils were to be both institutions for worker self-management – *autogestione* – and basic units of political democracy. The underlying thought was that power needed to be given to the producers: democracy was not about an abstract concept of equal citizenship, and socialism not about traditional trade unions (which always ended up dividing workers according to different trades and skill levels, and quickly became dominated by bureaucratic elites). For Gramsci, the councils were to be public institutions (unlike socialist parties and trade unions), comprising productive, legislative and executive functions. He claimed that 'the factory council is the model of the proletarian state'; it was the 'national territory' for the 'class that had no fatherland'. But he also, rather optimistically, envisaged it as the first building block of a whole new international communist economy.[38]

Gramsci was also enthusiastically in favour of the modernization of the factories, the introduction of 'Taylorism' as well as other kinds of what he called 'Americanism'. All would hasten the demise of the feudal remnants in the Italian state and economy, all would make workers more disciplined – a precondition for the proletarian state, in which work was to be both more efficient and yet somehow also more liberated. Where Lenin had wanted Russian workers to become Germans, Gramsci wanted Italians to become Americans. He never explained, though, how in the end more individual autonomy through self-management and more efficiency through national planning would go together; he also was largely unconcerned that American-style 'rationalization' and what he called the socialist 'regulated society' might reinforce the hardness of Weber's steely casing and permanently alienate workers if not from the products, then at least from the processes, of work.

What did Gramsci think he was doing? In 1919 he clearly assumed that he was merely emulating his great idol Lenin, whom he praised as 'the master of life' and the 'awakener of souls'. He hoped to follow the template of 1917, which, in his eyes, had been a revolution *against* Marx's *Capital*. Russia had been backward, so was Italy, but revolutionary will could succeed precisely at the periphery of the capitalist world. However, Lenin had of course already turned from 'all power to the soviets' to 'all power to the party', and had insisted that the party-state was crucial for implementing his own version of 'Americanism'.

As in Russia, the question of rule by councils or rule by party soon became acute. Were the councils merely schools of revolution or supreme instruments of revolutionary action?[39] Gramsci was clear: he claimed that both the socialist party and the trade unions should concentrate on creating favourable conditions for the growth and consolidation of the councils. But of course neither the party nor the trade unions were pleased by the subordinate role he had assigned them. The unions in the end settled for relatively minor gains and were taken in by the government's promise that parliament would study the problems of industrial democracy and pass an appropriate bill. The councils, which for Gramsci had seemed like the bridge to the new socialist fatherland, ended up as minor instruments of 'industrial relations'.[40]

The *biennio rosso*, however, had made the possibility of a repeat of the Russian Revolution in Italy seem very real. Fascism fed off that perception; the Fascists attacked party buildings in 1919 and Gramsci needed a bodyguard to go anywhere as early as 1921. He later observed that 'the class struggle has always assumed in Italy a very harsh character through the "human" immaturity of some sections of the population. Cruelty and absence of sympathy are two characteristics peculiar to the Italian people, who pass from childish sentimentality to the most brutal and bloody ferocity, from passionate anger to the cold contemplation of the sufferings of others'.[41]

Gramsci sought to respond to Fascism with a united front from below, which once more raised the question of national unity. He had closely followed the rise of the relatively progressive Catholic Popular Party after 1919 and opposed an understanding of socialism as mainly a form of anti-clericalism which belittled the hopes and concerns of simple people. He held that if one wanted to form an alliance of workers and peasants – in the way Lenin had managed in Russia – one needed the equivalent of the priesthood to educate and lead the peasants.[42] In Gramsci's eyes, intellectuals had to become 'permanent persuaders'; they had to be linked 'organically' to a 'national-popular mass'.[43] He claimed that 'history and politics cannot be made without passion, without this emotional bond between intellectuals and the people-nation'. This did not mean indoctrination of the workers by socialist intellectuals; rather, it was about creating a genuine culture centred in the institutions of society – schools in particular. As early as 1917 Gramsci had maintained, in contradiction to trade union leaders who saw culture as peripheral for the class struggle, that culture did not translate into 'knowing a little something about everything'. Instead, he asserted: 'I have a Socratic concept of culture: I believe it to be good thinking, whatever one thinks about . . .'[44]

Culture, for Gramsci, meant self-knowledge, self-mastery and, above all, thinking for oneself. He resolutely opposed any kind of educational initiatives – such as the party's Popular Universities – that he felt were condescending vis-à-vis ordinary people. The main point remained that 'every revolution has been preceded by a long period of intense critical activity, of new cultural insight and the spread of ideas through groups of men initially resistant to them'.[45] Thus a kind of passionate pedagogy had to be the essence of the formation of what Gramsci called a 'historic bloc' – a combination of 'base' and 'superstructure' and a notion which considerably refined the rather crude understanding among many Marxists of one simply being the reflection of the other.

Gramsci argued that socialist revolution and the permanent dominance of the proletariat required the conquest of 'hegemony', a translation of Lenin's concept of *gegemoniya*, which involved the Russian revolutionary class alliance of workers and peasants.[46] Hegemony did not so much indicate domination (as contemporary usage suggests); rather, it was revolutionary leadership successfully applied to carry several classes forward to fundamental change. Gramsci's preferred example of hegemony was the French Jacobins. Hegemony, as Gramsci wrote, 'necessarily supposes an intellectual unity'.[47] In practice, that meant everyone could properly conceive themselves as part of a revolutionary coalition – and everyone could do so, because, as Gramsci famously (and not at all frivolously) held: 'all men are intellectuals' (though he added, 'not all men in society have the function of intellectuals'). Party intellectuals were specialists in permanent persuasion, but all members of oppressed classes could be permanently persuaded.

Clearly, this strategy was designed specifically for Italy, with its lack of national unity, with its 'cosmopolitan' bourgeois intellectuals who did little to further national unity and with its large peasant masses ready to become, not Germans or Americans, but Italians. Like Bauer, Gramsci took nationalism seriously, though more as a means. Ultimately, he thought, class was the decisive factor. At the same time, he did not consider his Leninist approach suitable for more advanced countries, where the number of peasants had diminished dramatically, and where the party, embodying the 'collective will' of the proletariat, would have to proceed differently.[48] In particular, the further west one looked, the stronger bourgeois civil society became – which meant that simply overthrowing the bourgeois state by itself could not in any way ensure a long-term Communist victory. As Gramsci now put it in cautioning against the idea that the Russian Revolution could be repeated easily: 'In the East the State was everything, civil society was primordial and gelatinous; in the West, there was a proper relation between State and civil society, and when the State trembled a sturdy structure of civil society was at once revealed. The State was only the outer ditch, behind which there stood a powerful system of fortresses and earthworks.'[49] But where a frontal attack on the state – what Gramsci called a 'war of manoeuvre' – could not succeed, Communists should engage in a 'war of position': laying political and cultural siege to the bourgeois state.

In Italy neither revolution nor a united resistance to Fascism in the name of a 'national-popular collective will' was to be. Gramsci had been in Moscow during Mussolini's seizure of power; subsequently, he went along with the 'Bolshevization' of the party which the Comintern demanded and which prevented anything like a united front against Fascism. In 1924 this 'frail invalid held in both detestation and respect by Mussolini' (in Victor Serge's words) was elected to parliament, although he was only ever to deliver one speech there (upon which, according to legend, he was congratulated in the lobby by his prime enemy, the Duce).[50] He was arrested in November 1926 after exceptional legislation had been passed to revoke his immunity as a deputy. At the trial the prosecutor demanded: 'We must prevent this brain from functioning for twenty years.'[51] And Gramsci was indeed sentenced by Mussolini's Special Tribunal for the Defence of the State to twenty years, four months and five days in prison. But the Fascists failed to stop his brain from working: Gramsci was able to write his famous Prison Notebooks during his incarceration, thirty-five notebooks in all, which, written in code, contained most of his thought on the need to construct hegemony. Still, the Fascists did manage to kill him a little over ten years after his arrest. As a result of prison life, he died of a stroke in April 1937. He had just been released, after an international campaign for his liberation had finally succeeded. His brother and sister-in-law were at the funeral, easily outnumbered by police guards and secret agents.

The People's Home

In the end, the grand pro-socialist coalition that united workers and peasants, town and country, as well as the thorough conquest of cultural hegemony only really happened in one country. That country was Sweden. And it was brought about by a socialist mass party which allied itself first with liberals, then with peasants – the leader of the Sveriges Arbetarparti (SAP) in the early twentieth century, Hjalmar Branting, had in fact personally started out as more of a liberal. He collaborated with Sweden's Liberal movement to push through universal suffrage and, like Bernstein, conceived socialism as a form of making liberalism complete.[52] Branting also advocated cross-class alliances and a national vision for socialism: 'the goal . . . is through struggle to come to a solidarity that . . . stretches across the entire nation and through this . . . includes all human beings.'[53] Nominally, he remained a Marxist, but in his view Marxism had to be understood as a 'doctrine of development' and hence take account of the 'social conditions that since his [Marx's] time have changed completely'.[54]

Branting's strategy was further developed by Per Albin Hansson, chair of the SAP from 1928, and inventor of the idea of socialist Sweden as a *folkhemmet* or people's home. This concept had been associated with the nationalist thinker Rudolf Kjellén as well as with turn-of-the-century conservative proposals to provide homes and smallholdings for all, primarily to counter emigration.[55] Now the socialists sought to appropriate it for their own purposes (although some members of the party continued to reject the expression, finding it too paternalistic).[56] Hansson described the project thus:

> The basis of the home is community and togetherness. The good home does not recognize any privileged or neglected members, nor any favorite or stepchildren. In the good home there is equality, consideration, cooperation, and helpfulness. Applied to the great people's and citizens' home this would mean the breaking down of all the social and economic barriers that now separate citizens into the privileged and the neglected, into the rulers and the dependents, into the rich and the poor, the propertied and the impoverished, the plunderers and the plundered.

The home was to be created and administered by a party that increasingly understood itself as the representative not of specific class interests, but of 'the people' as whole. The home was to provide *trygghet* for all – meaning something like 'security' or 'feeling of security', only with warmer undertones. Similarly to 'chastened pluralists' such as G. D. H. Cole, Hansson stressed the importance of education in making the working class want, build and maintain their socialist home: 'socialist society will not come to us . . . before the masses are educated and . . . ways of thinking have been changed'.[57]

There was agreement that a 'home for all' could be achieved in a variety of ways and that, as self-taught SAP theoretician Nils Karleby in particular kept insisting, socialization was only one method, and not necessarily the best. Other theorists described the party's policies as 'provisional utopias' – clearly transformative, but always flexible and open to revision. It was a long way from Marxism understood as a precise social science enabling one to understand the past and the present and predict the future, but also from dogmatic modernization theories as pursued in Turkey and elsewhere on the European periphery.

The crucial reason for the SAP's long-term success was its ability to form a coalition with the peasants, based on the socialists' acceptance of protectionism for agriculture.[58] Thus in 1933 the SAP and the Agrarian Party worked out what came rather prosaically to be known as their 'cow-trade'. In 1938 the Saltsjöbaden Agreement was reached at a hotel in a suburb of Stockholm. It set a precedent, not just for Sweden, but for Western European Social Democracy as a whole: unions recognized the right of managers to manage industry, management recognized the right of unions to represent workers, and both tried to negotiate terms simultaneously to ensure full employment as well as high productivity.[59] They reached agreement not least so that the state would be kept from imposing solutions to the conflicts which unions and employers seemed unable to resolve.[60] Ownership and control over management were not touched; rather, the assumption went that rich companies would actually make for well-off populations. More ambitious demands for industrial democracy and worker self-management were shelved. But the principles of high social spending and active labour-market policies became entrenched.

Electorally, Swedish Social Democracy remained highly successful – the SAP was to stay continuously in power until the 1970s. It kept extending the welfare state further in the name of *folkpolitik*; after the Second World War, it returned to ideas about joint management of industry by workers and employers. Throughout it seemed to depend on highly specific circumstances: as Margaret Cole pointed out in a report by the New Fabian Research Bureau in 1938, Sweden appeared 'outside the main stream of European life and of European politics', which also meant that the Swedes were 'able to direct their home policy as they wish'. Sweden's national political culture, in the view of the British socialist, seemed remarkably free from the pathologies which afflicted other societies during the interwar period:

They are not perpetually mourning their lost glories or spinning fantastic dreams of reviving them like some of the peoples of Eastern and Central Europe; they do not celebrate elaborate festivals with ceremonies going back a thousand years, like the British coronation; and the Swedish royal family does not appear, at least, to be yearning to revive the laurels of the first Bernadotte.[61]

This might or might not have been an accurate description of Swedish *moeurs*, but the fact remained that Sweden had long-standing traditions not just of constitutionalism, but also of political consensus-building – there simply were no deep constitutional conflicts (mostly because there had been no need to fight feudalism).[62] With the exception of the Åland Islands, the country was also not facing minority questions in the way so many other societies did after the Versailles Treaty. Swedes had inherited a strong professional state admin-istration; its politics had long been characterized by egalitarianism and what Cole called an 'absence of fuss' – she was terribly impressed that the prime minister would take a tram to work.[63] However, other, more immediate factors also played a role: the unusual strength of the Swedish economy in the 1930s, when the world still depended on Swedish forest products; and the sheer weakness of a highly fragmented bourgeois right.

The SAP had accomplished what Gramsci had wanted to achieve with the Italian Communists: proletariat and peasants combined were essentially viewed as the entire nation; cultural hegemony appeared complete. In 1940 the programme of the SAP declared that Social Democracy was 'one with the Swedish nation'.[64] But all this was done without a party conceived as charis-matic hero – rather, it was about exactly what Max Weber's fellow social theorist Werner Sombart at the beginning of the century had feared most: the replacement of a 'heroic socialism' by an unheroic *Volksheim* idealism.[65]

Yet, as became apparent to many Swedes only much later, this stress on national community had a dark side: extensive eugenics legislation resulted in the sterilization of those deemed incapable of contributing to the national community. After 1935 more than 60,000 Swedes were affected, almost all of them women.[66] The policy was focused less on racial thinking than on who would be 'productive'; similar measures were taken in Denmark and Finland and parts of Switzerland.[67] Nonetheless, the leading social theorists Gunnar and Alva Myrdal, who set the agenda of the debate about population in the 1930s, had quite explicitly recommended combating any decline in the birthrate and creating a healthy Swedish population – as opposed to encour-aging immigration. The country abolished its sterilization policies only in 1975; revelations about the programmes sent a lasting shock through Swedish

society. Suddenly Per Albin Hansson's claim that 'people, like social conditions, must be thoroughly changed if socialism is to be implemented' appeared
in a very different light.[68]

The Party and the Evangelists

The Swedish and Austrian socialists, the pluralists with their programme of
worker schooling, Gramsci and his Socratic concept of education: they all
pursued experiments in the post-war European laboratory that crucially relied
on transforming culture. But for the most part their understanding of culture
was rather conservative: Red Vienna in particular was promoting what looked
more like petty-bourgeois 'cultures of uplift'. None really made a convincing
case for why any particular kind of culture – whether high-brow or socialist
realism or something else altogether – was an appropriate response to the
Marxist claims that workers were not just exploited but also alienated.

It was precisely this diagnosis of alienation which served as a starting point
for a number of thinkers with a much more radical cultural imagination. For
them, the First World War had appeared as a fiery prelude to a new world
being born; the end of the Age of Security had also liberated Europe from
stifling bourgeois conventions. Many of these thinkers saw political salvation
coming from Communist parties – which meant, if they joined the party, that
intellectual liberation had to have clear limits again, often imposed from
Moscow directly. To be sure, most Communist parties in Western Europe were
not particularly interested in intellectuals. But intellectuals were very interested in Communism, even if vanguard parties posed formidable challenges
for intellectuals who aspired to be 'in-between figures'. Two men in particular
exemplify the dilemmas of being a free-thinking intellectual *and* an official or
unofficial adherent of an organization that made a claim uniquely to be able to
chart the course to successful revolution: Georg Lukács and Ernst Bloch.

György Bernát Lőwinger had been born into a liberal, assimilated Jewish
family in Budapest in 1885.[69] His father, who eventually Magyarized his name,
was director of the Hungarian Central Credit Bank, and hence a pillar of
fin-de-siècle Pest society (he was ennobled as von Szeged in 1901). Like many
scions of highly assimilated Jewish businessmen, Lukács early on rejected his
bourgeois background and became part of a free-floating, self-radicalizing
intelligentsia moving around Europe on generous allowances (from their
usually despairing fathers). In fact, Lukács always appeared to be half travel-
ling, half fleeing; not by accident did the essay initially come to be his preferred
mode of expression, if one sees the essay as very much the genre of choice for
someone on the move. Like Bloch, he was appointed a professor late in life,

when the University of Budapest gave him the chair of aesthetics after the Second World War. He was frail looking – all thought and no body, as some observers noted. But he was also extremely charismatic, never without brilliant pupils buzzing around him. Thomas Mann supposedly portrayed him as the demonic figure of Naphta in the *Magic Mountain*, who exclaimed of the proletariat: 'Its task is to strike terror into the world for the healing of the world.'

In 1906 Lukács went to Germany to escape the stifling atmosphere of the Austro-Hungarian Empire. He tried to write poetry and novels, but decided that he lacked talent and burnt all his manuscripts when he was eighteen. Instead, he became noted for his writings of literary criticism, particularly on the history of the novel and of drama. At the time, he was still very much rooted in what he was later to describe as 'romantic anti-capitalism': tormented by a sense of tragedy in the face of modern rationalized life, but without much of an explanation of modern life itself, let alone a sense of how tragedy might be overcome. As a student of Simmel's in Berlin, he almost entirely absorbed Simmel's notion that life needed form to express itself – but that form always lacked what really mattered about life.

For now, Lukács remained primarily a literary theorist. In analysing the novel as the quintessential art form of bourgeois civilization, he diagnosed what he called 'the new loneliness' of the 'problematic man' as central to the genre. It was central, as he would later discover, because it came with capitalism. In the novel the hero also experienced what Lukács called 'transcendental homelessness'; he was constrained or even oppressed by what the Hungarian philosopher was to term 'second nature'. 'Second nature' – or what Lukács at another point referred to as one's 'self-made environment as a prison instead of a parental home' – was yet another variation on the overwhelming cultural forms Simmel had written about and the steely casing of impersonal forces Weber had prophesied.

According to Lukács, this crisis could not of course be overcome within the novel itself. Rather, as he concluded once he had discovered a thinker with whom to correct Simmel – namely Marx – the novel itself had become an indicator of 'reification', the reduction of human beings to mere things. He was to build on Marx's analysis of commodity fetishism – the phenomenon that capitalist commodities assumed a kind of magical character, seemingly generating relations among themselves as 'things', abstracted from their makers and their use value. Lukács extended this diagnosis by arguing that reification also characterized human consciousness under capitalism. Where commodities were fetishized, consciousness was reified. And this condition was not limited to the worker who, already according to traditional Marxism, was alienated both from his products and from his fellow human beings.

Lukács moved to Heidelberg next, where he was to frequent the salon run by Weber and his wife. Weber esteemed the young Hungarian dandy, claiming that 'whenever I have spoken to Lukács, I have to think about it for days'; he hoped his protégé would pursue an academic career in Germany. Lukács was becoming fascinated by Russia, planning to write a book on Dostoevsky as the one author who was pointing to a path beyond the bourgeois novel. But Russia also mattered politically: in the organic Russian village community Lukács saw a kind of social utopia foreshadowed – an ethic of brotherliness very similar to the ethics of conviction which, on its own, Weber found so problematic (and politically irresponsible). Together with Ernst Bloch, Lukács became a kind of spokesman for Slav culture in Heidelberg, but also for mysticism and what they both called 'the power of the Russian idea' as alternatives to the instrumental rationality supposedly predominant in the West. When the war broke out, Lukács lamented: 'the middle powers [the German and the Austria-Hungarian empires] will probably defeat Russia; this could lead to the fall of Czarism – I would agree with that. There is also a certain probability that the West will win against Germany; if that results in the fall of the Hohenzollern and the Habsburgs, I am also glad. But then the question arises: who saves us from Western civilization?'[70]

Was political action of some sort the answer to this predicament? Was politics ever capable, in Lukács' phrase, of 'filling the entire soul'? Could the right kind of political instruments at least create a different culture, without gelling into 'second nature' and becoming oppressive? For a period, Lukács flirted with syndicalist ideas, while remaining hostile to the Russian Revolution. Lenin's approach, he contended in an essay entitled 'Bolshevism as a Moral Problem', rested on an immoral wager that good could come of evil, that somehow class struggle would result in 'no class struggle'.

'Bolshevism as a Moral Problem' was published in December 1918. That same month, Lukács all of a sudden leapt into political praxis: much to the surprise of his friends, the grand-bourgeois aesthete joined the Hungarian Communist Party, just a week after it had been founded. He later explained his decision (or rather wager) by positing that one could not just 'sample Marxism' – one either became converted or stuck with 'bourgeois prejudices'.[71] And he had decided: 'October had given the answer' and was going to save him from Western civilization and what he had in his literary theory called 'the age of absolute sinfulness'. It also finally made him move out of his parents' villa. When the Communists assumed power in Budapest in March 1919, 'this mad Heidelberg philosopher', as the Hungarian Communist leader Béla Kun called him, was appointed deputy commissar for culture and education. Among many feverish activities, he found time to admonish young workers that 'the chief goal of your lives must be culture.[72] He had Ibsen plays staged, and opened public baths to workers' children.

The Hungarian socialist republic turned out to be an ill-fated experiment – it was, wrote Otto Bauer, a 'dictatorship of desperation' and quickly descended into chaos.[73] Since it opposed the Western Allies' Wilsonian schemes, the regime gained some nationalist legitimacy. But for the same reason it was under constant military attack, mostly from the Romanian and Czechoslovak armies. As in the Russian Revolution, power had fallen into the Bolsheviks' laps. Unlike the Russian revolutionaries, they made many tactical errors: they failed to redistribute land and thought a good cultural policy for socialists was to prohibit alcohol. They lost the civil war and never came close to erecting a counter-state through the party (they did unleash terror, however – to be followed by much crueller White counter-terror).

Lukács saw some action at the front, and became well known for dropping into kitchens incognito to inspect the quality of the food (which, together with mail delivery, he considered essential for morale). He also set up one court martial and had eight deserters shot in the market-place of Poroszló. In his capacity as political commissar he lectured his soldiers:

> If blood can be shed, and who would deny that it can be, then we are permitted to shed it. But we can't allow others to do it for us. We must take full responsibility for the blood that is shed. We must also provide an opportunity for our blood to be shed . . . In short, terror and bloodshed are a moral duty, or, more plainly, our virtue.[74]

As many critics noted, the ethics he had finally developed was in one sense very simple: good *could* come from evil, and the party line had to be followed because the party constituted nothing less than what he himself was to call the 'objectification of the proletariat's will'.

When the Soviet Republic fell, Lukács stayed behind in Budapest, while most other members of the leadership (including Kun, grabbing as much of the state's gold as possible) fled the country. Lukács later thought Kun had probably intended him to die a martyr's death and would always consider Kun 'disgusting' as a 'moral being'. But Lukács' family bribed a lieutenant-colonel to take him to Vienna. The philosopher pretended to be the officer's chauffeur – except that he could not drive, so they bandaged his arm, and had a story about an accident ready to explain why the officer was driving his own chauffeur. Several times Lukács was almost deported back to Budapest – had it not been for the intervention of luminaries such as Thomas Mann. Deportation would have meant certain death by execution. Otto Bauer also defended Lukács' activities in Red Vienna, arguing for the 'historical right of émigrés' to engage in propaganda.[75]

Max Weber, on the other hand, who had refused to add his name to the petition for Lukács, wrote to him with obvious disappointment:

> ... (I am absolutely convinced that these experiments *can* only have and will have the consequence of discrediting socialism for the coming 100 years.) ... whenever I think of *what* the present (since 1918) political goings-on cost us in terms of *unquestionably* valuable people, regardless of the 'direction' of their choice, e. g. Schumpeter and now you, without being able to see an end to all that, and, in my opinion, without achieving anything ... then I cannot help feeling bitter about this senseless fate.[76]

Others too were not impressed: Lenin and his followers essentially dismissed Lukács' early work in Marxism as an expression of the 'infantile disorder of left-wing communism'. In particular they took him to task for his position that Communist parties should not participate in parliaments; Lenin wanted to teach revolutionary enthusiasts a lesson that parliament was not 'historically obsolete' in advanced European countries, in the way his infantile or at least childish admirers were thinking.

In 1922 Lenin also announced that, five years after the Russian Revolution, the most important thing for comrades was to 'sit down and study'.[77] And Lukács, trying to overcome the 'left sectarianism' for which he had been rebuked by the *vozhd*, did finally find the time to revise the essays which were to make up *History and Class Consciousness* in a direction more in line with Lenin's thought. The book appeared in the Kleine Revolutionäre Bibliothek of the Berlin publisher Malik in 1923, alongside George Grosz's *The Face of the Ruling Class*. It was to constitute the single most important work to emerge from Marxist philosophy in the first half of the twentieth century. In a sense, it was the book that actually opened or at least reopened the possibility of Marxist philosophy – as opposed to Marxist 'science'.

How so? Because Lukács deployed what even opponents conceded were unrivalled dialectical skills against both the economic determinism associated with the Second International and the reformism that Bernstein and other 'Social Democrat opportunists' championed.[78] He began with a bold theoretical stroke, announcing that orthodox Marxism was a method and not a dogma. Even if all of Marx's own propositions and predictions could somehow be conclusively proven wrong, one could still be a Marxist. That was the first lesson for Bernstein and others concerned that empirically things simply had not been going the Marxist way (although, less obviously, it also allowed revisionist Social

Democrats not to feel like traitors to Marxism – tellingly, some of the Swedish socialists were saying more or less the same thing as Lukács, the faithful Leninist).

Lukács also insisted that deducing 'historical laws' of development – the position which had been encouraged by Engels' comparison of Marx with Darwin – was in fact a bourgeois 'contemplative' attitude. Rather than making history, it led Marxists to conform to what looked like the historical equivalents of the laws of nature – when in fact what could be observed in advanced countries was not in any way 'natural', but a specific consequence of capitalism. The supposed 'natural laws' could be broken through political action.

Thus Lukács gave both reformist revisionism and ossified 'scientific socialism' what he thought an authentically Marxist treatment, reinstituting the role of revolutionary will. He also tried to cut right through the long-standing debate about Marxism as a science versus an actual transformation of the world; in another bold move, he proposed that both were inextricably bound together. Only the proletariat could correctly understand the forces which oppressed it. But the moment of real comprehension (as opposed to bourgeois 'contemplation') was necessarily also the moment of revolution: the workers were both the subject and the object of knowledge, and both the subject and object of history. Hence splitting Marxism into a science of objective laws and a politics of the iron will (as exemplified, in the eyes of critics, by Lenin's putschism) was fundamentally misguided.

For Lukács, then, the proletariat would constitute itself as the first universal collective subject in history, derived from the consciousness of being a universal class and committed to what he called the objective possibility of historical liberation – and thereby also comprehend the world of which it was part in its totality, as the people uniquely capable of seeing the truth about capitalism. Only in this way could theory and praxis become a unity; only in this way could human beings, with Vico, really make sense of a world they had themselves created – bringing the tragedy of culture to a close, and making humans at last feel at home in this world.

But it was not quite so simple. A major complication arose with the meaning of the 'proletariat' and its capacities. Lukács agreed with Lenin that only the Communist Party, understood as a kind of brotherly community, could lead the way.[79] In fact, the Hungarian philosopher was to articulate the most philosophically sophisticated justification of vanguard-party dominance; where 'the greatest thinker to have been produced by the working-class movement since Marx' (Lukács about Lenin) had mostly written for the occasion and left many theoretical threads untied, Lukács rendered Leninist intuitions coherent and lent them philosophical subtlety. He seemed to have understood the Bolsheviks of 1917 better than they had understood themselves.

That understanding was obviously not an academic matter: like Lenin, Lukács insisted that successful party organization had to be based on a correct theory of the revolution. In the nether-world of theory, disagreements could be fudged, incorrect political diagnoses could remain without consequences – but not in organizational practice. Thus Lukács posited that there was no such thing as a purely proletarian revolution – the lead of the party as 'objectification of the proletariat's will' was indispensable. The party would have to carry other classes and recalcitrant parts of the proletariat with it; it would have to teach the workers that the crisis of capitalism would not automatically lead to socialism. Lukács reiterated time and again that if the proletariat failed its historical task – because it refused to be guided by the party's correct line – the result could be barbarism.

This world-historical urgency – as well as the crucial role of the party as an organization – then also justified not just the repression of the bourgeoisie as a class, but also the 'renunciation of individual [that is, bourgeois] freedom'. Lukács insisted on discipline and total participation as characteristics of the party, and, above all, the 'conscious subordination of the self to that collective will that is destined to bring real freedom into being . . . this conscious collective will is the Communist Party'.[80]

He was as good as his word. The Hungarian aesthete turned revolutionary did almost everything which the party, with all its crushing impersonal charisma, ordered him to do. For one thing, there was dangerous practical work – underground missions back in counter-revolutionary Hungary. But changes in ideological direction were also commanded. Lenin had been too ill to read *History and Class Consciousness*, and while the book provided the perfect theoretical justification for Lenin's party, by the time of the leader's death Lenin's successors had already moved on. Thus, in 1924, Grigory Zinoviev, head of the Comintern, was fuming: 'This theoretical revision cannot be allowed to pass without impunity. Neither shall we tolerate our Hungarian comrade, Lukács, doing it in the domain of philosophy and sociology. If we have a few more of these professors spinning Marxist theories, we shall be lost.'[81] Lukács eventually repudiated his major work as suffering from 'subjectivism'. But his advocacy of working with the peasants and moderate socialists for democratic reform within authoritarian Hungary in the late 1920s also backfired: the Comintern was just turning to the idea of attacking Social Democracy as 'social fascism', and Lukács was sharply reprimanded for wanting to 'fight fascism on the battleground of bourgeois democracy'. He again was to denounce his own ideas as 'opportunist' – in a way that he himself later on called 'completely hypocritical'.[82]

Lukács settled in Berlin at the beginning of the 1930s; when the Nazis took power, he fled to Moscow. Like most Communist émigrés, he was in danger of losing his life during the Stalinist show trials of the mid-1930s. Kun was not to survive them (his last words to his wife, after being arrested, were: 'Don't worry. Some misunderstanding. I will be home in half an hour').[83] Lukács kept a low profile, working in the Marx-Engels Institute, a kind of 'dumping ground for undesirable philosophers', mostly on innocuous literary topics. Still, he was arrested and interrogated – in German, as he had never learnt proper Russian. He had to spend a year in Tashkent, on Moscow's orders. His wife's son was sent to the camps. In the end, he claimed to have been the only Hungarian writer to have survived Stalinism intact.

Lukács always remained convinced that Stalin and the impersonal charisma of the party had been the only effective force against Hitler's National Socialism; excluding oneself from the party meant excluding oneself from the battle against fascism. Thus his self-denunciations, no matter how hypocritical, had been the necessary 'entry-ticket' for taking part in the only opposition to fascism that might work. Already in the late 1920s, he had maintained that one should not be silly and defy the party out of pride; patience, he explained to Victor Serge, was key and the unwavering conviction that 'history will summon us in its time'. Serge would later reflect: 'In him I saw a first-class brain which could have endowed Communism with a true intellectual greatness if it had developed as a social movement instead of degenerating into a movement in solidarity with an authoritarian Power.'[84]

In 1945, Mátyás Rákosi, the Hungarian Communist leader installed by the Red Army in Budapest, wrote to Lukács: 'We are waiting for you in Hungary to help the party influence the best members of the intelligentsia.'[85] Lukács flew home; and he could convince himself that at least for the moment the Communists seemed willing to work with bourgeois forces, just as he had advocated in the late 1920s. He lectured to packed audiences. He completed a book about 'the destruction of reason' in modern German thought, in which he attacked Simmel, his former teacher, for having expounded a 'philosophy of imperialistic rentiers' parasitism'. He also affirmed that there was no such thing as an innocent *Weltanschauung*. The party seemed happy to have him back.

Ernst Bloch was not a party man. He was born to petty-bourgeois Jewish parents in Ludwigshafen in 1885. Like Lukács, he was charismatic, but he was not at all frail; instead he was full of vitality, acting the role of the ancient prophet, exuding a kind of philosophical *eros*. His students claimed that one could not really understand him unless one had heard him speak, or rather thunder.

Bloch claimed that he had been struck when growing up in Ludwigshafen by the ugly face of capitalism which the city presented to him. In the evenings, he would see the downtrodden, ashen-faced proletarians walk through the streets; supposedly it was then that he decided to become a Marxist. The man who turned out to be a kind of Marxist philosopher of *Heimat* always detested his own hometown.

He began by denouncing every philosophy of his age, telling whoever would listen that it was time for an entirely new metaphysics. All he needed for this task, he announced, was what he had read in Hegel – and in Karl May, the author of Wild West romances. 'Everything else', Bloch claimed, 'is an impure mixture of the two' – Hegel and pulp fiction, so to speak – and, he asked, 'why should I read it?'[86]

According to the legend he spun about himself, his master idea had already occurred to him: where psychoanalysis had introduced the idea of the no-longer-conscious as part of the unconscious, Bloch uncovered the importance of the not-yet-conscious. His philosophy of hope and of what he called the 'not-yet' were to build on this insight. The vision of crossing the desert, just like the cowboys in the Wild West, followed by a homecoming, or return to *Heimat*, always remained central to his work.

Bloch went to Berlin to join Simmel's seminar, and there he met Lukács for the first time. Where Lukács had fastened on the idea of the tragedy of culture, Bloch took from Simmel the insight that life was always trying to transcend itself. Lukács was deeply impressed by Bloch. He claimed that Bloch convinced him that it was still possible to philosophize like the ancients or at least like Hegel. Lukács and Bloch then entered their state of near-symbiosis. Indeed, they had to demarcate a 'protected area of differences' (and sometimes artificially create differences in the first place), so that they would not always say exactly the same things at social gatherings.[87]

In Heidelberg they were an exceedingly odd pair: Bloch, the *enfant terrible* who enjoyed shocking the bourgeoisie by thundering prophecies, and the much more reserved, soft-spoken Lukács, who found himself roped into Bloch's schemes to marry a rich heiress. Bloch, whom Paul Honigsheim called a 'Jewish Apocalyptist', self-consciously adopted a kind of messianism, infuriating Weber – but also fascinating him, because of Weber's not-so-secret attraction to the extreme, the bohemian, the exotic and perhaps even the politically irresponsible: he once quipped that he would like to have only Russians, Poles and Jews at his Sunday *jours*. The philosopher Emil Lask in turn joked: 'What are the names of the four Evangelists? Matthew, Mark, Lukács and Bloch.'[88] And one could see why: Bloch went around Heidelberg declaring that 'human beings to whom I have been sent will experience and understand the returning god within themselves.'[89] Weber finally became irritated by Bloch's overblown rhetoric, just as much as by his lack of manners, while Bloch in turn was horrified by the fact that Weber, at the outbreak of the war, had greeted his guests in his reserve officer's uniform. Like Lukács, Bloch was profoundly disturbed by the jingoism of the war, not least among workers. He enthusiastically welcomed the Russian Revolution, even hailing Lenin as a kind of Messiah: *ubi Lenin, ibi Jerusalem* – where Lenin is, there is Jerusalem, he would say; or, with typical literary flair, Bolshevism was the 'categorical imperative with a revolver'.[90]

In the interwar years Bloch became an unusual diagnostician of fascism. Unlike the official analyses advanced by the Communist Party, which saw fascists as agents of a dying capitalism, Bloch pointed to a phenomenon he termed 'non-synchronicity'. He argued that while peasants and the middle class were objectively approaching a socio-economic situation similar to that of the proletariat, these groups had not evolved any proletarian consciousness, and to some extent remained stuck in pre-industrial ways of life. Their very justified grievances were then expressed in a romantic, anti-modern longing for the past. Rather than lecturing them on their objective interests, Bloch demanded that the Communists should take these longings seriously, particularly the utopian moments contained within them. Instead of abandoning the realm of myths, romantic symbols and even fairy tales to the fascists, Marxists should recapture their revolutionary potential. Bloch even went so far as to try to reclaim the notion of the Third Reich for the left.

Acute as his insights into fascism were, his anti-fascism led him to a blanket justification of the Stalinist show trials of the 1930s. Unlike Lukács, though, Bloch never became a party member and never spent time in the Soviet Union. Instead, after stops in France and Prague, he found asylum in the United States – which he intensely disliked. Most of Bloch's friends were not sure whether he had ever realized that people in Massachusetts did not speak German, so much did he deliberately cut himself off from life in his host country (though he was not above fabricating a story that he had been forced to work as a dishwasher at one point).

Even more than Lukács, Bloch rejected the economic determinism of scientific socialism and instead stressed the importance not just of will, but also of feelings and intuitions, especially of the not-yet. Bloch was eager to distinguish between a vulgar feeling of not-yet and the authentic utopian hopes which could be found especially in art and religion. He argued that 'if we walk on the street, and know that after three-quarters of an hour there will be a pub, then that is the vulgar not-yet. However, on that street which we are on in this precarious world, the pub . . . has not even been built yet. . . .'[91]

Real genesis, Bloch claimed, was not at the beginning, but at the end. All genuine religions were messianic in this sense, as were all authentically utopian images which people had formed in the past, including Paradise, the Land of Milk and Honey, works of great music like Beethoven's Ninth Symphony, and also slightly less highbrow conceptions like the Big Rock Candy Mountain and Robin Hood's refuge in Sherwood Forest. One word summarized them all: home, or *Heimat*.[92]

The search for cultural community and some sense of home, then, preoccupied, and often frustrated, left-wing thinkers during the interwar period; and the anxiety persisted that other political ideologies – fascism in particular – could provide more seductive visions of belonging and solidarity. Ironically, it might have been either the most pragmatic or the most utopian socialists who had an answer for what turned out to be a crucial strategic question in the interwar period: the relationship of socialists to the peasantry, or, put differently, the very possibility of hegemony in the original Leninist sense: an alliance of workers and 'poor peasants'. The Swedes managed to make farmers allies of the workers, helped by fortunate circumstances, while Bloch, for all his outlandish rhetoric, actually intimated something that might have been very important for a Europe where in countries such as Italy peasants still constituted more than half the workforce: a conservative socialism (inspired by the Russian village commune) that had a place for the non-industrial worker and his values. But these were exceptions, and in many ways Weber was to be confirmed in his belief that Marxism was unable to give an answer to the agrarian question.

As socialist and Social Democratic parties faced defeat in many European countries in the 1920s and 1930s – not least Italian Fascism, which initially promised 'sovereignty for the peasant' – there was still one great experiment in socialist people-making and in creating a comprehensive socialist civilization: what in the 1918 constitution of the Russian Soviet Republic had been called the 'dictatorship of the urban and rural proletariat and the poorest peasantry'. For many on the left – even if they could see that actually existing Bolshevism was not exactly the commune state – the Soviet Union appeared as the last dam against the rising tide of fascism and authoritarianism. There too the question what to do for, with or, as it turned out, against peasants was to become crucial.

New People

Stalinism was the most far-reaching experiment of the interwar period. However, it is far from obvious whether 'Stalinism' designates an ideology of any sort. Mussolini once answered the question 'What is Fascism?' by saying 'I am Fascism.' Within this logic it should have been clear enough who could best respond to the question 'What is Stalinism?' But Stalinism was a term used by Stalin's opponents to criticize bureaucratization and personality cults – and, unlike the word totalitarianism, it was not appropriated by those it was meant to attack. The designation Stalinism became in fact more widespread after Stalin's death – Stalinism, one is tempted to say, was a post-Stalinist concept.

To be sure, Stalin himself, like all men obsessed with their role in history, could not quite help pronouncing on the question. According to Khrushchev, when Lazar Kaganovich once suggested the term to him in the 1920s, Stalin replied: 'How can you compare a dick to a watchtower?'[93] And, accused of exploiting his father's name, Stalin's son Vasily cried out at one point: 'But I'm a Stalin, too.' Whereupon Stalin remarked: 'No, you're not. You're not Stalin and I'm not Stalin. Stalin is Soviet power. Stalin is what he is in the newspapers and the portraits, not you, no not even me.'[94]

At first sight Stalinism labels a clearly identifiable kind of regime that existed under Stalin himself and then in the Central and Eastern European countries effectively occupied by the Soviet Union after 1945. It was characterized by mass terror, by a personality cult, bureaucratization, forced industrialization, and – most importantly for disputes about Marxist doctrine – subordination of world revolution to the idea of 'socialism in one country'. Like a number of other interwar regimes, it can also be understood as a developmental dictatorship.

Despite such a seemingly clear laundry list of characteristics, Stalinism in certain respects remains more enigmatic than the reign of the Nazis. After all, the Great Terror and the Purges of the mid-1930s seemed to exhibit such a level of irrationality that people began to wonder whether the devil had arrived in Moscow to turn everything upside down – as in Mikhail Bulgakov's famous novel *The Master and Margarita*. Within Nazism there was a certain abhorrent predictability to mass murder (and therefore, some observers have claimed, a perverse kind of 'rationality'): certain groups were targeted, but not others. As Tzvetan Todorov observed, 'the inmates of Nazi camps knew why they were there, but the political deportees – often sincere Communists – did not, and could not comprehend their fate.'[95] In other words, the Nazis exhibited madness, but there was method to their madness. Stalinism, it seems, was both mad and methodless.

Any understanding of Stalinism has to start with Stalin himself – including his ideas. For Stalin had ideas, or, as his faithful henchman Kaganovich insisted, Stalin was, before anything else, 'an ideological person. For him the idea was the main thing.'[96] To be sure, most other close collaborators knew that theory was not exactly Stalin's strength; they even joked about it. He had himself tutored in Marxism in the 1920s (after which the tutor was shot), and added the designation 'Most Profound Theoretician of the Modern Age' to the many other sycophantic terms that had to be applied to him. But to believe that Stalin's main contribution to socialist theory was, as Hannah Arendt surmised,

' "you can't break eggs without making an omelet" ' (sic!) is to underestimate Stalin, and to misunderstand his regime.[97] In particular, Stalin sought to codify his particular interpretation of 'Leninism' (a word Lenin himself never used) – and thereby make himself the ultimate arbiter of which courses of action could be justified as authentically 'Leninist', sidelining the real theoretician (and, in Lenin's word, 'darling') of the party, Nikolai Bukharin. In fact, for Stalin, as Lukács pointed out in retrospect, even the most opportunistic tactical manoeuvres had to be explained and promoted by nothing less than the grandest and most abstract theoretical concepts.[98]

As with many successful politicians, Stalin's greatest asset was to be consistently underestimated – Trotsky called him an 'excellent bit of mediocrity'. As a young man he had engaged in some colourful revolutionary activities after being expelled from a theological seminary and dabbling in poetry: he robbed banks to fill the party coffers and acquired an aura of toughness. He himself adopted the name 'Stalin' – man of steel. But the important thing about him was that he turned out to be an excellent bureaucrat, nicknamed 'Comrade Card-Index'.[99] He rose to power through committees – unlike more charismatic (and vainer) revolutionaries, the ultimate *komitetchik* had understood early on that the staffing of committees and secretariats was crucial for building power in the Soviet system. His decisive break came when Lenin appointed him secretary of the Communist Party, which gave the rising Georgian access to a vast patronage machine. Lenin himself eventually understood this. In his 'political testament', he called Stalin 'too rude' for the position and tried to prevent a split between Trotsky and Stalin.

In a sense, Stalin's opponents were right to point out in 1929 that Stalin had not established the dictatorship of the proletariat – instead there was the dictatorship of the secretariat (Lenin himself had never been general secretary of the party). Nevertheless, being seen as a *'praktik*, a machine politician and state-builder who earned a reputation for getting things done' was by no means a bad thing in the late 1920s.[100] After all, bureaucratic domination – like other methods and styles of rule in the interwar years – seemed a credible response to a particular constellation of practical challenges: Stalin faced the need to keep building a new state (ideally, with new and not with 'former' people), and to figure out how to manage socialist-style production (which had never been tried before). This situation was very different from Hitler's in 1933. The Führer took over functioning state structures and could rely on the collaboration of at least some of the traditional elites. The Nazis inherited institutions, but had no real theoretical blueprint; Stalin had at least a very general blueprint (even if concepts like the commune state had already been disavowed), but by and large no tried-and-tested institutions. Thus Stalin's project was effectively transforming a continental empire recovering from revolutionary upheavals and civil war into a functioning state; Hitler's was expanding a traditional nation-state into a racist empire of a totally new type. One put ideological purification within an existing polity first, the other racial purification of a continent in the process of expanding a state.

Concretely, Stalin was faced with the results of Lenin's New Economic Policy: the NEP had created more independent, landowning peasants, more merchants in the city, and a lot of racketeering and profit-making by the so-called *nepmen*. In fact, it was a brief, almost golden moment for Russian peasants – driven by Nikolai Bukharin's idea of increasing the wealth of the peasantry so that they would supply plenty of food and buy industrial products. It was accompanied by the rise of what supposedly was a class of nouveaux riches, although the conspicuous consumption in the cities which was so much resented had a very practical reason: the *nepmen's* situation was so insecure, the taxes so high, that it made little sense to invest – while it did make perfect sense to consume everything as quickly as possible.[101]

The NEP posed a profound question for doctrine. If modernization through limited market activity continued, what role was there for the party? That question became more urgent, given that the charisma of the party, just as Weber's theory predicted, was becoming 'routinized' in day-to-day work: the party developed its own traditions, demanded piety towards its heroic founders and was in danger of losing its capacity to mobilize, or at least inspire. A response to these dangers – and a clear alternative to creeping marketization – appeared to be forced industrialization and collectivization, especially if it was presented as a return to the heady days of War Communism. Such a process also held out the promise of restoring doctrinal purity. After all, Lenin had stated that 'Communism is Soviet power plus the electrification of the whole countryside'. But there was also a more sociological rationale. In backward, peasant-dominated Russia the party had actually yet to create the proletariat in whose name it had been acting since 1917 (and whose will, according to Lukács, it objectified); they had the superstructure, now they needed to make or at least expand the base.[102] And once the number of peasants diminished dramatically, the old Leninist question of *gegemoniya* which Gramsci had picked up in Italy might also disappear.

Thus Stalin embarked on an immensely ambitious project of forced industrialization. It required either capital from abroad or relentlessly squeezing the peasants to provide both food and the required labour force (without at the same time paying them with consumer goods, as might have happened with a different strategy). Stalin chose the latter course and began to push the peasants into collective farms. Thus also began the process which Stalin liked to call the 'liquidation of the kulaks as a class'. 'Kulaks' literally meant 'grasping fists'. It was a metaphor applied to better-off peasants, in particular those who had taken advantage of the NEP and sold grain on the open market. Lenin had already failed to extract grain from the peasants by force in the early 1920s, when there had been widespread famines and unrest – now a new and even more brutal assault was waged.

From a theoretical perspective, it was highly debatable whether the kulaks could be described as a class in any meaningful Marxist sense at all. The most plausible justification was that they employed workers continuously – that is, did not just hire seasonal workers – and could thus at least count as a kind of permanent and possibly growing petty bourgeoisie which threatened to under-mine the socialist state. Or, even more simply put, as long as peasants so much as owned some of their own means of production, they posed a danger; after all, Lenin had famously warned, 'small-scale production engenders capitalism and the bourgeoisie continuously, daily, hourly, spontaneously, and on a mass scale'.[103] Nonetheless, this theory appeared more like window dressing. As Zinoviev had once admitted, 'we are fond of describing any peasant who has enough to eat as a kulak'.[104] This fitted with a general anti-peasant feeling among the Bolsheviks: Stalin's own grandparents had been serfs; the writer Maxim Gorky spoke disdainfully of the 'zoological individualism of the peasantry'.[105] And these prejudices were not entirely without precedents in the classics of theory: Marx himself had derided the 'idiocy of rural life', and called the peasants a 'sack of potatoes'.

In practice, rather than being anything like a piece of centrally planned social engineering, the policy came to resemble a country-wide pogrom, making use of the dictum of Foreign Commissar Maxim Litvinov that 'food is a weapon'.[106] State officials often simply grabbed what they could, drinking the kulaks' vodka on the spot and stealing their clothes, while the kulaks often preferred to slaughter their animals and smash their tools rather than hand them over to state officials.[107]

The results were in every respect disastrous: there was endemic violence – including cannibalism – and unprecedented famines in which millions died. The only success was achieved by Soviet propaganda. It managed more or less to hide this catastrophe both from the outside world and from many Russians (it was Stalin who had reintroduced the internal passport). The government also kept selling grain on the international market and refused any aid from the Red Cross. Lavish banquets were put on for Western visitors such as the writer André Gide; secret police agents dressed up as well-fed camp inmates to impress Western politicians.

Yet the failures of collectivization could only be hidden to a degree inside the country. And the more obviously these policies were failing, the more the regime needed scapegoats and conspiracy theories – hence it intensified the interminable, self-radicalizing search for 'wreckers', 'saboteurs' and 'spies'. The official language changed: 'enemies of the people' substituted for 'class enemies', suggesting that these could now also be found within the Communist Party. The term was even enshrined in the constitution.

Thus began the show trials of the mid-1930s (Lukács called them 'conceptual trials'), when, for the first time, the Communist Party demanded – and implemented – the execution of its own leaders. Lenin had initiated show trials, too (known as 'demonstrations'). But only Stalin had entire trials scripted beforehand, with every detail planned. He did not want to be seen as a 'legal nihilist', which is why he held trials in the first place, as opposed to shooting people in secret. The accused were as prepared as the prosecutors; the latter were even to produce calculated outbursts, such as calling Bukharin a 'mixture of fox and pig'.

Nonetheless, it seems the hunt for scapegoats can only partly explain the terror and the purges. Stalin also began to turn on the army, which bore no obvious responsibility for the many industrial accidents or the famines. Thus the purges seemed like a colossal exercise in state self-mutilation. Speculation abounded about Stalin's paranoid personality; people began to point to his occasional macabre pronouncements ('aphorisms' would be too much) with their perverse logic: 'Full conformity of views can be achieved only at the cemetery'; 'death solves all problems. No man, no problem'; 'one death is a tragedy, a million just statistics'.

There was indeed a personal, power-political side to all this – Stalin killed off his potential competitors, and he eliminated all the 'Old Bolsheviks' who knew that he had played a relatively minor role in the Revolution and the civil war. In that sense, the killings were not as random as Todorov's statement quoted above might suggest: there was a systematic annihilation of *witnesses*. This applied not just to comrades present at the creation. It applied also to Communists from outside the Soviet Union, many of whom had fled to the Soviet Union from Germany, Hungary and other countries, only to be killed by Stalin in the 1930s. A survivor like Lukács was in many ways an exception – he speculated later that he had escaped being shot partly because his Moscow apartment had not been all that attractive to the secret police. Most perversely, perhaps, a vast number of those who had somehow caught a glimpse of the West as prisoners of war in the 1940s were shot or at least sent to the camps after they had returned (or, at Stalin's insistence, been forcibly returned to the USSR) – they had been witnesses of some sort, too. No other state has ever treated its own soldiers this way.

While witnesses had to be eliminated, accomplices had to be created. Stalin always made it appear that major policy decisions were the outcome of a consensus among the leadership. Sometimes – as with the Katyń massacre of Polish officers – he made everyone who had been present when the measure was agreed put their name to it. The logic here was no longer that of a party as an impersonal charismatic force dictating the correct line on how to make history; instead it was the logic of the criminal gang or family, where it is crucial to implicate as many people as possible.[108] The infamous late-night feasts Stalin held were a symbol of this strangely informal way of rule, where everything – literally everything including one's life – depended on personal relationships. Hannah Arendt captured some of this mafia-like quality of Stalinism when she called the crimes of the terror 'old fashioned'.

The inner dynamics of the regime therefore was mostly one of a tightly knit gang opting for attack as the best means of defence. It might have seemed like a plausible choice for a leadership that felt constantly threatened, and that preferred to risk self-destruction rather than an erosion of its power. This leadership also found it harder and harder to read what was really happening in its society – hence the obsession with 'verification of implementation' (and establishing the 'true identity' of party members). But true identities and 'verified' social facts were all the harder to come by, because the terror created a party and a society permanently in upheaval. It unleashed fear and made people turn on each other. As a secret police officer once explained: 'Everyone was a traitor until he proved the contrary by exposing someone else as a traitor.'[109] Such a state would benefit the existing supreme leader and keep those just below him in check (if they had not been killed). Without trust, nothing resembling dissent, let alone opposition, could possibly coalesce.

But this is still not the whole story. Arguably another trigger for the terror was the introduction of a new Soviet constitution. The constitution was promulgated in 1936 (and hailed by Stalin as 'the only thoroughly democratic constitution in the world', while Lukács lauded it as giving '*real and concrete guarantees*' for everyone and also allowing 'equal opportunities of development for unequal personalities').[110] In particular, it codified the new concept of 'popularity'. In theory, the constitution had been shaped with large popular input: a draft had been produced for June 1936 and then been subject to 'public discussion'. Thousands of comments were sent to the constitutional commission; and, according to one estimate, up to fifty million Soviet citizens took part in half a million meetings to discuss the draft.[111] It was an enormous attempt to generate some kind of mass legitimacy, especially among the working class, and it was done in the name of democracy, though with democracy essentially understood not as the possibility of repeated political choice, but as participation in the impersonal charisma of the party. As Stalin put it:

For [the opposition] freedom of groupings and democracy are unbreakably linked. We don't understand democracy like that. We understand democracy as the raising of the activeness and consciousness of the party mass, as the systematic involving of the party mass not only in the discussion of questions but also in [the ability of] the leadership to work.[112]

This was not all that far removed from what Lukács had claimed in the early 1920s – namely that 'true democracy' was not 'formal freedom but the activity of the members of a collective will, closely integrated and collaborating in a spirit of solidarity'[113] – except that democracy was now no longer confined to the 'party mass'. Stalin himself had argued in the mid-1920s that 'there are arising entire ant-hills of self-governing organizations, commissions and conferences embracing millions of masses of non-Party workers and peasants – ant-hills which, by their everyday unperceived minute and noiseless work, are creating the source of strength of the Soviet State'.[114] Put differently: through participation in first the party and then the state more broadly a wholly new people was being created – the Soviet people.

As part of this new 'popularity', the electoral system was changed, from indirect to direct elections; unequal suffrage and positive discrimination for workers were abolished, thereby ending the institutionalized preponderance of urban and working-class voters.[115] By the mid-1930s, 'class antagonism' was held almost to have disappeared from the Soviet Union itself. The precondition of 'popularity' and what had always remained the declared goal of moving 'from a society with a proletarian dictatorship to a non-State society' was that the old society had been pulverized.[116] Now a wholly new people – the *sovetskii narod* – and a wholly new patriotism – Soviet patriotism – had to be created to implement socialism and, eventually, Communism.[117] As Hannah Arendt observed, 'by pressing men against each other, totalitarian terror destroys the space between them'. But part of the reason why they were pressed together was to create an entirely new people, beyond just the 'party mass', who, according to Leninist doctrine, were always supposed to remain an elite.

The whole language of class was becoming muted in favour of emphasizing the virtues of the 'new Soviet person', who seemed ideally to be a 'shock worker' with limitless energy for building socialism and highly cultured.[118] But Stalin's admission that there were only 'workers, peasants and the intelligentsia' left in the Soviet Union demonstrated just how sure of himself the leading *praktik* was now. In the early 1930s he had still resisted a push towards more 'socialist legality', fearing to be reduced to a mere 'chief executive'.[119]

Until this point, Stalin had always insisted that 'the abolition of classes is not achieved by the extinction of the class struggle, but its intensification . . . We must bear in mind that the growth of the power of the Soviet state will intensify the resistance of the last remnants of the dying classes.'[120] This precept often came to be viewed as Stalin's main – or only – contribution to political thought: class warfare would turn more severe, as socialism approached; and in the process the state would not wither away, but actually need to become more powerful. As Stalin had explained in 1933, 'the dying of the state takes place not through the weakening of state power, but through its maximum strengthening, necessary in order to kill off the rudiments of the dying classes and to organize the defence against the capitalist encirclement'.[121] While he held firm to the precept that socialism was possible (and progressing) in one country, the very fact that the country remained encircled by enemies further justified terror. His opponent Bukharin – shot by one of Stalin's henchmen in March 1938 – exposed the peculiar logic of this thought:

> This strange theory elevates the actual fact that the class struggle is now intensifying into some sort of inevitable law of our development. According to this strange theory, it would seem that the farther we go in our advance towards socialism, the more difficulties will accumulate, the more intense the class struggle would become, so that at the very gates of socialism, apparently, we will have to either start a civil war or perish from hunger and lay down our bones to die.[122]

What made the theory not quite so strange in the eyes of many contemporaries both inside and outside the Soviet Union was that the enemies of socialism *did* seem to prepare one final assault on the 'great experiment'. Nothing legitimated Stalin more in the 1930s (and after) than the rise of fascism, and the triumph of Hitler in Germany in particular gave credence to the idea that History was heading for some final dialectical clash.[123]

So fear of the capitalist world, terror, constitution-making and a new promotion of 'popularity' went together in 1936 and 1937: the Soviet Union no longer presented itself as a specifically proletarian society; rather, socialism was to be conceived as a 'truly popular system, which grew up from within the people'.[124] But potential 'people power' also carried its risks. When direct elections were first announced the party suddenly realized that things might not turn out the right way, not least given the one-and-a-half million people who had been expelled from the party and who could serve as a huge reservoir of candidates against the official ones.[125] Thus the push for purification was also an attempt to fashion a people without any possibility for dissent and 'deviations', a nominal 'democracy' from which disagreement (and uncertainty) had been eliminated once and for all.

In the end the leadership itself would never trust its capacities for people-making: at the last moment the party opted for allowing only pre-approved candidates (mostly party members, but also some non-party members) on the ballots.[126] Even so, the regime trumpeted that the constitution had been 'popularly' ratified. It turned out to be the longest-lasting Soviet constitution – in force until 1977.

There was one thing, however, that the leadership could be reasonably certain of with time: terror did not automatically endanger loyalty to the system; even those victims not so naive as to believe that Stalin's subordinates were proceeding without his knowledge would not come to question their identity as Soviet subjects. Evgenia Ginzburg, after months of terror (and before many more years of torment to come), could still reflect at the end of 1937:

Even now – we asked ourselves – after all that has happened to us, would we vote for any other than the Soviet system, which seemed as much a part of us as our hearts and as natural to us as breathing? Everything I had in the world – the thousands of books I had read, memories of my youth, and the very endurance which was now keeping me from going under – all this had been given me by the Soviet system, and the revolution which had transformed my world while I was still a child.[127]

Some of those directly affected by the Great Terror came to ask themselves whether they had not themselves already internalized too many of the regime's norms and interpretations. Nadezhda Mandelstam, suffering through the persecution and eventual death in the Gulag of her husband, the poet Osip Mandelstam, observed about herself: 'Our system, I felt, was harsh and brutal, but that was life, and a strong regime could not tolerate avowed opponents who, even though out of action, might make a comeback. I was not easily taken in by official propaganda, but I had swallowed some of their barbaric ideas of justice.'[128] Perhaps most disturbingly of all, there is evidence that Bukharin at his trial – while confessing some fantastic 'counter-revolutionary crimes' under duress – was also still trying to align himself with a proper understanding of Bolshevism and therefore History. He seemed to admit that his thinking, if not subjectively, then objectively, had constituted treason. After an intense period of study during his twelve months in prison awaiting trial (when, astonishingly, he wrote a book on socialist culture, a treatise on dialectics, a memoir and a cycle of poetry, all under inhuman conditions), he pleaded:

The motherland of socialism has set out on a heroic march into the arena of the greatest triumphant struggle in world history. Inside our country, a broad-based socialist democracy is emerging, founded on Stalin's constitution. A great creative and fruitful life is blossoming. Give me a chance, even behind prison bars, to participate in this as much as I am able. Let me – I beg and implore you – contribute at least a tiny bit to this life! Let a new, second Bukharin grow . . . this new man will be the complete antithesis of the one who has died. He has already been born.[129]

Stalinism – no one disagrees on this – meant personality cult. Stalin was not the only leader in the twentieth century to create such a cult. But he was special in that he had neither obvious charisma nor even a real presence in the lands that he led. Hitler would constantly move around the country and actually believed in a quasi-mystical unity with his *Volksgemeinschaft*. Stalin, on the other hand, was a recluse, and remained a figure distant from 'the masses' even during the famous Moscow parades; he insisted that his own secret police march without revolvers and he listened to pre-recorded cheering. While Hitler constantly talked, Stalin remained reticent and simply observed others, sucking on his pipe. In fact, most Russians had not heard Stalin's voice until 1941, two weeks after the war with Nazi Germany started; most were surprised by how thin the voice of their leader sounded when he began: 'Brothers, sisters, I turn to you my friends.'[130] Hitler built on genuine charismatic legitimacy; Stalin was not a personal presence, but, if anything, an icon or, as he had said to his son, a symbol, or even the idea of 'Soviet power'. And this was not just the case in the USSR; in the words of the Yugoslav Communist Milovan Djilas, Stalin had become 'the incarnation of an idea, transfigured in Communist minds into pure idea, and thereby into something infallible and sinless. Stalin was the victorious battle of today and the brotherhood of man tomorrow.'[131] This explains Stalin's curious habit of applauding himself after his speeches – he was saluting the idea, not his own person, a practice that would have been unthinkable for the Führer.[132]

Stalin mobilized genuine patriotism in the Second World War, but one that was at odds with his own ideology. Orthodox religion and Russian nationalism proved decisive, not 'Soviet power', and Stalin was now praised less as Soviet leader than as 'the unifier of the lands'. The young 'Koba' had developed his own conception of nationalism, which was substantially indebted to the Austro-Marxists and viewed nations as 'cultural communities' worthy of preservation (culminating in the famous 1930 formula of 'the flowering of national culture, socialist in content and national in form'). But the irony was that his real ideological aspiration – total unity in the state – could only be approximated with what Lenin and Stalin had derided as 'Great Russian chauvinism'.[133]

The victory over fascism, even if it owed little to anything derivable from Marxism, legitimated the regime like nothing else during the history of the Soviet

Union as a whole, not least on the outside. Simone de Beauvoir wrote of the post-war period: 'there were no reservations in our friendship for the U.S.S.R.; the sacrifices of the Russian people had proved that its leaders embodied its true wishes'.[134]

Unlike Nazism, Stalinism turned out to be a viable export. There was a template – quite independent of Stalin the person – which could be used in Central and Eastern Europe after 1945. This included camps, purges and show trials (where prosecutors lifted whole sentences from the Soviet proceedings of the 1930s). Personality cults were also fostered, focused on distinctly uncharismatic personalities, who were often as absent as Stalin and who conformed more to the image of the bureaucrat working late at night serving the people.[135] The regime also included forced industrialization, as well as attempts at atomizing entire societies, though with individual, rather than mass terror (but also with the classically Stalinist re-engineering of souls). Again, it could all look for a while as if it worked – until it obviously did not, whereupon most regimes switched to an implicit social contract in which at least some minimal consent was exchanged for at least some consumer goods.

Even up to 1989 there would be states which preserved features that could meaningfully be described as Stalinist and which in fact professed Stalinism as a model – in other words, long after Stalin and at least some of his crimes had been denounced by his successors. Nicolae Ceaușescu, socialist Romania's leader from the mid-1960s, felt he had to choose between the post-Stalinist USSR and Stalinism. He opted for the latter and carefully distanced himself from Moscow (although Romania never tried to leave the Warsaw Pact).[136] The self-proclaimed Conducător would still insist in a 1988 interview with *Newsweek* that Stalin had been proved right by history, although he confessed that he also felt inspired by North Korea. And he demonstrated that he meant it: there was the same emphasis on heavy industry and a thorough reconstruction of society from scratch – in particular, the wholesale destruction of traditional villages and urban neighbourhoods, and extensive resettlements to move people into newly built but completely dysfunctional mass housing. Like Stalin, Ceaușescu stoked a sense of the country being threatened by enemies inside and out, effectively drawing on nationalism to gain at least some support for the regime. As a high-ranking Romanian official put it to a Western diplomat, 'independence is our legitimacy'.[137]

Ceaușescu built lasting monuments to this whole style of politics, with its aesthetic of bigger as better – in particular, the House of the Republic in Bucharest, which still stands as the world's largest civilian administration building (and which had to be made from Romanian materials only).[138] The personality cult of the 'helmsman' (another self-designation) knew no bounds, and neither did his inferiority complex: every five years a tome called *Omagiu* would be published with quotations from world leaders about the virtues and achievements of the Conducător. Ideology and concept production did not lag behind to legitimize the supposed originality of this increasingly Byzantine (and often simply bizarre) regime: resettlements became 'systematization' in what was called a 'multilaterally developed socialist society' – a phrase with neither obvious nor hidden meaning.

In a sense, Ceauşescu's rule was more like personal tyranny than Stalinism. In 1989 he absurdly claimed that his 'personal hobby' was 'the building of socialism in Romania'. His wife Elena governed with him, becoming increasingly obsessed with making people believe that she was a great chemist (insisting that in every country they visited she should receive an honorary degree). The couple effectively designated one of their sons as successor, and there was contemptuous talk of 'socialism in one family'. All this looked more like traditional forms of despotism – where, in Marx's works, the state was 'nothing but the personal caprice of a single individual'. The cruel and vengeful execution of the leading couple at the end of 1989 also resembled traditional tyrannicide.

On the other hand, it was comforting but profoundly misleading to view Stalinism as a twentieth-century version of brutal Tsarism. It was really totalitarian. Not that Stalin's state actually succeeded in making total claims on Soviet citizens – the point is that the aspiration completely to reshape and homogenize the people was there, and many of the actual institutional and psychological mechanisms serving that aspiration had been put in place. A total fusion of state and society (what Stalin had termed 'the merging of the state with the masses'), the end of all social conflict and the absorption of all social power in one person who would no longer encounter any resistance to his actions – the 'Egocrat', as the French philosopher Claude Lefort, following Alexander Solzhenitsyn, put it – these constituted the hallmarks of the totalitarian Soviet ideal.[139]

In short, it amounted to a system, with its own political logic, and not just a matter of pathological personalities. But there was no single book that laid it out, no single ideologue who elaborated it. Despite the fact that it emerged from a family of political thought so obsessed with doctrinal refinement (and infighting), Stalinism could not be understood as having been based on a blueprint or as having produced any real theoretical self-justification. Nazism emerged from a philosophical background that was not nearly as sophisticated, but it did advance quite explicit claims for even its most inhumane aspects. With Stalinism there was no such theory; all there is are interpretations.

CHAPTER 3

Fascist Subjects
The Total State and *Volksgemeinschaft*

... National Socialism has no political theory of its own ... the ideologies it uses or discards are mere arcana dominationis, techniques of domination.

Franz Neumann, *Behemoth*, 1941

Conceptions and ideas, as well as movements with a definite spiritual foundation, regardless whether the latter is false or true, can, after a certain point in their development, only be broken with technical instruments of power if these physical weapons are at the same time the support of a new kindling thought, idea, or philosophy.

Hitler

National Socialism is a cool and highly reasoned approach to reality based on the greatest of scientific knowledge and its spiritual expression ... The National Socialist movement is not a cult movement; rather, it is a völkisch and political philosophy which grew out of considerations of an exclusively racist nature.

Hitler

National Socialism is nothing but applied biology.

Rudolf Hess

For us, Italian democracy is a human body that needs freedom, to shed its fetters and its burdens ...

'Futurist Democracy', 1919, reprinted in *Futurismo e fascismo*, 1924

All men of action necessarily move towards catastrophe as their conclusion. They live and end with this aura, either for themselves or for others.

Mussolini, 1939

M ANY DECADES after the fall of Hitler's and Mussolini's regimes a generally agreed theoretical account of fascism – or just a definition – has remained elusive. There is not even consensus about whether fascism is a strictly limited historical term, something that happened to Italians (or rather was perpetrated by Italians) between 1922 and 1945, or a universal phenomenon. The disputes surrounding fascism are not just a result of academic nitpicking; they point to what appear to be characteristics of the thing itself. At least rhetorically, fascism was opposed to 'reason'; it glorified will, intuition and sentiment. One could feel it, but one couldn't define it.

For a long time observers also took the view that fascism had simply been a kind of gutter ideology, at best an assembly of prejudices and nationalist clichés. Even the book that might qualify as a founding text – Adolf Hitler's *Mein Kampf* – has been dismissed by historians as 'dogmas which echo the conversation of any Austrian café or German beer-house'.[1] The leaders themselves did not help: Mussolini, when asked 'What is Fascism?', replied with characteristic modesty, 'I am Fascism' (to which a rival Fascist chief retorted, 'Fascism is not one man, it is an Idea').[2] Less absurdly, there was the fact that fascism from the beginning was centred on the nation and drew on nationally specific myths and values. This also explained why Mussolini would insist in 1932 that Fascism was not for export.[3]

In fact, an official fascist doctrine *was* eventually formulated by Mussolini and exports declared legitimate, but the point remains that fascists seemed self-consciously weak on theory. As the leader of a Romanian fascist group put it: 'The country is dying for want of men, not of programmes.'[4] During Stalinism arcane theoretical disagreements could literally be a matter of life and death. Hitler and Mussolini hardly cared about doctrinal purity (in the case of Hitler, only racial purity mattered) – although the National Socialists, once in power, outlawed citation of their earliest programme because their initial demands had been far more anti-capitalist than they cared to remember.[5]

And yet, for all its apparent theoretical weakness, fascism was one of the major ideological innovations of the twentieth century – especially if we measure innovation not by the production of sophisticated philosophical texts, but by a capacity to fuse ideas and sentiments to create new public justifications for the exercise of power. It is true that fascism had its roots in the late nineteenth century, but as a political belief system – and in fact quite an elaborate and internally coherent one, contrary to the notion of a 'gutter ideology' – it came together only with and after the First World War. The autodidact Hitler – who positively hated intellectuals and, unlike Mussolini, made no pretence at all of being interested in doctrine development – nonetheless did not have a purely instrumental and opportunistic relationship with ideas.

He would not always care whether his thoughts (let alone his proposed policies) were coherent, but that did not mean that on the road to power he would espouse whatever ideas he thought would get him there. In fact, he insistently claimed that he was that rarest of things, a theoretician and politician – the 'executor of the idea' – in one person.[6] The basic precepts of his *Weltanschauung* remained the same over decades, and so could also be elaborated by Nazi theorists without the kind of fear that Soviet thinkers necessarily felt because doctrines might change with the vagaries of power politics. For much the same reason the Nazis did not have party purges comparable to the Soviet ones. What fascists did fear, however, was that their ideas could be proved wrong by history: truth, for them, was a question of successful political action, of power. As an Italian Fascist put it, 'the truth of an ideology lies in its capacity to set in motion our capacity for ideals and action'.[7]

Crucially, fascist rule was not the same as that of the right-wing authoritarian regimes that flourished in interwar Europe: while National Socialism was a form of fascism, it was qualitatively different from the original Italian version; for that reason it will be treated separately at the end of this chapter. Most important, fascism was a response specifically to the age of mass democracy – an alternative which many political thinkers across Europe who viscerally hated both liberal parliamentarism (what the Nazis dismissed as 'the system') and socialism found plausible. Very large numbers of citizens found it plausible, too.

Sorel's Myths

Joseph Goebbels, the Nazi propaganda minister, claimed on the occasion of Hitler's seizure of power in 1933 that 'The year 1789 is hereby eradicated from history.'[8] The soundbite had much truth in it. Fascism opposed virtually everything which the Enlightenment stood for: the idea that humans could find the truth by reasoning together, that they could grant each other equal rights and freedoms through a social contract, and that reason and progress were inextricably linked. Thus fascists have been called misologists – haters of reason.

And yet this was not necessarily their key distinguishing feature. Many philosophers and politicians in the nineteenth century had been sceptical about the powers of reason, but they were identifiable – and self-identified – as conservatives. Fascism was different in that it wanted to be active, to mobilize people and to master history, rather than cautiously manage historical change and render it safe, in the manner of conservatives. It was not hostile to revolutions – in fact, it styled itself as a revolution, and especially as a revolution of dissatisfied youth.

Where did the imperative to mobilize come from? While it is a mistake to take much of what Mussolini said at face value, it is plausible that the Duce adopted such ideas from one of his favourite contemporary political thinkers, Georges Sorel. As Mussolini himself declared: 'What I am, I owe to Sorel.' Sorel in turn had already argued in 1912: 'Our Mussolini is not the usual kind of socialist. Believe me: one day you will see him leading a holy battalion and greeting the Italian flag with a sword. He is an Italian of the fifteenth century, a Condottiere.'[9]

Sorel must be considered one of the least classifiable political thinkers of the twentieth century. First he seemed like a conservative, then an orthodox socialist, then a revolutionary syndicalist, then a nationalist (and that is to leave out quite a few phases in between); his final ideological incarnation appeared to be as a Bolshevist praising Lenin. In one of history's most famous trials, he was first a Dreyfusard, defending the French army captain who had been falsely accused of treason, only then to deride the Dreyfusard parts of the French Third Republic's political establishment as a class of hypocrites most interested in doing well out of parliamentary government. The only constant in Sorel's life seemed to be that he was always shifting his allegiances; both friends and opponents were asking whether his thought had any coherence at all. One thing, though, everyone seemed to be able to agree upon in the 1920s and 1930s: Sorel's ideas were of the utmost importance. Wyndham Lewis, one of the few genuinely fascist writers in Britain, claimed in his book *The Art of Being Ruled* that 'Georges Sorel is the key to all contemporary political thought.'[10] Benedetto Croce, the Italian conservative liberal, praised Sorel for being the only original Marxist thinker, except for Marx himself. Gramsci admired him, using his theories to develop his own conception of the mass party as a modern version of the Machiavellian prince, a 'collective individual' and even a 'collective intellectual'; Georg Lukács conceded that his early romantic anti-capitalism had been influenced by Sorel. Lenin, however, did not return the compliments which Sorel paid him at the end of his life and dismissed the Frenchman as a notorious muddle-head, a 'councillor of confusion.'[11]

Sorel was indeed not a systematic thinker. He himself acknowledged that his writing style could be confusing, even infuriating, and that his thought was full of gaps which he could not be bothered to fill. In his most influential book, *Reflections on Violence*, he pointed out:

> I am neither a professor, a populariser of knowledge, nor a candidate for party leadership. I am a self-taught man exhibiting to other people the notebooks which have served for my own instruction . . . I put before my readers the working of a mental effort which is continually endeavouring to break

through the bonds of what has been previously constructed for common use, in order to discover that which is truly personal and individual. The only things I find it worthwhile entering in my notebooks are those which I have not met elsewhere; I readily skip the transitions between these things, because they nearly always come under the heading of commonplaces.[12]

In other words, Sorel strove to be utterly original in everything he wrote. He had 'never found anyone to teach me what I wanted to know'. So he had to work everything out by himself. And since he refused to build any system, he could reinvent himself ideologically every day, rather than becoming his own disciple.[13] Like many autodidacts, he remained an outsider, fired by a hatred of academic philosophers – who in turn refused to take him seriously.[14]

Intellectually adventurous though he might have been, the life of this self-consciously anti-establishment figure could not have been more conventional. He was born in 1847 to bourgeois parents in Cherbourg; he came from what Charles Péguy, a friend of his, was to call the 'old France', the traditional Catholic provinces.[15] He was sent to the École Polytechnique in Paris, France's leading scientific academy, and then went on to become an engineer for the Department of Public Works. He spent his Spartan life in the service of the Third Republic, one of countless obscure provincial officials. He had a somewhat bizarre relationship with a servant who had nursed him when he had fallen ill in Lyon in 1875. The servant was a devout, semi-literate Catholic, with whom Sorel set up a household after his recovery. He idolized this woman as a symbol of purity, taught her and, after her death, worshipped her memory for the rest of his life – in fact, all his books were intended as monuments to her. But Sorel had not just taught Marie David; he had also learnt from her. Even as a revolutionary Marxist, he would espouse values traditionally represented by the right – honour, the dignity of family and the sanctity of religious experience. Upon his retirement in 1892, when he had attained the rank of chief engineer, the French state awarded him the red ribbon of a Chevalier of the Légion d'Honneur. Sorel, the man who would relentlessly call for the destruction of the French state, was to wear the ribbon until the last days of his life in 1922.

By the time he retired Sorel had already published a number of articles and two books, one a study of the Bible, the other an account of Socrates' trial (the outcome of which he approved). He settled in a quiet suburb of Paris, living off a small legacy his mother had left him. One day a week, he would go into central Paris by tram, read at the National Library and talk passionately with friends (and random strangers) in the small bookstores around the Sorbonne. He rapidly established himself as a kind of Marxist political publicist at a time when

Marx was relatively little known in France. When he wrote his *Reflections* he was fifty-eight, with a reputation as something of a character. Friends affectionately called him *le père Sorel*.[16]

Many of Sorel's writings responded to the profound 'crisis in Marxism' discussed earlier in this book – the polarization between a doctrinaire and deterministic scientific socialism on the one hand, and a pragmatic revisionism prepared to accept liberal parliamentarism on the other. Sorel's distinctive contribution to the debate was this: he criticized everything he considered materialist and rationalist in late nineteenth-century Marxism; and he sought to recast the doctrine as a form of 'social poetry', as something that made people act heroically and could bring about moral rebirth. In theory, he seemed to agree with Eduard Bernstein's dictum that 'the goal was nothing, and the movement everything'. But for Bernstein this had meant that the goal of revolution should be replaced by gradual reforms achieved through legal means – with the workers' welfare and right to participate in democracy as the immediate goals. Sorel had only contempt for this kind of reformism, which he thought would turn proletarians into petty bourgeois; when he spoke about the movement being everything, he meant that strenuous, often violent *struggle* should be everything.

Sorel was one of the few nineteenth-century thinkers interested in Vico, who had argued that man could understand history, because man himself had constructed what the Italian had dubbed 'artificial nature'. For Weber and other early twentieth-century social theorists this fundamental insight of Vico no longer held true. Given what Weber had called the steely casing and what Simmel had lamented as the tragedy of culture, human beings could no longer understand the impersonal forces which they had created and which now inexorably ruled their lives. Sorel profoundly disagreed with this diagnosis. He still believed with Vico in human beings as primarily creators.[17] The question was under which conditions this creativity – and the moral greatness of which, according to Sorel, humans were still capable – could best be realized.

When Sorel turned to Marxism in the 1890s, he already had a highly eclectic and seemingly contradictory mixture of ideas at his disposal. He could argue that if human beings were properly to be creators, and if, in the last instance, virtue was formed only in combat, then the proletariat was the only creative class. Solely proletarians had a common consciousness which predisposed them to martyrdom and heroism, because they were already engaged in a constant struggle – both with the material they were working on, and of course with their employers. But the obverse side of this view of the proletariat as potential carrier of the highest human values was that any compromise – or even any actual improvement in the workers' welfare – had to be rejected.

This also meant that Marxism was not at all a matter of scientific truth. In Sorel's eyes, Marxism was pragmatically true, as the ideological expression of the only group of people who could morally rejuvenate mankind. And this group of people just so happened to be the proletariat. Sorel was quite ready to admit that at other times fundamentally different ideologies, such as early Christianity, had performed the same function and had therefore been similarly worthy of support. In that sense, Marxism as theory really did not matter; Sorel could easily switch to any ideology which seemed more likely to produce moral greatness in struggle.

Sorel perfectly fitted the picture that Weber had painted of the politician (or, in this case, the political thinker) of conviction. In fact, Weber had acknowledged that anarcho-syndicalism – the left-wing current to which Sorel belonged at the time of writing *Reflections* – might well be the most revolutionary movement of his time. Weber diagnosed that it was 'either an idle whim of intellectual romantics and . . . undisciplined workers . . . or else a religion of *conviction* which is justified even if it *never* provides a goal for the future that is "attainable" . . .'[18]

Sorel did not want a future of ease and leisure to be 'attainable'. He wanted men to be fired up to persist in struggle. That is why Sorel put the idea of class war at the centre of Marxism – an idea that had at all costs to be defended against the advocates of compromises with bourgeois democracy. More particularly, he distinguished between what he called the political strike and the general strike. The former aimed at material gains and better working conditions; for established working-class leaders it had the advantage that it did 'not generally imperil the precious lives of the politicians'.[19] The general strike, on the other hand, conjured up a final, almost apocalyptic confrontation between revolutionaries and the existing order. In an astonishing passage Sorel let it slip that heroism was more important than the actual outcome of any conflict: 'Even if the only result of the idea of the general strike was to make the Socialist conception more heroic, it should on that account be looked upon as an incalculable value.' Not surprisingly, then, he concurred with the judgement of his friend Daniel Halévy that 'the Wandering Jew may be taken as a symbol of the highest aspirations of mankind, condemned as he is to march forever without knowing rest'.[20]

Introducing his most influential idea, Sorel argued that in its violent march forward the proletariat was to be sustained by what he called social myths. Myths were undivided emotional wholes, drawing on what Sorel described as 'the profounder region of our mental life': the seat of intuition and emotion. Consequently they were not subject to analytical reason. As Sorel pointed out, 'people who are living in the world of "myths" are secure from all refutation'.[21]

Only myths, then, were 'capable of evoking as an undivided whole the mass of sentiments which corresponds to the different manifestations of the war undertaken by socialism against modern society'. 'We do nothing great', Sorel further insisted, 'without the help of warmly coloured images which absorb the whole of our attention'. The only way the revolutionary struggle could be undermined was if middle-class intellectuals, who, in Sorel's words, made 'the exploitation of thought their profession', took over the movement.[22]

Sorel opposed the tendency of parliamentary socialists to appeal to the humanitarian instincts of the middle class, thereby furthering social peace. He wanted the middle class to be not humanitarian, but strong, ruthless and conscious that the proletariat was the enemy. He celebrated the real captains of industry, as they were similar to warrior types, with their 'conquering, insatiable, and pitiless spirit'.[23] In fact, for Sorel, Marxism had always been a kind of 'Manchesterism' – he glorified the unshackled, free development of capitalism and production, hoping that society would be as polarized and thereby as energized as possible.

Thus revolutionary violence was also justified by its role of reinforcing the separation of classes, keeping the proletariat and the middle class pure, so to speak. It served what Carl Schmitt was later to theorize as friend–enemy thinking: according to Sorel, the threat of the general strike in particular would effectively group friends and enemies, keeping the demarcation entirely clear.[24] He argued that 'if a united and revolutionary proletariat confronts a rich middle class, eager for conquest, capitalist society will have reached its historical perfection'.[25]

All this might still have been seen as a tactical apology for violence. Sorel, however, went on to make what was probably his most paradoxical claim of all: 'proletarian violence', he argued, 'carried on as a pure and simple manifestation of the sentiment of the class war appears ... as a very fine and very heroic thing; it is at the service of the immemorial interests of civilization; it is not perhaps the most appropriate method of obtaining immediate material advantages, but it may save the world from barbarism'.[26] Violence saving the world from barbarism – it is here that Sorel touches directly on a theme that was to be central to fascist thought: since peace, tolerance and a liberal life at ease were all unmistakable signs of decadence, only perpetual struggle gave rise to the opposite of barbarism. In a genuine transvaluation of values, Sorel redescribed the bourgeois as the real barbarian.

But what would a non-barbaric life be like? Sorel, while trying to avoid the supposedly always 'rationalist' construction of a utopia, did attempt to outline what he called the 'ethics of the producers', to be characterized by traditional notions of duty and hard work. With this ethics of the producers, he shifted away from a primacy of politics – a sense that in the modern world meaning was to be derived from political struggle, similar to some of Weber's more illiberal moments. Instead he argued that epic, almost Homeric feats of production would take place in the factory. Under those circumstances there was also no longer any need for a state.

In the end, Sorel had expunged materialism and even economics almost entirely from Marxism, and instead injected it with a celebration of the human will to struggle. Even more strikingly, he cleansed Marxism of any notion of actually overcoming capitalism. He was a *moraliste* of sorts who cared less about actual proletarians than about the possibility of creating a collective body hardened (and ennobled) for and through struggle.

What Zeev Sternhell has called Sorel's 'antimaterialist revision of Marxism' was to inspire thinkers across the political spectrum in the first decades of the twentieth century – even if there were no direct disciples and no proper 'Sorel school'.[27] And it would take only one crucial conceptual switch to turn Sorel's basic ideas into something that already very much resembled fascist thought: the shift from the general strike or, more broadly, the class struggle to the nation as the most powerful myth. Fascists transposed the idea of class struggle to national groups, but retained a belief in violence as the motor of history and as indispensable to a new morality of heroism.

This conceptual switch happened soon enough. Sorel himself came close to making it when he turned to the proto-fascist nationalist Action Française, although he ultimately found the movement too royalist and too Catholic for his taste. He also despised the *union sacrée* of the French nation across all class boundaries at the beginning of the First World War: it was once again politicians using ordinary, honest people for their own ends, all in the name of national solidarity.[28] During the war, the young German jurist Carl Schmitt, hailing from a traditional Catholic background but intensely interested in new political thinking, had to read Sorel's *Reflections*, as he was working as a censor for French publications in Munich. He was deeply impressed and in 1923 was to write admiringly of Sorel's idea that 'out of true life-instincts come the great enthusiasm, the great moral decision and the great myth'.[29] He saw Sorel's irrationalist theory of 'unmediated concrete life' as an advance over 'intellectualist' Marxism and stressed that 'the great psychological and historical significance of the theory of myths could not be denied'.[30] While agreeing with Sorel on the sheer power of myths to generate enthusiasm and the courage necessary for any great moral decision, Schmitt profoundly disagreed on the question of what actually constituted the most powerful myth. He acknowledged the impact of the Marxist myth of the bourgeois, but argued that the Russian Revolution had been successful precisely because Lenin had managed to transform the myth of the bourgeois into a nationalist Russian myth. In this indigenous myth, the *burshui* became first and foremost a Westerner oppressing the Russian peasants. Only the fusion of socialism and Slavism therefore had brought the Communists to power. This demonstrated that 'the energy of the national was greater than that of the myth of the class struggle'. In Schmitt's words, what was needed was 'a sensitivity for difference as such; all that is moving today in the direction of national antagonisms, rather than class antagonisms'.[31]

As we saw in the last chapter, Schmitt himself turned into a major critic of liberal parliamentarism and the politics of compromise; in the mid-1920s he also began to laud Fascist Italy as providing a proper model for a specifically national democracy in the circumstances of twentieth-century mass politics. His development was yet more proof that Sorel's thought appealed to both the radical left and the radical right. Sorel's friend Daniel Halévy relates the story of how ten years after Sorel's death the ambassador of Fascist Italy approached him to propose to erect a monument over Sorel's grave which had fallen into disrepair. Soon after this, the ambassador of the Soviet Union came along with the same proposal on behalf of the USSR. Sorel's family, probably mindful of *le père*'s self-conscious outsider status, rejected both proposals.

Nevertheless, Mussolini kept claiming him as 'our master', alongside Friedrich Nietzsche, whose idea of *vivere pericolosamente* the Duce kept celebrating. And he had a point. Mussolini himself had started out as a socialist, and had then broken with the movement over the question of Italian entry into the war. Like Sorel, he rejected a socialism that culminated in the slogan 'bidets for everyone'. Glory, not comfort, had to be at the heart of a proper political morality. And soon enough, in Italy too, the conceptual switch from class to nation was made, through the work of Enrico Corradini, who replaced the proletariat as the agent of class struggle with the idea of the 'proletarian nation' which was being oppressed by stronger, capitalist nations.

The idea that nation beat class was given an immeasurable boost by the First World War. In 1914 socialists almost everywhere had rallied to their fatherlands. Fascism would not have emerged without what Mussolini himself called the 'trenchocracy' of the First World War – the aristocracy of proven fighters in the trenches. And it remained characterized throughout by a glorification of violence. As the Duce claimed, 'perpetual peace would be impossible and useless. War alone brings human energies to their highest state of tension, and stamps with the seal of nobility the nations which dare to face it.' There was even a kind of death cult: 'Long live Death' was only one of the many death-centred slogans of fascists (in this case, of the Romanian Iron Guard); a photograph of Mussolini's office as editor of a Fascist newspaper shows a loaded pistol on the desk and the picture of a skull on the wall.

Again, the belief in the value of war as such made fascists different from conservatives: Bismarck had claimed, 'I do not want war; I want victory.'[32] Fascists' faith in the absolute value of the nation, so that nationalism would trump all other ethical claims, also dissociated the nation from liberalism, with which it had mostly been allied in the nineteenth century. It was not an accident that Italian Fascism and Nazism arose in nation-states where national unification had come late and was widely perceived as incomplete – and where liberals were often blamed for this failure. Mussolini would eventually affirm that 'we have created our myth. The myth is a faith, a passion. It is not necessary for it to be a reality. It is a reality in the sense that it is a stimulus, is hope, is courage. Our myth is the nation, our myth is the greatness of the nation.' This was not an idiosyncratic Mussoliniesque interpretation of his own ideological creation; it became conventional wisdom among fascists across Europe. Individual myths meant to mobilize the masses differed among nations; the belief in myth as such did not.

Fascist Solutions

Fascists believed in an almost mystical unity of the leader and his people – a unity based on feeling or even 'spirituality'. This notion was underpinned by a whole pseudo-science of mass psychology dating back to the late nineteenth century, which was to influence Hitler in particular and which is faithfully reproduced in *Mein Kampf*. Fascism, unlike traditional conservatism, conceived of itself as a mass-based form of politics. In particular, it sought to appeal to the 'masses' who had mainly been politicized through a shared experience of sacrifice and suffering in the First World War.[33] Thus fascists also used the mass party as their vehicle to come to power. Unlike nineteenth-century liberals and conservatives, they did not cling to a tradition of small elite groups of notables or bureaucrats who paternalistically took care of the common good of society.

In the same vein, fascism did not object to 'modernity' – if by that term one understands technology and science. In fact, Italian Fascists in particular idealized aircraft, tanks and speed in general. Culturally, Fascism mixed the archaic with the ultra-modern and the avant-garde (a term that itself had been appropriated from military discourse), a fusion that went back to the period before the First World War. Already in 1909 F. T. Marinetti, later a fervent supporter of Italy's entry into the war, had declared in his 1909 'Futurist Manifesto':

we will glorify war – the world's only hygiene – militarism, patriotism, the destructive gesture of freedom-bringers, beautiful ideas worth dying for, and scorn for woman . . . we will destroy the museums, libraries, academies of every kind, will fight moralism, feminism, every opportunistic or utilitarian cowardice . . .[34]

Futurism (and the Fascist strands of thinking inspired by it) with its notion of *guerra come festa* proclaimed that 'war is the only rudder that can steer us through the new age of the airplane'; that rudder was not likely to get lost, because according to the Futurists' simple equations 'war cannot die, for it is one of the laws of life. Life = aggression . . . War = bloody and necessary trial of a people's strength.'[35] Futurism was comprehensively to refashion life, from high politics to crucial everyday matters such as cooking. The 1932 recipe book *La cucina futurista* proposed that Italians should stop eating pasta, which Marinetti associated with sloth, impotence and cowardice, and instead turn to some ultra-modern recipes – such as pineapples with sardines.[36]

The Nazis, by contrast, declared avant-garde art degenerate. But in Germany, too, a whole range of thinkers hoped that fascism could liberate technology from being subjected to the imperatives of capitalism – a more rational mobilization of all economic and technological forces for the national community than their haphazard use by individual capitalist entrepreneurs. What the writer Ernst Jünger termed 'total mobilization' translated into a full harnessing of modern technology and a complete regimentation of the *Volk* – understood as a fully mobilized collective body – for the sake of the nation. Thomas Mann tried to capture this strange mixture of combining the most up-to-date with nostalgia for an imagined past by coining the term 'highly technological romanticism'.[37]

This points to one reason why followers of fascism – and many observers of fascism – saw it not primarily as an irrational glorification of the will, but as a convincing practical answer to the problems of the age, especially but not only in the wake of the Great Depression. Fascists proposed economic policies of the 'Middle Way' or 'Third Way', which claimed to combine the best of socialism and capitalism. Parallel to Keynesian ideas, they advocated public works programmes to tackle unemployment. This explained the many curious in-between figures such as Oswald Mosley and Henri de Man, who – quite apart from and with much more serious thinking than Mussolini – started out as socialists but crossed over to fascism.[38]

But fascism also appealed to traditional elites: it seemed to offer them at the same time protection from radical socialism and a range of solutions to the worst failures of the free market. After all, Mussolini did not really march on Rome – he arrived in the sleeping car of the Direttissimo, the express train from Milan. He had been asked by the King to be prime minister, and promptly declared himself 'His Majesty's loyal servant'. His marchers were 'amateur soldiers playing at revolution, poorly armed (hunting rifles, old army guns, little ammunition)'; they would have been no match for the regular army, had it been willing to stop them (and most of them stopped anyway, about twenty miles from the capital).[39] Similarly with Hitler there was a sense among traditional elites – and among middle-class voters – that all else had been tried and that parliamentary government as a political form was finished. In fact, no fascist leader ever properly 'seized power' – they were all appointed, either by a king or by a conservative president or, outside Germany and Italy during the war, by the Third Reich. Hitler himself explicitly stated that revolutions in the twentieth century could, and should, be brought about without violent insurrection; instead, they were to proceed through initial collaboration with – and eventually the destruction of – old elites.

But just what was the supposed solution fascists offered for the problems of the age? In theory it was corporatism, that is, the division of society into distinct groups such as employers and workers in different industries, all co-operating for the good of the nation. Corporatism seemed to address both the challenge of class conflict and the demand for individual participation in decision-making where it mattered – the economy. Italian corporatism was, once more, deeply influenced by Sorel, in particular his rather sketchy 'ethics of producers' – except that none of the Italian corporatists envisaged abolishing the state in the way the French syndicalist had done.[40]

Mussolini trumpeted corporatism (or, as it was sometimes called, corporativism) as one of the major contributions of fascist political thought, which 'was of interest to the whole world'. Statesmen like Lloyd George echoed him, calling the corporate state 'the greatest social reform of the modern era'.[41] But it was theorized and elaborated at more or less the same time in many other European countries. There were similarities to the functional forms of representation that the Guild Socialists and G. D. H. Cole in particular had advocated – and there was in fact one major pluralist thinker, Ramiro de Maeztu, who went over to fascism.[42]

Above all, a rival, non-fascist version of corporatism was elaborated by Catholic thinkers – often with authoritarian leanings, to be sure. The influential Austrian sociologist Othmar Spann, for instance, put forward a holistic theory of what he called the 'true state'.[43] Spann, drawing on the German romantics, conceived of society as a body, whose limbs were constituted by corporations that were supposed to act together harmoniously. Reasonable social solutions and the reign of 'objective values' benefiting everyone should supersede arbitrary parliamentary compromises. It was, in Spann's convoluted terminology, about 'ranks' and organic inequality instead of democratic and therefore 'inorganic' equality; *Sachsouveränität*, something like rational administration, was supposed to replace *Volkssouveränität*, the irrational sovereignty of the people. And in Spann's vision, a state religion – which just so happened to be Catholicism – was supposed to hold society together as a whole. It did not seem all that surprising that some of Spann's students became leading members of the Heimwehr, the nationalist militia which was to play a crucial role in destroying Red Vienna.[44]

The main point of authoritarian corporatism (and all the strange organicist metaphors that someone like Spann put forward) was clearly this: to end class conflict. Once more it was Mussolini who made things explicit:

A country like ours, which has no rich resources in the earth, which has mountains for half of its area, cannot have great economic possibilities. If, then, the citizens become naturally quarrelsome, if classes have a tendency to strive to annihilate each other, civil life can have none of that rhythm necessary for developing a modern people.[45]

In Italy, the corporations were in fact official state organs, designed to impose discipline on labour and (in theory) employers, and accountable to the government for national production. The Fascist philosopher Ugo Spirito added that the scheme had begun as 'a grand experiment in economic conciliation ... as an effort in the reconciliation of class interests with the superior interests of the state'.[46] Eventually, it was supposed to lead to a complete transcendence of class differences and thus total social unity. As Spirito put it:

Corporativism is animated by the possibility of morally and technically unifying social life; it believes in the joy of giving and of sacrifice. It is opposed to every uniquely private goal in life and precisely for that reason, corporativism is not an economic notion, but the unique political, moral, religious, essence of the Fascist revolution.[47]

Spirito even wanted to see private property transformed into 'corporative property' and workers partly owning and managing firms. This predictably caused alarm among Italy's industrialists and was never realized – while Spirito himself was shunted off to Sicily.[48] It seemed not obviously inconsistent that he later became a Communist.

By the end of the 1930s, the Italian state or quasi-state agencies and 'institutes' controlled vital parts of the Italian economy; indeed, Italy had the largest state sector outside the Soviet Union. Corporatism was widely seen as a successful, or at least credible, approach to economic and social policy – not least in the United States, where some New Dealers were clearly taken with Mussolini's Fascism.[49]

The Myth of the Total State

After almost ten years in power, Mussolini finally presented the world with an official doctrine. It had actually been penned by the philosopher Giovanni Gentile. Gentile had begun his intellectual life as a liberal. In the early 1920s he even sought to provide a distinctly liberal justification of his support for Fascism, thereby reinforcing the sense that Italian liberals saw in Mussolini the last chance to save their system from socialism.[50] Gentile was invited by the Duce, immediately after the March on Rome, to serve in his first cabinet as minister of public instruction. He was committed to a notion of 'absolute idealism', which posited that reality was ultimately 'spiritual' and the product of human consciousness and moral choice. He put forward a moral imperative for all human beings fully to realize themselves. Self-realization, however, could be accomplished only in communion – human beings were essentially social beings; any other anthropological conception was an individualist illusion.

It followed that the modern liberal individual – as theorized by conventional liberalism – necessarily led an impoverished, not fully realized life which could never transcend a sordid compromise between self-interest and the contractually agreed interests of society as a whole. Instead, Gentile held, the nation should provide the foundation for moral choices, both individual and collective. This thought in turn led him to a conception of the 'ethical state' as a sovereign institution through which individuals would continuously realize and refashion themselves.[51] He explained, 'the Fascist State . . . is a force, but a spiritual force . . . It is the soul of the soul.' In ever so slightly more practical terms, this meant identification with a national leader who embodied the collective consciousness and the national will.

For Gentile the nation was a willed and imagined community. He had early on allied himself with the extreme nationalism of the Associazione Nazionalista of Corradini and Alfredo Rocco (the latter also aspired to be chief legal architect of the Fascist state). But Fascism was not simply extreme nationalism, as had been proposed by a number of thinkers in the nineteenth century. As Gentile later emphasized, the problem with conventional nationalism was precisely that it regarded the nation as something given, something external and transcendent. But for him there could be nothing beyond human will and moral choice, and traditional nationalism was too historical and 'naturalist' to make for a neat fit with his idealism. In his eyes, Fascism had to mean the continuous creation of the nation. Like so many Italian intellectuals, whether on the right or on the left (such as Gramsci), he held that the nineteenth-century Risorgimento had remained incomplete, that unification, as the famous phrase went, had made Italy, but not Italians. Gentile also conceived of himself

as fulfilling the ideals of Italian nationalism and claimed a liberal nationalist like
Mazzini as a direct ideological precursor, or even as a proto-*squadrista*, a kind
of Fascist guerrilla fighter *avant la lettre*.[52]

Still, even if it was grounded in individual will, it was not individualistic: the
citizen's total identification with the national state was a product of a specifically national and very comprehensive pedagogy. The modern state would not
just be an ethical state – it would also be an indoctrinating state.[53] In fact,
during his relatively brief period in government, Gentile initiated the largest
reform in public education in Italy since the mid-nineteenth century, stressing
what he saw as 'humanist' and nationalist values, and the importance of
the pupil 'merging' his will with that of the teacher. Mussolini praised the
philosopher's policy and also put him in charge of a commission tasked with
constructing a specifically Fascist state.[54]

What precisely had attracted Mussolini to Gentile, whose doctrines were
derided by Croce as a 'schoolboy's piece of work'? The future Duce – despite
all the boasting about 'I am Fascism' – had already claimed in August 1921 that
Fascism urgently required a doctrine if it was not to self-destruct.[55] While
Mussolini moved from socialism to Fascism, and substituted the proletarian
nation for the proletariat, he remained one thing throughout: a collectivist. In
a sense, all he had to do now was to switch from the materialism of his socialist
days to the supposed 'spiritualism' of Fascism. As Mussolini put it in 1922, 'for
a hundred years matter remained on the altars; today spirit is taking its place'.[56]
So what Gentile called his philosophy of 'Actualism', with its stress on the
communal and spiritual nature of human beings, would immediately appeal to
Mussolini, as would the pretensions that came with the expression 'ethical
state'. According to Carl Schmitt's (not entirely reliable) testimony, the Duce
told him during a one-to-one conversation in the Palazzo Venezia in 1936 that
'the state is eternal; the party is transitory; I am a Hegelian!'[57]

The ethical state would be a total state – or rather, a totalitarian state, which
meant that 'everything [was] in the state, nothing outside the state, and nothing
against the state'. But Gentile also kept insisting that it would be a genuine form
of democracy and best placed to generate a capacity for collective political
action.[58] In 1927 he informed the American readers of *Foreign Affairs*:

> the Fascist State . . . is a people's state, and, as such, the democratic state *par
> excellence*. The relationship between State and citizen (not this or that citizen,
> but all citizens) is accordingly so intimate that the State exists only as, and in
> so far as, the citizen causes it to exist. Its formation therefore is the formation
> of a consciousness of it in individuals, in the masses. Hence the need of the
> Party, and of all the instruments of propaganda and education which Fascism

uses to make the thought and will of the *Duce* the thought and will of the masses. Hence the enormous task which Fascism sets itself in trying to bring the whole mass of people, beginning with the little children, inside the fold of the Party.[59]

This vision described supposedly genuine democracy, because, according to Gentile, 'state and individual are one and the same thing, or rather, they are inseparable terms of a necessary synthesis'. Another word for this synthesis was 'totalitarian'. This concept, like so many political labels, had been created by an enemy of the phenomenon it ultimately came to designate:[60] the liberal anti-Fascist Giovanni Amendola had first talked about Mussolini's regime as 'totalitarian' in order to warn about further developments in the direction of dictatorship. However, in 1925 Mussolini himself began to speak about the 'ferocious totalitarian will' – *feroce volontà totalitaria* – of the Fascists. The Duce, who referred to himself as 'desperately Italian', also professed the totalitarian need to fashion a new man, or, more specifically, a 'new Italian' who would 'speak little, gesticulate less, and seem driven by a single will' (and, in line with Marinetti's cultural project, eat less pasta).[61]

This self-consciously totalitarian vision never even came close to describing the reality of Fascist Italy. Mussolini largely subordinated his party to what remained a traditional state apparatus; he left the King in place as head of state, with the monarch preserving a kind of 'reserve charisma' alongside the Duce's; schools would feature pictures of both King and Duce, and people would sing the Royal March alongside 'Giovinezza', the Fascist anthem.[62] Vittorio Emanuele III could even afford to refuse to salute the Fascist flag when Hitler came to visit Rome in 1938 (Hitler in turn was annoyed by the monarch, whom he referred to as 'the nutcracker king').[63] Gentile's and others' efforts to replace the Italian constitution – in essence the Albertine Statute of 1848, which had been extended from Piedmont to unified Italy – with a specifically Fascist one came to nothing. The only drastic change in a genuinely Fascist or at least post-parliamentarian direction was the substitution of the Chamber of Deputies by an – entirely unelected – Chamber of Corporations in 1939.[64] Doctrines were important, and so was indoctrination – but, if in doubt, the Fascists left traditional institutions undisturbed and demanded apolitical acquiescence rather than fanatical belief. As R. J. Bosworth put it, 'Himmler wanted the Germans to think in only one way; the Fascist secret police preferred that Italians did not think at all'.[65]

What all this meant for ordinary people is memorably depicted in Federico Fellini's film *Amarcord* (Rimini dialect for 'I remember'). In this profound meditation on what it was like to *remember* growing up under Fascism there is much 'normality' that belies any notion of the regime constantly making total claims on its citizens. And yet there are also the political harassment and the torture with castor oil. More subtly, there is the sense that people's inner lives are slowly being reshaped: they project their fears and desires onto the Duce – as when, during a Fascist parade through town, a giant mask of Mussolini suddenly comes to life in the imagination of a fat, unattractive boy for whom the leader gets the girl of his dreams. Eventually, one feels, the whole population is becoming infantilized, rather than directly repressed.

For all the supposed inner reshaping of citizens by the ethical state, it was surprisingly easy for the Duce to lose his grip on the nation. When the King and the Grand Fascist Council changed their minds about Mussolini's leadership in 1943, the regime simply collapsed, and the army switched sides very much as an eighteenth-century army might have done from one day to the next. In retrospect it seemed that the King had remained the ultimate source of legitimacy; when Vittorio Emanuele III ceased to lend his support to the Duce, and when the Fascist Party with its alternative institutional charisma lost faith in him, totalitarianism was over. As Mussolini himself had to admit, 'there was a monarchy before and there was a monarchy afterwards'.[66] Thus the regime which was first called and eventually called itself totalitarian had to make far too many compromises with traditional elites even to come close to achieving 'proper' totalitarianism.

One of these compromises was with Italy's most powerful non-state institution – the Catholic Church. The Vatican attacked Gentile's Actualism as akin to pantheism and as denying any transcendent reality. But even from within the Fascist movement Gentile was criticized, especially, but not only, after Mussolini's regime had turned racist and anti-Semitic from 1938.[67] For Gentile, racism could only mean a new form of materialism, which his absolute idealism had always rejected. Nevertheless, he continued in his support for the regime and even threw in his lot with the Republican Fascist State, the Republic of Salò, which the Duce created after 1943. He ultimately paid with his life for his decision to stick with Mussolini to the very end: he was killed by Communist partisans in April 1944 – according to at least one historical account, on the specific orders of the Communist leadership.

Trenchocracy versus Technocracy?

If Italian Fascism was not in actual fact totalitarian, it still profoundly differed from the right-wing authoritarian regimes which were established all over Europe in the 1920s and 1930s. In fact, these dictatorships became almost the default option after the heady days of democracy-building in the immediate post-war period and the subsequent crisis of parliamentarism which Schmitt had diagnosed. Almost all of these regimes sought to base their legitimacy on tradition or what was often touted as 'Christian national culture' – although these traditions were usually reinterpreted so as to fit political domination in the age of mass politics. When Horthy, the self-appointed 'regent' of Hungary, was actually presented with the possibility of restoring the King to the throne, he chased Karl I and his wife Zita out of the country.[68]

Leaders like Horthy and Portugal's António Salazar were not interested in permanently mobilizing their populations. They did not base their leadership on personal charisma or on the impersonal charisma of a vanguard party. Salazar's so-called New State is most instructive in this respect – after all, he made it to the cover of *Time* magazine as the 'Dean of Dictators'; he was widely admired by politicians and intellectuals across the continent and beyond; and among all the right-wing authoritarian governments in twentieth-century Europe, Salazar's lasted the longest. The regime was established in 1926 through a classic military coup – not with a 'heroic' or highly aestheticized march of paramilitary units. Salazar himself was a very self-effacing economics professor who left the major representative functions, such as the presidency, to others – which led an Italian observer to conclude that his was a case of 'personal rule without personality'. While Mussolini sometimes styled himself as the incarnation of a god, Salazar self-consciously sought to be seen as a humble civil servant. Mussolini wanted speed and had himself celebrated as Italy's premier aeroplane pilot; Salazar flew once and didn't like it. Mussolini's state claimed to challenge and to mobilize the masses; Salazar's Estado Novo put and kept people in their place.[69]

It is tempting to say that this kind of government was technocracy, rather than trenchocracy, or a West European version of Atatürk's rule. But that would be wrong, because Salazar and comparable leaders wanted neither social nor cultural revolution. Technological innovation did not matter either: their regimes were justified, above all, in the name of stability and some very controlled form of economic development, which left the interests of traditional elites – large landowners in particular – untouched. Because stability came first, there was also no attempt to go back to dynastic or other pre-democratic forms of legitimacy: Salazar never attempted to restore the monarchy or reverse the separation of state and church in Portugal. Tradition was constantly evoked; but an actual return to it was seen as politically too risky.

This kind of paternalism could coexist with – and to some extent be bolstered by – extremely limited forms of pluralism. The latter allowed at least some divisions in society to be represented, in contrast to the Soviet and fascist body politics, which were never conceived as anything but undivided. In some countries even parliaments still existed, elections were held and opposition parties (sometimes created artificially) kept in play – but power remained always in the hands of the dictator and his bureaucratic elite, or at the most in conjunction with a small number of parties faithful to the leader. In Hungary, the party permanently in power since Horthy's White Terror was simply known as 'the government party'.[70] Only about 30 per cent of the population could vote.[71]

Non-fascist authoritarian regimes were eager to present themselves as successful alternatives to parliamentary democracy. It was the post-democrat speaking when Salazar claimed in 1934:

> when the political systems of the nineteenth century are generally breaking down and the need for adapting institutions to the requirements of new social and economic conditions is being felt more and more urgently, we may be proud . . . because, with our ideas and our achievements, we have made a serious contribution to the understanding of the problems of and difficulties which beset all States . . . I am convinced that within twenty years, if there is not some retrograde movement in political evolution, there will be no legislative assemblies left in Europe.[72]

The main solution proposed for the 'problems and difficulties which beset all States' was corporatism, which, as we saw earlier, might well be called the most rational aspect of Italian Fascism. But corporatism in certain ways fitted better with Christian authoritarian regimes, because it had clear justifications in Catholic social doctrine. In particular, it had taken centre stage in the papal encyclical *Quadragesimo Anno* in 1931; it was also similar to Turkish 'populism' (one of Atatürk's founding principles of the republic), which sought to replace classes with occupations. In a non-authoritarian form, it was to make a comeback after the Second World War. Its authoritarian version survived in Salazar's Portugal until the early 1970s.[73]

Critics would always dismiss the holistic and organic images of modern society conjured up by corporatism as unrealistic or as being in bad faith, since corporatism actually benefited only capitalists. Max Weber had already derided proposals for a reordering of Germany along corporatist lines after the First World War as 'dilettante pipe-dreams', as 'non-ideas' (produced, as usual in his view, by confused German littérateurs).[74] He insisted that vocations and professions could not be clearly separated in a modern complex society; even if established, such separations could not last in a fast-changing capitalist economy; and, perversely, artificial separations would actually destroy whatever genuine solidarity might exist in a particular profession. Corporatism, Weber held, would be much less transparent than parliamentarism and, of course, lead to increased power for state bureaucracies.

But transparency and solidarity had not been the real purpose of corporatism in any event. The point was that corporatism would do away with the instability and conflict of representative democracy: members of corporations were not to pursue their interests like the isolated individuals of classical liberal theory, but were primarily to identify with the state (just as Gentile's Actualism had prescribed). Thus corporatism was of particular appeal to dictators like Salazar who put stability first; it was of less interest to regimes that believed in permanent popular mobilization and were opposed to a central role for Catholicism. Hitler had congratulated Othmar Spann after an anti-Semitic lecture in Munich in 1929. By the end of the 1930s, however, the National Socialists not only rejected Spann's application for party membership, but dismissed him from the University of Vienna. Eventually he spent eighteen months in a concentration camp.[75]

This logic also worked the other way around: authoritarian-corporatist regimes regularly suppressed more radical fascist groups, while borrowing from fascist style. In Romania, for instance, the royal dictator King Carol crushed the fascist Iron Guard movement, but created his own Front of National Rebirth and introduced a fascist salute.[76] Most of these authoritarian regimes denounced materialism and also what smacked of fascist paganism; instead, they emphasized Christianity – usually in contrast with 'godless Bolshevism'. Poland's de facto ruler, Marshal Piłsudski, was supposed to be responsible only to 'God and history'; General Franco was revered as *hijo predilecto de Dios*; and the Austrian 'clerico-fascist' constitution of 1934 was prefaced with the words: 'In the name of God, the Almighty, from Whom all justice derives, the Austrian people receive this constitution for their federal state based on Christian, German and corporative principles'.[77] Chancellor Dollfuss, on horseback, led a paramilitary march behind a huge wooden crucifix.[78] It was understood in a 'Christian Corporative State' that the state came first: neither the fascist movement nor for that matter the clergy were really to be in power.

Most of these authoritarian leaders engaged in what we might call a rhetoric of moral admonishment: they did not try to whip up the political passions of their people; rather, they sought to remind them that they had to return to traditional values of work, family and fatherland, and that any present hardships had to be endured because of past decadence and godlessness. Vichy France had looked to Salazar's state as a model, and Vichy's leader, Marshal Pétain, was a prototype of this kind of moral self-presentation. In New Year's addresses to his people, a morose-looking Maréchal would keep insisting that he had no idea what the future would bring, but that he was sure of one thing: France's present travails were part of the penance for its decadence in the prewar period.[79] In fact in the 1930s one of the many right-wing leagues had already predicted that 'the France of camping, of sports, of dances, of voyages, of collective hiking, will sweep away the France of aperitifs, of tobacco dens, of party congresses, and long digestifs'.[80] Vichy tellingly called itself *l'État français*: this was obviously opposed to *la République*, but it also indicated the primacy of a self-contained state over nation or empire, to say nothing of a political movement (Vichy had no mass party that supported the regime). In a fashion more similar to old-style monarchy, children were asked to pray, 'Our Father who art in charge of us, praised be thy name, thy kingdom come . . . And deliver us from evil, oh Marshal!'[81] In French classrooms it was illegal to place the mandatory picture of the Maréchal underneath the cross; it had to be above.

There was a crucial difference in thinking about foreign policy. Salazar and other authoritarian leaders tried to hold on to whatever colonies they had, but there was no in-built dynamism to expand and to engage in large-scale empire-building with civilizational-religious or racist overtones. The fascist movements which the authoritarians tried to keep in check would wax lyrical about imperial expansion, but the dictators remained cautious and often pursued an opportunistic policy. This opportunism partly explained why regimes like Franco's and Salazar's lasted such a long time. In contrast, regimes that constantly mobilized their people and based their legitimacy on political dynamism and conquests necessarily had to go to war – not least because successful wars would have allowed the elimination of any kind of pluralism and the remaining power of traditional elites such as the churches. As Sigmund Neumann put it in his 1942 analysis of fascism, 'the dictatorial regimes are governments at war, originating in war, aiming at war, thriving on war'.[82]

How regimes are formed and perish is of course always contingent. But there was a certain logic in the fact that fascism – exhibiting what Neumann called its 'boundless dynamics' – began with war and ended with war.[83] The same goes for the ultimate fate of the leaders. Men like Horthy did not end their lives by shooting themselves or by being strung up publicly at the hands of partisans – the fate of Hitler and Mussolini respectively. Rather, Horthy – by the end an admiral not just without a navy but without a country – enjoyed a comfortable retirement in a villa in Estoril, in Portugal – at the invitation of none other than António Salazar, who, like Franco, died a peaceful death, believing that he had lived a life of exemplary service for the stability and continuity of his nation.[84]

. . . versus Biocracy?

Fascism aimed to constitute purified national and racial subjects – through and for struggle to the death. War was not just inevitable; it was to be valued for generating specifically fascist characteristics. Political elites were to shape those collective subjects – although, ultimately, the quality of those subjects seemed to be determined not just by cultural but by biological characteristics which appeared to be entirely beyond the realm of political action. One thing was certain, though, in the fascist view of the world: ordinary human beings could not shape politics at all; they had to be mobilized (and regimented) by myths; they also had to act in conformity with a leader who embodied the collective subject. These were all characteristics of Italian Fascism. Every single one of them was radicalized by German National Socialism.

Aspects of Italian Fascism can usefully be understood as attempts at fashioning a 'political religion' – a comprehensive set of meanings, but also spectacles and rituals, which competed with those of the Catholic Church in particular. Unlike traditional religion, they promised redemption through politics.[85] Nazism's rhetoric – and its liturgical self-celebration – appeared even more pseudo-religious: Hitler frequently spoke about himself as an instrument of 'Providence', and some of his orations about 'faith in my *Volk*' actually concluded with the word 'Amen'. The religious and in particular the eschatological overtones which generally characterized continental empires were more audible in Hitler's speeches than ever before or after. The Nazis had appropriated the notion of the Third Reich as an *Endreich* – a final empire – from the right-wing prophet Arthur Moeller van den Bruck; they also insisted that Germany always had been and ideally always would be a *Reich* with the same racial substance.[86]

The official Nazi ideologue, Alfred Rosenberg, aggressively promoted a kind of neo-paganism that was directly opposed to the established churches.[87] Rosenberg, who hailed from Estonia and had fled after the Russian Revolution, had been instrumental in radicalizing Hitler's original anti-Semitism, introducing the young politician to *The Protocols of the Elders of Zion*. He also elaborated a peculiar 'spiritual racism'. His utterly unreadable (and, for all we know, mostly unread) magnum opus *The Myth of the Twentieth Century* cast what could have been mainly cultural and psychological claims in a racist idiom.[88] So a thought should always be evaluated by who had thought it first, and whoever had thought it first should be evaluated by their body, that is to say, their 'racial stock'. Otmar von Verschuer, a leading eugenicist and expert on 'racial hygiene', affirmed in the same vein that the Nazis understood *Volk* to be 'a spiritual and biological unity . . . the greatest part of the German people constitutes a great community of ancestors, which is to say a solidarity of blood relations'.[89]

Heinrich Himmler, head of the SS, also subscribed to this mixture of 'biocracy' (rule by biology), a convoluted 'spiritualism' and ancestor worship. He conceived of his 'order' as an advance troop in the struggle for de-Christianization, replacing the reigning religion with *Germanenglaube*, a Germanic ur-faith, whose contents and roots a vast SS research industry was expected to uncover and specify. The worship of ancestors was supposed to go hand in hand with – and strengthen – an ethical code focused on the imperative to keep Germanic blood pure.[90] Hitler himself opposed this kind of occultism; in private, he dismissed Himmler's and Rosenberg's *Germanenkult* as bizarre. But he fervently believed in the racist pseudo-sciences which informed the SS's policies, and admonished Himmler and others that Nazi 'philosophy does not advocate mystic cults, but rather aims to cultivate and lead a nation determined by its blood'.[91]

One of the distinguishing features of National Socialism was indeed that it put forward a comprehensive theory of historical and, above all, biological determinism. To be sure, racism had also been prominent in Italian Fascism from the very start; it was directed primarily against Slavs and Africans, but also against Jews.[92] Mussolini proposed the idea of *bonifica* – that is, the reclaiming of land and sea, as in Italy's *mare nostrum*, but also of culture (the infamous reclaiming of Italian words from foreign influences), and, ultimately, of human beings themselves (culminating in the project of the 'new Italian').[93] Italy wanted national (and eventually) imperial regeneration, and Mussolini sometimes spoke of the state's primary task as *curare*.[94] Reclamation, however, was not just to be complemented, but completed, by the elimination of the wrong people: the Duce presented himself as a 'racial clinician' in relation to 'unhealthy persons', claiming that 'we remove them from circulation as a doctor would an infected person'.[95] Thus, even if some of the language sounded almost harmlessly therapeutic, it left open the possibility of adopting more aggressive measures in the *difesa della razza* (defence of the race). This is precisely what happened towards the end of the 1930s, and it did not seem a radical break in self-presentation and self-justification. There had been slippage in Fascist rhetoric between *nazione* and *razza* all along.[96]

National Socialism, by contrast, was committed to the goal of a total remaking of the *Volkskörper* from the start, educating Germans to understand themselves primarily as Aryans (as opposed to members of a particular culture or religion, or even political movement for that matter). In the Third Reich the language of race never became muted, as it sometimes did in Italy; and it played a role in virtually everything that can plausibly be described as Nazi theorizing. As Rudolph Ramm, the chief Nazi medical 'ethicist', argued, 'unlike any other political philosophy or any other party program, National Socialism is in agreement with natural history and the biology of man'.[97]

Italian Fascism and National Socialism shared a conception, recognizable from Sorel, of the collective body hardened through and for struggle.[98] Sorel had stressed moralism over materialism, a tendency echoed in much of Mussolini's rhetoric. Hitler and his henchmen also kept evoking 'spirit' and willpower, but usually within a larger framework of biological forces that seemed to be beyond human volition.[99] There was simply no way to question the laws of biology, and no redemption for anyone deemed dangerous or unfit. This also constitutes one of the major differences with the Soviet Union even during the darkest days of Stalinism: there, at least in theory, class enemies or even 'enemies of the people' could redeem themselves through 'socially useful work' or, during the war, by joining the Red Army.

When Stalin invoked the 'laws of history', he sought to embed his regime in a story of progress, a moving forward in linear time from a backward civilization on the periphery of Europe towards a state when Soviet 'New Men' and joyous socialist life had become universally attractive and – ultimately – universally realized. There was no such story of progress for the Nazis, only a perpetual state of struggle and never ending dangers of degeneration. The Soviets wanted to claim the future, a time when an 'improved edition of mankind' (Trotsky) would be issued, all in a spirit of optimism; the Nazis, in a defensive posture throughout, wanted to claim and then defend their space against history – the vagaries of time – and against a hostile world which by definition could never find the Nazis' anti-universalism appealing.[100] The Soviet New Men were men of steel, but not because they needed to be protected from ever renewed enemy assaults. They fought with and forged the material world; the fascist men of steel always fought with other men, and expected that fight to last for ever.

Like Italian Fascism, National Socialism fashioned itself as a comprehensive 'ethical revolution' centred on values of solidarity and self-sacrifice for the sake of the *Volksgemeinschaft*, a thorough reshaping of the social body in the name of 'cleansing' and 'hygiene'.[101] *Volksgemeinschaft* – the tightly knit national community – had become a popular term in Germany during the First World War, when all class and status differences seemed to have been overcome in the face of a common enemy, so much so that *Volksgemeinschaft* and the idea of struggle became inextricably linked.

National Socialist theorists and jurists sought to refashion the meaning of *Volksgemeinschaft* as unambiguously one of racial community. It was to imply the inclusion and equality among *Volksgenossen* – literally, racial comrades.[102] Both public and private life were supposed to be reshaped comprehensively in line with this idea. In particular, conflict and division among *Volksgenossen* were to be abolished once and for all. Thus landlord and tenant were supposed to be united in a *Gemeinschaft*, as were employers and employees. And all should sacrifice for the undivided whole.[103] National Socialism therefore presented its own moral belief system – reprehensible as it was. It was a morality for *Volksgenossen* only. Its integrity was assured not just through the exclusion primarily of Jews and 'asocials', but also through tacit or not so tacit complicity in crimes against those who did not belong to the newly purified body politic.[104] *Gemeinschaftsfremde* – those alien to the community – had to be excluded and, ultimately, eliminated. Nazi jurists in fact attacked the very concepts of 'human being' and 'person' because they supposedly disguised and distorted 'the differences between *Volksgenosse*, citizen of the Reich, foreigner, Jew, etc.' As an exile political scientist commented, jurists like Schmitt were 'abolishing the human being'.[105] Nazi thought thus had an unprecedented anti-universalist thrust; less obviously, it also constituted a deeply illiberal response to a democratic age, in a manner that would not have been imaginable in earlier centuries.

The Death of the State

Yet Nazism was not all quasi-religious myths and medical metaphors. It is important to realize that fascism *partly* played on the register of democracy: Gentile had insisted that Fascism was 'the most genuine form of democracy' which 'finds expression at those times when the consciousness and will of the few, even of one, manifests itself in the consciousness and will of all'.[106] Carl Schmitt, who became one of the leading jurists of the Nazi regime, having joined the party in 1933, argued that democracy could be divorced from the idea of representation. Genuine democracy was based on identity between the governors and the governed – a principle from which it followed that the popular will could be concentrated in one individual, making a dictatorship like Mussolini's a much more credible expression of democracy than liberal parliamentarism.[107]

True, most leading Nazis time and again explicitly dismissed democracy – theirs was the only major twentieth-century ideological movement that made almost no semantic concessions to it. Hitler himself would always denounce liberal democracy as a means of weakening the nation, and as a de facto form of plutocracy – that is, rule by the rich; others suggested that in Western democracies small 'clans' always effectively excluded 'the masses'.[108] When a prominent Nazi philosopher sought to honour Rosenberg as the chief ideologue of the movement in the introduction to the latter's collected works, he found it most appropriate to laud him as a leading 'enemy of democratic-Jewish internationalism'.[109]

Nonetheless, at least some National Socialist theorists felt it important to develop a concept of 'Germanic democracy' – centred on the importance of 'trust' between rulers and ruled, as opposed to mechanical electoral accountability. Hitler himself insisted that 'I am not a dictator and never will be a dictator'; he even went so far as to claim that 'National Socialism takes seriously the idea of democracy, which had degenerated under parliamentarism' and 'we have overthrown outdated institutions precisely because they no longer served to maintain a fruitful relationship with the nation as a whole . . .'[110]

To be sure, these were partly tactical statements designed for consumption outside Germany during the early years of the regime. But the point remains that Hitler and his intellectual henchmen felt compelled to employ the rhetoric of popular participation and inclusion, and great care was taken to make the idea of actual popular participation plausible. As Tzvetan Todorov has pointed out, Nazism (and Stalinism, for that matter) required a gigantic spectacle of pseudo-democracy (and what Franz Neumann called 'pseudo-egalitarianism'): a theatrics of popular acclamation and parades, where 'the people' appeared to be directly present and affirming their belief in the Führer. The leader (unlike the emperor or the king) was a man of and with the people; yet he also transcended them, and not only because of the charisma that made him different from the Soviet bureaucrat-leader. His will did not conform to that of a self-determining populace; rather, he sought to recognize and act according to immutable racial laws, and, based on correct interpretation of these laws, fashion a collective body capable of perpetuating itself, permanently dominating or even eliminating inferior races, and dealing with any challenger.

National Socialism, much more than Italian Fascism, based its claims on a total unity of leader and *Volk*. In Italy, some Fascist leaders had seen themselves as the trustees of the collective charisma of the Fascist movement and held that Mussolini's charisma was derived from the party. While they affirmed that Fascism would always require the office of leader, charisma could primarily be lodged in the party as an institution. As one jurist put it, 'if the new state is to become a permanent way of being . . . it cannot do without the role of Leader because of its hierarchical structure, even if this Leader does not have the extraordinary magnitude of the Man who promoted the revolution in the first place'. Others directly invoked Weber to claim that 'in reality, Fascism has been the first complete realization of the "charismatic" theory of national societies'.[111] National Socialism, on the other hand, showed no tendency whatsoever to separate an impersonal office of *Führer* from the person of Hitler; and there was no equivalent to the internal Fascist opposition to the personality cult of *mussolinismo*.[112]

Personal *Treue* or faith was at the heart of the Nazi notion of law, as opposed to cold, 'formal' legal positivism, or even just decrees by an authoritarian ruler. Hence also the highly peculiar fact that, after the death of the last democratically elected president, Field Marshal von Hindenburg (himself a kind of *Ersatzkaiser*), in 1934, the German army swore an oath to Hitler personally. Oaths to kings had the institution of monarchy as their object, not the particular person of the king; during the Weimar Republic soldiers had vowed to defend the constitution.

The emphasis on persons, instead of institutions, resembled Stalin's rule in the Soviet Union: it relied on the logic of the gang, rather than that of the impersonal state. Unlike Stalin, however, Hitler did not want an informal social life to go along with this logic – he prohibited *Bierabende* with his cabinet.[113] He was never interested even in the fiction of being just the chief bureaucrat among bureaucrats (in fact, unlike Stalin, with his genuine bureaucratic authority, Hitler himself was averse to paperwork, prompting some historians to call him a 'lazy dictator'). But, also unlike Stalin, Hitler was not afraid of his own people. He really did believe in the authority of his own charisma and would never have claimed that 'Hitler' was simply a symbol of 'Nazi power', in the way that Stalin – positively postmodern in this respect – thought the image of himself actually had little to do with the reality of Comrade Card-Index.

In line with this logic of personal loyalty, Nazi jurisprudence was centred on the notion of 'concrete order', a set of institutions as well as individual and, even more so, collective dispositions which were – once more – rooted in race. Ideally, rule was to be based not so much on legal coercion by a state as on supposedly Germanic faith, trust and honour – not 'biological values' as such, but supposedly biologically determined. So the state did not play much of a role at all in this scheme, and certainly not the German tradition of the *Rechtsstaat*, the rule of law. Schmitt argued that the liberal rule of law had been superseded by the 'immediately just state'. The younger generation of Nazi intellectuals, Reinhard Höhn foremost among them, went one better and tried to expunge the concept from legal thought altogether (it supposedly threatened to contaminate its users with traces of liberal jurisprudence). Hence Höhn and his followers would insist, for instance, that the expression *Volksfeinde* – enemies of the people – should be substituted for *Staatsfeinde*.[114] Their opponents within jurisprudence, on the other hand, claimed that a *Volk* still had to become 'political' through legal and administrative structures, whether of a state or an empire; they also worried that individuals – even if of the right racial stock – would lose all legal protection vis-à-vis the *Volk* as a whole.[115]

Nazi political theorists therefore had no truck with the Hegelian visions of a Gentile; in fact, it was telling that on 30 January 1933 Carl Schmitt declared that 'today Hegel's state has died'. True, on a very abstract level, Gentile's aim was also that of the Nazis: integrating 'the masses' into the state. But it was not so much that the state was an educator above and beyond the *Volk*; rather, political order consisted of an unholy trinity of state, movement (that is, the party) and people, as Schmitt entitled one of his first major publications under the Hitler regime.[116] The movement, according to Schmitt, was to provide the 'dynamic' element between the (static) state and the homogeneous but apolitical *Volk*. As Hitler declared at a rally in Nuremberg in 1934: 'the party commands the state'.[117] Schmitt also insisted that with the Nazi seizure of power Germany had regained a genuine political leadership, which – here Schmitt echoed Weber's old anxieties – it had lost under the merely bureaucratic state of the Weimar Republic. If one asks what held this entire construction together, the answer could once again only be race. 'Homogeneity' – Schmitt was explicit about this – meant racial homogeneity. The *Volk* could thus almost literally be embodied in the figure of the Führer – who was to be of the same racial 'substance'; hence this model conformed to Schmitt's supposedly democratic principle of 'identity'.[118]

Of course the Nazis did not completely abolish the state – nobody in the twentieth century did, least of all those whose proclaimed aim it had been. As critics like Ernst Fraenkel and Franz Neumann already understood in the late 1930s and early 1940s, the Nazi state became highly fragmented and operated with increasingly deformalized law. Fraenkel discerned the emergence of a 'dual state': a 'normal' state based on traditional 'positive legality', and a highly arbitrary one ruling by measures – what he distinguished as the 'Normative State' and the 'Prerogative State'.[119] Simply put: one could get married or be convicted for theft according to normal law that remained thoroughly predictable; but basic questions about who was fit or unfit to live were subject to arbitrary decisions by increasingly chaotic bureaucracies working at cross-purposes or trying to outdo each other in 'anticipating' or working towards the Führer's will.[120] This chaos and incoherence were not entirely unrelated to the bases of Nazi ideology: 'biology' as such could not legislate; *Volk* did not by itself constitute a political agent (let alone become institutionalized). But to admit this would have been to concede that biology had always been defined politically rather than the other way around, and to let go of the historical certainty promised by the supposed insight into biological determinism.

It is revealing that the Nazis, like the Italian Fascists, did not create a new constitution and in that sense never finalized the new structure of their polity – although Hitler promised that eventually a Nazi constitution would be promulgated. There was an abundance of Nazi law and decrees, but no basic template for Nazi rule and no single officially endorsed Nazi jurisprudence to make sense of it all. Neumann highlighted the fact that the Nazi Reich existed in a permanent state of emergency, and that, if anything, it had turned into a chaotic 'non-state', its constitutional life characterized by 'its utter shapelessness'. The Nazi polity resembled more the quantitative total state – the state absorbed by interest groups in society – which Schmitt had decried in the early 1930s and to which he wanted to oppose the qualitative total state above all divisions in society, a vision with clear parallels to Gentile's conception. Rule was exercised by informal compromises between different groups, who came to resemble feudal clans, consisting of individual Nazi leaders and their personally loyal retinue.[121] According to Neumann, there appeared to be less and less of a 'need for a state standing above all groups; the state may even be a hindrance to the compromises and to domination over the ruled classes'.[122]

What did stand above all groups, however, was the person of Hitler, who set bureaucrats and political groups against each other, consciously promoting a kind of 'institutional Darwinism'. There was a certain logic to this: Hitler himself could remain completely unconstrained, in both thought and action; he would refuse to commit to a constitution or even a clear political theory, disappointing all those thinkers who fancied themselves as 'leading the leader'. The desire to be unconstrained went so far that citations from *Mein Kampf* became virtually taboo.[123] As Hannah Arendt understood, the Nazis sought to prove that anything can be done, that 'everything is possible'.[124]

At first sight, this emphasis on unconstrained leadership might resemble the self-conception of the Leninist party – except that the latter, even in its most charismatic phase, was an institution, with rules and a capacity to renew itself. Hitler was, obviously, just one person; he put everything into permanently mobilizing the *Volksgemeinschaft*, making it into a racial *Kampfgemeinschaft*, a community of struggle, both as a means and as an end.[125] But he did not build institutions. Even as a head of state and then empire, he tried to rule primarily by public speaking and agitation.[126]

As the war went on, the German state, which he had inherited and already partly made into a 'non-state', started to fall apart. The Nazi Party – which, according to Schmitt, was supposed to have been the 'dynamic' element vis-à-vis the state all along and, had the famous Law for Ensuring the Unity of Party and State become reality, would even have taken over the state – tried to grab more power.[127] But it had never gained the independent existence that even under Stalin the Bolshevik Party retained; and, in any event, it had never developed the ethos of discipline and formalism which Lenin had established. It simply could not substitute for the state, because it had never developed a proper bureaucracy (which was yet more confirmation of Weber's view of revolutions). Nazi rule, in the end, was all mobilization and virtually no institutions. It was concrete chaos.

Great Spaces – without Peoples

A somewhat similar divergence between theory and practice developed in the international realm. 'Concrete order thinking' underpinned the European – and ultimately global – visions of Nazi order which Hitler's willing intellectual executioners fashioned in the late 1930s and during the Second World War. They envisaged a world divided into 'great spaces' or 'realms' (*Großräume*), which each featured an empire, or *Reich*, at its centre, and a number of essentially satellite nations around it. Again, Carl Schmitt had been at the forefront of elaborating such a distinctive Nazi approach to international law and international relations. In 1939 he had called on the Führer to declare a 'European Monroe doctrine' and make the Third Reich the centre of a new *Großraum*, in which non-European powers (the United States in particular) were not allowed to intervene. This fitted with Hitler's wish consciously to create an empire and prevent Germany from ever becoming a 'second Holland', a 'second Switzerland' or even a 'slave people'. Schmitt insisted that economic developments were also pushing in the direction of greater spaces. But the crucial point was that empires of the sort he prescribed supposedly enjoyed genuine popular legitimacy. Even in the international arena, then, Nazi thought oscillated strangely between quasi-democratic appeals and a complete biologization of politics, a subjection of politics, that is, to historical and racial laws supposedly beyond human will. Hitler did indeed call himself a 'liberator of humanity', but insisted at the same time that individual human beings did not matter.[128]

The idea of a *Großgermanisches Reich* sometimes simply seemed to revive the old notion of a continental, even multinational empire, though Hitler had always been disgusted by the Habsburg Empire with its multiplicity of nationalities; for him, it was a horrific 'Babylonian' mixture. So instead *Reich* might actually have suggested a very large nation-state or a national community somehow without a state – except that some National Socialists were even distrustful of the idea of the nation, since, like the concept of the state, it smacked too much of a liberal past.[129]

Again, the contrast with Italian Fascism is instructive: the Italians also claimed to want *Lebensraum* – what they called *spazio vitale* – and officially shared the Schmittian vision of dividing up the world into a *grande spazio* for each empire. But they retained essentially nationalist principles of rule. In the only country they conquered without Germany's help – Albania – they replicated the dual structure that characterized Italy itself: Vittorio Emanuele III became king of Albania and Mussolini the head of a newly created Albanian fascist party – but in theory the Italians maintained the claim that the Albanians should and would continue to run their own affairs. As the foreign minister Count Ciano declared in May 1942, 'it was not possible to export Fascism to a country and simultaneously deny it the principle of nationhood, which is the essence itself of the [Fascist] doctrine . . . Our action in Albania constitutes concrete proof before the world that in the new order envisaged by Rome nations will not be subjugated but valued'.[130]

Even if these claims were thoroughly hypocritical, the point is that the Germans would never have made them in the first place. To the extent that there were coherent conceptions of the *Reich* at all, the Nazi empire was to be entirely racialized, that is, defined by 'racial blood' (*Volksblut*) and separated from Slavic Asia by a 'blood wall' (*Blutswall*).[131] As Hitler had asserted on the very first page of *Mein Kampf*, 'One blood demands one *Reich*.' During the war, when the struggle against Bolshevism was increasingly presented as a fight to save 'Europe', he would insist that 'Europe' was a 'blood-determined concept'.[132] Hence the ever expanding 'race bureaucracy' tasked with classifying and certifying people, with issuing 'race cards' and with gathering every last drop of German blood into a single political community. Hannah Arendt noticed this peculiarity and called the Nazis an 'anti-national international movement';[133] the Russian-French philosopher Alexandre Kojève, in a memorandum for Charles de Gaulle after the war, also put his finger on the ambiguous, if not outright contradictory, Nazi endeavour of running an empire like a large racially defined *Volksgemeinschaft*. He argued:

> the German national State pressed 80 million nationals into service, whose military and civic (if not moral) qualities revealed themselves to be above all praise. Nonetheless, the superhuman political and military effort of the Nation served only to delay an outcome which can truly be called 'fatal'. And it is certainly the eminently and consciously national character of the German State which is the cause of this 'fate'. For to be able to sustain a modern war, the Third Reich had to occupy and exploit non-German countries and import more than 10 million foreign workers. But a nation-State cannot assimilate non-nationals, and it must treat them politically as slaves. Thus Hitler's 'nationalist' ideology would have been enough by itself to ruin the imperial project of the 'New Europe', without which Germany could not, however, win the war. It can therefore be said that Germany lost this war because she wanted to win it as a nation-State. For even a nation of 80 million politically 'perfect' citizens is unable to sustain the effort of a modern war and thereby to ensure the political existence of its State.[134]

This paradox had quickly become apparent, as the supposed *Volk ohne Raum* conquered an empire: it confronted ever more *Raum* without *Volk*.[135]

Anti-Semitism was central to these thoroughly racialized visions of the world: it was Hitler's initial political obsession (already in 1919 he had demanded the 'removal of the Jews altogether', in the name of an anti-Semitism based on 'reason');[136] it guided the actions of what one might see as the ultimate conviction politician in the Weberian sense to the very self-destructive end. Hitler had insisted from early on that the next war had to be both a *Weltanschauungskrieg*, a war of deeply held worldviews, and a '*Volk* and race war' at the same time: the complete exclusion of the German Jews was to be a precondition of Germany being victorious in this war, while the destruction of European Jewry as a whole – in Hitler's eyes the 'anti-nation' as such – was to be its consequence.

Was there anything in Nazi thought that directly connected the conquest of *Lebensraum* and the Judaeocide? It seemed that the successful claiming of space depended on being as brutal as possible; and since Hitler identified the principle of the sanctity of life with Judaism, the destruction of the Jews – and the weakening of traditional universalist ethical codes – was a condition for forming a pure collective body capable of successful political action, even of world domination and, ultimately, mastering history.[137] Hence Hitler also proclaimed that 'never before has there been a war so typically and at the same time so exclusively Jewish'.[138]

Thus race thoroughly structured both foreign policy and the inner life of the Nazi state. *Führerprinzip* and *Rassenprinzip* belonged together in the 'theory of transubstantiation', as Franz Neumann put it: the leader had a mystical connection to his people, but ultimately he did so because they were of the same 'racial stock', united against an enemy race and its universalist ethical beliefs, which could only weaken the *Volk*'s authentic will. In the last weeks of his life, when Hitler looked back on his 'career' and his fateful choices, he insisted that his defeat had been due to the Jews and that 'alcoholic *verjudete* half-American' Winston Churchill – dominated, in Hitler's mind, by Jewish advisers. Moreover, his 'political testament' would end with the words: 'Above all I charge the leaders of the nation and those under them to scrupulous observance of the racial laws and to merciless resistance to the global poisoner of all peoples, international Jewry.' The Führer lamented that the Germans had lacked 'moral preparation' for the war; and, in particular, that twenty years would have been required to rear a proper Nazi elite that would have imbibed 'the National Socialist way of thinking' with their mothers' milk.[139] He also told the few remaining people around him on his very last day that as an idea National Socialism was dead for ever.

And he was right. Fascism and National Socialism had not just been defeated on the battlefield. Their unprecedented cruelties and atrocities, especially those of the Nazis, were to come to light and make it impossible ever to gain very many 'hearts' alongside 'minds' for fascism in the future. Moreover, they really had been defeated as *ideas*: for fascists, truth was proven in action, and the fascists' actions had failed; worldviews predicated on the value of war and the valour of engaging in eternal struggle had lost in war, and the leaders had admitted it. Fascism simply could not afford to lose – ever. In that sense, fascism turned out in the end to be what Thomas Mann had called a *Zeitkrankheit* – a disease of the times: possible only in the age of mass democracy, mass social upheaval and mass war – but, once defeated, impossible beyond its own time.[140] Thus reconstruction – and the ideas animating it – had to be in the broadest sense anti-fascist and antitotalitarian. But of course this did not in itself mean that it would turn out to be particularly democratic.

CHAPTER 4

Reconstruction Thought
Self-Disciplined Democracies, 'People's Democracies'

The state is an important instrument; hence the struggle to control it. But it is an instrument, and nothing more. Fools will use it, when they can, for foolish ends, and criminals for criminal ends. Sensible and decent men will use it for ends which are decent and sensible.

R. H. Tawney, 'We Mean Freedom', 1946

It is fatal for a capitalist government to have principles. It must be opportunistic in the best sense of the word, living by accommodation and good sense.

John Maynard Keynes

It is obvious that the vitality nurtured on impassioned battles of ideas cannot be maintained in the successful democracy's atmosphere of levelling and compromise. We cannot have it both ways . . . The problem is whether or not more eagerness, a more universal and lively interest, discussions on principles and the personal efforts of the citizen can be kindled whilst maintaining security and a sufficient community of values.

Herbert Tingsten, 'Stability and Vitality in Swedish Democracy', 1954

Our victims know us by their scars and by their chains, and it is this that makes their evidence irrefutable. It is enough that they show us what we have made of them for us to realize what we have made of ourselves. But is it any use? Yes, for Europe is at death's door.

Jean-Paul Sartre

The basic lesson is that no people should be written off – and so many have been, from Germans to Malaysians – as lacking the desire for freedom.

István Bibó

Post-war reconstruction in Europe presented formidable, in fact unprecedented, tasks. They were, above all, material. But the challenges were also moral and symbolic. While the Holocaust was to remain marginal to thinking about the war at least until the 1960s, the meaning of mass violence and atrocity was immediately debated by political thinkers across the continent. After all, from the late 1930s to the late 1940s more people had been 'killed by their fellow human beings than ever before in the history of humankind'.[1]

Mass death in the Second World War was not seen in the same way as in the First: there was no heroic myth of the trenches – but there were no Sassoons or Remarques of the Second World War either.[2] As the German historian Reinhart Koselleck – himself a Wehrmacht soldier who had spent years in Russian captivity – was to observe: death was 'no longer understood as an answer but only as a question, no longer as providing meaning, only calling out for meaning'.[3]

Hannah Arendt predicted that 'the problem of evil will be the fundamental question of postwar intellectual life in Europe – as death became the fundamental problem after the last war'.[4] She also insisted that the experience of totalitarianism had constituted a profound break in European history; that the past no longer shone a light on the present; and that consequently a world that had witnessed the Nazis trying to do things nobody had thought possible also needed fundamentally to re-evaluate its political thinking.

Yet the answers that many European intellectuals felt compelled to offer to the 'problem of evil' failed precisely to take seriously totalitarianism as a caesura in European political experience. Their diagnosis of the times was entirely conventional in that they held the cataclysms of the twentieth century to have originated in the rise of 'the masses'. Tellingly, a book like Ortega's *Revolt of the Masses* remained *the* philosophical bestseller in a number of West European countries from the early 1930s until the late 1950s. The story about the fateful entry of the masses into politics had begun with the French Revolution; it could now simply be extended further and further and include the Second World War – which, after all, had been started by a man who seemed to have come from nowhere and seemed perfectly to represent 'mass man'. The German historian Friedrich Meinecke, writing in 1946 about the causes of the 'German catastrophe', claimed that the masses were still 'advancing' – after having explained 'Hitlerism' (away) as a form of 'mass Machiavellianism'.[5] Arendt put forward the idea that the emergence of the masses had been a precondition of totalitarianism, with the masses characterized by a feeling of being 'superfluous' and 'selfless', in the sense of having no proper self. She also insisted that 'the chief characteristic of the mass man is not brutality and backwardness, but his isolation and lack of normal relationships'.[6] Not everybody was as comparatively charitable to 'mass man'.

In response to the war, then, West European intellectual life went through a kind of Indian summer for defences of high culture as a barrier to barbarism; Meinecke, for instance, thought there should be 'Goethe communities' organized all across Germany. In fact, though, with a further erosion of traditional hierarchies and patterns of deference during the Second World War, 'masses' could now quite plausibly refer to everyone – not just workers and the lower classes, as had still been the case in the interwar period.[7] Whatever power the aristocracy might have had left after 1918 now vanished for good; the last remnants of the European old regimes were finally going. Some of the quasi-aristocratic rhetoric they had inspired even in the age of democracy persisted for just a bit longer.

To be sure, high cultural pessimism was not the only response to the war. The longing for a real tabula rasa – as nothing less than a moral necessity – was widespread on the continent. That a more moral politics was possible seemed to have been proved by the experience of solidarity within the various European resistance movements. The French Resistance newspaper *Combat* chose as its motto: 'From Resistance to Revolution'.

Existentialism promised the cleanest break with the past. It also emphasized the most radical notion of freedom: human beings could create themselves from scratch – there was only existence, and no predetermined 'human essence'. True, there was history, and Europeans had just experienced it in its most terrible form. But even with *that* past, and in the absence of any assurance of progress, there remained the individual possibility of self-transcendence, of choosing oneself in new kinds of action and of facing any situation in a moral manner.[8]

Did that sound abstract or slightly adolescent? Despite or because of that, existentialism was enormously influential as a cultural style. But it did not successfully translate into any party politics. Jean-Paul Sartre, its leading philosopher, was for a brief period involved in a kind of anti-party party consisting of sections of the middle class and workers, the Rassemblement Démocratique Révolutionnaire. The RDR searched for a neutral 'third way' (but different from the fascist 'Third Way') between Western liberal capitalism and Eastern Communism – in existentialist fashion refusing to be determined by the world's split into two camps. Like many of the idealistic associations emerging from the Resistance it had foundered by the late 1940s – not because of any obvious intellectual weaknesses, but because, under the conditions of the incipient Cold War, the political odds were massively in favour of choosing one of only two possible ways.

To be sure, the atmosphere of the immediate post-war period had seemed no less revolutionary than the years 1918 and 1919. Capitalism appeared discredited because of the Great Depression; in the eyes of many intellectuals, it had at least paved the way for fascism (while even non-Marxists saw merit in the view that fascism had been a tool in the hands of capitalists to preserve their power).

Unlike after the First World War, however, there was no great strike wave (and no factory councils sprang up): there appeared still fewer instruments for radical change than thirty years earlier.[9] The vanguard parties officially committed to revolution – in particular French and Italian Communists, who derived enormous moral prestige from their leading roles in the Resistance – eventually supported the emerging liberal-democratic orders. In Italy this support was explicitly justified by the party's theorists, while the French, remaining ideologically closer to Moscow than any other Western European Communists, de facto acted as a 'party of order' (which, as we shall see in the next chapter, became all too apparent in 1968).

Another difference with the interwar period was obvious or was made obvious to everyone who somehow failed it to see it: Europe as a whole was no longer the master of its own fate. Continent-wide and national ideals of self-determination could still capture the political imagination – but would quickly meet their limits with the strategic plans of the superpowers. The cruel fact was that, from the perspective of traditional ethnic nationalists, the preconditions for national self-determination seemed much more favourable, as European states virtually everywhere had become more homogeneous: unlike after the First World War, hardly any borders were moved, but millions of people were officially expelled or pressured to move.[10] Ironically, as we saw in the last chapter, the Nazis were profoundly anti-nationalist, but they ended up remaking a continent with more clearly defined and demarcated national collectives. It would be wrong to think, however, that this in itself provided stability in the post-war period. What provided stability (as well as the dread of nuclear annihilation, making this yet another Age of Anxiety, in Auden's phrase) was something else: the Cold War.

Stability was to become a major goal – in fact the lodestar – of the post-war Western European political imagination. Party leaders, no less than jurists and philosophers, sought to build an order designed, above all, to prevent a return to the totalitarian past. The past, in their view, had been about limitless political dynamism, unbound masses and attempts to forge a completely unconstrained political subject – the purified German *Volksgemeinschaft*. In response, Western Europeans fashioned a highly *constrained* form of democracy, deeply imprinted with a distrust of popular sovereignty – in fact, even distrust of traditional parliamentary sovereignty.

This was a new kind of democracy, whose novelty, however, was often obscured by the fact that its innovative institutions were publicly justified with highly traditional moral and political languages. Not just conventional cultural pessimism about the masses gained yet another lease on life; religiously inspired natural law thinking also underwent a major renaissance after the war (as did Christianity more broadly). Intellectuals hoped it would provide immutable ethical foundations for right political conduct – as opposed to the relativism, if not outright nihilism, which supposedly had characterized fascism and, as many intellectuals now asserted, liberalism. Often the deployment of such traditional languages crucially depended on misinterpretations of the fascist experience. Legal positivism, for instance, was accused of having paved the way for Hitler, as it had no substantive moral content – when in fact it had been enemies of legal positivism such as Schmitt or Idealists such as Gentile who had been most useful for the masters in Berlin and Rome.

Despite the various quests for 'third ways', it proved highly seductive to present the post-war era not as the beginning of something new, but as a moral return to something safely known. But no known set of institutions in any way 'returned' and neither was 'liberalism' in any nineteenth-century sense (as a matter of ideas, let alone in terms of a social base) revived after 1945. What emerged instead might best be described as a new balance of democracy and liberal principles, and constitutionalism in particular, but with both liberalism and democracy redefined in the light of the totalitarian experience of mid-twentieth-century Europe.[11] While many of the central institutions and values of the post-war period could be seen as functional equivalents of certain liberal ideas, the inherited political languages of liberalism were almost universally rejected as relativistic, or simply unsuitable for the age of mass democracy.

In other words, in post-war Western Europe a new, chastened Weberian politics triumphed: not charismatic, but firmly centred on the executive and pragmatic leaders; not geared towards generating meaning, but based on more than economic success (namely, moral foundations, such as natural law); not animated by a comprehensive liberal vision, but attempting to integrate citizens through shared values rooted in a rejection of the fascist past and the Communist threat from the East in the present. By contrast, in what were first 'people's democracies' and then 'people's republics' (we will have occasion to discuss the difference further below) across the Iron Curtain, a deradicalized Leninism persisted: without mass terror and other imperatives of 'war communism'; but still fully committed to the idea that the vanguard party – whose leading role came to be inscribed in the various constitutions – was uniquely qualified to make and lead a socialist people to a Communist commune state, where the subordination of man to man had finally ceased. Democratization kept being invoked, but not once did it mean party pluralism; rather it conjured up active participation in a single political project, or at least reducing the gap between the people and the party-state.

The 'people's democracies' and 'socialist democracies' were in many ways not new: Stalinism provided the initial template. By contrast, what emerged in Western Europe was not a restoration of any previously existing liberal order but was emphatically a post-post-liberal order, a set of institutions and attendant justifications (and less explicit moral intuitions) deeply imprinted with antitotal-itarianism.[12] This constellation – and new intellectual synthesis – cannot be summed up as any kind of established 'ism'. It was never formulated by a single thinker – though it had its thinkers, some of whom are almost entirely forgotten today.

New quasi-liberal institutions and decidedly non-liberal, if not outright anti-liberal, political idioms – this, then, is the great paradox of the relationship between political thought and political institutions in the late 1940s and 1950s. It was clearly revealed in the triumph of one political movement in the Western half of the continent: Christian Democracy, the most important ideological inno-vation of the post-war period, and one of the most significant of the European twentieth century as a whole.[13] It is often said that the decades after 1945 in Western European finally witnessed the full flowering of Social Democracy. But this was hardly so. In some countries Social Democracy had been flowering all along: Sweden and, to a lesser extent, Denmark. But in the core countries of continental Western Europe – Germany, Italy, the Benelux countries and France – it was actually Christian Democracy which proved central to constructing the post-war domestic order, and the welfare and modern adminis-trative state in particular.[14] Its leaders were willing to innovate politically, while its intellectuals could present innovation in the guise of largely traditional languages. In the *longue durée* of European history, post-war Christian Democracy brought about the reconciliation of Catholicism to the modern world. It also achieved peace (or at least truce) between different confessions – in a country like Germany arguably for the first time since the Reformation. The leading scholar of the movement has spoken of Christian Democratic parties' 'undeniable dullness'. But dullness was just the point: Christian Democracy promised a decent enough form of public life, while allowing citizens to turn away from politics if they so desired. Many citizens desired nothing more.

Christian Democracy also played a central role in realizing the idea of supranational European integration, not least because Catholics had long been wary of the nation-state and traditional notions of sovereignty. It was easy to give up parts of what was feared in the first place. And as in domestic politics, there was a tendency to leave politics – here in the form of international negotiations – entirely to high-minded elders.

The Decent State

The truly unusual path in Western Europe was actually taken by Britain, where the Labour Party had come to power just after the war.[15] The government under Clement Attlee was exceptional in both aims and methods: universal provision, national insurance and nationalizations of industry; all were means to what the influential social theorist Richard Titmuss called 'the search for equity' through extending the power of the state which had been vindicated by the victory over Nazism – when almost everywhere else in Europe state authority had been eroded by the war.[16] As the Labour Party intellectual Dick Crossman put it: 'The National Health Service is a by-product of the blitz.'[17]

The main beneficiaries of the welfare state turned out to be the middle class. But this was justified as a legitimate outcome in a free democracy, where workers simply were not in the majority. As the sociologist T. H. Marshall wrote:

> It may look at first sight as if the bourgeoisie had, as usual, filched what should have gone to the workers. But in the circumstances, that was bound to happen in a free democracy and is bound to go on happening in the Welfare State. For the Welfare State is not the dictatorship of the proletariat and is not pledged to liquidate the bourgeoisie.

This proved really just another way of saying that the welfare state was there to stay, because it could not be construed as a victory in some form of class war – in which case there would have remained an incentive to reverse that victory. Rather, it benefited (almost) everyone. Not least, it reconciled the middle classes (who had suffered traumas such as inflation in the interwar period and had been particularly tempted by extremist solutions) to post-war democracy: after all, they received most of the welfare benefits (and often were themselves employed in the large new welfare bureaucracies).[18]

Such reconciliation was made easier by the fact that the welfare state was justified not so much by way of long-standing socialist ideals, but rather as a form of – a major word in the 1940s and 1950s – decency. Its architects – William Beveridge, above all – were actually liberals, devoted to an evolution of the existing state, rather than to revolutionary breaks. On the other hand, the Labour Party itself soon seemed to be running out of programmatic ideas. It had simply been assumed that 'wartime standards of corporate solidarity and devotion to a common cause would survive into peacetime' and that no new public justifications for further institutionalizing 'solidarity' were required.[19] As the introduction to the *New Fabian Essays* from 1952 stated, 'the election of the Labour Government in 1945, and the rapid completion of the Fabian programme, had been followed by a dangerous hiatus both of thought and action.'[20]

Socialism had been implemented from above to constrain capitalism, but it had not been presented – or accepted – as a new way of life (in contrast to Sweden, for instance). It stood in the collectivist tradition of the Fabians, who, as we saw in the second chapter, had long been accused of ordering people around for their own good, rather than letting them participate in making decisions about what was good for them. Crossman claimed that 'the impression was given that socialism was an affair for the Cabinet, acting through the existing Civil Service. The rest of the nation was to carry on as before, while benefits were bestowed from above . . .'[21]

The British welfare state thus ended up short on 'theory' and extensive public justifications. Beveridge himself came to disown the term, which he associated with the 'Santa Claus state' (he preferred the expression 'social service state').[22] Nevertheless, it proved very popular, but less because of principles than because of practical success. As Crossman lamented:

> the continental Marxists certainly blunted their capacity for practical reforms by forcing their politics into conformity with a rigid doctrine. The Labour Party has gone to the other extreme. It capsulated its theory into a number of measures. Once these reforms had been accomplished, its only guide for future action was a tradition, which could be interpreted in any number of contradictory ways . . . but tradition, and the Conservative Party which is its guardian, is democracy's brake on social change. The dynamics can only be provided by a party which challenges the *status quo* on grounds of principle and uses theory to expose the inadequacy of tradition as a guide to action.[23]

The Christian Democratic Moment

Christian Democracy often did speak the language of tradition. This is the main reason why in retrospect it is easy to miss the momentous turn in European history – and also in the history of the Catholic Church more generally – that mid-twentieth-century Christian Democracy constituted. After 1789 there had been a continuous counter-revolutionary tradition (though in many different national versions); and while repeated attempts had been made to reconcile the church with the modern world (the French Catholic thinker Lamennais had even spoken of 'baptizing the Revolution'), the Vatican had remained locked in a battle with liberal democracy. Clericalism and anti-clericalism had deeply split many European countries, sometimes even turning into separate and explicitly opposed ways of life: French anti-clericals would aggressively defend the ideals of lay education and ostentatiously eat meat on Fridays and *tête de veau* on 21 January (the day of the beheading of the king); in Italy the conflict between the Vatican and the newly unified state led to the Pope forbidding Catholics to vote in national elections, resulting in a kind of continuous cold culture war.

Christian Democracy had emerged from and against these drawn-out *Kulturkämpfe*. The church had begun in the late nineteenth century to organize politically against the threats from liberal, anti-clerical governments.[24] Simultaneously, it sought to rise to the challenge of socialism by presenting its own solution to the social question. Leo XIII's 1891 encyclical *Rerum Novarum* constituted the manifesto of what came to be known as 'social Catholicism' – which was explicitly anti-socialist. The Pope affirmed that 'the first and most fundamental principle . . . if one would undertake to alleviate the condition of the masses, must be the inviolability of private property'. He also stressed the importance of family and voluntary associations, alongside a principled suspicion of the state. Overall the idea of social harmony – foreshadowing the ideals of corporatism we came across earlier – proved central to this vision:

> Just as the symmetry of the human frame is the result of the suitable arrange-
> ment of the different parts of the body, so in a State is it ordained by nature that
> these two classes should dwell in harmony and agreement, so as to maintain
> the balance of the body politic. Each needs the other: capital cannot do without
> labour, nor labour without capital. Mutual agreement results in the beauty of
> good order, while perpetual conflict necessarily produces confusion and savage
> barbarity.

Arguably, this was one step towards accepting parts of 'social democracy' in the sense of workers' economic rights – without, however, thereby necessarily legitimating political democracy. The encyclical *Diuturnum* from 1881 had still affirmed categorically that 'to make [political power] depend on the will of the people is, first, to commit an error of principle and, further, to set authority upon a foundation both fragile and inconsistent'. Improving the workers' lot was one thing, trusting them to make political decisions another. In fact, the church cast a wary eye on the Catholic parties that had formed in the late nineteenth century. Rome kept affirming that what mattered was 'Christian action', not Christian party politics, and sometimes Catholic parties found themselves attacked as signs of 'modernism' per se. In one sense this suspicion was understandable: the Catholic (and therefore universal) faith could not just be one party among (or like) all the others, let alone a mere interest group.[25] Pluralism as such had to be a problem for an institution with genuinely universalist aspirations.

In actual fact, even the words 'Christian Democracy' did not necessarily indicate a commitment to democracy, but were merely supposed to signal 'popular' or 'among the people'. Participation in elections to advance one's interests was one thing, actually endorsing the idea of popular sovereignty another. Catholics continued to play by the rules of democracy not because they believed in them, but because it was more advantageous to be inside the game than outside.

As with so much else, the First World War and its aftermath proved a watershed. In Italy Pope Benedict XV lifted the ban on Catholics participating in the political life of the Italian nation-state, and in 1919 Don Sturzo, a Sicilian priest, appealing to *tutti i liberi e i forti*, founded the Partito Popolare Italiano, Italian Catholics' first sustained experiment in mass politics. The party immediately became the second largest after the Socialists; it played a somewhat unfortunate role during the rise of Fascism, with some of its politicians joining the first Mussolini government alongside Liberals. The Vatican itself maintained a highly ambiguous relationship with the PPI: its secretary had initially called it the 'least bad' of all Italian parties. But eventually the Holy See turned against Sturzo and supported factions that were unquestioningly prepared to collaborate with Mussolini.[26] The PPI was dissolved in 1926, and its main leaders and theoreticians had to go into some form of exile. Alcide De Gasperi, the last party secretary and the first Christian Democratic post-war prime minister, found shelter in the Vatican library; Sturzo himself lived in New York for most of the *ventennio nero* (the two 'black decades' of Fascist rule).

In the end, the interwar years proved disastrous for Christian Democratic parties in most European countries – in Italy and Germany in particular. Much more fruitful were developments in Catholic thought. Of special importance proved to be the personalist movement in France, often associated with Emmanuel Mounier and the group around his magazine *Esprit*. Personalists sought to distance themselves simultaneously from both Communism and liberal individualism, condemning these supposedly opposed ideologies as forms of materialism. Liberal individualism, in particular, was held responsible for what Mounier derided as *le désordre établi* – his designation for the corrupt parliamentary politics of the Third French Republic; as he put it, 'on the altar of this sad world, there is but one god, smiling and hideous: the Bourgeois'.[27] As an alternative to the materialist twins of liberalism and Communism, Mounier tried to reconcile Catholicism and a soft version of socialism: the 'person' – as opposed to the isolated 'individual' – always realized himself or herself in community, while also retaining a spiritual dimension which could never be absorbed into politics in this world. Practically, personalists called for a society with a flourishing group life (not unlike what the English pluralists had advocated), as well as decentralization of decision-making. While this might sound rather harmless by way of concrete proposals, the rhetoric (and personal expectations) of Mounier were never anything less than revolutionary and aggressively anti-liberal. Hence Mounier could briefly see a place for the personalists in the Vichy regime (whose leader had also affirmed that 'individualism has nothing in common with respect for the human person') and support Soviet Marxism after the war.[28]

The intuition about decision-making having to be as decentralized as possible – now worked up into the theory of 'subsidiarity' – also appeared in the 1931 encyclical *Quadragesimo Anno*, which was explicitly directed against both Communism and market liberalism. Pope Pius XI admonished that 'it is not rightful to remove from individuals what they are able to achieve with their endeavour and industry in order to give it to the community, it is unjust to assign to a larger and higher society what can be done by smaller and lower communities'. The church condemned fascism as a form of atheistic statism. But by and large it took a favourable view of the Catholic corporatist (and authoritarian) regimes of the interwar period.

Fascism, as we saw in the last chapter, was completely discredited with the war. The Catholic authoritarian regimes now distanced themselves from whatever fascist tendencies they had harboured – in short, they became *more* Catholic. While Franco and Salazar soldiered on for a few more decades (and retained many admirers in other countries), it is not an exaggeration to say that the war had also put an end to the long counter-revolutionary tradition in Western Europe. This was most obvious in the original context of counter-revolution, that is, France: the Vichy regime's failed 'National Revolution', under the shadow of occupation, had also discredited the long-held dreams of royalist and religious right-wing movements.

The main change, however, was that Christian Democrats in post-war Europe were no longer in the business of grudgingly and resentfully accommodating the modern world – Christian Democrats really became democrats. Don Sturzo insisted in 1945 that in the past liberty had been 'badly understood by clericals', but now had to be 're-linked to the Christian tradition of popular sovereignty and to the democratic regime'.[29] Christian Democrats also embraced human rights as indispensable to a proper Catholic view of the world – a development which can hardly be understood without the role of the French philosopher Jacques Maritain.[30] Maritain had been born into a prominent republican family and started his intellectual life as a philosophy student at the Sorbonne, supporting Colonel Dreyfus against the forces of the right. In 1901 he had met fellow student Raïssa Oumansoff, daughter of Russian Jewish immigrants. So began a lifelong intellectual and spiritual collaboration which had few parallels in the twentieth century – not least in its dramatic moments. In 1903, on a sunny summer day in the Jardin des Plantes, the lovers vowed to commit suicide together within a year if they could not find answers to life's apparent meaninglessness. Eventually they did find an answer: Catholicism.

Maritain became a fervent Catholic – and clearly a right-wing one. In the 1920s, he moved close to the proto-fascist Action Française and was perceived by some as the unofficial philosophical spokesman of this stridently nationalist and royalist movement. In 1926 the movement was condemned by the Vatican; the Pope accused the AF of instrumentalizing Catholicism for political purposes, while actually being atheist. For a while, Maritain tried to mediate between the Vatican and the movement's leader, Charles Maurras; then he abandoned the Action Française for good. He remained highly critical of the modern world, however, and of Protestantism and liberalism in particular. His beliefs shaped the emerging personalism, and for a while he acted as a mentor to Mounier and the *Esprit* group.[31] Unlike many European Catholics, he refused to endorse Franco's actions in the Spanish Civil War as a kind of modern crusade. He also began to work out a philosophical rapprochement between Catholicism and modern conceptions of human rights and democracy.

American and Canadian universities had begun to invite Maritain for lecture series in the mid-1930s. When the war broke out, he found himself in North America and decided to stay; the Gestapo searched his house outside Paris in vain. He spent the following years on the East Coast, teaching at Princeton and Columbia. He remarked that there existed in the United States a fundamental tension between the structures (or 'logic') of advanced industrial civilization and the generous, humanist spirit (or 'soul') of the American people. He was convinced that the soul would emerge victorious over capitalism.[32]

Partly inspired by the example of the US, Maritain began to propagate what he saw as the inner connections between democracy and Christianity more openly. In 1942 he authored a pamphlet *Christianity and Democracy* that was dropped by Allied planes over France. There he claimed that 'democracy is linked to Christianity and that the democratic impulse has arisen in human history as the moral manifestation of the inspiration of the Gospel'.[33] More boldly, he declared that 'democracy is the only way of bringing about a moral rationalization of politics. Because democracy is a rational organization of freedoms founded upon law.' And on an even more emphatic note, he announced that 'democracy carries in a fragile vessel the terrestrial hope, I would say the biological hope, of humanity'.

True, Maritain's intellectual-political *aggiornamento* was highly selective: it did not let go of elements which had constituted core elements of Catholic political thought at least since the late nineteenth century. He was sceptical of the state and of the notion of sovereignty in particular. Rousseau, the apparent originator of the idea of popular sovereignty, but also Luther kept being blamed for the cataclysms of the mid-twentieth century. Maritain argued that 'political philosophy must eliminate Sovereignty both as a word and as a concept – not because it is an antiquated concept . . . not because the concept of Sovereignty creates insuperable difficulties and theoretical entanglements in the field of international law; but because, considered in its genuine meaning ... this concept is intrinsically wrong and bound to mislead us if we keep using it'.[34]

For Maritain, 'sovereign' meant 'separate' and 'transcendent' – and neither kings nor peoples could properly be separate from the body politic. Only God was sovereign. At the same time, the notion of 'person' was precisely to signal openness to the transcendent. Maritain's 'theocentric' humanism, which he wanted to realize in a pluralist and personalist democracy, sought to do justice to 'man in the wholeness of his natural and supernatural being'. But theocentric did not mean theocratic: Maritain insisted that 'a new Christian temporal order, while founded on the same principles (analogically speaking) as that of the Middle Ages, will imply a *secular Christian*, not a consecrated, conception of the temporal order'.

What underpinned Maritain's views was a strong Thomist notion of natural law which ultimately derived from divine law and which specified human beings' proper ends. Freedom for Maritain therefore meant not licence or arbitrarily following one's desires, but the full realization of these ends. It is against this background that he insisted on the importance of workers' rights and even general rights of subsistence, because they were indispensable for such a proper realization of the person.

Maritain's conceptions did not remain confined to debates among Catholic philosophers: he was a central player in drafting the UN Declaration of Human Rights. De Gaulle persuaded him to serve as French ambassador to the Vatican after the war. The Holy See itself would eventually ratify many of his ideas, and it was highly fitting that he was presented by the Pope with the 'Message to the Philosophers' at the closing of the Second Vatican Council. However, Maritain – who after the death of his wife in 1960 had lived in a monastic order near Toulouse – now thought that the church was going too far in its 'modernism'. His harsh criticisms of its more liberal positions were greeted with anger and incomprehension by many of his followers – was he disowning his life's philosophical work? Even so, unrepentant right-wing Catholics like Carl Schmitt would consistently denounce him as 'Cauche-Maritain' (Night-Maritain), while conservatives such as the Hungarian thinker Aurel Kolnai never found his efforts expended in 'dressing up poor Thomas Aquinas in the rags of a laicist apostle of democracy' very credible.[35] East of the Iron Curtain, the Polish philosopher Leszek Kołakowski attacked the whole neo-Thomist tendency as a desperate measure to justify and preserve private property rights.[36]

However, for the newly formed Christian Democratic parties of Western Europe Maritain's thought constituted an important reference point, although the French Thomist had not necessarily been in favour of founding explicitly Christian parties; Christianity, he felt, should be something like the 'yeast' of political life. Maritain's philosophy proved particularly significant for a group of left-leaning Christian Democratic thinkers involved in the drafting of the Italian constitution.[37] At their centre were the intellectuals Giorgio La Pira (who was to become mayor of Florence) and Giuseppe Dossetti from the Catholic University in Milan, who were nicknamed *professorini* (young, or fledgling, professors). They had avidly read the personalists, criticized individualism and, above all, endorsed the point that the person was always embedded in community; in La Pira's words: 'the human person unfolds through organic belonging to the successive social communities in which it is contained and via which it steadily develops and perfects itself'.[38]

Dossetti, an expert in ecclesiastical law, had fought in the Resistance and served on the Committee of National Liberation. In 1945 he was made vice-secretary of the Democrazia Cristiana and tried to open the party to personalist, pacifist and even socialist ideas. He had been deeply impressed by the Labour Party's 1945 election victory in Britain; he and his allies had studied Beveridge and Keynes (who they wrongly believed to have been Labour politicians); and they were hoping for an Italian version of a personalist, labour-based 'substantial democracy', which realized Christian solidarity throughout the state, society and the economy.[39] Their central beliefs about the economic reordering of post-war Italy could be summed up in their slogan 'First the person and then the market'.[40] What this meant in terms of political institutions and policies often remained unclear, however, and, as we will see in a moment, any more left-leaning visions of Christian Democracy were soon sidelined in favour of more market-friendly versions. At least there were some symbolic victories for the *professorini*: article 3 of the Italian constitution read, in perfect personalist language: 'it is the Republic's duty to remove obstacles of an economic or social order physically constricting the freedom and equality of citizens and thus impeding the full development of the human person'.[41]

A Bargain of Ideas

It was not personalist philosophers – nor even the general revival of Christianity – that ensured the party-political success of Christian Democracy after 1945. It was a particular electoral alliance of the middle class and the peasantry (an alliance supportive of and benefiting from European integration, too). Perhaps more importantly still, Christian Democrats became the quintessentially anti-Communist parties of the era, helped by the fact that the traditional right had been so thoroughly discredited alongside fascism. One reason why human rights proved so attractive to Catholics was that the language of personal rights could be deployed against the threat of 'godless Bolshevism'.

To be sure, Christian Democrats had not been completely unaffected by the revolutionary atmosphere of the mid-1940s. For instance, the German Christian Democratic Union (CDU)'s initial party programmes were almost socialist in some of their aspirations – including large-scale nationalizations and the co-determination of workers and employers; they sought to appeal not least to Catholic unions and the worker-priest movement. Georges Bidault, the founder of the French version of Christian Democracy, the Mouvement Républicain Populaire, summed up this approach as 'to govern in the centre, and pursue, by the methods of the right, the policies of the left'.[42]

By the early 1950s, however, this slogan seemed not nearly as plausible as it had been in the late 1940s. The CDU now emphasized the importance of small business, small peasant holdings and (ideally not so small) families. In fact, rather than pursuing any 'policies of the left', as in Bidault's phrase, the German Christian Democrats brokered a compromise between economic liberals and socially conservative Catholics who might have had socialist leanings: if the former accepted traditional morality, the latter would live with the market. This intellectual bargain also needed particular 'in-between figures' capable of speaking to both sides and of credibly representing free-market and Catholic ideals at the same time. In Germany, Oswald von Nell-Breuning, who had been the main author of *Quadragesimo Anno* and later served as an adviser in Ludwig Erhard's liberal Economics Ministry, performed precisely such a role. He and others forged what turned out to be both an intellectually and electorally highly successful formula.

Over time Christian Democratic parties turned themselves into genuine mass parties, following the model of the Social Democrats, but broadening their electoral appeal still further and fashioning themselves into what the erstwhile socialist legal theorist Otto Kirchheimer – now a political scientist at Columbia University – called 'catch-all parties'. Even in Italy De Gasperi did not want to shape a party that understood itself as exclusively Catholic (or, even worse, was perceived as the political arm of the Vatican); instead, the Democrazia Cristiana, in De Gasperi's mind, was to become a genuine *partito nazionale* cutting across classes and regions, thus actually modelling itself on the Fascist Party (while in Germany the Nazis had arguably been the first *Volkspartei* cutting across class and region).

True, in order to highlight the contrast with Communism, party leaders kept affirming that democracy necessarily had to rest on Christian foundations, and that the only alternative to Christian Democracy was totalitarianism. But more and more, the Christian Democratic parties were losing the odour of incense which had clung to the movement earlier in the century.[43] By the early 1970s, the Austrian Christian Democrats could declare with a straight face that their party was open to 'Christians and all those who from other motives believe in a humanistic view of man'. In other words, atheists may apply, too.

While in France the political space available for the Mouvement Républicain Populaire was eventually closed by Gaullism, the Italian Democrazia Cristiana became the most successful party machine in post-war Western Europe. It was effectively a state party, or at least a party colonizing areas of the state, continuously in power to keep out the Communists, always employing in varying positions the same personnel representing the different party factions or *correnti*, and throughout relying on clientelism (and sometimes corruption) – something that thinkers like Dossetti had predicted would happen if the DC failed to offer Italy genuine ethical renewal. The 'libertas' in the DC's coat of arms appeared to signify mostly freedom *from* Communism and freedom *to* plunder the state. The party always held on to – of all ministries – the post office, because it provided the amplest opportunities for patronage. Some drew the consequences early on: Dossetti, always as much a religious mystic as a politician, dissolved his left-wing faction in the party, founded a monastic order called the Piccola Famiglia dell'Annunziata and became a priest.

And yet, for all its increasingly conspicuous failings, it is important to remember what the DC did not do – it resisted pressure from the Vatican to keep the option of a more authoritarian Catholic state open (after all, Salazar's Estado Novo remained attractive for Rome). De Gasperi was perhaps no Don Sturzo, that is, no great believer in an egalitarian version of Catholic social doctrine – but the point is that he was no Franco either.

Also, for all the sordid and not so sordid material reasons that ensured the triumph of Christian Democracy, it has to be remembered that some body of thought had to be available publicly to justify Christian Democratic politics – and, in particular, thoughts which credibly spoke to believers, while reassuring non-believers that religious parties had genuinely accepted pluralism and that they would not reignite a *Kulturkampf*. The very vagueness of a philosophy such as personalism probably ensured its broad appeal (leading Jean-Paul Sartre to claim in 1948 to a Swiss writer, 'you personalists have won . . . everybody in France now calls themselves a personalist'). More specifically, its professed anti-liberalism could help Catholics build bridges to modern democracy without feeling that they had betrayed their own convictions. Maritain's thought in particular provided reasons from within the Catholic tradition to embrace liberal politics – in fact, if not in name – while also reassuring non-believers that Catholics would not revert to some form of authoritarianism if they gained the majority. It was a delicate philosophical balancing act. It did not necessarily make for profound philosophy. But it made West European politics more moderate.

Like the CDU in Germany, Democrazia Cristiana turned out to be much more pro-market in economics than one might have thought in the late 1940s. However, like the CDU, it was consistently conservative in questions of morality. Already in 1946, at the first congress of the DC, Guido Gonella declared in a rousing speech:

> an invisible and silent bomb has destroyed the family unit. The family, if it is not already dispersed, is more likely to unite around the radio, which is a deafening and dulling window on the world, than around the domestic hearth . . . The family is a fortress which cannot be defended from inside the fortress. Certainly we must also issue forth and fight the enemy in open battle.[44]

But Christian Democrats were clearly losing this particular battle. They could try to combine their belief in modernization and traditional morality rhetorically, as when the leader of the Bavarian Christian Social Union, Franz Josef Strauβ, declared that 'to be conservative today means to march at the head of technological progress'. But in reality the trends of the time were summed up in the opening scene of Fellini's *La dolce vita*, when a gigantic Christ statue is flown across Rome, followed by paparazzi and watched by some scantily clad women sunbathing on a roof below: the symbols of traditional Christianity (and morality) were still there, but life on the ground was changing inexorably. The fusion of technology and tradition seemed less and less coherent.

Longer-lasting (and more coherent) was the specifically Christian Democratic approach in international affairs: the founders of the European Community – Alcide De Gasperi, Konrad Adenauer, Robert Schuman – were all Christian Democrats. Not by accident did they hail from the margins of their respective nation-states; all had been marked by the sometimes brutal homogenization of the 'late' nation-states Italy and Germany: De Gasperi had studied in Vienna and served in the pre-1918 Austrian Reichsrat; Adenauer had been mayor of Catholic Cologne – very much on the margins of the Reich; Schuman's family had fled Lorraine from the Germans to Luxembourg.[45] All could, if they desired to do so, speak German with each other. National sovereignty was neither a value in itself for them nor a precondition for creating political meaning, in the way it had been for Max Weber. On the contrary, it was something to be feared. These leaders advocated subsidiarity and a Europe united in its 'Christian-humanist' heritage (the particulars of which were not to be discussed all that much, as long as they added up to anti-Communism). They believed in supranationalism as something done by well-connected elites of high-minded planners and bureaucrats – the kind of diplomacy that had been foreshadowed by Keynes' dealings after the First World War, but which, for the most part, had so spectacularly foundered in interwar Europe. Jean Monnet, the French bureaucrat-cum-intellectual who was one of the major architects of European integration, famously claimed: 'We are not connecting states, we are connecting people.' But in fact they were first of all connecting well-intentioned, but not necessarily internationally well-connected, politicians and civil servants.

Thus the creators of the European Community followed an indirect way of gaining legitimacy for their project: rather than having the peoples of the initial member states vote for supranational arrangements, they relied on technocratic and administrative measures agreed among elites to yield what Monnet time and again called 'concrete achievements' – which were eventually to persuade citizens that European integration was a good thing.[46]

In retrospect, the official approach has often been derided as European integration by stealth. At the time, however, it appeared as a credible response to the dangers of popular sovereignty, of which Christian Democrat leaders, even as leaders of people's parties, would remain particularly wary. On the other hand, some architects of integration did seek to instil real political passion for Europe in their people. Adenauer told the members of his cabinet in February 1952 that 'the people must be given a new ideology. It can only be a European one.'[47] And De Gasperi claimed in a speech to the Italian Senate:

> some said that the European federation is a myth. It's true, *it is a myth in the Sorelian sense*. And if you want there to be a myth, then please tell us what myth we need to give to our youth concerning relations between one state and another, the future of Europe, the future of the world, security, and peace, if not this effort toward unification? Do you prefer the myth of dictatorship, the myth of power, the myth of one's nation's flag, even if it is accompanied by heroism? But then, we would create once again that conflict that inevitably leads to war. I tell you that this myth is a myth of peace.[48]

Nevertheless, European integration was from the beginning a political end mainly pursued by taking seemingly small economic and administrative steps, and not so much by promoting Sorelian myths (even if the Sorelian notion that continuously moving is everything – and the end nothing – sometimes seemed to sum up what Euro-enthusiasts were really saying).

In retrospect all these changes seem momentous, in particular the devaluing of national sovereignty and the creation of (relative) social peace among classes, but also among confessions. At the time, however, the Christian Democratic moment was often deplored as a 'restoration' of traditions which had failed at least once already. Critics levelling this charge did have a point: measured against the hopes of many political thinkers in the Resistance, the post-war landscape looked profoundly dispiriting: there was too much capitalism, and too little direct participation in democracy. Younger generations felt this even more acutely. The philosopher Jürgen Habermas, who had been a member of the Hitler Youth and then served as a field nurse in the final phase of the war, was deeply shocked when he learnt more and more about German atrocities and what he called 'the fact of collectively realized inhumanity', as he listened to the reports of the Nuremberg trials on the radio. Habermas explained later that 'we believed that a spiritual and moral renewal was indispensable and inevitable'. The apparent failure of such renewal then led to a fundamental sense of distrust vis-à-vis the post-war polity: 'if only there had been some spontaneous sweeping away, some explosive act, which then could have served to begin the formation of political authority. After such an eruption we could have at least known what we couldn't go back to.'[49]

The 'Euthanasia of Politics'?

The 1950s and 1960s are often characterized by the concept of 'consensus politics'. This seems a highly plausible diagnosis: the centre expanded, as the extreme right had been discredited by fascism, while the post-war left became more and more moderate, shedding almost all remnants of Marxist theory. True, the notion of consensus hides persistent disagreements on policy, which remained rooted in different political principles (and different political imaginations). But there really were shared goals: in particular, the vocabulary of 'stability' became ubiquitous after 1945.

Tellingly, 'stability' had entered political language only in the nineteenth century and was itself imported from the sphere of technology, and engineering in particular. In the post-war world stability was to be ensured not least by 'the politics of productivity' – the co-operation of employers and unions for the sake of higher productivity and greater wealth all round. One reason that both former class enemies seemed able to collaborate was the stress on 'technocracy': conflict could be reduced significantly, because there really were technically correct solutions to social and economic problems; it simply made no sense to keep fighting about them. What automatically fell by the wayside were ideals of industrial democracy and worker self-administration: there seemed no point in giving decision-making power to unqualified workers, as opposed to qualified experts. Workers should remain content as unions obtained the best possible deal for them. As the British union leader Hugh Clegg put it, 'the trade union . . . is industry's opposition – an opposition which can never become a government'.[50]

The means for attaining stability, then, seemed uncontentious. Keynes talked about the 'euthanasia of politics' in economic policy-making;[51] the Swedish analyst Herbert Tingsten claimed as early as 1955 that 'as the general standard of values is commonly accepted, the functions of the state become so technical as to make politics appear as a kind of applied statistics'.[52] Consensus was justified by the overriding importance of stability, and stability in turn was justified in the language of security. The German Christian Democrats' most famous election slogan simply demanded, 'No experiments'; another imaginative one ran, 'Safe is safe' (*Sicher ist sicher*). Even when there was change – as with the entry of the German Social Democrats into government in 1966 for the first time since 1930 – change was presented as a means of gaining even more stability. The Social Democrats thought the best they could do by way of an election slogan in 1966 was: 'Sicherheit ja!'

The craze for large-scale planning was the clearest expression of this belief in the capacity of governments to steer, stabilize and secure entire societies. It cut across left and right. Most famously there was Jean Monnet, who insisted that 'the plan, like life, is continuous creation' and that 'the only alternative to modernization is decadence'.[53] Even in the country where planning was viewed somewhat warily because of its associations with both Communism and Nazism – West Germany – 'plans' proliferated: from the Green Plan to the Federal Youth Plan to the Golden Plan (for the Olympics).[54]

Planning had to be 'scientific', of course. The Labour politician (and two-time prime minister) Harold Wilson demanded in 1963 that 'in the Cabinet room and the boardroom alike, those charged with the control of our affairs must be ready to think and to speak in the language of our scientific age'. They were supposed to be helped in that endeavour by the social sciences – sociology and economics in particular – which had become supremely self-confident in the post-war period and seemingly capable of vanquishing the three evils which Keynes had already identified in the interwar period as the greatest threats to liberal democratic stability: 'risk, uncertainty, and ignorance'.[55]

In actual fact, planning was to be least practised in Britain (even if there was a great deal of talk about 'democratic planning'). As both idea and practice, planning could be separated from the welfare state (which kept expanding in the UK). British unions supported the latter, they resisted the former. Planning could also be separated from nationalization; observing the development of the latter made G. D. H. Cole revert to his Guild Socialist principles and claim that nationalization policies constituted a 'bad cross between bureaucracy and big business'.[56]

Unlike in the major continental European countries, there was also a noticeable British philosophical opposition to technocracy, and to planning in particular. Its protagonists could speak self-assuredly in the name of national tradition. Ernest Barker, who still retained pluralist sensibilities – but now thought only those with the right national character could sustain pluralism – criticized what he called 'the managing and manipulating state'; he felt disturbed by 'the nervous tension in planning . . . which hardly accords with our instincts or the general tradition of our life'. The gentleman-scholar remained fundamentally opposed to the technocrat-planner, and what Barker saw as the quintessentially English 'anti-professional modes of government' appropriate to a state conceived as a gentlemen's club. Amateurism, he held, would also prevent 'life from being too hugely serious' and leave 'a space for fun'.[57]

Nevertheless, there appeared on the continent an unashamed endorsement of technocracy, or, put differently, of Weber's steely casing – because there seemed actually to be security in that casing. And while it might not have been exactly Barker's 'space for fun', in the new age of consumerism it at least proved comfortable. Never mind that critics such as the French Communist poet Louis Aragon derided it as a 'civilisation de frigidaires'.[58]

It was tempting to conclude that industrial society, or what the French sociologist Raymond Aron called 'scientific' and 'rationalized' society, could now somehow stabilize itself – without too much help from the state. The German legal theorist Ernst Forsthoff, a pupil of Schmitt, announced in the late 1960s that 'the hard core of the social whole is no longer the state, but industrial society, and this hard core is characterized by the notions of full employment and increase of the GNP'.[59] Whether or not Forsthoff was right in this diagnosis, there was a widespread sense that Western Europe was modernizing rapidly, and that modernization would spell the end of long-standing ideological conflict, or, more bluntly, class warfare. The German sociologist Helmut Schelsky diagnosed a 'levelled-down middle-class society'. Harold Wilson, when asked to which class he belonged, claimed: 'Well someone who started at elementary school in Yorkshire and became an Oxford don – where do you put him in this class spectrum? I think these phrases are becoming more and more meaningless.'[60] The language of class conflict was fading.

And even 'the masses' disappeared. While it is impossible to say when exactly they ceased to be central to European intellectual debates, there can be little doubt that by the early 1960s the value-neutral 'society' or 'industrial society' had taken their place.[61] For a while at least, sociology, with its highly abstract concepts – rather than cultural criticism – tended to be the basso continuo of political thinking.

It has to be remembered, though, that modernization proceeded under auspices which did not seem modern at all: a paternalistic form of politics – embodied in figures such as the German chancellor Adenauer, who governed until the age of eighty-seven, De Gasperi, who was already sixty-four when he became Italian prime minister, the French president Charles de Gaulle and the German president Theodor Heuss – often referred to simply as 'Papa Heuss'. Most of them – de Gaulle being an obvious exception – sought a dedramatization of politics. These old men – self-consciously anti-charismatic and conventionally bourgeois in their appearance – could not have marked a greater contrast with the fascist and, in general, pre-war cult of youth.[62] For most people it was a very reassuring contrast.

The Post-War Constitutional Settlement: Disciplining Democracy

It would be a mistake, however, to think that stability was supposed automatically to follow from the 'politics of productivity', from planning and from consumerism. Political institutions were expected to play a role, and the post-war period saw crucial innovations in what Hans Kelsen had called 'constitutional techniques'. One of the most important in twentieth-century Europe as a whole was the creation of constitutional courts. These were not simply a copy of the American Supreme Court. Instead this particular conception of judicial review dated from thirty years earlier – Kelsen had included it in the Austrian constitution which he had crafted after the First World War (he himself had served on the court until 1930, when anti-Semitic attacks forced him out).[63] Austria had been only the third country to have such judicial review of the constitutionality of statutes (after the US and Australia), and the first to centralize tests for constitutionality and task a specific separate court with it. Kelsen defended judicial review as a form of checks and balances; he did not concede that it might be inherently undemocratic, as many opponents were to claim. In the early 1930s, in a major controversy with Carl Schmitt, the Austrian jurist argued that only such a court could be the ultimate 'guardian' of a constitution. Schmitt, on the other hand, assigned this role to the president, in a manner that was closer to Max Weber's thinking.[64] At the time, German political elites had gone with Schmitt rather than Kelsen.

After 1945, even in countries which had traditionally been highly suspicious of judicial review – above all, France, with its aversion to *gouvernement des juges* – the idea of testing for constitutionality was accepted eventually. Constitutional courts appeared to limit or even contradict traditional notions of popular sovereignty – but, in a post-war age that was suspicious of the dangers of potentially totalitarian democracy, having more checks and balances was precisely the point. What was unexpected was that constitutional courts also contradicted executives. As Adenauer, one of the architects of the West German

Basic Law, complained after the court had began to go against his plans to rearm the country: 'This is not how we imagined it.'[65]

Constitutional courts were also instrumental in the rise of so-called militant democracy – a concept that had first been defined by the German exile political scientist Karl Loewenstein in 1938, at a time when one European country after another had been taken over by fascist and authoritarian movements using democratic means to disable democracy.[66] Loewenstein had argued that democracies were incapable of defending themselves against such movements if they continued to subscribe to 'democratic fundamentalism', 'legalistic blindness' and an 'exaggerated formalism of the rule of law'.[67] Part of the new challenge was that, according to Loewenstein, fascism had no proper intellectual content, relying on a kind of 'emotionalism' with which democracies could never compete on its own terms. Consequently, democracies had to take legal measures against anti-democratic forces, such as banning parties. They should also restrict the rights to assembly and free speech.[68] As Loewenstein argued, 'fire should be fought with fire', and that fire, in his view, could be lit only by a new, 'disciplined' democracy.[69]

One country in particular in post-war Europe was prepared to fight fire with fire: the Federal Republic of Germany. The West German Constitutional Court invoked the idea of militant democracy to ban the quasi-Nazi Socialist Reich Party and the Communist Party in the 1950s; in the 1970s the concept was evoked in support of draconian measures against those guilty of (suspected) association with terrorists. Critics charged from the beginning that this anti-extremism could easily be instrumentalized against legitimate opposition (especially left-wing opposition), while, at the same time, it did little to help deal with the Nazi past. If anything, its implicit equation of Soviet Communism (and its alleged foreign agents) and Nazism seemed to relativize the evils of the latter.

Militant democracy was most pronounced in West Germany, but the imperative of democratic self-defence became pervasive across Western Europe. In Italy the Christian Democrats sought to establish a 'protected democracy' – *una democrazia protetta* – that was to restrict civil liberties but was also to justify electoral laws benefiting major parties.[70] But the initiative failed in the Italian Senate, most likely because the Vatican had an interest in preventing a ban on right-wing parties and thereby keeping its political options open.[71] While the Italian constitution had explicitly prohibited the re-establishment of the Fascist Party, the Italian Social Movement, a de facto successor to Fascism, established itself as a minor party. Once more, the theory and the reality of militant democracy differed markedly – and the reality, for the most part, favoured the right.

For all these failings, though, there emerged after the war a new constitutional settlement, with a particular 'constitutionalist ethos'.[72] It was informed by the perceived lessons of the interwar period: whereas fascists (and Stalin) had tried to create new peoples, the point now was to constrain existing ones. Neither major political thinkers nor actual political leaders were interested in 'people-making' of any kind; the latter in particular were content with the peoples they found and to let them be (or let men make themselves in the market, so to speak). The fact that the war had brought about more homogeneous state populations and that class divisions were decreasing among them obviously helped.

In concrete terms the imperative of constraining peoples translated into weakening parliaments and, in particular, restricting the ability of legislatures to delegate power – preventing them, so it was hoped, from the kind of democratic suicide the Weimar Republic and the French Third Republic had committed: never again should an assembly abdicate in favour of a Hitler or a Pétain. Thus what the German lawyer Hugo Preuss – father of the Weimar constitution and responsible for involving Weber in its drafting – had described as the danger of 'parliamentary absolutism' was to be banished once and for all.

At the same time, many of the functions of the ever expanding post-war welfare and regulatory states were delegated to administrative agencies, but these were in turn made subject to strong judicial and administrative oversight. The latter was to alleviate the kind of liberal anxieties about the rule of law which Lord Hewart had voiced in the 1920s (and which had been exacerbated for continental observers of the neo-feudal Third Reich: there, as we saw in the last chapter, power had been delegated to numerous unaccountable and self-radicalizing agencies).[73] Karl Loewenstein concluded in 1966 that the task of checking the bureaucracy which Weber had assigned to parliament was now effectively fulfilled by courts, while 'parliamentarism, which in the nineteenth century seemed to be the ultimate in political wisdom, has . . . undergone such widespread devaluation'.[74]

Constitutional courts in turn were to protect this new order as a whole, especially by safeguarding individual rights. These were also to be out of reach for parliaments and grounded in natural law or other systems of absolute values (which directly contradicted one of Kelsen's major philosophical positions, namely that democracy necessarily entailed a form of value relativism).[75] Even sceptical liberals would affirm the necessity of such supposedly unshakeable foundations of objective values as a direct lesson of the past. Isaiah Berlin answered the question 'what has emerged from the recent holocausts?' by saying, 'something approaching a new recognition in the West that there are certain universal values which can be called constitutive of human beings as such'.[76]

European integration was part and parcel of the new 'constitutionalist ethos', with its inbuilt distrust of popular sovereignty, and the delegation of bureaucratic tasks to agencies which remained under the close supervision of national governments.[77] Member countries consciously gave powers to unelected institutions domestically and also to supranational bodies in order to 'lock in' liberal-democratic arrangements, and to prevent any backsliding towards authoritarianism.[78]

Two fundamental decisions by the European Court of Justice reinforced this sense of 'Europe' as another set of constraints on electoral democracy. Landmark cases in 1963 and 1964 established that European Community law was to have supremacy over national laws and that it took direct effect in member states – that is, EC legislation could be invoked by individual citizens in national courts and be enforced against member states. The court confidently announced that 'by creating a Community of unlimited duration . . . the Member States have limited their sovereign rights, albeit in limited fields, and thus created a body of law which binds both their nationals and themselves'. In 1969 the judges even added the opinion that fundamental human rights were in fact 'enshrined in the general principles of Community law and protected by the Court' – when in fact the original treaties had made no mention of such rights. This discovery or, rather, invention of rights was prompted by the fear that the German and Italian constitutional courts could oppose European law in the name of basic rights contained in national constitutions. Thus, in line with the general West European trend towards review by a special court, the European Court of Justice had more or less bootstrapped itself into a position of extraordinary judicial power (and was, for the most part, accepted as possessing that power both by national courts and by national governments).

A central element of the post-war constitutional settlement, then, was that outside Britain the idea of unrestricted parliamentary supremacy cased to be seen as legitimate. The flipside of the weakening of parliaments was a strengthening of executives, a process which went furthest under General de Gaulle, who turned the Assemblée Nationale into the weakest legislature in the West. Justifications of democracy centred less on having one's views effectively represented in parliament than on ensuring the regular turnover of responsible political elites through elections.

It was very much the notion of democracy which Joseph Schumpeter – Weber's sardonic adversary in the café debate on the Russian Revolution – put forward at mid-century. Like Weber, Schumpeter, who had briefly (and disastrously) acted as Austrian finance minister after the First World War, held that there was no such a thing as a coherent popular will; he also denied that participation in politics mattered in the least for ordinary people; but unlike Weber he attributed no particular dignity to the public realm. Competition for votes among elites was a good thing, the rest of democratic ideology an illusion, as was Weber's hope for politics as a sphere independent of the economy and capable of creating collective meaning. Many post-war thinkers shared such assumptions, with leading Labour Party intellectual Tony Crosland, for instance, claiming that 'all experience shows that only a small minority of the population will wish to participate', while the majority would always 'prefer to lead a full family life and cultivate their garden'.[79]

Politics, then, was not supposed to be a major source of meaning; in fact it was not supposed to be a source of meaning at all. But with such expectations for meaning (and possibly personal fulfilment through politics) also went any sense of the public realm as a site of collective freedom – or so Hannah Arendt (and other critics who could not be suspected of either Nazi or Soviet sympathies) complained. European liberals emphasized 'negative freedom', that is, absence of interference in one's life. It was supposedly the only kind of freedom that could not be turned into a totalitarian nightmare in the name of ideals centred on 'positive freedom' understood as individual or collective self-direction. But for critics this seeming self-restriction – promoted not least to mark the difference from socialism in the East – made for a diminished form of democracy. In the eyes of observers like Arendt, such a restrictive liberalism actually reinforced 'mass man's' isolation and, perversely, made a return to totalitarianism more likely. There were also some self-designated 'classical liberals' tormented by the fear of a return to totalitarianism: not because of the post-war order's restrictive liberalism – but because of the very consensus politics that promised stability.

Liberals in the Wasteland

Friedrich von Hayek, a distant cousin of Wittgenstein, had grown up in the Vienna of the early twentieth century when it had been a laboratory for many of the century's most important intellectual trends.[80] He spent some time in New York in the 1920s, supposedly having arrived with exactly twenty-five dollars and ready to do the proverbial dishwashing in a restaurant on Sixth Avenue if a research position had not finally opened up at New York University. He left Austria in 1931 for the London School of Economics, the first foreigner to be appointed there.

In Britain he quickly made a name for himself with a number of direct attacks on Keynes, but he was widely perceived to have lost the battle that he had fought with Keynes in specialized academic journals. Their heated exchange apparently did not damage the respectful personal relationship between the two gentlemen-economists: Keynes made sure Hayek was put up properly when the LSE had to be evacuated to Cambridge during the war; and they even did fire watch together on the roof of King's College Chapel.

1 Lecturing German youth on what's what: Max Weber (with hat) at a conference in Burg
Lauenstein (Thuringia) in 1917, which was intended as a place for different generations of German
intellectuals to meet (and which Weber later called a 'department store for Weltanschauungen').
It was at this gathering that Weber directly (and passionately) confronted a number of young left-
wing intellectuals (or littérateurs) who opposed the War. The writer Ernst Toller (*centre, back*) was
one of them. Eventually Toller was put on trial for his role in the Bavarian council republic. Weber,
despite all his misgivings about Toller's politics, was to come to his defence. Toller was spared the
death penalty.

2 A workers' home in Red Vienna (also more or less functional as a fortress for class warfare): Karl-Marx-Hof, 1927–30, Heiligenstädter Strasse, in the 19th district of the city. The complex contained more than 1,300 apartments; balconies and private toilets were distinct innovations – sometimes perceived as luxuries – for workers' homes. The Hof remains the longest residential building in the world.

3 The intellectual joins the battle: 'Commissar Lukács thanks the proletariat for its help in overcoming the counter-revolution', or so the official caption of this still from a newsreel tells us. Lukács is reported to have lectured his soldiers: 'If blood can be shed, and who would deny that it can be, then we are permitted to shed it. But we can't allow others to do it for us. We must take full responsibility for the blood that is shed. We must also provide an opportunity for our blood to be shed ... In short, terror and bloodshed are a moral duty, or, more plainly, our virtue.'

4 Stalin touted his constitution as the 'most Democratic in the World':
fold-out poster by El Lissitzky, 'The Stalin Constitution', from *USSR
in Construction* (1937). Another 1937 El Lissitzky poster bore the
inscription, 'Stalin's Constitution is the Soviet People's Happiness'. The
supposed 'Happiness' only came to an end in 1977: Stalin's constitution
turned out to be the Soviet Union's longest lasting.

5 Fascism finally has its doctrine and Italy its Encyclopedia: Mussolini, caught fumbling with his tie, looks anxious, but the others – *(from left to right)* Giovanni Treccani (the publisher), Calogero Tumminelli (the editor), Giovanni Gentile (the main philosopher of Fascism) and Ugo Spirito (who would later turn from Fascism to Communism) – seem rather confident.

6 No political thinker did more to reshape the Catholic Church's attitude towards liberal democracy and human rights: Jacques Maritain consults with Pope Paul VI in 1964. While a great proponent of Christian Democracy, Maritain was no friend of Christian Democratic parties; in the mid-1960s he declared: 'until today – and despite (or because of) the entry on the scene, in different countries, of political parties labeled "Christian" (most of which are primarily combinations of electoral interests) – the hope for the advent of a Christian politics has been completely frustrated'.

7 French students defy the bourgeois Right's lingering anti-Semitism – and, inadvertently, bring about a bit of European integration: 'Nous sommes tous des juifs et des allemandes' (we are all Jews and Germans), poster depicting 'Red Danny' – Daniel Cohn-Bendit (1988 reprint of the 1968 original).

8 The fourth 'M': Herbert Marcuse, maybe or maybe not looking like a messiah, lectures at the Free University in Berlin, 1967. He is surrounded by what Jacques Maritain might well have called 'prophetic shock minorites'.

9 Human Rights as a post-ideological – or perhaps post-political – consensus reconciling Left and Right: Jean-Paul Sartre (*centre*), André Glucksmann (*left*) and Raymond Aron (*right*) attend a government conference at the Elysée Palace on 26 June 1979. Glucksmann, the flamboyant New Philosopher, had brought the twentieth century's greatest French socialist philosopher and the twentieth century's greatest French liberal together to support Un Bateau pour le Vietnam, a group which provided assistance for Vietnamese refugees.

10 The general and the special intellectual unite forces for a
common cause: Jean-Paul Sartre and Michel Foucault protesting
about the treatment of Arab immigrants in the Goutte d'Or
quartier in the 18th arrondissement of Paris, 1971. This after
Foucault had observed of one of Sartre's major works: 'The critique
of dialectical reason is the magnificent and pathetic effort of a man
of the nineteenth century to think the twentieth. In this sense,
Sartre is the last Hegelian, and I would even say the last Marxist.'
Foucault certainly thought he would have the last laugh in the
battle over defining the role of the intellectual in twentieth-century
European politics.

Hayek now branched out into popular political pamphleteering. In 1944 appeared his bestseller *The Road to Serfdom* – which was adapted for an American audience by the *Reader's Digest* under the heading 'One of the Most Important Books of Our Generation', and even became the subject of a 'radio dramatization'. Hayek declared that the creation of the welfare state would necessarily lead down the road of totalitarianism. While the Nazis had lost the war, they could still win the battle of ideas, if Western European states – and Hayek's beloved Britain in particular – elected socialist governments. Hayek insisted that socialism, no matter how humane and well intentioned its leaders, necessarily meant the establishment of a central authority in charge of planning. There were two problems with such an authority: a practical one and a moral one. First of all, Hayek argued,

socialism . . . overlooks that the modern society is based on the utilization of widely dispersed knowledge. And once you are aware that we can achieve the great utilization of available resources only because we utilize the knowledge of millions of men, it becomes clear that the assumption of socialism that a central authority is in command of this knowledge is just not correct. I think the nicest form to put it is to say that socialism, protesting against production for profit and not for use, objects to what makes the extended society possible. Profit is the signal which tells us what we must do in order to serve people whom we do not know. By pursuing profit, we are as altruistic as we can possibly be, because we extend our concern to people who are beyond our range of personal conception.[81]

While he was trying to say nice things about socialism, Hayek could not help pointing out that it was plagued by a crucial moral problem: a central authority could never just benevolently distribute goods; it would have to make choices about priorities and values and thus ultimately need to impose one vision of the good life on society, rather than allowing citizens to co-ordinate their activities spontaneously. In short, there could be no such thing as a non-totalitarian socialism.

Hayek insisted that he was no anarchist, but that states should simply establish a framework of general and predictable laws – at times going so far as calling for a uniform minimum income for all citizens. Keynes would take him to task for the apparent indeterminacy of where general laws ended and arbitrary state intervention started:

you agree that the line has to be drawn somewhere, and the logical extreme is not possible. But you give us no guidance whatever as to where to draw it.

It is true that you and I would probably draw it in different places. I should guess that according to my ideas you greatly underestimate the practicability of the middle course. But as soon as you admit that the extreme is not possible, and that a line has to be drawn, you are, on your own argument, done for, since you are trying to persuade us that so soon as one moves an inch in the planned direction you are necessarily launched on the slippery path which will lead you in due course over the precipice.[82]

The British social theorist R. A. Tawney was also eager to show respect for Hayek's work. According to Tawney, 'he writes, as Burke was said to speak, with the expression of a man confronted by assassins. His honesty and competence are beyond question.'[83] But he insisted that the most important insight was that 'it all depends' on what he called 'the debatable land between economics and politics'. Planning, he argued, 'like parliaments and public education, is not a simple category. Its results depend, not upon the label attached to it, but on the purposes which it is designed to serve, the methods which it employs in order to realise them, and the spirit which determines the choice of both.'

The Road to Serfdom ended up playing a minor role in the 1945 general election in Britain when its ideas appeared to have been picked up by Winston Churchill. The Tory war hero argued in one of his election speeches that:

socialism is inseparably interwoven with totalitarianism and the object worship of the state. It will prescribe to every one where they are to work, what they are to work at, where they may go and what they may say . . . They would have to fall back on some form of Gestapo, no doubt very humanely directed in the first instance.[84]

The press promptly charged that Churchill was using 'Second-Hand Ideas from an Austrian Professor'.[85] He lost the election, and the Labour government seemed to go down the very road that the Austrian professor had warned about. Hayek, on the other hand, took what for an academic was an altogether less travelled path. He proceeded to found the Mont Pèlerin Society – a self-described 'nonorganisation of individuals',[86] but de facto an elite advance troop in the war of ideas, especially equipped to engage in close intellectual combat on the debatable land between economics and politics. Hayek demanded that 'we must raise and train an army of fighters for freedom'. He advocated a focus on intellectuals – professors, bureaucrats, teachers and journalists – as 'second-hand dealers in ideas', who, according to him, would always end up shaping public opinion in the long run. He also insisted that the young could be easily influenced, as long as they were given something to be enthusiastic about. Hence his urgent call for the construction of a 'liberal utopia'.

At the first meeting of the society in Switzerland, however, it was far from clear what exactly the right first-hand ideas for a liberal utopia were meant to be. Some argued for laissez-faire, some thought a renewal of Christianity was most important, some sang the old lament about mass society. One participant suggested that the association should be named the Acton–Tocqueville Society – an idea that was opposed with the observation that a mid-twentieth-century club for the refashioning of classical liberalism could not possibly be named after two nineteenth-century Catholic aristocrats. Karl Popper put forward the notion of the Pericles Society and pleaded for the inclusion of democratic socialists. In the end, having failed to find agreement, the founding members decided to name the Society simply after the place where the meeting had been held.

Until this point it all sounded rather second hand, but at least the 'fighters for freedom' were well financed. Hayek kept raising money for the Society from various American funds, while in Britain the chicken magnate Antony Fisher, wanting to repeat what the Fabian Society had done for the Labour Party, established the Institute of Economic Affairs in 1955. This think tank was essentially devoted to the promotion of Hayekian ideas – again, specifically among 'second-hand dealers in ideas', as opposed to political parties.

For now Hayek and his followers had little success with their crusade in Britain (or in the US for that matter). The only place where economic liberalism seemed to have experienced a lasting renaissance was Germany. There intellectuals of the so-called Freiburg School were close to the economics minister Ludwig Erhard – the father of the German 'economic miracle' – while also serving as members of the Mont Pèlerin Society.[87] In fact, when the society appeared to break up into different factions in 1960, Erhard offered to serve as a mediator.[88]

However, some representatives of German economic liberalism complained that Hayek had stolen the label 'neoliberal', when in fact he was nothing but a 'palaeoliberal', a man of the eighteenth century who sought the reinstatement of laissez-faire.[89] The social philosophers Wilhelm Röpke and Alexander Rüstow (Rüstow occupied Max Weber's chair in Heidelberg after the war) maintained that the old liberalism had been wrong to believe in a primacy of the market. States had to regulate markets tightly; in particular, they had to break up monopolies and ensure – even, if necessary, engineer – economic competition. Beyond that, Rüstow argued, governments had to engage in what he termed 'liberal interventionism' aimed at improving the concrete situation of individuals – or what he called their *Vitalsituation*. The ideal 'vital situation' was that of independent property owners – small peasants, for instance – which stood in

starkest contrast to the degraded life of the 'urban masses'.[90] Given that Europe
could not possibly return to the world of the smallholder, new ways would have
to be found to encourage self-reliant economic agents. Markets, then, were not
natural; they had to be guaranteed and often unclogged by states (which, to be
sure, always faced the danger of being captured by particular interests). But
neither was there anything natural or given about proper market participants;
they might have to be as much the creation of states.

Thus German neoliberalism absorbed some of the cultural pessimism
typical of the interwar and immediate post-war periods. It also had a curiously
authoritarian conception of the state: it wanted governments to engage in a
kind of popular pedagogy to educate 'the masses' about the virtues of a free
economic order.[91] But it was also much more social than caricatures of neoliberalism later assumed. The term 'politics of society' or *Gesellschaftspolitik* – a
concept unknown to earlier versions of liberalism – encapsulated the idea that
the state should mould society for the sake of freedom, while the phrase 'social
market economy' was partly justified by appealing to the ideal of property-
owning workers and entrepreneurs competing within a just framework set by
the state. It was the compromise formula on which liberals and Catholics could
agree and which served the German Christian Democrats so well.

Hayek, on the other hand, objected to the very term 'social' in 'social market
economy' and fell out with Röpke (who had also tried to interest him in
Christian personalism – unsuccessfully).[92] He persisted in what, with the
triumph of the post-war welfare and administrative state, seemed an increasingly quixotic quest. One day, though, he would emerge from what for now
appeared to be an ideological wasteland.

Decolonizing the European Mind

Western Europe (as opposed to the continent as a whole) appeared internally
pacified – it was divided up into nation-states that at least for the moment seemed
to have no claims on each other (and had they tried, the superpowers surely
would have stopped them). But European nation-states had also been making
claims on the rest of the world for centuries. Fascism had discredited imperialism,
and not just the continental-religious type of empire. After 1945 Western Europe
began to disengage from the world – not least to build its own Community more
effectively. But it also went into almost immediate denial about its imperial past.
Moreover, there was no inner connection between the particular post-war
European model of democracy and what Europeans were doing in and to the rest
of the world. It was indicative that the European Convention of Human Rights,
which came into force in 1953, was, for the most part, to apply only to Europeans.

Britain was the sole major European empire to extend the Convention to its dependencies (although it categorically refused a right of individual petition and the jurisdiction of the European Court of Human Rights, treating the Convention as largely symbolic).[93] Belgium did not extend the Convention to the Congo, and France did not ratify it until 1975.[94] Effectively, how empires behaved when decolonizing was very much left to their own conscience.

Impressive as they might have looked in terms of colouring the map, European empires had long been 'a vast confidence trick'.[95] On the eve of the Second World War, the British Empire in Africa involved 1,200 British colonial administrators ruling over a population of forty-three million black Africans, backed by around 900 Colonial Service police and military officials.[96] Imperial control could not have been accomplished without the collaboration of local elites to do what Orwell called 'the dirty work of Empire', and at least some form of acquiescence, or, put differently, rudimentary belief in legitimacy.

The Second World War changed all that, both because of the way it had progressed and because of the programmes which the victors had announced. For one thing, the early Japanese victories in the Far East destroyed the myth of white superiority, in particular symbolically charged events like the fall of colonial Singapore. As a British governor in the South Pacific had realized even before this disaster, 'the Heaven-born Big-White-Master theory of colonial administration began to crack up'.[97]

But programmes also mattered – even if they were disingenuous – because leaders became trapped by their own lip service to ideals. After all, the Allies fought in the name of anti-racism and anti-imperialism. As a member of parliament had announced on 3 September 1939 in the House of Commons, it was a war 'in its inherent quality, to establish, on impregnable rocks, the rights of the individual, and it is a war to establish and revive the stature of man'. And even Churchill, for it was he who had thus defined the war aims, could not easily backtrack from this.

Yet a surprising number of British politicians in particular persisted in the belief that all this would somehow not apply to them. But the leaders were taken at their word – and the great confidence trick could no longer be performed when people (or peoples) had lost confidence. As the Javanese nationalist leader Sukarno asked in October 1945:

Is liberty and freedom only for certain favoured peoples of the world? Indonesians will never understand why it is, for instance, wrong for the Germans to rule Holland if it is right for the Dutch to rule Indonesia. In either case the right to rule rests on pure force and not on the sanction of the population.[98]

Colonialism as fascism – or fascism as colonialism brought back to Europe: this was a compelling thought and it was articulated by thinkers as different as Hannah Arendt and the poet (and politician) Aimé Césaire, who hailed originally from Martinique.[99] The latter diagnosed in his highly influential 1951 *Discourse on Colonialism* that 'a poison has been instilled into the veins of Europe and, slowly but surely, the continent proceeds towards *savagery*'. Nazism treated Europeans like Africans: 'and then one fine day the bourgeoisie is awakened by a terrific reverse shock: the gestapos are busy, the prisons fill up, the torturers around the racks invent, refine, discuss'. Césaire extended this assessment to Europe's present and future:

> Whether one likes it or not, at the end of the blind alley that is Europe, I mean the Europe of Adenauer, Schuman, Bidault, and a few others, there is Hitler. At the end of capitalism, which is eager to outlive its day, there is Hitler. At the end of formal humanism . . . there is Hitler.[100]

Many in Europe concurred with the call by Frantz Fanon – originally also from Martinique – to 'leave this Europe where they are never done talking of Man, yet murder men everywhere they find them'. Fanon also most forcefully articulated the belief that violence might be a moral necessity and a precondition for creating a proper political identity. This view was famously endorsed by Jean-Paul Sartre in his preface to Fanon's *Wretched of the Earth*:

> he shows perfectly clearly that this irrepressible violence is neither sound and fury nor the re-emergence of savage instincts nor even a consequence of resentment: it is man recreating himself. I believe we once knew, and have since forgotten, the truth that no indulgence can erase the marks of violence; only violence itself can eliminate them. And the colonized are cured of colonial neurosis by thrusting out the settler through force of arms. Once their rage explodes, they recover their lost coherence, they experience self-knowledge through recreating themselves . . .[101]

And Sartre affirmed that 'aside from Sorel's fascist chatter, you will find that Fanon is the first since Engels to focus again on the midwife of history'.[102] The Algerian War (1954–62) – and the theses of Fanon, whom *Time* magazine derided as a 'prisoner of hate' – deeply split intellectual opinion in metropolitan France and elsewhere. For many observers such conflicts appeared to externalize the violence that, at least for the moment, had been expunged from Europe itself.

With the exception of Britain, empires not only disappeared from the map, they also vanished quickly from the political imagination. To some degree decolonization helped the left in countries like France to become reconciled to the very idea of 'Europe' – both as a civilization and in the concrete form of the newly created European Community (though it was of course tacitly assumed that 'Europe' meant Western Europe). During Vichy, French fascist leader (and active collaborator) Jacques Doriot had announced that France had to prove itself worthy of 'Europe' – that is, a Nazi European *pax Germanica*.[103] Decolonization was a precondition that 'Europe' might again be associated with and worthy of an egalitarian universalism. According to the French sociologist Edgar Morin, for instance, it was only through decolonization that the idea of Europe itself became 'purified' for his generation.[104] In a sense, Sartre, for all the shocking claims about violence in his preface to Fanon's book, had been right: Europe, too, had to be decolonized. By the 1970s it had become thinkable that both left and right (mainly in the form of Christian Democracy) could sign up again to something like a common European project.

The New Class Takes Over

Western Europe appeared like a (slightly bland) island of the blessed, sheltered from the harsh winds of world history by the United States. Certainly, the Cold War posed a kind of permanent apocalyptic threat, but it also offered a curious kind of protection. Obviously, Central and Eastern Europe had not been so lucky. Their post-war regimes initially followed the model of 'people's democracies' – 'popular front'-style governments by anti-fascist, strongly left-leaning and, crucially, pro-Soviet coalitions that undertook expropriations and consolidated homogeneous nation-states, mostly by expelling the German minorities. Stalin thought such a model moved the countries under his control closer to his kind of socialism, but also preserved a sense of national independence (though not too much of it: both notions of Slav unity and feelings of socialist brotherhood were to make what were also sometimes called 'new democracies' toe the Soviet line). To be sure, in 1945 many people in Central and Eastern Europe felt that both the interwar authoritarian regimes and Western capitalism had shown themselves to be conclusive failures – and that it was time for a revolutionary change. Nowhere did Communists come to power through democratic means, but it would be wrong to think that all experiments in establishing 'people's democracies' therefore obviously lacked legitimacy at the beginning.[105] It was just not always certain which way they were going – whereas intimidation and rigging elections, the course Stalin and his local followers eventually chose, left no uncertainty.

Almost all emerging Communist leaders had either spent the war years in Moscow or resisted the Nazis in their own countries. Younger converts to Communism had been deeply marked by the fear of what it would be like to live in Hitler's New Europe as 'subhumans'. Especially for this group, Stalin's victory over Nazism seemed to prove the historical truth of Soviet-style Communism. The Czech Communist intellectual Zdeněk Mlynář described the peculiar mentality of those who were around twenty at the end of the war and who turned into fervent Stalinists:

> My generation was made prematurely aware of politics by the stormy events of that period; at the same time we lacked political experience. The only experience we had was of the war years and the Nazi occupation of Czechoslovakia, and during some of this time we were still children. One of the chief results of this was a black-and-white vision of the world, with the enemy on one side and his adversary on the other . . . Thus our unique experience drummed into us the notion that the victory of the correct conception meant quite simply the liquidation, the destruction, of the other . . . We were children of the war who, having not actually fought against anyone, brought our wartime mentality with us into those first postwar years, when the opportunity to fight for something presented itself at last.[106]

As in Stalin's Soviet Union, the Central and Eastern European regimes also played on the register of democratic values: they invoked 'national fronts' of nominally independent parties and unions working together for socialism; they called for continuous mass participation as the only genuine form of democracy. In 1949 in Hungary 200,000 agitators were sent around the country to mobilize six million electors. Even though the outcome of the election was then a foregone conclusion, leaders were anxious about the actual numbers and keen to put on a convincing theatrics of democratic participation.[107] The 'people's democracies' of Central and Eastern Europe presented themselves as being in direct *democratic* competition with the West. Georg Lukács declared at a conference of European intellectuals in Geneva in September 1946,

> Europe today struggles for its new face. Formally, this struggle is between different types of democracy. The real issue revolves around the question of whether democracy remains legal and political in form, or becomes the real life-form of the people. And behind this problem lies the nature of political power. Should it be confined to the two hundred families or transferred to the working masses? In my view, only an ideological and political identity with the masses can create the new Europe.[108]

Not long after, Stalin switched tactics and tried to make all 'people's democracies' follow the Soviet model – which is to say, Stalinism.

The illusion that Stalin's Soviet Union was furthest ahead on the way towards an 'ideological and political identity with the masses' was shattered by Khrushchev's 'secret speech' at the Twentieth Party Congress in 1956. It is often overlooked that Khrushchev mainly denounced Stalin out of prudence and to pre-empt an investigation into his own conduct. He only really condemned Stalin for 'ignoring the norms of Party life' and for 'trampling on the Leninist principle of Collective party leadership', while sparing the Stalinist system more broadly. He exalted the role of the Leninist party (and its 'indissoluble unity with the masses') as the right model in contrast to 'all efforts to oppose a "hero" to the masses and the people'. In other words, people had to be reminded of who the real hero was: the party.[109]

Still, Soviet citizens could not fail to notice that things did begin to change, and that the public justifications the regime offered to its people changed with them. Khrushchev did not arraign his opponents at show trials and kill them, but rather sent them to be the heads of remote cement factories.[110] Some space opened up for intellectual and artistic dissent, although this was mostly the result of intra-Kremlin feuds. In 1962 Alexander Solzhenitsyn was able to publish, with Khrushchev's personal permission, his short story 'One Day in the Life of Ivan Denisovich', an unvarnished account of a day in the camps (though a rather bearable day, compared to the accounts of Ginzburg, for instance, or what Solzhenitsyn himself would describe in the *Gulag Archipelago* a decade later).

The principle of 'socialist legality' had been officially proclaimed in 1953 (which did not immediately raise high hopes: it had also been used by Stalin's prosecutors in the trials of the 1930s). With this new emphasis on juridical formalism came attempts at constitutional clean-ups – in particular, the offices of head of state and of party secretary were to be properly separated. Rule in the name of (manufactured) collective and, in the case of Stalin, individual charisma gave way to rule that at least in theory adhered to legal procedures and therefore could be called, in Weber's sense, 'rational' – even if central planning made for high levels of economic irrationality. The latter did not go unnoticed, but the solution Khrushchev imagined – 'more democracy' understood as narrowing the gap between the bureaucracy and the people by periodically replacing party officials – only contributed to his downfall. The leaders of the coup against him promised 'stability of cadres' instead of 'democratization campaigns'.[111]

The Polish poet Czesław Miłosz had written that 'when one considers the matter logically, it becomes obvious that intellectual terror is a principle that Leninism-Stalinism can never forsake, even if it should achieve victory on a world scale'. In a sense, the point still held true, except that intellectual terror became more intermittent and affected ordinary people less and less. A bargain seemed to take shape (though that is in many ways too positive a term, given that the people, as opposed to the party, had little to bargain with): acquiescence or, even better, political resignation in return for material goods, at least something that could look like implied consent for the sake of consumption. Professions of heartfelt ideological identification were demanded less and less. The personality cult was effectively over; if anything, it was replaced with a half-hearted 'cult of the state', which now at least got to share some of the party's (fading) charisma.[112] What under Stalin could plausibly be called an 'ideocracy' – the domination of and through ideas – gave way to what the Franco-Greek philosopher Cornelius Castoriadis would later label 'stratocracy', that is, domination by the military and a bureaucracy that accumulated power for power's sake (and, of course, for its own personal benefit). Speaking Bolshevik was still required, but especially younger people could easily see that they were simply confronted with an elaborate (and tedious) façade – what the Bulgarian intellectual Tzvetan Todorov, looking back on his youth in the 1950s, called a 'pseudo-ideocracy'.[113] In other words, hardly anybody believed in it – and everybody knew that hardly anybody believed in it. Stalinism seemed to be gone for good; after a 1956 trip to the USSR Isaiah Berlin reported his interlocutors as saying that 'a return to those horrors was unthinkable', although he added, 'save in so far as in Russia nothing was unthinkable'.[114]

And sometimes the unthinkable did happen in the world of Communism: Yugoslavia proved that Stalin could be rebuffed in the name of nationalism, while still claiming that one was building proper socialism. The country's leader, Marshal Tito, erstwhile leader of the only fully successful resistance movement against the Nazis, thereby also shattered the notion of a global, unified Communist movement by de facto committing the sin of 'factionalism' at the level of states.[115] It was a momentous event in the history of Communism: for the first time a Comintern-trained leader, a man promoted by the Kremlin, successfully defied the Soviet Union and Stalin's (and his successors') claim to a monopoly on truth.[116]

Subsequently, Yugoslavia became the subject of many Eastern and, especially, Western hopes – which largely turned out to be illusions. The country prided itself on the practice of worker self-management – in a sense trying to make good on the promises of genuine soviets which the Soviet Union had failed to keep. However, self-management was essentially imposed from above to shore up popular support at a time when the regime felt extremely threatened by Stalin and the 'socialist brother countries', whose economic and political systems the Yugoslavs now denounced as 'state capitalism'.[117]

The prime theoretician of the specifically 'Yugoslav road to socialism' was Milovan Djilas, a Serb Montenegrin from a remote mountain village. His father had been an officer, his grandfathers and great-uncles had been outlaws in the rugged little country on the Adriatic. He had fought as a Communist partisan, had met Stalin in Moscow in 1944, and was widely seen as Tito's potential successor. In the early 1950s, by then vice-president and a member of the Executive Committee of the Central Committee, he wrote a number of penetrating analyses of the way Yugoslavia was developing. His calls for more democracy earned him expulsion from the government and loss of all party positions in 1954 (his party number had been four). He subsequently gave an interview to the *New York Times*, hoping that outside attention would yield some personal security. However, rather than celebrity translating into political protection, Djilas' sensational revelations resulted in trial, conviction and time in prison. There he penned a novel and translated Milton's *Paradise Lost* on toilet paper.

He managed nonetheless to have a manuscript smuggled out of Yugoslavia to New York: *The New Class*, which pinpointed the emergence of a stratum of privileged bureaucrats who had betrayed the revolution to amass spoils. According to Djilas, 'the Communists were unable to act differently from any ruling class that preceded them. Believing that they were building a new and ideal society, they built it for themselves in the only way they could.'[118] In particular, he claimed, the relationship of the New Class to the means of production was one of political control, which the party bureaucrats would ceaselessly try to increase, in order to satisfy their vanity and desire for material goods. Summing up his indictment, Djilas argued that 'in contrast to earlier revolutions, the Communist revolution, conducted in the name of doing away with classes, has resulted in the most complete authority of any single new class. Everything else is sham and an illusion.'[119]

Saving the Honour of Socialism

It was only consistent that Djilas would support what turned out to be the most powerful challenge to these New Class dictatorships: the Hungarian uprising (or revolution – to name it is to make a judgement) of October and November 1956. Hungary's Stalinist regime had been exceptionally repressive; an attempt at a somewhat more moderate course under the reform Communist Imre Nagy after 1953 had failed, with Nagy being dismissed as prime minister and even excluded from the party. By 1956 discontent was widespread even within the party. The Petőfi Circle (named after Hungary's national poet, who had played a major role in the 1848 war of independence against the Habsburg Empire) acted as a kind of officially sanctioned inner opposition, encouraged by Khrushchev's secret speech. Its members, together with increasingly radicalized students, supported reform in Poland; they also called for the reinstatement of Nagy.

On 23 October, when the student demonstrations had swelled to mass rallies, the Petőfi Circle demanded: 'The Central Committee and the government should adopt every method possible to ensure the development of Socialist democracy by specifying the real functions of the Party, asserting the legitimate aspirations of the working class and introducing factory self-administration and workers' democracy.'[120] This was not the language of counter-revolution or quasi-fascist nationalism, as asserted by an increasingly panicky government. Demonstrations by workers and students appeared uncontrollable short of outright violent repression; the government was paralysed (which led Lukács to comment: 'nothing is worse than a weak-handed tyranny!').[121] In this highly combustible situation Nagy – just readmitted to the party – was pushed to address the huge crowds gathered outside the parliament building; when he started with the customary 'Comrades!', he was greeted with shouts of 'We're not comrades, we're not comrades.' He found no way to break out of party jargon. In the end he sang the national anthem. People sang with him. As two Marxist observers pointed out, a highly trained Bolshevik of thirty years' experience, a man who had worked closely with Bukharin, did not seem to know what to do with a genuinely revolutionary situation.[122]

Eventually Nagy was appointed prime minister. He edged towards party pluralism and was prepared to recognize all the parties that had been legal before Stalinist repression began in earnest in 1946 (it was decided to exclude the revival of fascist parties). Meanwhile, workers took over factories and formed their own councils; then they went on general strike. Nagy began to appoint non-Communists to his cabinet, while reiterating his commitment to building socialism in a neutral Hungary, outside the Warsaw Pact.

Someone else was appointed by Nagy: Georg Lukács. The philosopher had been purged from his university post in the late 1940s and had to engage in 'self-criticism' – not for the first time, as we saw, and, as it turned out, not for the last time. He now entered Nagy's government as minister of education and the arts – three and a half decades after having been a people's commissar in Kun's regime. The Soviet emissaries Anastas Mikoyan and Mikhail Suslov reported back to Moscow that 'chosen . . . was . . . Lukács, who is a famous philosopher, and although he caused a lot of confusion in the field of philosophy, is more trustworthy politically and authoritative among the intelligentsia.'[123] Lukács felt that Nagy was lacking any kind of coherent programme and that in any event 'Uncle Imre' was not a 'real politician.'[124] Lukács voted against withdrawing the country from the Warsaw Pact. Nagy, however, announced Hungary's neutrality, upon which the workers' councils resumed work. The Soviets invaded. Lukács never even set foot in his own ministry.

For all its brevity, there was one undeniable fact: this had been the first anti-socialist revolt (or, as some theorists put it, anti-totalitarian or at least anti-bureaucratic revolution) in which the working class had played a central role. This was clearly seen by the Hungarian politician and political theorist István Bibó, initially a member of the peasants' party, who observed that 'a party made up largely of bureaucrats and policemen [was] *standing against* the entire working class'.[125] Bibó was an intellectual known for his careful historical analyses and principled calls for moderation (some would dub him the Isaiah Berlin of *Mitteleuropa*). He had been appointed minister of state and ended up as the last major politician left in the parliament building next to the Danube when the Soviets closed in. He holed up on the second floor with a machine gun and sought desperately to make contact with the United Nations and the great powers. On the afternoon of 4 November, mistaken for a simple clerk, he was able to get out a declaration that 'Hungary does not wish to pursue an anti-Soviet policy. On the contrary, Hungary's full intent is to live in the community of free Eastern European nations which want to organize themselves on the principles of liberty, justice and freedom from exploitation.' Then he was arrested, imprisoned and put on trial. He escaped execution and, after an amnesty, was allowed to work as a librarian. Imre Nagy and other leaders – as well as Lukács – were flown to Romania. Nagy was tried. He claimed that the trial violated socialist legality. His last words in public were:

> I have attempted . . . to save the honour of the word 'socialism' in the basin of the Danube . . . In this trial . . . I have to sacrifice my life for my ideas. I willingly sacrifice it. After what you have done to these ideas, my life has no value any longer . . . One thing alone would repulse me: to be rehabilitated by those who will murder me.[126]

He received the death sentence and was hanged in June 1958. Lukács was permitted to return to Hungary in 1957. He later claimed that the Romanian guard assigned to work on him ideologically eventually had to be sent to a psychiatric clinic.

What did '56 mean? Some observers thought the result of a successful uprising and secession from the Soviet bloc might have been the creation of a real council democracy, or at least a dual power of parties on the one hand and councils on the other (without this dual power becoming unstable in the way it had in Russia in 1917).[127] Hannah Arendt saw 1956 as evidence that a people freed from the constraints of government would not be lawless, but form councils and committees to organize their affairs – the old dream of self-management appeared to be alive in the ruins of Budapest.

And indeed the programme which János Kornai and other young economists were working on for Nagy was to contain elements of 'market socialism'
as well as 'workplace democracy'. Kornai and his colleagues also insisted that
nationalizations and welfare programmes were not to be scaled back.[128] This
matched the 'Draft of a compromise solution of the Hungarian question',
which Bibó had worked out: his constitution was to be based on a dual rejection of fascism and Stalinism by the Hungarian people; it was to contain full
civil liberties and democracy. But Bibó also dismissed the idea of reversing
the land and factory expropriations of the 1940s – an implicit admission that
even the worst kind of state socialism had meant some measure of modernization, in that it had broken the power of the reactionary landed magnates.
Potentially, then, there might have been a unique combination of socialism
and worker self-management in industry, economic liberalism in agriculture, parliamentary democracy and, finally, some form of 'anti-imperialist
nationalism'.[129]

However, things simply moved too quickly for any real institutional
blueprint to emerge, or for any obvious social consensus – other than an anti-
Stalinist one – to crystallize. The aspirations of a genuinely popular movement
from below outran the (in any event highly improvised) goals of reform
Communists at the top.[130] Thirteen days were too short for a revolution, when
the one self-declared revolutionary superpower would not stand for it – even
though, as critical Marxists pointed out, what had happened in Budapest was
probably as close as the dry party slogan 'self-education of the masses in the
revolutionary process' would ever get to reality.[131]

The crushing of '56 did not mean that nothing would change. In one sense,
the triumph of consensus politics in Western Europe now also found at least a
small parallel in the East – which is not to suggest that there was 'convergence'
between East and West, as a number of analysts began to argue in the late 1950s.
Hungary's post-1956 government offered consumerism – albeit a drab version
compared to Western Europe – in exchange for political acquiescence or (from
the regime's point of view, even better) cynicism. It was stability at almost any
price, and one price – from the perspective of the vanguard party – was ideological apathy. János Kádár, the post-insurrection leader who served at Moscow's
discretion, announced what amounted to the exact opposite of a principle of
totalitarian mobilization: 'He who is not against us is for us.' Kádár even went on
record as claiming that 'people don't exist just so that we may test out Marxism
on them.'[132] As much as possible, he removed politics from people's lives.
Analysts in the West began to speak of 'welfare Communism', or, in a more
homely phrase, of 'goulash Communism', sometimes going so far as to claim that
the regime had achieved 'legitimation through compromise', when in fact it had

merely pacified society.[133] The shrewd Kádár himself carefully avoided calling what he was doing a 'model', so as not to provoke Moscow.[134]

But welfare Communism was costly, and increasingly the countries of Central and Eastern Europe would rely on Western credits to keep up the implicit social contract. None could solve the problem of what Kornai had called the 'softening of the budget constraint' – the fact that there was no market to punish inefficient enterprises, and hence no constraint on spending. There appeared to be an irresolvable conflict between efficiency considerations and the ethical principles of a truly socialist economy.[135]

Ironically, just as some of the 'people's republics' more or less openly retreated from totalitarian aspirations, disillusionment spread among the intellectual supporters of Communism in the West. After 1956, one heard much less of arguments along the lines that 'over the dream of a socialism without defect, Russian socialism had the immense advantage of existing' or of ledgers that compared 'the misfortunes of the people imprisoned by the Russians' with the victims of Western colonialism. Sartre could still write: 'must we call this bloody monster that tears at its own flesh by the name of Socialism? My answer is, quite frankly, yes.'[136] For more and more people on the left the frank answer had to be: no.

The Skull that Would Never Smile Again

The limits of Moscow's tolerance of its satellites – and, above all, the capacity of Communism to change itself – were to be tested once more: the 'Prague Spring' in 1968 was the last major effort at a reform of Soviet-style socialism from within, before Mikhail Gorbachev came to power. Under the leadership of Alexander Dubček the Czechoslovak Communist Party set out to construct what they optimistically referred to as 'a new model of socialist society, deeply democratic and adapted to Czechoslovak conditions' – or, as the catchphrase went, 'socialism with a human face'. Market elements were introduced and price controls loosened, as theorized by the leading reform economist Ota Šik. In retrospect Dubček insisted that 'neither my allies nor I ever contemplated a dismantling of socialism, even as we parted company with various tenets of Leninism . . . We also believed that socialism could function better in a market-oriented environment.' And yet, as he had to realize soon enough, the Soviets might not stand for it:

This proposal, I should say, was immediately viewed by the Soviets as the beginning of a return to capitalism. Brezhnev made this accusation directly during one of our conversations in the coming months. I responded that we needed a private sector to improve the market situation and make people's lives easier. Brezhnev immediately snapped at me, 'Small craftsmen? We know about that! Your Mr. Bata used to be a little shoemaker, too, until he started up a factory!' Here was the old Leninist canon about small private production creating capitalism 'every day and every hour'. There was nothing one could do to change the Soviets' dogmatic paranoia.

Still, this outcome had not been easily predictable. Czechoslovakia in the early 1960s had faced an undeniable political and economic crisis.[137] Once a highly developed part of the Habsburg Empire – far richer than Italy – it now had the lowest living standards in the Eastern bloc. Many highly trained younger people, professionals in particular, could work only in positions for which they were vastly overqualified. De-Stalinization was explicitly rejected: in 1957 the party newspaper *Rudé Pravo* editorialized: 'the ambiguous word "de-Stalinization" stands only for the idea of weakening and giving way to the forces of reaction . . .'[138]

In a new constitution promulgated in 1960 the government declared that socialism had been achieved (changing the name of the country to the Czechoslovak Socialist Republic); they also insisted that there were no longer 'class antagonisms' in what was now termed an 'all-people's state' – a concept inspired by Khrushchev and, arguably, by Stalin's project of Soviet people-making. This claim led to jurists demanding real 'socialist legality' instead of the violence associated with the Manichaean thinking described by Mlynář. He and others who had become fervent Stalinists in the 1940s were now in their mid-thirties or even early forties. Mlynář himself had travelled to Yugoslavia and been much impressed with self-management; he had been even more impressed during visits to Italy and to Belgium at the time of the Brussels World Exposition. His political cohort could see every day that state socialism had not kept its promises, and many of them sincerely sought to understand why. Sociology was rehabilitated as a discipline. Its practitioners promptly demonstrated that social stratification remained a fact.[139]

However, all remaining problems, or so the regime itself now suggested, would be addressed by pushing further the 'scientific-technological revolution' – a claim that seemed not completely implausible, given that the Soviets had recently sent the first satellite into space and appeared to be competing head to head with the West in at least some technologies. The party set up a number of research commissions, led by experts. The experts pointed out that technology was now really driving economic progress, and that technocrats ought to be seen as members of the progressive working class. The Marxist revolutionary would be an engineer or computer programmer; 'the liberated, unalienated free agent of history now wore a white collar'.[140]

Intellectuals felt and then furthered the changes. Karel Kosík had been a Stalinist in his youth and participated in the resistance against the Nazis; eventually he was imprisoned in Theresienstadt. He had studied in Leningrad and subsequently became a philosophy professor at Charles University in Prague. Now he promoted the idea of 'praxis' as central to a humanist Marxism; others began to engage with existentialism and Gramsci. Socialist realism in art was abandoned alongside Stalinist political thought. Ironically, a more subjective and humanist Marxism emerged with the ascendancy of the new technocratic intelligentsia.

After Dubček's ascent to power in January 1968, censorship was first relaxed and then effectively abolished – with Dubček insisting all along that the party's monopoly on power must not be abandoned: reform was in no way to threaten the 'party-state'; it was just about expanding 'space' or 'scope' for participation.[141] The party, whose leading role had been codified in the 1960 constitution (an example to be followed by many other socialist states), would now have to earn its position and serve as the vehicle to advance progress. It was to attract the best and the brightest to solve society's problems; it would become an instrument of cognition, rather than coercion.[142] After all, there was still the fact that unlike anywhere else in Central and Eastern Europe Communists had actually won elections (though not in Slovakia) after the war. This fostered the illusion that somehow Communism could still enjoy full popular legitimacy.

Mlynář went further. He co-authored the Communist Party's 'Action Programme' of April 1968 and called for a synthesis of socialist economics and full-fledged pluralist democracy, though carefully hedging his bets with the corollary that all groups and interests could eventually be 'united' again. This vision was to be realized in some form of corporatism, with state-guided interest representatives articulating the demands of workers in industry, agriculture and services.[143] According to Mlynář, the party itself was to retain its leading role for now, but rather than being the 'universal "caretaker" of society', it was to revert to its charismatic role in order to 'inspire socialist initiative . . . and to win over all workers by systematic persuasion and the personal example of communists'.[144] The party should have been ready to contest (and win) free elections towards the end of the 1970s. By contrast Lukács, in the course of '56, had assumed that a thoroughly renewed Communist Party might get 10 per cent of the votes.[145]

Dubček seemed to calculate that Moscow would not intervene as long as the country made no move to leave the Warsaw Pact; this, he thought, had been Hungary's crucial mistake. In the eyes of many observers, the 'controlled liberalization' from above did strengthen whatever legitimacy the Communist Party might have had at that point.[146] Unlike in Hungary – and unlike Poland in the early 1980s – people did not organize themselves *against* the state, because the real opposition appeared to be between the old party elite on the one hand and the 'party masses' and the 'non-party masses' on the other, as Kosík put it.

And yet there was no way Moscow would countenance the possible loss of power by a Communist Party. On 21 August Warsaw Pact troops rumbled through the streets of Prague. Mlynář much later, in a conversation with Mikhail Gorbachev, described what happened to the leadership – including their beliefs about socialism:

> We . . . were in a conference room together with Dubček, when bursting into the room there came soldiers of the Soviet Taman division and one of them took his place behind each of us and aimed a Kalashnikov submachine gun at our backs. One's concept of socialism at such a moment moves to last place, but unconsciously at the same time you know that it has a direct connection of some sort with the automatic weapon pointing at your back.[147]

Dubček was forced to implement what euphemistically came to be known as 'normalization'; then he was pushed out, expelled from the party and made to work in the Czech forestry service. Kosík had to leave the party and was prohibited from publishing anything; the secret police repeatedly seized even his research notes. Mlynář was also expelled, almost exactly a quarter-century after he had joined the party; he devoted himself to the study of beetles in the National Museum. And Šik, Dubček's deputy in the summer of 1968, emigrated to Switzerland; he claimed that the West was moving closer to a 'state-bureaucratic' form of economy, while the East remained caught in Soviet-style 'state monopoly capitalism', and that only the third way of a genuine democratic socialism was legitimate.[148] Others became more sceptical. The Hungarian Kornai – now part-time at Harvard – insisted that 'history does not provide such supermarkets in which we can make our choice as we like'.[149]

In response to events in Prague, Leonid Brezhnev announced that the 'weakening of any of the links in the world system of socialism directly affects all the socialist countries, and they cannot look indifferently upon this'. This naked reaffirmation of Soviet power – soon known as the 'Brezhnev doctrine' – led the Czech writer Milan Kundera to conclude rather apocalyptically:

> What was actually at stake behind the smokescreen of political terminology (revolution, counter-revolution, socialism, imperialism, and so on, and so forth) was nothing less than a shift in the borders between two civilizations: the Russian imperium had once and for all conquered a piece of the West,

a piece of Europe ... Some day Russian mythographers will write about it as a new dawn in history. I see it (rightly or wrongly) as the beginning of Europe's end.[150]

But the political terminology *did* matter; and the events of 1968 signalled not the decline of Europe, but the beginning of Communism's end. The Prague Spring was the last instance of 'reform Communism' or 'revisionism' with any real credibility in East or West. In 1974, after having been forced out of Poland, Leszek Kołakowski declared categorically apropos the Marxist revisionism of which he had been a leading proponent in the 1950s: 'This skull will never smile again.'[151]

The Hungarian revolt had largely – but by no means completely – discredited ideological fellow-travelling in the West. The crushing of the Prague Spring, as a kind of late 'offshoot of Khrushchevism', ended all hopes that a governing Communist Party could reform itself – as long as there was an unreformed Soviet Union.[152] Many Western socialists now gave up on all 'people's democracies'. The British socialist Ralph Miliband, for instance, who had continued to view the Soviet Union favourably on a visit there in 1961, wrote to a friend in 1968, apropos the 'Czech business' (and also apropos student unrest in France), that 'I haven't got a proper grip' and that 'I am ... very muddled.' But for many left-wing observers the muddle disappeared as soon as they observed Czech 'normalization' unfolding. Miliband now declared the Eastern bloc as consisting of 'bureaucratic collectivist' states.[153] The conscious or often only half-conscious assumption of so many on the Western left – that these polities, for all their momentous failings, might somehow be moving towards socialism – was shattered.

'Reform Communism' had to be a structural contradiction, as long as there was no account of how a Leninist vanguard party should undo itself on the road to Communism – and there was no such account by the late 1960s, and there would be no such account until the very end of the Soviet Union. Thus the 'leading party' itself could not exorcise what Imre Nagy had called 'the Bonapartist spirit of minority dictatorship' – unless, like some of the Czech reformers, it saw a one-time election in the past as providing enough legitimacy to reach some more or less unknown point in the future when realized socialism had become so irresistibly attractive that somehow the electionless period in between could be justified.[154]

But this was clearly a bit of a stretch. None of these vanguard parties – half self-appointed, half Soviet-appointed – could ever claim to be a charismatic institution. In the immediate post-war period anti-fascism had given them some credibility initially – but, with that gone, there remained the worst of traditionalism and 'bureaucratism'. And it seemed to be getting worse still. In Poland Adam Michnik drew the conclusion that 'there is no such thing as non-totalitarian ruling communism', although the post-1956 development of Hungary might have suggested that there was indeed such a thing; there was just no such thing as *non-authoritarian* Communism: terror could be dispensed with, but not the police state. This is precisely the lesson Mlynář drew in retrospect: the best one could get, he thought, was something like Kádár's Hungary, a version of how Khrushchevism might have developed, with extra doses of cynicism – but 'in that case there was hardly any point in starting at all'.[155] Václav Havel put the point simply: 'the fun was definitely over'; and now began an 'era of gray, everyday totalitarian consumerism'.[156] The claim that Georg Lukács made until the very end of his life was hardly self-evident any longer: the worst form of socialism was better than the best form of capitalism.[157]

Czechoslovak reform Communism had always had a strong technocratic trait – with its faith in comprehensive social engineering (or, rather, re-engineering) by experts, and economists and sociologists in particular. True, there were calls for workers' councils and self-management, but given the ideological constraints (unlike in Hungary), what else could reformers have said? There was thus little similarity with the other, Western '68 – to which we now turn – the '68 that was politically inconsequential in comparison with the Prague Spring, but that was the clearest expression of a rebellion against technocracy, what Lukács had called the 'cybernetic religion' which imagined machines increasingly running the world all by themselves. But it was also directed more specifically against post-war consensus politics, against the notion of democracy as tightly constrained parliamentarism, and the seemingly ever more powerful administrative state. Prague had been about a reform movement for a modicum of pluralism and constitutionalism. By contrast, the Western '68 was, in a deep sense, anti-constitutionalist.

CHAPTER 5

The New Time of Contestation
Towards a Fatherless Society

The State exercises the monopoly of physical violence and claims thereby the exorbitant privilege of distinguishing what belongs to the commerce of ideas and what constitutes an exchange of blows. With the pretext of protecting the freedom of pure ideas, it gives itself the freedom to define what is an idea and what is not. Monopolizing the use of force, and thereby determining the use of ideas, the State proclaims in the last analysis: 'I am the only philosopher.'

André Glucksmann, July 1968

We have no desire to seize the state, like Trotsky or Lenin, but to take over the world, a necessarily more difficult passage, as well as being more general and more gradual, less spectacular. Our methods will vary according to the empirical facts we meet here and now, there and later . . . taking over the world must be in the largest sense cultural.

A member of the Situationist International

democracy has no ground which is favourable to the principle of authority in general and to the Fuehrer-ideal in particular. Insofar as the father is the archetype of authority, because the original experience of all authority, democracy is, according to its idea, a fatherless society.

Hans Kelsen

Men must learn to be silent. This is probably very painful for them . . . One has scarcely the time to experience an event as important as May '68 before men begin to speak out, to formulate theoretical epilogues, and to break the silence. Yes, these prating men were up to their old tricks during May '68.

Marguerite Duras, 1973

Illusions, in so far as they guide political action, can have real historical conse-
quences. They open up alternatives and do not dissolve without a remainder in
a history that is essentially determined by laws of movement and structural
constraints.

Ulf Kadritzke, German student leader

THE TWENTIETH century demonstrated that Europe was no longer central to world politics. It had done so brutally in the First and Second World Wars; in a less obvious – and, of course, less brutal – way the 1960s were also to drive home this point. The decade seemed to synchronize political and cultural dissatisfaction around the globe – what the CIA at the time referred to as a 'world-wide phenomenon of restless youth' (another American institution, *Time* magazine, would actually declare youth the 'Man of the Year' in 1967). Outside Western Europe, the political stakes were clearly very high: the Vietnam War, the brutal crushing of student protest in Mexico, the Cultural Revolution in China and, in East-Central Europe, the suppression of the Polish March (in fact, the first '68 student uprising – brutally suppressed by a party-state which also unleashed a vile anti-Semitic campaign to divide intellectuals from workers) and the Prague Spring. It was Western Europe that seemed to have the least at stake, though it nevertheless produced the iconic images of '68. As was often pointed out, west of Czechoslovakia 'no one died', no government fell and there was certainly nothing comparable to 170,000 Warsaw Pact troops invading a small country seeking socialism with a human face. For a number of not even partic- ularly conservative observers, '68 – and the 1960s more broadly – seemed to have been about a small minority of spoilt children playing revolution. Raymond Aron, the leading French liberal of his time, was to heap scorn on what he perceived as a mere 'psychodrama' (a diagnosis also endorsed by Communists such as Eric Hobsbawm); Ernest Gellner, the British social anthropologist of Czech background, diagnosed the 'mad logic of a family quarrel'; and even some of the protagonists themselves ultimately came to the conclusion that they had just been engaged in a huge 'costume drama'.[1]

So many myths or, to use a more neutral term, collective memories were to surround the various 'events' of the 1960s that it is hard to get a real sense not just of what, if anything, actually happened, but also of what the intentions of the protagonists might have been. Some observers saw '68 as the birth of a form of left-wing libertarianism in Europe; others lamented it as a return of political romanticism, or of anarchism, or even of fascism. As one historian noted, 1968 seemed more like 'an interpretation in search of an event'.[2]

Interpretations revolving around unintended consequences have had a particular appeal. It has often been claimed that the revolt had largely positive effects, but effects very much contrary to the intentions of the protagonists: the line between high culture and low culture was blurred, social life became less hierarchical, and dissent and even civil disobedience more accepted as part of normal democratic politics. Jürgen Habermas was to speak of a 'fundamental liberalization', others mentioned 'modernization' and even Americanization.[3] Many protagonists agreed with such interpretations, while admitting that in retrospect the events made them cringe. Daniel Cohn-Bendit, the Franco-German student leader often dubbed 'Red Danny', claimed: 'When one watches footage of '68 today, listens to the speeches, it's a catastrophe. It really hurts.'

Conservatives, meanwhile, would not just agree with the French writer and Gaullist politician André Malraux that '68 was a 'crisis of civilization'; they maintained that the '68ers exhibited a basic contempt for democratic institutions, because they were averse to *any* institutions. Why? Because institutions as such implied recognition of some authority. This anti-authoritarianism, so the charge continued, had inflicted long-term damage on the political cultures of Western Europe. In the most extreme version of this argument '68 had led directly to the terrorism of the 1970s: the Red Army Faction in Germany and the Red Brigades in Italy.

Understanding the political thought of '68 is not obviously the best way into comprehending the phenomenon of 'restless youth'. Yet the participants themselves clearly believed that their actions were inseparable from political theory: they were driven by theory, but, so they thought, their practical experiences would in turn push theory further. And theory necessarily had to loom large, because of the particular historical situation the students felt they were facing – the post-war constitutional settlement with its highly constrained understanding of democracy, and the self-consciously anti-ideological consensus politics of the 1950s and 1960s which froze out the radical left and sometimes led to banning Communist parties altogether. The seemingly 'thoughtless' emphasis on stability and productivity, as well as depoliticized private life and – not least – the continuous dominance of political patriarchs like de Gaulle, reinforced a sense of political suffocation. Hence many students not just in the US were receptive to what the sociologist C. Wright Mills articulated in his famous 1960 'Letter to the New Left':

> The end-of-ideology is on the way out because it stands for the refusal to work out an explicit political philosophy. And alert men everywhere today do feel the need of such a philosophy. What we should do is to continue directly to confront this need. In doing so, it may be useful to keep in mind that to have a working political philosophy means to have a philosophy that enables you to work . . .

Thus theorizing as such already seemed a highly political gesture against consensus politics.

Yet it would be wrong to assume that what the Italians were to call the great *contestazione* was simply rooted in some kind of cultural opposition to what Aragon had derided as a *civilisation de frigidaires*. The most immediate motivation for protest was the Vietnam War or, more broadly speaking, a sense of Western hypocrisy vis-à-vis the Third World. Many French leftists had first been radicalized by the experience of the Algerian War, while the German student movement really took off with the brutal suppression of demonstrations against the Shah of Iran's visit to Berlin in June 1967 – for many a symbol of a cruel and corrupt dictatorship not just condoned but actively supported by the West.

Thus while not all students knew what they were for, almost all knew what they were against: according to German student leader Rudi Dutschke '68 started with 'existential disgust'.[4] The flipside of the anger about Western hypocrisy, however, turned out to be an idealization of Third World liberation struggles, and the mystique of the guerilla leader in particular (a frequent slogan ran: 'War no, guerilla action yes'). It was not an accident that the terrorist groups of the 1970s would style themselves as 'urban guerillas'.[5]

Vietnam was one cause of 'existential disgust', but there were others of a quite different nature, and closer to home: the Europe-wide crisis of higher education effectively precipitated by the heavy expansion of universities without any change to inherited institutional frameworks. In 1958, there had been 175,000 university students in France; in 1968 there were 530,000. In Italy the number almost doubled after examinations for university entrance were abolished in 1965.[6] The problem hardly went unnoticed by state officials – though there were also many conservatives who opposed the whole trend as such: the British writer Kingsley Amis, for instance, insisted categorically that 'more will mean worse'. But, as so often, the explosion came just at the moment when state reforms were first showing results.

It was partly a matter of style. Change-from-above was usually presented in an entirely technocratic and managerial idiom; an infamous Italian book even analysed the university as an 'entreprise'.[7] In response to such top-down, efficiency-driven approaches, the so-called Strasbourg Manifesto, entitled *On the Poverty of Student Life* and authored by radical student activists, had declared in 1966:

> the student is the most universally despised creature in France, apart from the priest and the policeman ... Once upon a time the universities had a certain prestige; the student persists in the belief that he is lucky to be there.

But he came too late. His mechanical, specialized education is as profoundly degraded ... as his own intellectual level, because the modern economic system demands a mass production of uneducated students who have been rendered incapable of thinking.[8]

Something else still gave decisive shape to the movements of the 1960s, and also profoundly affected not just the practice but also the purposes of political thought: the small screen. This was the first revolution that would be televised. As Cohn-Bendit pointed out later, the various student leaders effectively met through television and, not least, got inspired by what others were doing. Europeans were to import many of the methods of the American civil rights movement and US student protest, such as sit-ins, go-ins and teach-ins (very few young people had actually been to the United States, though there were exceptions – for instance, the German student leader K. D. Wolff had been on a freedom ride in Mississippi). But theorists like Dutschke also insisted that, with the internationalization of communication, the revolution now necessarily had to have an international character: 'student rebellion in one country' was not an option. Less tangibly than all this, television gave everyone a sense of immediacy – and, above all a sense of their world-historical importance. What was happening had to be important, since, after all, it was on television.

What came to be known as May '68 had partly been started by an often narrated encounter. In January 1968 the French minister for youth and sports, François Missoffe, was visiting the new university of Nanterre, a concrete monstrosity which had no co-ed dormitories; he was to open a new swimming pool (to avoid anything funny from happening, no students had been invited). Outside he was accosted by a young red-haired, baby-faced student who asked for a light and calmly demanded: '*Monsieur le ministre*, I have read your white paper on youth. In three hundred pages there is not one word on the sexual problems of young people.' The minister, he continued, had no right to speak about young people. Missoffe, a decorated *Résistance* fighter, responded by saying that he was there to promote sports programmes. The redhead – none other than Cohn-Bendit – persisted, until the minister tried to shake him off with the immortal words: 'I am sure with your kind of face you actually know these problems. I suggest you take a dip in the pool.' Cohn-Bendit shot back: 'Now there's an answer worthy of the Hitler Youth!'[9]

In general, the reaction of the authorities to protest was heavy-handed and appeared to betray a surprising amount of insecurity. On the one hand, they would not take them seriously. De Gaulle claimed that May '68 was simply about students not wanting to take their exams; at one point he announced:

'reforms yes, but no bedwetting'. The British Labour minister for education thundered about 'thugs of the academic world' who – this clearly made matters worse – were 'not even respectable Marxists' (a statement echoed by the French Communist Party whose leader dismissed Cohn-Bendit as a mere 'German anarchist').[10]

On the other hand, students were demonized as a grave threat to the state. In fact, de Gaulle himself eventually lost his calm and, at the height of the *événements*, mysteriously disappeared to Germany for a day to consult with General Massu, the notorious strategist of the Battle of Algiers. After his return and a steadying of nerves, the General called on his followers, and a million Frenchmen marched on the Champs-Elysées, with almost everyone singing the Marseillaise and some apparently shouting 'Send Cohn-Bendit to Dachau.'[11]

Theory? No, Thanks

Did 'restless youth' have any positive political programme? The paradox is that the sound of the 1960s was heavily philosophical: Marx exegesis by highly idiosyncratic and difficult thinkers like Louis Althusser in Paris, the rediscovery of the writings of the Marxist–Freudian Frankfurt School from the interwar period, and the conscious turn of British left-wing thinkers such as Perry Anderson and others associated with the recently founded *New Left Review* to continental theory (and away from allegedly superficial British empiricism). And yet, despite all the theoretical work – and not least the tortured theorizing of the relationship between theory and praxis – there remained a sense that everyone simply had to be learning by doing, or, put more simply, making it up as they went along. It was not an accident that 'en route' became a favourite phrase among French student leaders. Cohn-Bendit also spoke of 'learning through action', while Dutschke talked about a 'unity of action and reflection'. Almost all radicals ultimately appeared to trust that events themselves would somehow 'practically problematize' – as one of the most telling phrases went – the elements of theory which seemed doubtful or confused.

But there was also the temptation to jettison theory altogether, and instead put all energy into creativity and spontaneity, and hope for shock and imagination as the real revolutionary instruments. Slogans such as 'Imagination should take power' and 'Be realistic: demand the impossible' seemed far more inspiring than convoluted Marxisant theorizing. In Italy, 'book fetishism' became an accusation in its own right;[12] even the German student movement – supposedly most weighed down by turgid political philosophy – produced the slogan 'Theorie? Nein, danke.'

Yet, with all the retrospective myth-making and selective memory of cute slogans such as 'It is prohibited to prohibit', one thing is most easily forgotten: the leaders actually did speak the language of revolution (though often interestingly hedged: the leaders of the 22 March movement in France, for instance, talked about a 'non-catastrophic revolution'). They did not regard themselves as 'reformers' or 'liberalizers'. Even the 'long march through the institutions' which Dutschke famously advocated was not a kind of 'reform from within', a fact immediately obvious when the formula is read in context: 'the long march through the institutions is the subversive use of the contradictions and possibilities within and outside the political–social apparatus, so as to destroy this apparatus in a long process'.

To be sure, revolution was commonly presented as a revolution in consciousness. In almost all theorists' accounts, revolution had to be initiated by a minority who, through provocation or 'direct action', demonstrated to majorities the sham nature of merely 'formal democracy' and the pathologies of capitalism. In Germany the students were often officially dismissed as 'a small radical minority'. That was precisely the point, and soon enough the students themselves were shouting as they marched, 'We are a small radical minority!'

Many leaders shared a perception of what they were up against: 'formal democracy', or, as Dutschke characterized it at one point, 'unreasonable democracy', or an 'authoritarian welfare state' and 'repressive tolerance', in Herbert Marcuse's seminal formulations. At the same time, it is surprising that many theorists' descriptions of what had gone wrong with democracy and liberal institutions like parliaments relied on naive ideals and implausible historical accounts of what *liberalism* had been like in nineteenth-century Europe. Contrasting institutions as they actually functioned under conditions of mid-twentieth-century industrial mass democracy with an imaginary golden age was a typical theoretical move – one that showed affinities with Carl Schmitt's anti-parliamentarism of the 1920s.

Also actually quite liberal was the master concept of '68: autonomy. What was not liberal in any historical sense of the word were the institutions which students and workers proposed to bring about autonomy: self-management as realized in workers' councils, students' councils, peasants' councils, 'direct democracy' and 'direct action in factory and street' – all invoked to replace the existing 'industrial and administrative monarchy'.[13] Established left-wing forces, especially the Communist trade unions, dismissed concepts such as *autogestion* as 'formulas without content'. But many of these institutions were in fact quite 'old left', derived from long-standing socialist, syndicalist or anarchist traditions.[14] As many observers noted, the political language of '68, as far as positive prescription was concerned, seemed sometimes strangely archaic, almost like a last hurrah for nineteenth-century radicalism. Even the highly unorthodox Situationists – whom we shall shortly look at more closely – sent a telegram to the politburos in Moscow and Beijing which affirmed the old dream of workers' councils, though in typically shocking style: 'Tremble Bureaucrats Stop The international power of workers' councils will soon sweep you away Stop Humanity will not be happy until the day when the last bureaucrat will be hung with the entrails of the last capitalist Stop.'

What is most striking, given the developments in Western European political thought and practice which we traced in the previous chapter, is that self-management and most other student demands specifically denied the principles which had been central to the post-1945 constitutional settlement. The French student leader Alain Geismar and many others explicitly opposed all 'delegation of power', and in fact the 'refusal to delegate' became characteristic of student movements across Europe. In Italy, for instance, the slogan went 'We are all delegates' and the 'sovereignty of the general meeting' was declared.[15] Direct democracy was to take the place of the highly cautious and restricted conception of democracy that European elites had endorsed after 1945.

The political failure of '68 is explained less by what critics saw as the utopian nature of proposals such as self-management and more by the complete absence (with the partial exception of Italy) of a social basis for the movement. The search for what the American sociologist C. Wright Mills had called 'historical agencies of structural change' and the famous 'question of organization' were symptoms of this problem. The latter especially never came even close to any kind of answer, although until about 1970 there appeared to be a consensus against forming Leninist vanguard groups.[16] At the end of what one sociologist derided as 'shopping for the revolutionary subject' the basket remained empty. Increasingly desperate attempts to find inspiration among thinkers who had shaped Marxist debates in the interwar period remained fruitless. Sometimes they were explicitly rebuffed: Lukács, for instance, claimed that 'we all went wrong, and today it would be quite mistaken to try to revive the works of those times as if they were valid now. In the West, there is a tendency to erect them into "classics of heresy", but we have no need for that today. The twenties are a past epoch; it is the philosophical problems of the sixties that should concern us.'[17] When Dutschke went to visit him in Budapest, Lukács told him to stop studying obscure party documents from the interwar period and concentrate on the 'relations of production' in the Third World.[18]

What options remained when the revolution failed to materialize? Few could simply convert to liberal democracy and set out on a 'long march' now actually understood as 'reform from within'. The immediate winners were the Maoists, because they had a long-standing answer to the 'question of organization': first have a disciplined organization, then go out into the factories and work on the workers.[19]

The Revolution of Everyday Life

The long-term winners, however, were certainly not the Maoists. The Strasbourg Manifesto quoted above had been formulated by members of the Situationist International – arguably the most original group of thinkers of the 1960s, with the almost mythical figure of Guy Debord at its centre. The movement owed more to the artistic avant-garde than to traditional left-wing political doctrines. In particular, they wanted to go beyond what they saw as an intellectually exhausted surrealism and its concern with language. Instead, they sought to return to the Dadaists' focus on aesthetic shocks as a means of profoundly transforming social relations. They aimed at a fundamentally 'different life' from the one dominated by consumer capitalism. The latter made people chase after things instead of authentically interacting with others; given the choice between love and garbage-disposal units, according to the Situationists' diagnosis, young people now opted for the disposal units.[20] Debord had been influenced by Lukács' theory of reification; he also found inspiration in the work of Johan Huizinga, the Dutch cultural historian who had focused on human beings' 'ludic instinct'. *Homo ludens* opened a way to perceive true humanity as play, rather than production, let alone planning. As Debord wrote, 'it is now a question of converting the rules of play from an arbitrary convention to a moral foundation.'[21]

But what were they playing at or for? At the core of Situationism was the idea of creating situations as moments of poetic intensity, of glimpses of what a different, real life could be like. A new 'psycho-geographical' experience would be had in cities, where *dérive* – drifting around the streets, without purposes imposed by society – could be practised.[22] *Dérive* was shorthand for a kind of subversive *flâneur* existence, which could be fashioned even in an urban environment that had been constructed in the name of soulless rationality by high-handed post-war planners. But what might have seemed like idling, with a fancy concept attached to it, was also to have a strategic element and long-term political impact. As Debord put it, 'more than one to whom adventures happen, the adventurer is one who makes them happen ... The construction of situations will be the continuous realisation of a great game, a game the players have chosen to play ...' He also insisted that 'what changes our way of seeing the streets is more important than what changes our way of seeing painting'.

Another Situationist thinker, Raoul Vaneigem, declared: 'Guerilla war is total war. This is the path on which the Situationist International is set: calculated harassment on every front – cultural, political, economic and social.

Concentrating on everyday life will ensure the unity of the combat.' What the 'Situs' called 'immediate participation in a passionate abundance of life' was therefore not a hedonist distraction from political struggle: in a productivist and consumerist society it *was* political struggle. Beyond that, the tactical repertoire of Situationism also contained new 'experiments in living', and 'harassment' by parodying and provoking the authorities. A German section of the SI was, in an ironic allusion to Adenauer's election slogan, to call one of its pamphlets *Nervenruh! Keine Experimente.*

Was this simply an update of *épater les bourgeois* by thinkers whom the *Nouvel Observateur* called 'Saint-Justs in leather jackets'? The same magazine asserted: 'Certainly, Situationism is not the spectre which has been haunting industrial civilization, any more than communism was truly the spectre haunting Europe since 1848. But it is an ideological sign.'[23] An ideological sign of what? observers kept asking. Clearly, it was a sign of an intense dissatisfaction with what came to be seen as an ever more manipulative consumer and media society. Lest there be any doubt, this was given theoretical expression in Debord's November 1967 treatise *The Society of the Spectacle*. Neatly divided into numbered paragraphs, written in a self-consciously ice-cool style, the treatise started out with the assertion that 'the whole life of those societies in which modern conditions of production prevail presents itself as an immense accumulation of spectacles. All that once was directly lived has become mere representation.'[24] In Debord's view, the spectacle served 'as total justification for the conditions and aims of the existing system';[25] it appeared to be all-powerful, beyond human control, although its shape could ultimately be explained by the fact that it reflected the prevailing relations of production. In a sense, Debord was updating familiar Marxist ideas – about false consciousness in particular – for the media age. Suggestive, even poetic formulations abounded: 'the spectacle is the bad dream of modern society in chains, expressing nothing more than its wish to sleep. The spectacle is the guardian of that sleep.'[26] Or, again paraphrasing a rather conventional leftist idea:

> At the root of the spectacle lies that oldest of all social divisions of labor, the specialization of power. The specialized role played by the spectacle is that of spokesman for all other activities, a sort of diplomatic representative of hierarchical society at its own court, and the source of the only discourse that society allows itself to hear.[27]

In the same vein Debord insisted that 'the social cleavage that the spectacle expresses is inseparable from the modern State, which, as the product of the social division of labor and the organ of class rule, is the general form of all social division'.[28] Anti-statism was not central to Situationism, but its basic analysis implied as much.

Anti-statism also explained what Debord proposed in the latter sections of *The Society of the Spectacle* as the antidote to an alienated society dominated by images as much as by the threat of physical violence:

> That 'long sought political form whereby the economic emancipation of labor might finally be achieved' has taken on a clear outline in this century, in the shape of revolutionary workers' councils vesting all decision-making and executive powers in themselves and federating with one another through the exchange of delegates answerable to the base and recallable at any time.

And he went on:

> Once embodied in the power of workers' councils – a power destined to supplant all other powers worldwide – the proletarian movement becomes its own product; this product is the producer himself, and in his own eyes the producer has himself as his goal. Only in this context can the spectacle's negation of life be negated in its turn.[29]

After all the conceptual fireworks used up to illuminate the all-powerful spectacle, the 'solution' was – workers' councils? It seemed a rather conventional leftist idea, not to say a theoretical letdown.

In 1973 Debord made a film about what he had called 'the concrete manufacture of alienation', also entitled *The Society of the Spectacle*: fashion shoots were intercut with John Ford movies, images of Castro, missile launches and speeches by President Valéry Giscard d'Estaing – all of which were supposedly part of the spectacle. The film was a flop, but in retrospect it seemed much more suggestive and insightful in its criticism of modern media power than agit-prop like *Tout va bien*: there *nouvelle vague* director Jean-Luc Godard (whom Debord detested for offering 'pseudo-liberty' and 'pseudo-critique') had Jane Fonda and Yves Montand trapped in an occupied factory, with non-Communist left-wingers, the *gauchistes*, earnestly rehearsing speeches against both capitalism and the French Communist Party.[30]

By the time Debord's film was shown in the Quartier Latin, the Situationist International had already been formally dissolved. Debord, who had always prided himself on never spending a day without drinking, descended into ever more self-destructive behaviour. He left Paris for good and retreated to a simple farmhouse hidden behind high stone walls in the Haute-Loire, poring over Clausewitz's *On War*.[31] On the last day of November 1994, as daylight was fading, he shot himself through the heart. He was sixty-two.[32] It was not a fantastic notion to say that he had been the most innovative Marxist thinker in Europe after 1945 – or that, at least, he had convincingly updated Marxist ideas about alienation for the media age (even if his antidotes to alienation had been far less original).

While seeming minuscule and marginal in so many ways, Situationism had arguably been at the heart of the '68 that later on came to be remembered and that appeared to matter in the long term: the slogans about liberated subjectivity, the emphasis on everyday life and, in the broadest sense, culture. As self-declared 'pariah-elites', the Situationists had sought to stage 'events' which might or might not find an appropriate interpreter at the time and which were free from all supposedly bourgeois concerns about 'legitimacy'.[33] Situationist action had to be direct and immediate; its protagonists were a vanguard, but one devoted to creating new passions and inspiring new desires, redrawing the entire map of the 'psycho-geography' of the modern city.[34] The form might have looked Leninist at some points. But the content never was.

To be fair, the importance of any of this was rarely seen at the time; and to the extent that he was known to the more obviously political leaders of '68 Debord was disliked, or even despised. Cohn-Bendit did not hesitate to call him a 'nasty bastard', while Debord himself heaped scorn on all traditional theorists, as well as on the 'official avant-garde' consisting of artists such as Godard. In Germany, too, a deep split separated Situationists like Dieter Kunzelmann from the anti-authoritarian Dutschke and the more orthodox socialist theorists.[35] The latter were still preoccupied with the correctness, even purity, of Marxist theory – strongly flavoured with a Protestant devotion to the revolutionary cause. Where the anti-authoritarians were struggling to reconcile their beliefs with the fact that all effective politics seemed to demand some measure of hierarchical organization, the Situationist *Subversive Aktion* announced that the meaning of organization was its failure.[36] No wonder the *Marxisant* theorists charged them and the leaders of the new *Kommunen* (famous for slogans such as 'Fuck for Peace') with quasi-anarchist 'false immediacy' as the prime theoretical (and practical) sin.[37]

As it turned out, the libertarian 'experiments in living' were not nearly as liberating as their intellectual promoters had promised: they often resulted in the worst kind of sectarianism and intense psychological terror for some of the participants – a perversion of ideals of brotherhood and sisterhood that might have been recognizable to Weber. Still, some of these experiments provided a model for the large 'alternative' and 'autonomous' areas in Europe (few of which still exist today). It is true that some also became hotbeds of violent anarchism, but most were clearly devoted to peace, environmentalism and feminism. In a sense, their inhabitants sought to develop their own 'politics of prefiguration': demonstrating to bourgeois majorities what a truly liberated egalitarian life could be like, in the absence of a forceful overthrow of existing political institutions. It was a kind of Red Vienna from below.

The Transformation of Democracy

One reason why liberal and conservative observers were quick to speak of 'left-wing fascism' in the face of student rebellion was the apparent return of anti-parliamentarism – which had been such a distinctive feature of the 1920s and which seemed much more specific in its target than the general anti-statism of a thinker like Debord. With anti-parliamentarism came the renaissance of thinkers from the beginning of the twentieth century, such as Weber's friend Robert Michels and other 'elite theorists' who held that sooner or later all institutions would be controlled by oligarchies. These thinkers were now being used to show that liberal democracies had failed to make good on their promises of civic equality.

In many ways the students and other critics had a point when they saw post-war parliaments as merely stages behind which real power was negotiated in corporatist backrooms – and always with the same cast of players. The formation of the grand coalition in West Germany meant that there was only a small opposition party left in the Bundestag – which led to calls for an 'extra-parliamentary opposition'. In Italy, the Christian Democrats were constantly in power, refining their tactics for co-opting nominally competing parties like the Socialists. In France, on the other hand, de Gaulle's reign – though it had ensured a level of political continuity unknown under the previous Third and Fourth Republics – increasingly looked like a presidential dictatorship.

Arguably *the* political theorist of the German 1968 was Johannes Agnoli – his criticism of pluralism and parliamentarism was central to the movement and would continue to form the basis of much left-wing thinking into the 1970s and 1980s. He also enjoyed an astonishing intellectual career, reminiscent of the interwar phenomenon of *rechte Leute von links und linke Leute von rechts* (that is, intellectuals seemingly switching back and forth between extreme right and left).[38] He had been born Giovanni Agnoli in Valle di Cadore, a village in the Dolomites, in 1925. His family had been well off. His father, after shouting obscenities outside the local church, had fled to Latin America – where he had made a lot of money from smuggling alcohol. He eventually became an engineer and turned into a highly respected notable in what was a rather left-wing community – though he lost his wealth in the Great Crash. As a teenager Agnoli – always a contrarian, if those who knew him well are to be believed – penned hymns to the Duce as a 'defender of culture'. In 1943, just after leaving school, he volunteered for the Wehrmacht. He saw some combat with partisans in Yugoslavia before being captured by the British and sent to a re-education camp in Egypt. In the 1950s he studied in Tübingen, wrote a dissertation on Vico and became a German citizen (in 1955). For a while he was a member of the Social Democratic Party. Most witnesses agree that he never tried to hide his fascist past and in fact often spoke openly about it.

Agnoli and his followers started from the premise that under conditions of capitalism no genuine democracy could ever be realized. The bourgeois state systematically shrank the space for the autonomous expression of the people's desires. However, rather than reverting to fascism – which was, after all, a failed strategy for controlling and diverting the mass desire for political self-determination – the bourgeois state transformed the existing institutions of parliamentary democracy in such a way as to render change impossible, but without having to resort to open oppression. This 'transformation of democracy', Agnoli argued, meant a 'modernization of the state in the sense of an adjustment to the new forms of collective life (the so-called mass society) as well as an improvement in the sense of a modernization of the means of domination'.[39]

The need for modernization was caused by 'technical–economic progress', but was also driven by the 'unified interests of the dominating groups'.[40] These 'dominating groups' shared an interest in defusing democracy as a potential means of what Laski had called 'revolution by consent'.[41] Parliamentary democracy was not the most secure guarantee for capitalism. It was by nature ambivalent, since, in theory, parliament could accurately reflect the basic social antagonism in society and serve as a springboard to socialism.

The kind of political uniformity which the fascist state could impose only by one-party rule was now achieved through 'aligned pluralism' – in other words, it looked like ideological diversity, but ultimately it was all the same thing. Society had not overcome the basic antagonism between capitalists and workers, but the pluralism on display in parliament veiled this fact most effectively. Through the negotiations between different parties and 'social partners' such as employers' associations and unions, social peace and the illusion of democratic participation for the masses could be maintained. Just as Vilfredo Pareto, the supposed 'Marx of the bourgeoisie', had advised Mussolini to keep parliament as an 'ornament' while transforming the Italian state into a fascist one, so the West German elite had erected a particularly perfidious form of pseudo-democracy.[42]

Throughout this 'transformation', the official ideology of democracy was left intact – the only change was that languages of humanism and technocratic necessities were supposed to supplant the language of class struggle among the workers' representatives. Parties, trying indeed to 'catch all', no longer knew workers and capitalists – only human beings as such. They no longer implemented platforms; they only observed the objective imperatives of technology. What a conservative politician had called 'the abolition of the proletariat' simply meant that class consciousness could be eroded through increasing mass consumption and other 'grand attempts at collective corruption'.[43] It was Aragon's diagnosis of a *civilisation de baignoires et de frigidaires* all over again.

Thus arose what in retrospect appears to be a full-fledged anti-liberal anti-parliamentarianism, reminiscent of the contempt Sorel had expressed for the socialists in parliament who only furthered their own interests. But what was the remedy for this situation? The answers to this question remained not only vague but often contradictory. On the one hand, Agnoli hinted that 'transformed democracies' were beyond reform. But then again, the presence of Communist parties in some Western European countries might somehow mitigate its effects. Ultimately, however, the process seemed essentially unstoppable within the current parameters of legality, and what really followed was an imperative to abolish the bourgeois state with its fake parliament.[44]

Agnoli and his fellow theorists never wavered in making two assumptions: that liberalism had brought about fascism and could do so again any time, and that advanced capitalist societies had reached an age of abundance in which the abolition of 'irrational domination' had become possible.[45] Consequently, '68 had to be about a genuine 'change of political form' – any integration into existing institutions was condemned to failure. Yet that still left the question of who the revolutionary subject was going to be, if workers could be bought off with fridges. Agnoli did not really give an answer. But others did.

The Prophet

An important value – perhaps even the core concept of the international '68 moment – was autonomy. The 1962 Port Huron Statement, the intellectual founding document of the American student revolution, had declared that 'the goal of man and society should be human independence'. Autonomy – understood as individual but also collective self-direction – was most obviously opposed to a post-war world seemingly dominated by technocracy and bureaucracy: Weber's steely casing. Technocracy in particular appeared to have expunged political will from politics, even from one's personal life, which had to be fashioned according to the work and consumption imperatives of industrial society. In the eyes of critics such as Hannah Arendt, any distinctively political realm seemed to have been swallowed by industrial 'society', just as Forsthoff and others had claimed; the post-war world was so stable because conformist (and entirely predictable) 'behaviour' was replacing individualist action. The European 'societies of jobholders' required its members to abandon any remaining individuality in favour of a 'functional type of behaviour'. As Arendt so sharply observed, 'the trouble with modern theories of behaviourism is not that they are wrong but that they could become true'.[46]

So the protest movement, according to the socialist academic Oskar Negt, was all about restoring both the individual and collective 'integrity of political will'. Whatever this meant in practice, in theory it had to mean that the movement was anti-authoritarian and, in particular, anti-bureaucratic. Geismar, pressed about his philosophical principles, declared: 'I am not a theoretician. For me, socialism can be defined negatively, with respect to existing structures, by a rejection of all bureaucracy, of all centralized direction . . .'[47] All authority – even delegated authority – was suspect; all could immediately be connected to the political catastrophes of the twentieth century: on posters de Gaulle would remove his mask to reveal himself as Hitler; French students supporting Cohn-Bendit would chant, 'We are all German Jews.'

Yet individual anti-authoritarianism was hard to square with the idea of a revolution, which, after all, appeared to require a revolutionary collective with some measure of organization and even, *horribile dictu*, authority. It was a wide-open question which revolutionary subject could act perhaps in a charismatic yet consistently anti-authoritarian way – and thus *not* turn into something like a Leninist vanguard party.

One theorist offered at least a tentative answer, a man whom the *New York Times* declared in 1967 the 'most important living philosopher': Herbert Marcuse. Marcuse had studied with Martin Heidegger during the Weimar Republic. He fled the Third Reich, then operated on the margins of the Frankfurt Institute of Social Research (which later became known as the Frankfurt School) in American exile, but also worked for the OSS (the precursor of the CIA). In the 1950s, with Rockefeller money, he provided analyses of Soviet Marxist theory (which he charged with 'extreme poverty and even dishonesty').[48] Efforts to return to Germany after 1945 proved unsuccessful. By the 1960s he was teaching in California, but his political-philosophical reach became global in a way that arguably has not been emulated by any philosopher since. Marcuse embodied the curious mixture of European high theory and American popular culture which dominated much of the 1960s. It is hard to think of other Marxists featured in *Playboy* magazine.[49]

Marcuse's global impact had at least two major, seemingly contradictory reasons: on the one hand, his bleak assessment of 'the reigning ideology of advanced industrial society', most famously outlined in his *One-Dimensional Man*, simply rang true; on the other hand, there was optimism too: he also claimed that the completely marginalized in industrial society, as well as Third

World liberation movements, just might be capable of bringing about radical transformations (if not the revolution). There was even some role for students.

This peculiar combination of despair and hope made sense in the context of Marcuse's overall diagnosis of a society characterized both by affluence and by a kind of *gleichgeschaltete* culture. He took for granted a society of surplus riches, which existed, in his view, alongside poverty and oppression. It is crucial to remember that '68 happened towards the end of a very long boom in Western economies that started with the Korean War and only finally came to a close with the oil crisis in 1973/4 – although it is equally important to remember that thinkers argued for a socialism that would mean not just abundance but a different quality of life.[50]

In many ways, Marcuse actually shared the diagnosis of what he called 'advanced industrial civilization' with some of its conservative and liberal defenders, such as Forsthoff in Germany or Aron in France: the system seemed self-stabilizing and could absorb dissent. Unlike many technocratic thinkers, however, Marcuse insisted that technology was not a neutral instrument, but a means of domination and was crucial in shaping a particular kind of person, fully adapted to the needs of industrial society. Like so many of his left-wing contemporaries, Marcuse criticized the rampant consumerism with which, in his view, the capitalists had effectively bought off the proletariat – in the process achieving a new synthesis of the welfare and the warfare state.

Apart from affluence, a notion of what can only be described as false consciousness constituted the other axiom of Marcuse's thought. In particular, he argued that what had previously served as a means of contestation – great art as a means to refuse social conformism, for instance – had now become a way of reinforcing the status quo or, even worse, of generating profits. 'The music of the soul', he claimed, 'is also the music of salesmanship.'[51] Not just individual person-alities but culture as a whole had become one-dimensional. And most shocking of all for his liberal-democratic listeners: democracy, at least in its constrained post-war shape, 'would appear to be the most efficient system of domination.'[52]

Until this point, these were all diagnoses which would have struck a left-wing theorist of the 1930s as familiar: the proletariat was not living up to its assigned role; the wrong kind of culture could stunt revolution. But Marcuse also attempted an original synthesis of Freud's theories and Marxism, claiming that advanced industrial civilization did not simply 'repress' sexu-ality; rather, he argued, a pseudo-liberation of the libido went hand in hand with a 'de-eroticization' of the contemporary world for the sake of intensifying domination. To drive his point home, he would ask his readers to 'compare love-making in a meadow and in an automobile, on a lovers' walk outside the town walls and on a Manhattan street'.

Under advanced capitalism, then, people were still profoundly repressed sexually. And Marcuse was adamant that civilization did not have to be repressive, or at any rate not as repressive as this. The present system, he insisted, was characterized by 'surplus repression' – a repression which could be overcome not just by a release of sexuality, but by what Marcuse called 'the transformation of the libido': namely, from 'sexuality constrained under genital supremacy to eroticization of the entire personality'. It remained rather unclear what precisely Marcuse meant by this. But the gist of his argument was clear: the preconditions for a genuinely free subjectivity had been met with the present state of Western capitalism; the task was to help that subjectivity to emerge through political struggle. Already at the end of *One-Dimensional Man* there had been a glimmer of hope. Marcuse spoke about:

the substratum of the outcasts and outsiders, the exploited and persecuted of other races and other colours, the unemployed and the unemployable. They exist outside the democratic process; their life is the most immediate and the most real need for ending intolerable conditions and institutions. Thus their opposition is revolutionary even if their consciousness is not. Their opposition hits the system from without and is therefore not deflected by the system; it is an elementary force which violates the rules of the game and, in doing so, reveals it as a rigged game.[53]

In more confident mood towards the late 1960s, Marcuse added that 'the militant Liberation movements in the developing countries represent the strongest potential force for radical transformation'. At the same time, he left no doubt that students as such were not carriers of the revolution; being confronted with many claims that he was corrupting youth everywhere (but especially at his university in La Jolla, where members of the local, highly conservative community wanted to buy out his professorship, and where an effigy with a sign saying 'Marcuse Marxist' was hanged), he insisted:

I have never said that the student opposition today is by itself a revolutionary force, nor have I seen the hippies as the 'heir of the proletariat'! Only the national liberation fronts of the developing nations are today in a revolutionary struggle. But even they do not by themselves constitute an effective revolutionary threat to the system of advanced capitalism.[54]

However, Marcuse still held out hope for a confluence of forces: Third World liberation movements, marginalized groups in Western societies and students somehow all working together. Whatever the details of the diagnosis, the main point was this: Marcuse seemed to be faithful to the original project of the Frankfurt School in that he linked a theorizing that was grounded in empirical studies but framed by normative philosophical goals with actually existing historical subjects capable of bringing about change. It was this special combination which significantly contributed to Marcuse's international stardom.

But the particular tone of his writings mattered, too – there was an existential urgency to it that few contending theorists could match. And try as he might to refuse the role of father-figure to the movement, he was regarded as a kind of patron.[55] There was talk of the three 'Ms' who were all-important for the students: Marx, Mao and Marcuse. He was received like a 'messiah' in West Berlin in 1967 (his own observation, adding a fourth 'M').[56] He seemed to understand the students and their motivations like few others. Marcuse himself had been formed by the German Youth Movement at the beginning of the century; he now advocated a heady mixture of 'politics and eros', a 'new sensibility'. Not least, he was able to make sense of the idea of total refusal which could not be bought off with a few reforms. He praised the hippies for their 'aggressive non-aggressiveness'; in the 1970s he endorsed Cohn-Bendit's formula of a 'unity of resistance and life'.[57] Unlike other older representatives of the Frankfurt School, he was willing not only to engage with the students, but also to encourage them to go beyond his own theories. He wrote to Theodor Adorno that he was ready to put up with (theoretical) patricide – even if he had to admit that it hurt.[58]

Most important, Marcuse, as an advocate of libertarian socialism, took the students seriously in a way that few others did – even if he said again and again that by themselves students were not a revolutionary subject at the present time.[59] In France the workers – though not the Communist Party, the 'party of order', and the Communist trade union, the CGT – joined the students. But no workers joined the students in Germany, and Marcuse, with his idea of all-pervasive manipulation and 'moronization' (his expression), had a theory why this was so.

As demands for concrete organizational instruments for radical change became more fervent, Marcuse began suggesting a particular mode of political action which did not centre on mass parties or a centrally organized coup. Instead, it was aimed at a more 'diffuse disintegration of the system', through local and regional 'open' and 'autonomous' groups.[60] Ultimately, however, like many of the student leaders, Marcuse argued that the precise nature of revolutionary goals and the best ways to oppose what he called the 'neoimperialist, global reorganization of capitalism'[61] had to be discovered en route. Practice could not be deduced from theory, but experiments in political action and local 'reformism' were to help theory-building along.[62] As Marcuse put it, 'praxis does not come at the end, but at the beginning of theory, without thereby entering an area that would be foreign to theory'.

In retrospect, it is astonishing how many basic assumptions advocates of the counter-culture shared with their opponents: they took the extent and further rate of modernization for granted alongside economic abundance; they shared the technocrats' tendency to downplay the importance of the state; and like them they refused to use a traditional vocabulary of political power.[63] Almost all these assumptions were to be disproved soon after '68 – although in some countries this took much longer than in others.

The Lasting May: Autonomy

Italy, even apart from '68, holds a special place in post-war European political thought. No other European country has thrown up as many radical popular movements from below – all against the background of an unbroken continuity in conservative rule at the top.[64] But the Italian '68 was special, too: nowhere else was social insurgency as drawn out as in Italy (with some observers speaking of a 'creeping May').[65] *Contestazione* continued at least until the end of the 1970s and produced an enormously rich (but also confused and confusing) outpouring of radical political thought. Precisely because of this *longue durée* it was credible for a theorist like Antonio Negri to claim that in Italy revolutionary experience and its theoretical formulation could proceed together – as opposed to theory having to precede praxis (as the Germans were wont to think), or theory always trying to catch up with a fleeting moment that might not have lasted even a month (as allegedly was the case with France).[66] Most importantly, only in Italy did the post-1968 political languages of anti-authoritarianism and older idioms of class conflict come together in a sustained manner – even if there were also major tensions between Old and New Left, between workers and the *movimento studentesco*, between Maoist and other radical left-wing groups and the by and large pro-Soviet Communist Party, the PCI.[67]

Already in the late 1950s – after Khrushchev's secret speech and the crushing of the Hungarian uprising had cost the Communist Party thousands of members – space had opened up beyond the PCI. Under the leadership of Gramsci's friend Palmiro Togliatti, the post-war Communists had essentially opted for a Gramscian approach: at least rhetorically supporting bourgeois democracy as it was (despite being permanently excluded from government by the Christian Democrats), but slowly building cultural hegemony in its many regional and urban strongholds (such as Tuscany and Emilia-Romagna). The Italian republic was essentially split between red and white culturally – but what looked like permanent *Kulturkampf* settled into a stable, mutually respectful arrangement not entirely dissimilar to the conflict between the priest Camillo and Communist mayor Peppone famously depicted in Giovanni Guareschi's satirical stories. No wonder more radical left-wing thinkers concluded that the PCI had essentially given up on radical political change. At the same time, such intellectuals did not think *fare come in Russia* (that is to say, emulating the Soviet Union) could possibly be the answer to Italian problems.

The socialist theorist Raniero Panzieri had written during the 1950s specifically against the studied ambiguities of *togliattismo* – in particular, Togliatti's concept of 'progressive democracy', which seemed designed to oscillate between reform within the system and revolution. Panzieri instead affirmed the necessity to return class struggle to the factories, rather than hope for change through an alliance of the working class with progressive members of the bourgeoisie.[68] According to Panzieri, the Italian left as a whole – that is to say, Socialists and Communists – should reunify around the old ideas of factory councils. When the Socialists joined the Christian Democrats in government, Panzieri essentially gave up on his party. In 1961 he founded the journal *Quaderni Rossi* to provide a platform for theoretical reflections around 'workerism' (*operaismo*) – a particular focus on actual class struggles in factories, as opposed to political parties' manoeuvrings within the established institutions of the republic and the corporatist 'politics of productivity'.

A new enthusiasm for sociology informed the founding texts of the Italian *nuova sinistra*. In particular, research conducted in the 1950s in the FIAT and Olivetti factories served to demonstrate that the production process itself could be a primary form of domination and that it was plainly not enough to seize the means of production – the conditions of production themselves had to change and were a better starting point for revolutionary transformations than the state-centred 'neo-reformism' of Togliatti's PCI. So these radicals did not just break with Gramsci's cultural approach – at least as interpreted by party officials – they also rejected the Sardinian's favourable view of 'Americanist' modernization of factories. Panzieri and his followers were duly attacked by PCI representatives for 'infantile leftism' and 'spontaneism'.[69]

Two of Panzieri's disciples radicalized this programme further: Mario Tronti and Antonio Negri. Both had been deeply impressed by the FIAT worker riots in Piazza Statuto in Turin in 1962; unlike Panzieri, they had seen it as evidence that revolutionary worker autonomy could in fact smash capitalism immediately. But they also enlarged the potential revolutionary subject: Tronti argued that the focus should be shifted from factories in a narrow industrial sense to the notion of the 'social factory', that is, processes of domination in society as a whole. Negri claimed that the idea of the 'mass worker', that is, the unskilled, most downtrodden worker who had been at the centre of *operaismo* initially, should be replaced with that of the 'socialized worker' – like Tronti, he thought that factory discipline and domination had spread through society as a whole, 'like a virus'. Negri also pointed to a range of groups outside the working class as traditionally defined: 'precarious workers', students, the women's movement – basically anyone suffering from the conventional family and traditional forms of education. Such a theoretical shift was obviously designed to stoke revolutionary hopes. Even if the working class was content with fridges, there were other groups which might be willing to assert their autonomy – a thought that clearly paralleled Marcuse's ideas about the marginalized elements of a one-dimensional society.

Thus worker-centred *operaismo* came to be replaced with general *autonomia*; what remained the same was a rejection of any Leninist conception of a vanguard party. Instead, the theorists of autonomy advocated local committees and networks, and direct action by anyone willing to go on strike in the 'social factory': rejection of work, but also what came to be known as *autoriduzione*, the refusal to pay transport fares or rent.

The State as Enemy

It has often been pointed out that the '68 student movement broke up into many groupuscules, each devoted to seemingly ever more esoteric doctrines. But the movement had never been that unified to start with, and especially in Italy (less so in Germany and less so still in France) the *contestazione* of the 1970s was actually more of a mass phenomenon than '68: '68ers as such numbered in the tens of thousands, whereas the highly fractured oppositional cultures of the 1970s numbered in the hundreds of thousands. Often, the more doctrinaire they became, the less intellectual in any traditional sense, and sometimes the less intelligent. As early as December 1968 the older British socialist Ralph Miliband, teaching at the LSE, had voiced his despair:

> I am struck here by the intellectual poverty of the student movement, which is accompanied by a worrying totalitarianism, despite its anti-authoritarian claims. [One of the protesting students] . . . told me yesterday that in a socialist regime, 'sociology would wither away'. I asked him what would replace it. 'Marxism,' he told me. 'Meaning what?' I asked him. 'The reading of Marx, Engels, Lenin, Gramsci etc' he told me, adding that this wouldn't prevent people from reading other things if they wanted to. What strikes me in this silliness, is the total lack of respect for intellectual activity, for research, for scientific elucidation of very complex problems, even a refusal to consider that very complex

problems exist. These people want a social science that the masses can whistle, to use the expression that . . . Zhdanov used in relation to socialist music.[70]

Some groups now sent their members into factories to mobilize or at least organize workers, but most remained self-involved and turned increasingly sectarian. None, it seemed, could solve the persistent 'question of organization' and construct a credible revolutionary subject. The Italian Lotta Continua, for instance, adopted as its motto 'the organization is a process' – except that the process appeared never ending and lurched between the principle of centralization and the ideal of *spontaneismo*.[71] In the same vein, there remained a tension between trying to mobilize marginal groups, as Marcuse had advocated, and the appeal to broader constituencies. Radicals also wavered between instigating more conventional mass protest and individualized, almost anarchic approaches – such as the Italian innovation of the 'hiccup strike' (*singhiozzo*), as well as new initiatives in areas that had not really been included in any revolutionary agitation previously: the army and prisons.[72]

Some activists eventually opted for the route of 'direct action' – understood as violent attack on the state and capitalism. As so often, those who made that choice actually saw themselves as engaged in a defensive struggle: the state or 'the system' had attacked first. Their (self-appointed) task was to engage in an anti-imperialist or, as it was most frequently put, anti-fascist struggle. This was somewhat more plausible in Italy, where, after all, parts of the state were collaborating in a 'strategy of tension' to provoke an authoritarian takeover of the country. It was utterly implausible in Germany. To be sure, the German state had overreacted to student protest, and the 'disciplined democracy' Adenauer had created could appear not just as stuffy but as potentially authoritarian. Gudrun Ensslin, one of the founders of the Red Army Faction – better known as the Baader–Meinhof gang – is supposed to have reacted to the shooting of an unarmed and entirely peaceful student protester during the anti-Shah demonstrations in 1967 as follows: 'They will kill us all . . . You know what kind of pigs we are dealing with. This is the generation of Auschwitz which we are dealing with. One cannot discuss with people who have done Auschwitz. They have weapons and we have none. We have to arm ourselves.'[73] That is not what the students had concluded. But RAF leader Ulrike Meinhof always insisted that her organization had emerged from the remains of the failed student movement. RAF manifestos saluted the achievement of the latter as having anchored Marxism-Leninism in the consciousness at least of the intelligentsia as the one proper theory to explain the 'political, economic and ideological facts' and their relations.[74]

Obviously, the question of organization was no longer answered with regard to any of the anti-authoritarian ideals of the students. The terrorists looked to

Third World models, in particular the Brazilian Marxist theorist Carlos Marighella's *Minimanual of the Urban Guerilla*, published in German in May 1970. They also adopted Mao's formula that 'armed struggle constituted the highest form of Marxism-Leninism' and presented his imperative of 'drawing a clear line between ourselves and the enemy' as their very first task.

Despite some protestations to the contrary, the Baader–Meinhof group essentially demanded a primacy of practice over theory. It was a wager whether Germany really was in a revolutionary situation, and only 'revolutionary praxis' could give the answer. They explicitly argued that they could not wait for 'the masses' to give their consent to what they were doing – but their actions, or so they hoped, would actually generate explicit consent. As they put it flatly: 'we have to start an attack to awaken the revolutionary consciousness of the masses'.

Often a decidedly anti-theoretical tone pervaded the pronouncements of the RAF: the student leaders had talked, the RAF would act. It fitted with the macho self-image of the highly charismatic Andreas Baader in particular: he would laugh when other members of the group started citing Marx and Engels, and ridicule them until they shut up. The RAF leaders were also fond of quoting a slogan by the Uruguayan guerilla group Tupamaros: 'at the present stage of history nobody can deny that an armed group, however small it may be, has a better prospect of transforming itself into a large people's army than a group which limits itself to pronouncing revolutionary doctrines'.[75]

Was history repeating itself as tragedy or as farce? Sometimes the RAF seemed closer to the insurrectionist tradition of the anarchists, sometimes they looked like a reincarnation of the late nineteenth-century Russian terrorists, whom Chernyshevsky, Lenin's idol, had celebrated as 'new people'. They obviously thought themselves a vanguard, hoping to be the core of an entirely new, ideologically reformed people. In the eyes of some leftist sympathizers they might also have looked like a charismatic organization, with the police-car chases, the unconditional devotion to the cause going so far as starving themselves to death in prison. But they certainly were not a Leninist institution by any stretch of the imagination, nor were they a direct consequence of '68 thinking. Yet they were also unimaginable without the larger context of Communist theorizing in and on twentieth-century Europe – especially the idea that capitalism had used fascism to preserve itself and that, consequently, capitalist states could reveal their fascist face at any moment.

As it turned out, 'praxis' *did* give the answer to the question of whether West Germany was in a revolutionary situation. Nineteen-sixty-eight had been the last chapter in the history of insurrection in Europe, not the first one of a new revolutionary era. A small armed group could not awaken 'the masses' – who almost unanimously abhorred their methods. But it could still profoundly shake the self-confidence of a self-styled militant democracy: during the so-called 'German autumn' of 1977, politicians faced the simultaneous kidnapping of the industrialist (and former Nazi) Hans-Martin Schleyer and the hijacking of a Lufthansa aircraft to obtain the release of the remaining leaders of the Baader–Meinhof group from prison (Meinhof had hanged herself in her cell in 1976, having been alienated from her fellow terrorist inmates). In this extraordinary situation, West German political elites seemed to come close to losing their nerve and crossing the boundaries of normal parliamentary politics. In secret meetings among key government and opposition leaders in 1977, some politicians were even said to have raised the possibility of taking terrorists as 'counter-hostages' who could be shot in turn. Such measures would not only have recognized the terrorists as equal combatants, they would also have implied a moral equivalence between the state and the terrorists challenging it in a new 'state of nature'.

Ultimately, the government of Chancellor Helmut Schmidt resisted these temptations and continued officially to treat the members of the RAF as criminals. On the other hand, the actual treatment of RAF prisoners and new legislation hastily adopted in response to terrorist acts made it plain that the Baader–Meinhof gang was not an ordinary gang. German militant democracy also led to Communists being banned from civil service positions. Terror never threatened a state like the Federal Republic, but it revealed just how nervous about their own stability, and ultimately their own democracy, some of the post-1945 regimes remained.

Italy in particular was nervous, and in many ways it had reason to be so. The Red Brigades had been founded in 1970 by Roberto Curcio, a student at the new and progressive university of Trento, at the time the only Italian university with a faculty of social sciences. They were the most radical group within the much larger movement of left-wing militancy (promptly theorized as 'mass intellectuality'). In general, these militants remained closer to established parties than any of the doctrinaire groupings in West Germany. On the other hand, the range of Italian terrorists' targets was also much more 'democratic': It was not just prominent politicians and leaders of industry who lived in fear, but middle-managers and mid-level bureaucrats who were knee-capped, kidnapped and sometimes killed.[76]

The Italian left was preoccupied less with imperialism and more with the emergence of what was increasingly seen as a 'double state': official legal and political institutions on the one hand and, on the other, a shadowy world of secret circles bent on defending Italy against Communism with all means – if necessary dictatorship. The 'strategy of tension' and the 'black terror', undertaken by extreme right-wing political groups, were designed to exacerbate the polarization between left and right, with the goal of a coup d'état to defend democracy, since a supposedly *democrazia protetta* (the Italian version of militant democracy) actually could not defend itself.[77] As with many right-wing thinkers in post-war Europe, an authoritarian–bureaucratic presidential system, a kind of radicalized Gaullism, also remained their ideal.

The apparently ever increasing polarization of Italian society led a number of left-wing theorists to claim that a real revolution had actually become possible in the 1970s, and that a final clash between the forces of reaction and 'the real proletariat' – including all kinds of marginalized groups – might be imminent. It is here that the thought of Carl Schmitt became important for the Italian left – with Schmitt understood as the theorist of life-and-death political conflict and, in a sense, as an antidote to Gramsci's thought, in which there always seemed more culture to be conquered before real political struggle could be unleashed.[78] In other words, the young theorists wanted a war of manoeuvre, not just Togliatti's endless war of position, and they thought Italy might be ready for it. They demanded the complete destruction of the state; even more so than the Germans, they returned to an all-out insurrectionary strategy.

The state, in the end, responded in a deeply illiberal, but seemingly effective, manner. The 'years of lead' after the murder of the popular five-times DC prime minister Aldo Moro by the Red Brigades in 1978 saw mass arrests and the imprisonment also of some of the theorists of the *autonomia* movement – such as Antonio Negri, who was accused not just of 'insurrection against the state', but also of being the mastermind behind the Red Brigades (a charge of which he was cleared eventually). Many fled into exile in France, where President Mitterrand had promised not to extradite those who had not caused 'bodily harm' and had also repented. Many were to return to Italy only at the beginning of the twenty-first century.

The eruption of '68 had been a real blow to the stodgy French Communist Party, who had revealed themselves, when the chips were down, as guardians of the established order. Something similar happened in Italy, though for better reasons than the narrow-minded orthodoxies of the French. The leader of the Italian Communist Party, Enrico Berlinguer, had already learnt a (bitter) lesson from the 1973 coup against Salvador Allende in Chile. Through the 'Historic Compromise' with the Christian Democrats he sought the broadest possible democratic consensus to defend the Second Republic and thereby also counter the 'strategy of tension'.[79] 'Eurocommunists' such as Berlinguer and the Spanish Communist leader Santiago Carrillo now unambiguously pronounced themselves in favour of a 'legal revolution', echoing Laski's theories of revolution by consent.[80] Rather than engage in violent revolutionary activity, they sought a parliamentary road to power – and to the revolutionary transformation of the state.

In the end, Italy managed to avoid the kind of radical breaking of a stalemate which had happened in Austria during the interwar period. In fact, the Italian Communists became the defenders of democratic legality, even the 'shield of the constitution'. But shielding a corrupt state exacted its own costs through significant electoral losses in the 1980s. 'Eurocommunism' generated hopes among the European left at a time when all hope for the Soviet Union had long been abandoned – but it ended with a whimper.

Intentions and Consequences

It is easy to see in retrospect why alarm bells rang for conservatives, but also for liberal anti-totalitarians: the students seemed to despise parliament much as the extreme left and right had done in the 1920s, and their emphasis on spontaneity, on chasing after 'immediate experience', appeared to go directly against any kind of Weberian ethics of responsibility (and so confirm the Weberian diagnosis that the rule of impersonal forces such as technology would always generate a highly excitable subjectivist culture as its seeming antidote). The hard-won gains for a more liberal political culture in countries like France and Germany seemed to be squandered for nothing, as Raymond Aron, the leading French Weberian, complained bitterly.

Yet the real long-term effects of what Aron called a 'charade' were rather different from what was imagined at the time. To be sure, the month of May did not 'cause' some large-scale social and cultural transformations. But in many European countries it became shorthand for them. Because changes there were: in particular, the rise of a new quasi-libertarian language of 'self-realization', culminating in the narcissistic 'me decade' of the 1970s and what Marcuse had warned about as a 'politics in the first person'. But this was not just Weber's 'sterile excitation'. All over Europe, what came to be seen as a major constraint on self-expression – the traditional family – came under attack, in some countries such as Italy for the first time.[81] Students, the sons and daughters of the *Mittelstand* and of the *ceti medi*, who had been on the right for most of the twentieth century (and leading in the promotion of fascism in the 1920s and 1930s), were now for the most part on the left.

At the same time, there was widespread loss of belief in the capacity of societies for collective self-transformation through mass political action, whether inside or outside political institutions like parliaments. Individual, rather than collective, transformations mattered. The events as well as the thought of '68 and after called into question traditional concepts of the political, tearing down the ideological barricades between the public and the private and making everyday experience explicitly political – just as the Situationists had hoped, though they would have liked workers' councils, too.

Perry Anderson had been jubilant that the 'long night of theory' was finally over in the 1960s (in Britain, at any rate), but the dawn did not herald anything like a conventional political revolution. Instead, there was revolution in values and culture, which, at least for the moment, left major political institutions intact. It also completely sidelined established (and in a sense loyal) oppositions such as the French Communist Party, which reacted with impotent fury to the students, as did some leading intellectual supporters of Communism. Already in June 1968 director Pier Paolo Pasolini had published an anti-student poem in the magazine *Espresso*, which began: 'Now the journalists of all the world (including / those of the television) / are licking your arses (as one still says in student / slang). Not me, my dears / You have the faces of spoilt rich brats . . .'[82]

The most important of the *real* revolutions was undoubtedly feminism, or what is commonly referred to as 'second-wave feminism', in contrast with earlier struggles for political rights, and suffrage in particular. Consensus politics had been paternalist, and in many ways patriarchal. Women having the vote did not obviously change this fact. To be sure – and this is often overlooked, not least in the self-celebratory accounts of participants – second-wave feminism was not a part of '68 in a narrow sense, it was a reaction against it. 'Student leaders', after all, was a designation for men who sent women to make the tea or coffee, who had them copy the flyers – and who generally liked having them around as revolutionary groupies, not to mention what came to be know as 'sozialistischer bumszwang' (the socialist imperative to fuck). For instance, Barbara Görres, the wife of Johannes Agnoli, had to get up at five to take care of their daughter, then make the theorist's breakfast; when she was made 'general secretary' of a revolutionary 'society', this meant she would do all the typing.[83] As French feminists eventually concluded, frying the steak of a revolutionary took as much time as frying the steak of a reactionary.[84]

Time and again, there seemed to be a moment of shock, but in the end also liberation, when left-wing women realized they had to do their own thing. When a debate contribution by Helke Sander, a film and theatre director and a founder of the Action Committee for the Liberation of Women in Germany, was simply ignored, women threw tomatoes at the male student leaders. Italian feminists organizing a march in Rome to draw attention to injustices in family law had requested that women from the various left-wing radical groups participate as women, not as representatives with signs and slogans from the respective groups. On Via Cavour a group of men from Lotta Continua tried to force their way in; when they met resistance, they pushed and kicked the female marchers.[85]

Such moments confirmed feminists in their belief that they could no longer be content with subsuming 'women's concerns' within a larger socialist movement – a movement, where, if in doubt, male workers' interests always came first. True, there were parallels with other struggles: the fact that the oppressed did not even have their own language to start with, the difficulties, even embarrassment of trying to articulate their own situation and possible remedies. Existing 'theory' did not help – on the contrary. As Sheila Rowbotham pointed out in 1969:

> there is the labour of making connections. Theory and the removed language in which it is expressed presents a means of going beyond the immediate. It crystallises innumerable experiences, it puts a canopy over the world which enables it to be regarded as a relating whole. It makes reality intelligible. But this theory is constructed from the experience of the dominators and consequently reflects the world from their point of view; they however present it as the summation of the world as it is.[86]

The point was that women's liberation should not simply operate with existing theories of exploitation and oppression in particular accounts of class. As Rowbotham argued:

> These exploitations are part only of the oppression of some women. The full extent of our oppression is not fully revealed by the isolation of these particular forms of exploitation. The woman question is not comprehensible except in terms of the total process of a complete series of repressive structures. Thus the particular form of domination changes but the process operates in both pre-capitalist and post-capitalist society. The function of revolutionary theory is to keep track of this moving shape of these subordinations.[87]

Of course, there had been feminist theory before, in particular Simone de Beauvoir's *Second Sex*, which had famously argued that woman served as 'the Other' of man and that one became a woman, rather than being born one. Beauvoir had called on women to realize that their ovaries would not have to condemn them 'to be on their knees for eternity'. But the feminism of the late 1960s was more radical than Beauvoir's existentialist feminism (which she herself, in any event, later disavowed for being insufficiently materialist: in 1963 she held that 'only a revolution' would change 'woman's condition' – thereby going against the trend of decoupling questions about labour and feminism).[88] But a few years later Beauvoir also came to realize 'the specificity of women's struggles'. As she explained in a conversation with – or rather interrogation of – Jean-Paul Sartre in 1970:

you accepted *The Second Sex*. It did not change you at all. Perhaps I should add that it did not change me either, for I think we had the same attitude at that time. We had the same attitude in that we both believed that the socialist revolution would necessarily bring about the emancipation of women. We have been disillusioned since then . . . This . . . is what decided me, around 1970, to take up an openly feminist position. What I mean by this is, to recognize the specificity of women's struggles.[89]

The new feminism focused clearly on concrete legal strategies for change. Partly as a consequence, it also had more immediate results: the 1970s saw reforms of divorce laws (or the introduction of divorce laws for the first time, as in Italy), and, most importantly, the relaxation or de facto abolition of prohibitions on abortion. European states finally began to relinquish the right to control what was happening inside women's wombs.

Thus feminism also reinvigorated an anticipatory or prefigurative conception of political action that would have been familiar to the Austro-Marxists: even if the state as such had not yet become socialist, social change in the family, the personal, should be implemented – here and now. The slogan of the American feminist organization NOW – that the personal was the political – was taken up all over Europe.[90]

Consensus politics had led to a great extension of state activity. But it had not necessarily increased state authority. With '68 and after, state authority – and deeply ingrained habits of deference – came under severe attack. The consensus politics shared by 'smug conservatives, tired liberals and disillusioned radicals' (C. Wright Mills) was taken to task for its 'elitist', top-down approach; people wanted not just to be represented, but also to participate, the '68ers insisted; and different people, while still wanting to be represented, wanted to be represented differently – most importantly women. 'Autonomy' had not just been a slogan.

States and even constitutions survived all this. What changed for good, however, were *mœurs*, not least because '68 succeeded spectacularly as a form social-cultural criticism, or, in the words of British New Left theorist Stuart Hall, 'cultural rebellion'. One might as well use the term so prominent at the time: 'cultural revolution'. As Umberto Eco pointed out: 'Even though all visible traces of 1968 are gone, it profoundly changed the way all of us, at least in Europe, behave and relate to one another. Relations between bosses and workers, students and teachers, even children and parents, have opened up. They'll never be the same again.'[91] The German social theorist Niklas Luhmann put the point even more succinctly: after '68 one could walk across the lawn. So the conservative Gaullists had been right, in a sense: '68 was about a 'crisis of civilization' (as well as a crisis of political representation). And that crisis was resolved by a change in civilization.

One can debate whether this cultural liberalization in the end was not exactly the kind of 'repressive desublimation' of which Marcuse had been afraid. One can even lament that the much discussed 'pluralization of lifestyles' actually made capitalism more legitimate. One can also ask whether liberalization would not have happened even without '68. What cannot really be doubted, however, is that '68 (and after) demonstrated that the basic constitutional post-war settlement was largely compatible with a liberalization of culture. For those with larger ambitions for institutional political change there remained the two virtues which Agnoli deemed essential for the true revolutionary: irony and patience.

CHAPTER 6

Antipolitics, and the Sense of an Ending

Sovereignty is always shaped from below, and by those who are afraid.

Michel Foucault

Being a democrat means, primarily, not to be afraid . . .

István Bibó

Economics are the method; the object is to change the soul.

Margaret Thatcher

*I think the end of communism is a serious warning to all mankind. It is a signal
that the era of arrogant, absolutist reason is drawing to a close, and that it is
high time to draw conclusions from this fact.*

Václav Havel

*It is ridiculous to ascribe to high capitalism . . . an elective affinity with 'democracy' or 'freedom'. The question can only be: under its domination, how are
these things 'possible' at all in the long run?*

Max Weber

IN RETROSPECT the mid-1970s seem like the high point of a profound crisis
affecting not just Western Europe, but the West as a whole. At the very least
they were the culmination of an acute consciousness of crisis in the West. The
famous 1975 Report to the Trilateral Commission, a high-level group of politicians and bureaucrats in the US, Western Europe and Japan, fretted that
European countries might become 'ungovernable': the oil shock of 1973 had
brought the *trente glorieuses*, the 'thirty glorious years', of unprecedented
growth and social peace (compared to the first half of the twentieth century)

to a definitive end; the hitherto unknown phenomenon of stagflation – combining high unemployment and runaway inflation – seemed there to stay. The German philosopher Robert Spaemann claimed that the oil shock was, from the point of view of intellectual history, the most important event since the war.[1] In 1976 the British prime minister James Callaghan announced to a stunned Labour Party conference that 'we used to think that you could spend your way out of a recession and increase employment by cutting taxes and boosting government spending. I tell you in all candour that that option no longer exists.' In the same year, the Swedish Social Democrats lost power for the first time in four decades. The days of technocratic fine-tuning of the economy – the supposed key to post-war prosperity and, above all, stability – seemed over.

Stability was also threatened in another way: both domestic and international terrorism, from right and left, were on the rise. Terrorism cast doubt on the one seemingly unquestionable attribute of the modern state, there to stay even when technocratic illusions had been dispelled: the monopoly of violence. Terrorism could be contained, but the great social mobilization which had begun in the late 1960s continued unabated, with all the demands for more and different representation, and, in any event, more direct participation in politics.

Above all, there appeared to be a failure of nerve. Alexander Solzhenitsyn declared in his 1978 address to the graduating class at Harvard that 'a decline in courage may be the most striking feature that an outside observer notices in the West today. The Western world has lost its civic courage, both as a whole and separately, in each country, in each government, in each political party.' He pointed out that 'such a decline in courage is particularly noticeable among the ruling and intellectual elites, causing an impression of a loss of courage by the entire society.'[2]

How then did Western Europe get from what Habermas had called the 'legitimation crisis of late capitalism' in the 1970s and what Michel Foucault had already announced in the late 1960s as 'the death of man' (which, among many other things, seemed to spell the end of the illusions of liberal individualism) to the supposedly triumphalist liberalism of a Francis Fukuyama in the late 1980s, to the apparent vindication of apologists for capitalism, such as Hayek, and to the apparently conclusive discrediting of the Leninist model of politics? Was this a case of a rapid liberalization of West European thought, following perhaps the example set by the turning of many dissident thinkers in the East to some sort of liberalism, as many observers were to claim? Or was it the victory of a neoliberal conspiracy which had already begun on Mont Pèlerin in 1945, but whose chief conspirators – Hayek and Milton Friedman – only conquered the commanding heights of intellectual discourse in the 1970s, as critics on the left alleged? And what did this return – or reversal, depending on one's point of view – mean for conceptions of democracy and for the fate of the post-war Western European constitutional settlement in particular?

'The Crisis of Democracy'

The Crisis of Democracy was the matter-of-fact title of the influential 'Report on the Governability of Democracies to the Trilateral Commission' published in 1975. The report claimed to respond to a widespread perception of 'the disintegration of civil order, the breakdown of social discipline, the debility of leaders, and the alienation of citizens'.[3] The social scientists who had written it feared a 'bleak future for democratic government'; more specifically, they were concerned about an 'overloading' of governments by demands emanating from society, and in particular what one of the principal investigators, Samuel Huntington, was to describe as a 'democratic surge' afflicting the United States and Western countries more broadly. Too many people wanting too many things *from* government and ultimately also too much participation *in* government made statecraft ever more difficult. Or so the diagnosis went.

In addition, Michel Crozier, Huntington and Joji Watanuki stated in their introduction that 'at the present time, a significant challenge comes from the intellectuals and related groups who assert their disgust with the corruption, materialism, and inefficiency of democracy and with the subservience of democratic government to "monopoly capitalism" '.[4] They lamented the rise of the 'adversary culture' of 'value-oriented intellectuals' bent on 'the unmasking and delegitimation of established institutions'.[5]

One possible way forward seemed an increased role for what the Trilateral Commission's rapporteurs had hailed as the 'technocratic and policy-oriented intellectual' – the non-adversary culture, so to speak. Its greatest late twentieth-century advocate was arguably the German sociologist Niklas Luhmann. Not because he had vast influence on policy (in fact, quite the contrary), but because he offered the most coherent and sophisticated theoretical justification for why policy-making should be shielded from widespread participation and essentially be left to bureaucrats. Luhmann had actually been a *Beamter* (civil servant) himself in Lower Saxony, before winning a scholarship to Harvard to study with the social theorist Talcott Parsons (who had been instrumental in introducing Weber to American academia). Luhmann subsequently – and in record time – completed a Habilitation, the second doctorate required of all German academics, before becoming a professor at the newly founded university of Bielefeld – itself a concrete manifestation of the technocratic optimism of the 1960s.

Luhmann's 'systems theory' was deeply influenced by Parsons who in turn had formalized and systematized many of Weber's thoughts. The former German civil servant, radicalizing one of Weber's and Parsons' central insights, held that modern societies were steadily evolving, and, in particular, becoming divided into ever more 'systems' which operated according to their own logic or 'function' (such as the economy, the arts and the government).[6] Systems reduced complexity: they made the world around them comprehensible to themselves. Any attempted interference by one system in another was prima facie counter-productive. So any expectation that governments could realize 'values' from outside the system of state administration constituted a kind of category mistake. And what it meant for politics to try to dominate the economy could be observed every day east of the Iron Curtain.

The upshot of Luhmann's theory was that the business of government should be left to politicians and, ultimately, to bureaucrats – and that social-movement activists listening to nothing but their conscience could inflict much damage on modern societies if governments acceded to their misguided demands and illusionary hopes for participation. Such a diagnosis – ostensibly inspired by Weber's criticism of the ethics of conscience – often went along with contempt for members of the 'adversary culture'. Luhmann's teacher, the sociologist Helmut Schelsky, for instance, derided intellectuals as a 'new class of high priests' trying to gain power, while 'others are actually doing the work'.[7] However, the more original and more disturbing lesson of Luhmann's theory was that politics (and the state) were simply not as important as most people assumed: governments could not 'steer' societies as a whole, and states were simply the 'self-descriptions' of specialized, self-contained 'political systems' – without any possibility, for instance, of reforming the economic system.[8]

Unlike in Weber's thought, there was no special place for politics in generating meaning, no chance of the public realm becoming a home for 'sublime values'. Conversely, no over-arching belief systems – civil religions or ideologies – were needed to 'hold societies together'. Luhmann's ideas were thus not so much a sign of an Indian summer for the technocratic thinking that had dominated the 1950s and 1960s; rather, they were perfectly suited to an age of diminished political and economic expectations, in which, according to Luhmann, evolution rather than the planning of society should inform thinking about the future.

Luhmann was to be cast in the role of prime theoretical adversary of Jürgen Habermas, the most prominent heir to the Frankfurt School of Critical Theory. Habermas had distanced himself from the '68 rebels, but tried to hold on, broadly speaking, to hopes for democratizing the state administration and the economy.[9] He became the most important philosopher for the environmental and feminist social movements that emerged in the 1970s alongside the revolutionary groupuscules which the aftermath of '68 had produced. He stressed the need to protect the integrity of what he called the 'lifeworld', that is, the realm of family and other inter-personal relations, as well as civil society, which ought to be shielded from the instrumental logic – or ruthless strategic thinking – which characterized the economy and public administration. The market and the state would always, so Habermas argued, have a tendency to 'colonize' the lifeworld. Social movements and, not least, intellectuals in the public sphere could work against such a colonization, and perhaps even achieve gradual decolonization.

Luhmann, who saw himself as being in the business of 'sociological enlightenment', treated such hopes with irony, rather than opposing them polemically. To understand societies and their evolution one had to look at systems, not at individuals or movements fighting for or against political values. In one sense his systems theory seemed to affirm the Weberian diagnosis of a steely casing and Simmel's tragedy of culture: social complexity had far outrun any capacity for real individual autonomy. But Luhmann insisted that the kind of sociological disenchantment he offered was also liberating, even if 'the systems' (never just '*the* system') had their own iron logic. As the British New Left theorist Perry Anderson observed, 'if Habermas told his readers that things could be as they should be . . . Luhmann's message was dryer, but no less reassuring: things were as they had to be'.[10]

It was telling that Habermas eventually incorporated many elements of Luhmann's theories into his own thinking, seemingly giving up any wider aspirations for democratizing the economy and state administration. Instead, the best that could be hoped for was a lively public sphere, an alert press and, as a result, a vigorous public opinion that would relate to the state like a permanent siege relates to a fortress.[11] This gave legitimacy to activists and social movements challenging the state, but the other, perhaps more obvious, implication of the image was that the fortress of the state actually could not – and should not – be conquered.

France's Antitotalitarian Moment

A persistent suspicion of bureaucracy – whether in the state or in capitalist enterprises – animated a range of French intellectuals who came to prominence after the upheavals of the late 1960s; they did not want to subscribe to orthodox Marxism (they viewed the established Communist parties in Western Europe as themselves prime examples of bureaucratic ossification) or invest in Maoist or other exotic hopes. Older philosophers such as Cornelius Castoriadis and Claude Lefort, who had emerged from a Trotskyist background, advanced an ingenious analysis of bureaucracy under state socialism; their concepts were to inspire younger intellectuals looking for new forms of social organization with autonomy as a central value. One of the watchwords of the mid- to late 1970s was *autogestion* (roughly, self-management), which had already appeared in the mid-1960s, but which was to be properly theorized only by members of what in the 1970s came to be called *la deuxième gauche*.[12] Pierre Rosanvallon and other intellectuals around the non-Communist, originally Christian trade union CFDT (Confédération Française Démocratique du Travail) advanced a political agenda that was meant to invigorate the French Socialist Party, but also draw a clear line vis-à-vis the Communists. As a slogan *autogestion* could serve a range of political currents, from libertarian to technocratic; as a theory, it was supposed to describe and prescribe a new, anti-bureaucratic form of democracy that was directed as much against state socialism in the East as against traditional Social Democracy in the West.[13] In particular, *autogestion* was to rehabilitate the notion of civil society, with autonomous individuals freely associating and governing their own affairs as much as possible without state interference. But, unlike for nineteenth-century liberals who had endorsed civil society, self-government was to extend to the economy, too. Hence Rosanvallon would quote the Christian Democrat Marc Sagnier to the effect that democracy could not be realized as long as monarchy reigned in enterprises.[14]

The debates around *autogestion* eventually became enmeshed with the wide-ranging disputes about totalitarianism in mid-1970s France. By the beginning of the decade, the myths of Gaullism had been shattered for good. Almost logically, it seemed, it was now time for what had always been Gaullism's great adversary in the Fifth Republic – Communism – to come under attack. Politically and culturally, the two had divided up the republic between themselves, so to speak, with the French Communist Party offering not just a 'counter-culture' but even a kind of potential 'counter-state'.[15]

The major myth of Gaullism had of course been the General himself, who had left with a whimper in 1969, having lost what many considered a minor referendum. But then again there was a certain logic to the idea that a man who was supposed to embody *la France* could not possibly lose a popular vote. De Gaulle's shadow proved long. But from the early 1970s onwards France began to conform more to the post-war Western European constitutional settlement (even though the disempowering of parliaments had been part of the Gaullist constitution from the very beginning). In particular, a landmark decision by the Conseil Constitutionnel in 1971 established the principle that human rights were to be protected by the court. After de Gaulle, plebiscitary leadership was never to be quite the same again.

Communism's myths had mainly been of a moral and intellectual nature, rather than centred on individual charisma and the ideal of strong executive power de Gaulle personified; it was only logical, then, that left-wing intellectuals themselves had to dismantle them.[16] Many claimed to have been shaken out of their ideological slumber by what came to be known as the *choc Soljenitsyne*. Arguably nowhere else did the publication of *The Gulag Archipelago* have such an impact as in the Hexagon – but not because what Solzhenitsyn described had been completely unknown. True, there was the undeniable literary power of Solzhenitsyn's work, in particular the frequently sarcastic tone that demanded one take a stance and that made its readers angry as much as saddened. But the attack on Communism was also prompted by concrete domestic concerns: in 1972 François Mitterrand had created the Union of the Left between Communists and Socialists, with a five-year Common Programme for governing. In the run-up to the 1978 elections, there was a real sense that a Communist–Socialist government might actually be voted in. This possibility made it all the more important who would win the battle for political – and intellectual – dominance within the Socialist–Communist coalition.

It was therefore not an accident that a new intellectual anti-Communism – though phrased in the language of 'antitotalitarianism' – peaked at precisely this moment. The reaction of the Communist Party to Solzhenitsyn was widely interpreted as a sign of its authoritarianism; PCF leader Georges Marchais claimed that the Russian dissident could of course publish in a socialist France – 'if he found a publisher'.[17] Left-wing magazines like *Esprit* argued forcefully that the PCF had not really broken with its Stalinist past and that the Common Programme proposed far too state-centred an approach to building socialism.

And then the so-called New Philosophers burst on to the scene. Young and telegenic, André Glucksmann and Bernard-Henri Lévy produced a string of bestsellers, much fêted in popular magazines and on the small screen. They argued that socialism and Marxism and in fact all political thinking inspired by Hegel was fatally contaminated with authoritarianism. The ex-Maoist Glucksmann especially appeared as strident in his condemnation of more or less all recent philosophy as he had previously been in his endorsement of Mao's Little Red Book. He railed against the '*theoretical cretinism* proper to our century' and argued that 'our century produces and reproduces this invention which is proper to it: the concentration camp'; East and West both shared what he called the imperatives of 'Colony, Order, Work'. His polemic culminated in the notion that 'to think is to dominate', while Lévy in turn proclaimed that the Gulag was simply 'the Enlightenment minus tolerance'.[18] An opposition to the state, in fact to all forms of power, as well as a thoroughgoing historical pessimism, pervaded the literary output of the New Philosophers – to the extent that older liberals like Raymond Aron consciously distanced themselves from *les nouveaux philosophes*, whom they suspected of black-and-white thinking, in which black and white had simply changed places.[19]

More serious intellectuals were moving in a similar direction, though. The historian François Furet, a brilliant organizer and institution-builder no less than an outstanding historian, relentlessly attacked Marxist interpretations of the French Revolution; he argued that totalitarianism had been present in the Revolution from the very start and that the Communists were quite right to draw a direct line from 1789 to 1917 – except that the continuity in question was one of terrorism and totalitarianism. He claimed that 'the work of Solzhenitsyn raised the question of the gulag everywhere in the depths of the revolutionary design . . . Today the gulag leads to a rethinking of the Terror by virtue of an identity in their projects.'[20]

It was not just that the revolutionary imagination had been depleted in the wake of 1968's obvious failure as a political revolution; rather, the very logic of glorifying 1917 by thinking of it together with 1789 now went into reverse: retroactively, parts of the French Revolution became contaminated with Leninism and Stalinism.[21] And revolutions elsewhere in the world – China and Cuba in particular – lost their glow. In April 1976 Michel Foucault had argued that 'the role of the intellectual today should be to reestablish for the image of the revolution the same level of desirability that existed in the nineteenth century.'[22] Only a year or so later he had to concede that 'for the first time . . . this entire body of thought of the European left, this revolutionary European thought which had its points of reference in the entire world . . . thus a thought that was oriented toward things that were situated outside itself, this thought has lost the historical reference-points that it previously found in other parts of the world.'[23]

A large ideological void seemed to have opened up. Human rights appeared to be one area where – after Solzhenitsyn – long-standing liberals, renegade leftists and, for that matter, even some unreconstructed leftists could unite in a moral project which transcended deeply entrenched ideological disputes. They were a kind of minimalist moral-default option after so many other ideological blueprints for the future seemed to have failed.[24] Thus everyone experienced it as an emblematic moment when Sartre and Aron shared a podium in 1978 to campaign on behalf of the Vietnamese boat people. Brought together by Glucksmann, they shook hands, and this after Sartre had publicly claimed in 1968 that Aron did not deserve the title professor.[25]

Nevertheless, it was soon questioned whether by themselves human rights would actually be sufficient to constitute a positive political programme. Marcel Gauchet, a pupil of Lefort and an editor of *Le Débat* (which had been launched in 1980 and established itself quickly as France's premier intellectual magazine), asked whether human rights were enough: they were crucial for criticizing tyrannies, but of little use when it came to constituting groups capable of political action in their own right.[26] Rights, in other words, were perceived as positively corrosive of repressive regimes, but emphasizing them to the exclusion of collective goals could undermine positive ideals of statecraft – social democratic ones in particular.

Socialists and Communists finally triumphed at the ballot box in 1981. But rather than realizing anything resembling the Common Programme, or advancing on the road to self-management, François Mitterrand presided over a radical turnaround: under intense pressure from international financial markets, he had his prime minister abandon any ambitious nationalization plans in 1984. The age of diminished expectations that had begun in the early 1970s could not be transcended by an act of political will.

Intellectually, antitotalitarianism succeeded in corroding any bien-pensant benevolence towards Communism, but its attacks on social engineering and bureaucracy also tainted other left-wing politics – Social Democracy in particular – that understood itself as explicitly anti-Communist. The immediate effect of the latter was not yet obvious in France; the only visible change was the almost complete dismantling of the Communist counter-culture by the end of the 1980s – in a way that had no parallel in Italy. But there the PCI also gradually declined: the high-minded, in its original inspiration Gramscian, emphasis on self-improvement (and high culture) continued, and the party never came to grips with the blurring of the borders between high and popular culture that characterized the 1970s and 1980s. But Communist theory continued to flourish; in France, on the other hand, what remained of socialism was theoretically uninspired and politically uninspiring. The more exciting ideals of the *deuxième gauche* were never put into practice, not least because Mitterrand was obsessed with destroying the political ambition of Michel Rocard – the leading political exponent of the Second Left – to succeed him as president.

Social Democracy under Pressure

It was, above all, old-style Social Democracy that came under threat in the late 1970s and the 1980s; the most conservative politician at the time – in the literal sense of not wanting change – was 'the right-wing Social Democrat', according to Ralf Dahrendorf.[27] Pressure came from two sides simultaneously. On the one hand, there was the New Left and the social movements it had spawned – including the peace movement which was growing rapidly in opposition to the deployment of 'Euro missiles'. On the other hand, there was what observers alternatively construed as a revival of classical nineteenth-century liberalism or, conceding that something theoretically new was in the air, as neoliberalism. Quite apart from these two obvious threats, there was postmodernism – not a political movement but certainly a political mood of sorts, characterized by a distrust of 'grand narratives' of human progress and, in particular, of the technocratic, 'modernist' vocabulary that had been central to the age of mass democracy.

The lasting legacies of the New Left turned out to be feminism and environmentalism – although, as was pointed out in the last chapter, neither was directly related to '68 or 1960s theory as such, and certainly owed nothing to anything that was particularly Marxist. Feminism could to a considerable extent be integrated into parties which traditionally had understood themselves more or less without saying so as consisting of males and as working for males – especially males employed in industry. Environmentalism, however, was initially institutionalized separately, in green parties – which in fact at first presented themselves as 'anti-party parties'. It was clearly much more difficult for thinkers and political parties of an ultimately Marxist inspiration to break with a belief in the beneficial nature of industrial production.

A pioneer of such a break was the social philosopher André Gorz, who, as a consequence, was much maligned by traditional Marxists. Born Gerhard Hirsch in Vienna in 1923, he was the son of a Jewish merchant and a Catholic secretary. During the war he had been sent to study in Switzerland, where he obtained a degree as a chemical engineer. He came to the attention of Jean-Paul Sartre and Simone de Beauvoir when they visited Lausanne in 1946; subsequently, the man who now called himself Gorz (after the company that had produced his father's army fieldglasses) moved to Paris and became a close collaborator of the world's most famous philosopher. Initially he aspired to be a writer and his first novel, *The Traitor*, appeared in 1958, with a preface by Sartre. But subsequently Gorz worked mainly as a journalist, co-founding the influential left-leaning weekly *Nouvel Observateur*.

He eventually turned to social philosophy, trying to elaborate strategies for the working class under 'advanced capitalism'. These in many ways paralleled the ideas expounded by Marcuse and by the Italian New Left in the 1960s. But then his orientation changed more radically than that of the Italians ever did: by the mid-1970s he began to stress the importance of ecology; in 1982 he published his most controversial book, *Farewell to the Working Class: An Essay on Post-Industrial Socialism*. He urged a 'future Left' to give up on the proletariat as a revolutionary subject and instead to envisage 'the liberation of time' as well as the 'abolition of work' – that is, the end of labour for a wage. In practical terms, Gorz advocated a basic income for all citizens irrespective of employment – the ultimate step in overcoming 'workerism', that is to say, the exclusive focus on the proletariat and the obsession with labour as central to human fulfilment. The demand for the end of work, Gorz argued, was not at all utopian; it was perfectly in line with developments actually under way in Western societies. Keynes, he claimed,

> is dead. In the context of the current crisis and technological revolution it is absolutely impossible to restore full employment by quantitative economic growth. The alternative lies rather in a different way of managing the aboli-tion of work: instead of a society based on mass unemployment, a society can be built in which time has been freed.[28]

Gorz also identified a new 'non-class of non-workers' as carriers of radical change – men and women in non-industrial, 'intellectualized' jobs, as opposed to the traditional industrial working class, as well as the under-employed and the unemployed.

'Non-class of non-workers' was not exactly a rousing call to a dormant revo-lutionary subject. But Gorz's theory as a whole was among the most radical in the latter third of the European twentieth century: it challenged not only particular Social Democratic policies, but the post-war left's political imagina-tion in general. It called into question the gospel of never-ceasing economic growth; it also suggested that being on the left was not a matter of being (or being for) workers. As Gorz wrote, 'it is no longer a question of winning power as a worker, but of winning the power no longer to function as a worker'. Thus Gorz even opposed ideas of workers' control (as production would still ultimately be determined by the 'giant machine' of society).[29]

Environmentalism, while also featuring thinkers opposed to any further economic growth, demanded nothing quite as radical. That is perhaps why environmentalist ideas eventually ceased to be represented primarily by green anti-parties and were at least partly adopted by virtually all parties in Europe. If there ever was such a thing as an end of ideology (at least in Europe), it could be found here: while everyone disagreed about policies, nobody was prepared to deny anything like a basic imperative to save the planet.[30]

Both feminism and environmentalism were intimately tied to the peace movement. Opposition to nuclear war became closely aligned with efforts to end 'male violence', as well as what Edward Thompson referred to as the general 'exterminism' of the industrial system.[31] The philosopher Rudolf Bahro insisted that 'militarism is a natural consequence of the dependence on raw materials of our over-worked production system'.[32] Thus 'eco-pacifism' mandated nothing less than what thinkers such as Bahro referred to as 'indus-trial disarmament' – even if it remained unclear what an industrially disarmed society might look like. But, then again, Bahro and others claimed that 'it is in general wrong to believe that social change can only be achieved if people have first been given a scientific explanation of what precisely can be done'.[33]

Social movements were thriving throughout the 1980s, but their visions were, for the most part, negative, if not outright apocalyptic. As Bahro announced in 1982:

> the plagues of ancient Egypt are upon us, the horsemen of the apocalypse can be heard, the seven deadly sins are visible all around us in the cities of today, where Babel is multiplied a thousand fold. In 1968 the promised Canaan of general emancipation appeared on the horizon, and this time at last for women as well. But almost all of those who believe in this have tacitly come to realise that first of all will come the years in the wilderness. All that is lacking now is the pillar of fire to show us the route of our exodus.[34]

Habermas did not know where to look for the pillar of fire, but he shared the sense of a new intellectual wilderness. In 1985 he diagnosed the 'new confusion' – or *neue Unübersichtlichkeit* – and the 'exhaustion of utopian energies'. In particular, the utopias centred on labour had conclusively lost their appeal. Dahrendorf had already declared a few years earlier the end of the 'Social Democratic Century'.[35] What did this mean, given that the Social Democratic parties obviously had not disappeared from the political landscape? It was a question of confidence and unspoken assumptions, not electoral outcomes: the belief in large-scale collective self-transformations of society, often but not necessarily couched in the language of technocracy, seemed to have been undermined, perhaps fatally.

Habermas saw this ideal – which he identified with the Enlightenment and, broadly speaking, with rational progress – as coming under attack from what he called 'neoconservatives' (a usage only partially related to what the term was to designate in the United States). Neoconservatives, according to Habermas, believed in a kind of 'foreshortened' or 'arrested' Enlightenment: capitalism was here to stay, and traditional values and culture were to compensate for any damage capitalism might be inflicting on individuals and the lifeworld – a kind of consolation through pleasing (and never provocative) aesthetics. In any event, in the eyes of the neocons (as construed by Habermas) the traditional family and the nation-state were institutions that simply could not be further changed, let alone transcended altogether – they were, in a sense, where the Enlightenment met its institutional limits. Unlike Habermas, supposedly neoconservative thinkers such as Hermann Lübbe denied that the family and values of friendship would be undermined by the kind of thinking and feeling required to do well in a capitalist system. According to them, market economy did not have to mean market society.

The End of the End of Alienation – and Cutting Off the King's Head

In Habermas' eyes, the Enlightenment was also coming under attack from a quite different angle, namely from postmodern and post-structuralist thinkers who supposedly denigrated 'reason' and represented a dangerous celebration of the 'spontaneous powers of the imagination', 'the immediacy of the affects' and even the individual's 'will to power' – all in contrast with 'reason'. In other words, what these intellectuals were after could only be evoked and not discussed, a matter of will and gestures, not of deliberation – a highly problematic, or so Habermas hinted, step back into the 1920s, with potentially sinister political consequences.

Indeed, drawing primarily on Nietzsche and Heidegger, a number of French thinkers cast fundamental doubt on any notion of rational autonomy. With Jean-François Lyotard (who had once been close to the undogmatic left around Castoriadis and Lefort), they not only diagnosed but in fact demanded an 'incredulity towards meta-narratives', ideals of rational progress in particular. A proper understanding of history – especially the history of the most high-minded ideals – required an appreciation of the fact that their origins were often unsavoury or bound up with violence, and that the past, when looked at closely, was a story not of progress but of never-ending power struggles. In a sense, Habermas was justified in seeing the emergence of postmodernism as yet another symptom of Western Europe's 'loss of confidence' in itself: for the postmodernists history was a matter of debunking and deflating, not of finding hope.

Added to all this, postmodern thinkers renounced any search for a fully authentic way of life, which had still been assumed to be available somewhere somehow by the theorists of the late 1960s. The philosopher Jean Baudrillard admitted, not without nostalgia, that 'I was very, very attracted by Situationism' and 'even if today Situationism is past, there remains a kind of radicality to which I have always been faithful'.[36] Situationism was past because postmodernists no longer held out hope for a realm beyond the spectacle that could be recovered through political (or just cultural) action. Ending alienation, completely and conclusively – that was an illusion, and a dangerous one.

All that seemed to remain were either radical gestures without radical programmes or a philosophical style emphasizing irony and pastiche (also without programmes). The tragedy of culture was still tragic, but it no longer elicited tears, only knowing smiles. This is what alarmed the critics of postmodernism on the left – social hope seemingly giving way to nostalgia: while progressive mass politics waned, museums boomed. To be sure, it was usually ironic nostalgia, or at least nostalgia different from the cultural pessimism which had suffused left-wing and, even more so, right-wing political thought for so long. But did this mean that at the end of a century of political passion and self-righteous ideologies stood . . . relativism?

Not all was what it seemed, and the political meaning of postmodernism and post-structuralism very much depended on the perspective from which one was perceiving (or even creating) it. The trajectory of Michel Foucault is telling in this regard. Foucault was born in 1926 into a bourgeois family based in Poitiers.[37] He refused early on to follow in the footsteps of his father, a highly respected provincial doctor. He had grown up under Vichy (his parents were discreetly opposed), decided to become an academic and eventually made it to Paris' elite academic institutions, in his case the Lycée Henri IV and the Ecole Normale Supérieure, where he studied philosophy and psychology (and where he briefly joined the French Communist Party, only to leave in disgust, as Stalin, just before his death, seemed to launch a new wave of terror). Rather than being condemned to teach in the provinces for a few years before starting a proper academic career back in the capital, Foucault was lucky enough to serve as a cultural diplomat abroad: he headed French cultural insti-tutes in Uppsala (where he found Swedish Social Democracy, promising a future in which everyone would be 'happy, rich and ascepticized'), in Warsaw (where he experienced 'the stubborn sun of Polish freedom' trying to melt a frozen 'people's democracy') and in Hamburg (where he took visiting cultural luminaries on tours of the red-light district).

By the mid-1960s, Foucault had become well known in France as the author of a history of madness and was widely identified as a star of structuralism, even if he himself did not directly associate himself with a strand of thinking which critics viewed as a form of determinism: originally part of linguistics, structuralism eventually claimed to explain the behaviour of whole societies, emphasizing the unchanging and the unconscious. In the eyes of its enemies, structuralism was the perfect philosophical fit for the era of technocracy; Jean-Paul Sartre derided it as 'the last barricade that the bourgeoisie can erect against Marx'. It seemed to deny human beings any capacity to make their own history.

Structuralists and those sympathizing with its methods did not hesitate to hit back. Apropos existentialism's emphasis on individual freedom Foucault claimed in 1968, 'man is disappearing in philosophy, not as an object of knowl-edge, but as a subject of liberty and of existence'.[38] Foucault also dismissed the ideal of the general intellectual – who speaks moral truth to power – that

Sartre had embodied like no one else, and this was meant to be a blow against both existentialism and Marxism. Foucault drove the point home in criticizing the notion of the intellectual as 'being the consciousness/conscience of us all': 'I think we have here an idea transposed from Marxism, from a faded Marxism indeed. Just as the proletariat, by the necessity of its historical situation, is the bearer of the universal . . . so the intellectual . . . aspires to be the bearer of this universality in its conscious, elaborated form.'[39]

But Foucault came to change his mind, not so much about the limits of the general intellectual as about the capacity of human beings to make their own history. And what changed his mind? The short answer is '68 and after (one of whose larger lessons was summed up in the famous one-liner that structures don't demonstrate in the streets).[40] True, Foucault had not himself been in Paris during the May events; he was teaching philosophy in Tunisia. There, however, he had witnessed a far more brutal (and often deadly) suppression of student protest by the authoritarian Bourguiba regime. Back in France, he became deeply involved with a post-'68 (and partly Maoist) association, the Groupe d'Information sur les Prisons (GIP).[41] After the Maoist Gauche Prolétarienne had been banned by the government and some of its leaders incarcerated, the remaining members sought to draw attention to the appalling conditions in French prisons. Prisons themselves were off limits for researchers, but question-naires could be handed out to wives visiting inmates, and former inmates them-selves could be encouraged to write about their experiences (the results of these investigations were then published in a book series with the title 'Intolerable').

It was labour-intensive political activism: Foucault was not above stuffing and addressing envelopes. It also allowed the man who now held the chair in the History of Systems of Thought at the Collège de France, the country's most prestigious academic institution, to get his hands dirty, so to speak – outside the archives, in line with his notion that ever since 1956 had discredited Marxism as a framework providing an interpretation of all political events, philosophers should really become journalists. And, not least, it furnished Foucault with some of the ideas which he was to develop in the 1970s. In particular, he began to emphasize that 'power' was not just repression exer-cised by the state from above, but functioned in much more subtle ways, espe-cially in the form of being disciplined by seemingly benevolent institutions like hospitals and, not least, by oneself: not so much the society of the spectacle as the society of surveillance; not so much the state as executioner as the state in the role of a sanatorium director who wants 'docile bodies'.

A related but much more positive lesson could be drawn from '68, however: that political change did not primarily have to be about confronting the state head-on (and, on the Leninist model, seizing centralized bureaucratic power).

At first sight, this seemed to make individual liberation easier. One should simply, as the Situationists had suggested all along, behave differently, in everyday life. But in fact liberation could also be said to have become a much more problematic endeavour. Foucault, like other thinkers sceptical of the inherited languages of 'alienation', did not believe that there was an 'authentic self' to be liberated. But he also thought that the modern state – and in particular the liberal state – reinforced the self-disciplining of subjects in ways that were much harder to perceive and to break free from.

Foucault claimed that 'the political, ethical, social, philosophical problem of our days is not to try to liberate the individual from the state . . . but to liberate us both from the state and from the type of individualization which is linked to the state'. The focus thus shifted to liberal 'governmentality', the set of techniques and 'arts' of government which effectively made liberal subjects govern themselves, rather than have states directly repress them, as premodern and authoritarian states did. As Foucault explained: 'It is not that the beautiful totality of the individual is amputated, repressed, altered by our social order; it is rather that the individual is carefully fabricated in it, according to a whole technique of forces and bodies.' Modern liberty, Foucault thus claimed, had been 'produced', too, and was not a direct opposite to state power in the way that was conventionally assumed by liberals.[42] And liberal governmentality, he argued, was reaching a new stage of sophistication during his own time, with Hayek's thought and the German neoliberal Freiburg School whose members had been advising Ludwig Erhard.

This was a strong, counter-intuitive punch-line: liberalism was not about not interfering with people's freedom; rather, it was about the state much more subtly 'conducting the conducts' of individuals who thought themselves free. The modern state, Foucault now added, was a biopolitical enterprise. It controlled not just the quantity but also the 'quality' of its populations and sought to augment it. The idea that states acted directly on individuals' bodies could be derived from some of Foucault's own more unusual political experiences: seeing his Tunisian students disappear into basements, only to re-emerge with bloodied faces; noticing his Polish interlocutors lower their voices (and discreetly burn their letters). But it was also a question that had been posed as long ago as Weber's political writings: how did modern self-disciplining and 'the quality of people' (which Weber sought unashamedly) relate to each other? Was Nazi biocracy perhaps much less of an aberration in Western history than generally thought; was it in fact 'the dream of modern power', as Foucault wrote?[43] The answer was clear and shocking: according to Foucault, 'the modern state can scarcely function without becoming involved with racism at some point'.

At the same time, Foucault remained adamant that power should not be conceived as a top-down affair – an image which might have been appropriate for an age of kings, but which no longer captured the workings of modern states and societies. He claimed that 'in thought and political analysis we have still not cut off the head of the king', since 'political theory has never ceased to be obsessed with the person of the sovereign' – and this obsession had led to a distorted conception of power which remained indebted to 'the juridico-political theory of sovereignty'.[44] It was urgent, Foucault argued, to break with a tradition which conceived power only in terms of law (and repression), and therefore privileged states in any analysis. In a tone of exasperation with the received wisdom, he explained that:

in defining the effects of power as repression, one adopts a purely juridical conception of such power, one identifies power with a law that says no ... Now, I believe that this is a wholly negative, narrow, skeletal conception of power, one that has been curiously widespread. If power were never anything but repressive, if it never did anything but to say no, do you really think one would be brought to obey it? What makes power hold good, what makes it accepted, is simply the fact that it doesn't only weigh on us as a force that says no; it also traverses and produces things, it induces pleasure, forms knowledge, produces discourse. It needs to be considered as a productive network that runs through the whole social body, much more than as a negative instance whose function is repression.[45]

In a curious way, Foucault's thought paralleled Luhmann's: both claimed that an essentially outdated political language from centuries back led theorists, and ordinary citizens, vastly to overestimate the role of the state. Both advanced the idea that power was not located 'at the top' in the official domain of politics. And so the ideas of both could resonate in particular during a time when states, confronted with new economic challenges and social discontent, did seem curiously 'powerless' – even if the political imperatives the two theorists derived from their work were diametrically opposed.

Power, if it was 'circulating' and dispersed, clearly needed to be studied in its 'micro-physics'; it was also at the micro-level, so to speak, that Foucault now firmly located the work of the intellectual. He both diagnosed and advocated a shift from the universal or general intellectual – that is to say, Sartre – to the 'specific intellectual'. Where for Luhmann the ideal intellectual was the adviser to the bureaucracy, in Foucault's eyes he or she might have been the expert working with prisoners, psychiatric patients or gays. It was again a very post-1968 thought: the intellectual elite was not to represent the universal from on high, but to work with (and only very indirectly for) particular others. Foucault elaborated the argument:

> the work of an intellectual is not to form the political will of others; it is, through the analyses he does in his own domains, to bring assumptions and things taken for granted again into question, to shake habits . . . to take the measure of rules and institutions and, starting from that re-problematization (where he plays his specific role as intellectual), to take part in the formation of a political will (where he has his role to play as citizen).

In the end, Foucault was no less globally engaged than Sartre – omnipresent, it seemed, from California to Iran, where he reported for an Italian newspaper on the 1978 revolution (which he lauded initially as a new 'political spirituality', 'a groundswell with no vanguard and no party').[46] Whether he admitted it or not, like Sartre he still pursued a distinctly moral agenda, one that came to be centred on the practical demand for respecting human rights: he drove supplies to Poland in the early 1980s, when the Solidarity trade union had been repressed;[47] and he lauded the work of New Philosophers like Glucksmann.[48] But he no longer spoke a confident universalist moral language. His new understanding of power and his (admittedly cagey) calls for specific moral engagement hung together; and, practically, both pointed to an imperative of subversion – as opposed to calls for insurrection (let alone acceptance of charismatic vanguard party leadership). But both visions also remained incomplete, lacking any kind of larger and positive orientation once the work of subversion was done. Foucault demanded that 'we should be looking for a new right that is both antidisciplinary and emancipated from the principle of sovereignty'.[49] That search had only just begun when Foucault died prematurely, in 1984, one of the first prominent victims of AIDS.

Foucault had wanted his books to be mines, bombs or at least fireworks. In his eyes, exploring 'the History of Systems of Thought' was a kind of war for subversion, an attempt loudly to question or quietly to undermine the most common assumptions about the social and political worlds. It would be hard to claim that he had been an 'in-between figure' exercising influence on policy (though serious prison reform was undertaken after the highly visible work of the GIP). But nobody who had read Foucault – even if they continued to endorse the 'decent state' which Tawney and other welfare-oriented thinkers had created – could ever view the state with quite the same eyes.

There had seemed to be an unbridgeable difference between Foucault and post-structuralists on the one side and Habermas and his many followers in continental Europe on the other: here, a suspicion of universalism and inherited left-wing languages of liberation as always annihilating differences and

particularity; there, a willingness to hold on to languages of the Enlightenment –
a chastened Enlightenment, to be sure – because its values still promised the best
route to social and political amelioration. Ultimately, however, Habermas and
the French theorists shared a great deal more than either seemed to have realized
initially. Both clung to an ideal of autonomy, except that the prime threats
to autonomy were perceived very differently on opposite sides of the Rhine:
Habermas, a self-identified 'product of American re-education', feared a return of
political irrationalism; his philosophical opponents in France were apprehensive
about an oppressive rationalism (including structuralism). Symptomatic was an
admission by Foucault who at one point – outrageously, it seemed – had asserted
that reason equalled torture. Pressed by a German interviewer, he conceded that
for him the word *raison*, unlike the German *Vernunft*, had no ethical dimension.
Thus 'for us in French, torture, that is reason. But I understand very well that in
German torture cannot be reason.'[50]

So at least some skirmishes in the epic philosophical battles between
modernists (or defenders of the Enlightenment) and postmodernists (or
critics of the Enlightenment) had been based on terrible generalizations (such
as '*the* Enlightenment' rather than 'the Scottish Enlightenment' or 'the French
Enlightenment') and, it seemed, a few terrible mistranslations.[51] More important, while their ways of articulating moral agendas for politics differed
profoundly (Habermas called Foucault 'crypto-normative'), and while their
assessments of the post-war constitutional settlement were generally at odds
(Habermas was much more positive about what had been achieved by way of
democracy), their practical conclusions were often similar. Apart from that,
they were also increasingly united against a common enemy: neoliberalism.

The Descent from Mont Pèlerin

The greatest threat to Social Democracy (and, by extension, to social versions
of Christian Democracy) was neither neoconservatism – which was not in
principle hostile to the welfare state – nor postmodernism. It was altogether
unexpected, and it was in many ways based on a renewal of 'utopian energies' –
except that the utopia in question was that of the unfettered market and the
strong state.

As we saw in Chapter 4, it did not emerge from nowhere. Ludwig von Mises,
an economics professor fully in favour of laissez-faire, had stipulated as early as
the 1920s that 'only ideas can overcome ideas and it is only *ideas* of Capitalism
and of Liberalism that can overcome Socialism'. Based on this insight, Mises'
pupil Hayek had been working all along with and through his 'non-organisation
of individuals', the Mont Pèlerin Society, which was often also plagued by a

'non-organisation' of opinions. Many of the most influential members saw no need for anything 'neo' and remained wedded to ideals of laissez-faire, feuding with representatives of the German social-market economy in particular. Mises once stormed out of a meeting with the words 'You are all communists!'[52]

Even if the 'army of fighters for freedom' was sometimes in disarray, Hayek's clarion call for 'second-hand dealers in ideas' had been heard clearly. Think tanks were set up and some eventually gained influence on major politicians such as Sir Keith Joseph, a cabinet minister in a succession of Tory governments with a serious interest in political philosophy (which earned him the nickname 'mad monk'), as well as a tendency for ideological self-flagellation: he confessed that he had not really been a Conservative until 1974, when he had been converted to the virtues of a strong state combined with a free economy.[53]

With the apparent failure of Keynesian policies, Hayek slowly ceased to be viewed as a kind of intellectual crank. He received the Nobel Prize in 1974 (though it was suspected he was chosen to 'balance' the socialist Gunnar Myrdal).[54] Hayek himself had also toned down his rhetoric somewhat and now did without apocalyptic predictions; although Labour in '45 had seemed to be the first step towards totalitarianism, he later conceded that socialism had probably peaked with the 1945–51 Attlee government.

But Hayek made no concessions in political theory. Writing more as a social philosopher than as an economist from the 1950s onwards, he advocated a strong state, in the sense of a state able to resist the demands emanating from society – meaning special-interest groups, and trade unions in particular. But in actual fact, an opposition of state and society was already conceptually dubious; Margaret Thatcher, seemingly faithful to Hayek's methodological individualism, claimed in an interview with the magazine *Woman's Own* in 1987 that there was no such thing as society. Instead, 'there are individual men and women and there are families and no government can do anything except through people and people look to themselves first'.

Even Thatcher, however, might have underestimated the radical nature of some of Hayek's proposals. The Austro-British professor presented himself as rehabilitating a classical nineteenth-century conception of liberalism, in particular the primacy of the rule of law over democracy, and argued that the limits, rather than the source, of political rule were decisive for good government. As early as 1944 he had affirmed that he had 'no intention . . . of making a fetish of democracy': 'It may well be true that our generation talks and thinks too much of democracy and too little of the values which it serves . . . Democracy is essentially a means, a utilitarian device for safeguarding internal peace and individual freedom. As such it is by no means infallible or certain.'[55] But, according to Hayek, there were means of generating more certainty against 'arbitrary power'. And in specifying them, he finally put forward what he had been promising from the mid-1940s onward: a liberal utopia. He proposed a new constitutional settlement ensuring that only abstract universal laws (that is, laws not serving special interests) would be enacted and individual liberty maximized. To that end he advocated the creation of a parliamentary upper house with a small membership – 'an assembly of men and women elected at a relatively mature age for fairly long periods, such as fifteen years, so that they would not be concerned about being re-elected'.[56] In short, power should be delegated as much as possible to political bodies insulated from the people – that is to say, from pressure groups and elections.

Much as he admired Britain, Hayek's self-described 'model constitution' owed more to nineteenth-century continental conceptions of the monarchical state and its unitary executive than to a Britain where parliament – until the very last years of the twentieth century – was to reign supreme. Still, Hayek's thought proved popular, because it appeared to offer a solution to the 'governability crisis' of the 1970s, putting an end to consensus politics or what Hayek himself called 'the muddle of the middle'. In particular, it justified the crushing of militant trade unions. When Mrs Thatcher proceeded to do just that, she was told to stay the course by letters to the editor in the London *Times* by none other than Hayek.[57]

However, Hayek was not the only intellectual patron saint of Thatcherism. One of the philosophically most sophisticated defences of a strong, centralized state disengaging from society (and from planning in particular) was proposed by the unlikely figure of Michael Oakeshott – in the eyes of many observers a quintessentially English gentleman-scholar averse to any radicalism, including a radical reconceptualization of statehood. Yet in many ways he recast the notion of the state as it had evolved in twentieth-century Western Europe more fundamentally than even the supposed classical liberalism of Hayek did.

Oakeshott had been part of the wave of British Idealism in the 1920s and 1930s, before analytical philosophy essentially demolished it.[58] He had studied theology in Germany in the mid-1920s, but then veered away from religious topics. His first teaching assignment was in Cambridge, where he acquired a reputation as a dandy and a ladies' man. He also took on seemingly risky academic topics: he was the first don to lecture on Marx, in 1938. Earlier he had published a book entitled *A Guide to the Classics* – though the classics in question were horse races, and the subtitle appropriately read, *How to Pick a Derby Winner*. Not much indicated that this man would one day play an important role in twentieth-century conservative political thought.

After the war Oakeshott moved to the London School of Economics, then a hotbed of student radicalism. Faithful to the Fabian tradition, the School also remained a training ground for bureaucrats to staff the emerging welfare state.

In a number of elegant essays Oakeshott began to register his opposition to planning and what he called 'rationalism in politics'. He claimed that 'a centrally planned society is the ideal of all rationalistic politics', and that liberal democracy was increasingly obsessed with what he called – using a phrase from D. H. Lawrence – 'the plausible ethics of productivity'. But politics, Oakeshott insisted, was not about far-sighted planning, and not for the intellectual-as-planner. He claimed that 'it is not the clear-sighted, not those who are fashioned for thought and the ardors of thought, who can lead the world. Great achievements are accomplished in the mental fog of practical experience. What is farthest from our needs is that kings should be philosophers'. Rather, politics was to be characterized by what Oakeshott termed 'the pursuit of the intimations of tradition'; the source of political activity, according to Bernard Susser – gently parodying Oakeshott here – could only be 'the rhythms, textures, resonances, whisperings, cues, recollections . . . that animate a given tradition of public life'. To discern these, in turn, 'a finely tuned yet inarticulable sensibility' was needed.[59]

Practice, informed by tradition, was the exact opposite of rationalism – of which Oakeshott, in 1947, had already given a rather incongruous-seeming list of examples: 'the project of the so-called Re-Union of the Christian Churches, of open diplomacy, of a single tax, of a civil service whose "members have no qual-ification other than their personal abilities", of a self-consciously planned society, the Beveridge Report, the Education Act of 1944, Federalism, Nationalism, Votes for Women . . . the destruction of the Austro-Hungarian Empire, the World State . . . and the revival of Gaelic as the official language of Eire'.[60] One might detect as a common denominator here a certain technocratic scheming, but also the ever busy activity of the New Man over-eager for reform, at whom Oakeshott sneered without too much of an attempt to disguise his feelings. The rationalist in his hubris, like the self-made man or woman, denied that his achievements depended on the services rendered by others – in the present, but also, above all, in the past. Oakeshott put the point with a typically homely metaphor: 'the cookery book is not an independently generated beginning from which cooking can spring; it is nothing more than an abstract of somebody's knowledge of how to cook; it is the stepchild, not the parent, of the activity'.

The cricket and cooking metaphors, the evocations of long summer evenings in the Home Counties and warm beer hid a very hard political edge, however.[61] The real force of this theory derived from Oakeshott's distinction between what he called civil and enterprise association, or the contrast between *societas* and *universitas*. Oakeshott claimed that:

> the idea of *societas* is that of agents who, by choice or circumstance, are related to one another so as to compose an identifiable association of a

certain sort. The tie that binds them, and in respect of which each recognizes himself to be *socius*, is not that of an engagement in an enterprise to pursue a common substantive purpose or to promote a common interest, but that of loyalty to one another, the conditions of which may achieve the formality denoted by the kindred word 'legality'.[62]

In contrast, enterprise associations did have a common substantive purpose, to which its members had to subordinate themselves. In modern times, citizens of such associations would act with what Oakeshott called 'warm, compensated servility'; they would also most likely be those to whom he referred in unflattering terms as individuals *manqués* – human beings incapable of bearing the burden of making their own choices; of belonging to themselves and being, as he put it, 'self-employed'. The individual *manqué* apparently 'had feelings rather than thoughts, impulses rather than opinions, inabilities rather than passions'. These mass men, Oakeshott implied, were fit only for a *régime administratif* whose rulers acted either like chairmen of a board of technocrats or like 'the directors of a sanatorium from which no patient may discharge himself by a choice of his own'.[63]

Oakeshott was painting the supposedly paternalist post-war welfare state in the most unflattering light possible. He contrasted the state as sanatorium with the vision of a strong state possessing undisputed authority that set itself no goals, had no pretensions to scientific management and let its citizens get on with their lives – or 'adventures' and 'travels', as he often put it. Oakeshott thought that there was a specific human type – the modern European individual – who alone was fit to inhabit such a state. This type had been a particular civilizational achievement, celebrated by Montaigne, Hegel and Tocqueville. And now it was in danger of dying out.

In a style unmatched by any political theorist writing in English in the twentieth century, Oakeshott had given philosophical credibility to an all-out assault on post-war consensus politics, and on the very idea of harnessing state power for the collective self-transformation of society – the political imaginary that had become so plausible after the First World War and that had been cast in indisputably democratic terms after 1945. Oakeshott's attack, though, seemed all the more effective because it came in harmless-sounding language. In a letter to Karl Popper on the topic of rationalism he pronounced himself in favour of conversation:

> . . . I would say that the politics I have in mind is the *politics of conversation*, as against your *politics of argument*.
> I don't believe that reason is the *only* bond which unites men, not because men are unreasonable sometimes, but because there is something else much

stronger that unites them e.g. a common civilization (where it exists), common habits of behaviours (where they exist) – neither of which are rational, dependent upon argument or common to *all* men. There is *nothing*, I think, common to *all* men.

In short, the trouble with your true rationalism is not that it is impossible, but that it is impossible by itself. The place of reason, in politics & in life, is not *to take the place of* habits of behaviour, but to act as *the critic* of habits of behaviour, keeping them from superstition etc. And what the rationalist is trying to do is, so to speak, to make a literature which consists *only* of literary criticism.[64]

But Oakeshott himself was not just a critic. To the extent that it could be articulated as a coherent philosophy, he appeared to have formulated Thatcherism.[65] The Iron Lady wanted to give him an honour. He refused, saying that honours should go to those who wanted them. But he probably also had his own reasons for disliking what was happening in British society in the 1980s. In 1964, he had written in his private notebooks that ' "achievement" is the "diabolical" element in human life; and the symbol of our vulgarization of human life is our near exclusive concern with achievement'. Moreover, he had no truck with family or any other kind of Victorian values, and he insisted that 'it is not at all inconsistent to be conservative in respect of government and radical in respect of almost every other activity'.

Such quasi-aristocratic (or perhaps bohemian) *dégout* contrasted sharply with Thatcherism's insistence on moral self-discipline as a product of the market: Keith Joseph had already called in 1974 for a 'remoralisation of our national life' (which in concrete terms meant that unmarried, uneducated girls should have fewer children).[66] Thatcher herself, the grocer's daughter and ardent Methodist, would not have recognized a contradiction of market and morality; quite the contrary, the market was a way to make people moral by forcing them to adopt virtues of self-discipline, responsibility and so on. Even if in actual fact she unleashed greed and made social irresponsibility pass for virtue, she never simply recommended *Enrichissez-vous*, in the way the original proponents of laissez-faire had done. She thus also disagreed with the German neoliberals, such as Rüstow and Röpke, who feared the market as a threat to morality and hence wanted a 'politics of society' (and strong doses of Christianity) to contain its consequences. But in a sense she did agree with, of all people, Foucault: both state and market could produce a certain kind of 'individualization' – which, however, had led Foucault precisely to demand liberation 'both from the state and from the type of individualization which is linked to the state'.

Oakeshott eventually retired to his cottage in Dorset, revered by a steadily increasing number of admirers. Yet, in his view, there was of course no dogma to be reproduced, and no cookbook to be copied. His criticism of rationalism even extended to Hayek. The self-confessed Tory declared that 'a plan to resist all planning may be better than its opposite but it belongs to the same style of politics'. Fittingly, Hayek in turn kept repeating that he was in fact no conservative or Tory at all – and thus very different from Oakeshott. He noted: 'it has . . . invariably been the fate of conservatism to be dragged along a path not of its own choosing . . . What the liberal must ask, first of all, is not how fast or how far we should move, but where we should move.'[67]

But where did everyone move? In the end, what was propounded as 'classical liberalism' (ironically, only the Germans were truly comfortable with the term 'neoliberalism' – and they were the least laissez-faire) turned out to be vastly more influential in the United States than in Western Europe, as opposed to Central and Eastern Europe after 1989. It was a perfect fit with a political culture that always had a place for the not exactly European ideals of rugged individualism.[68] If anything, in Europe Hayekian liberalism was often still cloaked in the language of consensus politics. In 1975, for instance, Keith Joseph claimed that 'the objective for our lifetime, as I have come to see it, is embourgeoisement'; he went on to explain that 'our idea of the good life . . . in the sense of life-style, behaviour pattern and value-structure – has much in common with that traditionally held by Social Democrats, however we may differ about the kind of social economic structure best capable of bringing about and sustaining the state of affairs we desire'.[69] Much more so than in Thatcherite Britain (let alone Reaganesque America), even nominally conservative politicians on the continent agreed that things should change only in such a way that everything could essentially stay the same. Like Dahrendorf, they seemed to concede that 'the consensus is in a certain sense the most in terms of progress that history has ever seen'.[70]

In the end, the post-war constitutional settlement was not fundamentally renegotiated in line with anything that could plausibly be called neoliberalism. But that was partly because it already conformed to some of the institutional schemes neoliberals tended to advocate – the rule of law and checks and balances, in particular. Hayek himself seemed not have realized how Hayekian post-war politics – outside the United Kingdom – had been all along. And his more outlandish ideas, such as the senate of elders, were always unlikely to be implemented.

One of Margaret Thatcher's chancellors of the exchequer, Nigel Lawson, once claimed that the National Health Service was the closest thing the British had to a national religion – and they were not to be converted to another. In fact, under

Thatcher public spending as a percentage of gross domestic product did not shrink significantly (according to some estimates, it actually grew). Numbers, of course, do not tell the whole story of Britain in the 1980s (or of continental countries later on). Something did change in how states were conceived, and in what was seen to constitute legitimate political action. The British state – rather along Oakeshottian lines – was rigidly centralized, and local government effectively disempowered. In the political imagination the figure of the planner was replaced by that of the consultant – advising on efficiency and how to introduce 'market logic' into state bureaucracies (as well as the health service and universities). The citizen as participant in politics yielded to the citizen as consumer, who could claim their rights to compensation if the trains failed to run on time; economic audits replaced traditional notions of democratic accountability. That the latter routinely created *more* bureaucracy (in the form of regulatory agencies) was rarely appreciated. Even less appreciated was the fact that the lesson about the control of bureaucracy leading to more bureaucracy could have most plausibly been learnt from the Soviet Union.

The Politics of Antipolitics under Post-Totalitarianism

Thinkers like Hayek and Mises had accorded pride of place to ideas and intellectuals, essentially turning Marxism with its primacy of economics on its head. Yet it was debatable – and it was widely debated – whether in Western Europe intellectuals did not in fact matter less and less. It could hardly be doubted, though, that they mattered in Central and Eastern Europe. Their dissident strategy from the mid-1970s onwards was based on a very simple and very radical idea: they wanted to take their regimes at their word, especially after socialist governments had signed the Helsinki Accords of 1975 and officially committed themselves to upholding human rights.[71] The regimes themselves had assumed that the human rights basket meant nothing – an assumption shared with Western realists like Henry Kissinger, who sneered that it might as well have been written 'in Swahili for all I care'.

Taking 'socialist legality' seriously – a kind of legal positivism with unstated political intentions – had been pioneered in the mid-1960s by the Russian poet and mathematician Alexander Yessenin-Volpin.[72] He was the son of the popular folk poet (and one-time husband of Isadora Duncan) Sergei Yessenin and the poet Nadezhda Volpin – although his father, who committed suicide in the Hotel Angleterre in Leningrad at age thirty, never knew him. A contrarian by nature and an early author of 'anti-Soviet poetry', he had been declared 'schizophrenic' and 'mentally incompetent' by Soviet psychiatrists several times, was sent into exile in Kazakhstan in the late 1940s and was held again in mental hospitals four times in the 1950s and 1960s (according to himself, he faked mental illness in order to avoid a state prison like the Lubianka, where he had briefly been incarcerated).[73]

According to Ludmilla Alexeyeva, a founder of the Moscow Helsinki Watch Group, Volpin had already in the early 1960s praised the Stalin Constitution to her – and explained the possibilities of radical civil *obedience*: 'What would happen if citizens acted on the assumption that they have rights? If one person did it, he would become a martyr; if two people did it, they would be labeled an enemy organization; if thousands of people did it, they would be a hostile movement; but if everyone did it, the state would have to become less oppressive.'[74] Volpin's idea not only posed a challenge to the state, it also posed a challenge to a Russian intelligentsia that found formalism – legal and otherwise – suspect, and favoured, if anything, direct heroic confrontation (and martyrdom). Volpin thus aimed at nothing less than what he called a 'meta-revolution' – a revolution, that is, in the way revolutions are made.[75]

After the arrest of the writers Andrei Sinyavsky and Yuli Daniel, Volpin organized a protest for 5 December 1965 – the Soviet Constitution Day. A few days earlier he had handed out leaflets with a 'civic plea' around Moscow University: it called for a 'strict observance of legality' on the appointed day of protest; protesters should ask for nothing more than an open trial for Sinyavsky and Daniel, thus very consciously limiting the demand to transparency of the judicial proceedings, rather than judging the prosecution's case. Placards and leaflets distributed on Constitution Day around Pushkin Square stated that the treatment of the dissidents had violated article 3 of the constitution as well as the Criminal Code. Yessenin-Volpin and about 200 other demonstrators (the figure remains disputed, because many of those around were probably plainclothes KGB agents) also held up banners demanding 'Respect the Soviet Constitution!' The protesters, mostly students, were promptly arrested and brought to a psychiatric ward. Yessenin-Volpin himself eventually emigrated to the United States, though not without demanding the *legal* right to return.

Yessenin-Volpin's example became known in parts of Central and Eastern Europe, but opposition to the regimes could also draw on rich local traditions of resistance and subversion to hegemonic powers. More recently, the dissidents had learnt at least three hard lessons from the Prague Spring and the troubles in Poland in the late 1960s: 'leading parties' could not be expected to reform themselves out of their leading roles; direct confrontations with the regimes could not be won, but pressure from workers might have some effect; and, perhaps most importantly, intellectuals and workers should not be played off against each other, as had happened with the state's anti-Semitic campaigns in Poland in the late 1960s. In 1976 Adam Michnik advocated a 'new evolutionism' in civil society, but also made it clear that the most effective way to confront an ostensible workers' state was through working-class pressure. He argued:

'new evolutionism' is based on the faith in the power of the working class which, with a steady and unyielding stand, has on several occasions forced the government to make spectacular concessions. It is difficult to foresee developments in the working class, but there is no question that the power elite fears this social group most. Pressure from the working class is a necessary condition for the evolution of public life toward a democracy.[76]

The dissidents also recognized existing geopolitical realities, in two senses. On the one hand, they drew the lesson especially from 1956 that they could not expect any substantial help from the West. In Michnik's words: 'Imre Nagy's appeal for aid and the silence of the Western governments were much too clear a signal of . . . the fact that no one will help us if we do not help ourselves.' On the other hand, they took account of the dominance of the Soviet Union and the resulting lack of room for manoeuvre for the satellite regimes. Consequently, they committed themselves to political action that was consciously 'self-limiting', mainly just taking their regimes at their word. The goal was not revolution, but reform through targeted pressure from below; or what the Hungarian philosopher János Kis referred to as 'radical reformism'.

After the Helsinki Accords, which Brezhnev had celebrated as an undiluted victory for the Eastern bloc, the Czechoslovak group Charter 77 was founded in 1977. Its signatories described themselves as a 'free, informal, open community of people of different convictions, different faiths and different professions united by the will to strive, individually and collectively, for the respect of civic and human rights in our own country and throughout the world'. Indeed, it was a motley group, which included reform Communists like Zdeněk Mlynář, Trotskyists, Catholic conservatives and rock musicians: some of the founders had first come together to defend the underground group Plastic People of the Universe, several of whose members were imprisoned on a charge of 'extreme vulgarity with an anti-socialist and an anti-social impact', and this despite the fact that their lawyer had argued that they were merely following a long Communist line of forthright and effective self-expression, starting with Lenin's supposed 1922 saying, 'bureaucracy is shit'.[77]

Like similar groups inspired by Yessenin-Volpin's example in the Soviet Union, Charter 77 sought to subscribe to a strict legal positivism and merely 'help' the Czechoslovak state to implement the Helsinki Accords. As Václav

Benda, a leading Czech dissident, put it, 'this tactic of taking the authorities at their word is, in itself, a shrewd ploy'.[78] Milovan Djilas hailed it immediately as 'the most mature and accomplished program produced by Eastern Europe from the war up to today'.[79]

As Tony Judt, one of the most astute Western observers of dissident strategies, pointed out, the focus on rights reminded everyone of their very absence – but this reminder served less to prompt the regimes to change than to 'talk past them'.[80] This constituted the crucial step beyond Yessenin's notion of legal positivism as a dissident weapon: the Russian poet had tried to address the state; the Central and Eastern Europeans of the 1970s tried to talk to society. They had realized that speaking to the regimes in Marxist language, as the revisionists had done, simply fell on deaf ears; the point now was to address fellow citizens with an uncontaminated moral vocabulary. As Michnik put it, they tried to 'give directives to the people on how to behave, not to the powers on how to reform themselves'.[81] He went further by claiming that 'society must transform itself from a "sack of potatoes" (we owe this apt metaphor to Marx) into the executor of its own interests and aspirations' – an idea with parallels in the aspirations associated with *autogestion* in Western Europe around the same time.

Of course, the establishment of political organizations outside the leading party and its various organizational offshoots was strictly forbidden. So, almost by definition, any associations being formed had to present themselves as a-political or perhaps even antipolitical. This also made conceptual sense, as the regimes were almost uniformly described by the dissidents as totalitarian. The political language of totalitarianism, as we have seen, was not only rediscovered in Central and Eastern Europe, it became crucial for French left-wing intellectuals in the mid-1970s. It was also to make a comeback with older liberal anti-totalitarian thinkers such as Karl Dietrich Bracher in Germany, who strenuously opposed the peace movement because of its alleged blindness to the threats emanating from a totalitarian Soviet Union.[82] But in Central and Eastern Europe a strategic lesson could be drawn from theories of totalitarianism, which in the West mostly served as polemical weapons. The concept revealed a particular point of weakness in the regimes: 'precisely because totalitarian governments politicize daily life, daily life [could become] a vast terrain on which totalitarianism can be opposed'.[83] Seemingly a-political action could potentially have vast political consequences.

In many respects, the dissidents shared more concerns with intellectuals in the West than has often been acknowledged. They focused on everyday micropolitics, rather than changing the state as such. And like Habermas, they sought to protect a lifeworld of undamaged interpersonal relations – even under totalitarianism. This intuition was particularly important in the thought of the Czech philosopher Jan Patočka. Patočka had emerged from the phenomenological school and had studied with both Husserl and Heidegger, whose ideas he attempted to use in the service of a vision of individual dignity. Crucial was the notion of 'care for the soul', which Patočka viewed as a distinctive European idea going back to Plato. This kind of care implied both resisting an inauthentic self-forgetting in everyday business and refraining from violent attempts to transcend everydayness, such as in war.[84] Patočka also formulated the ideal of a 'community of the shaken' in the face of totalitarianism and insisted on the specifically moral – as opposed to political – character of dissidence, claiming that morality 'is not here to make society work, but so that man can be man'.[85] He was one of the first spokesmen for Charter 77, describing it as an attempt to demonstrate the primacy of spontaneous solidarity and the 'sovereignty of moral sensibility' over mere state sovereignty. He was arrested by the Czech secret police and died after a number of severe interrogations. Even in death, the authorities would not leave him alone: they tried to disrupt his funeral with a motocross race next to the cemetery and a helicopter hovering above.

But the dissidents' voices could no longer be drowned out or silenced altogether. Václav Havel, who described himself as 'a philosophically inclined literary man', carried forward Patočka's legacy, also drawing on Heidegger to formulate a comprehensive critique of modernity and human beings' dependence on technology in particular – a critique that was supposed to be applicable to the West as much as the East and that took up themes developed earlier by Marxist revisionists such as Kosík and Bahro.[86] The playwright saw state socialism as a 'convex mirror of all modern civilization', supposedly characterized by its 'anthropocentricity'.[87] As a tentative response Havel suggested a different understanding of politics – not as a kind of technology, but 'as practical morality, as service to the truth, as essentially human and humanly measured care for our fellow humans'.[88] Again, a supposedly a-political virtue – care – turned out to have potentially vast political implications.

Antipolitics also translated into an opposition to the external politics of the superpowers, practised with high technology and nuclear weapons in particular. As the Hungarian writer György Konrád wrote,

> antipolitics strives to put politics in its place and make sure it stays there, never overstepping its proper office of defending and refining the rules of the game of civil society. Antipolitics is the ethos of civil society, and civil society is the antithesis of military society. There are more or less militarized societies – societies under the sway of nation-states whose officials consider total war one

of the possible moves in the game. Thus military society is the reality, civil society is a utopia.[89]

More important than any comprehensive (and, in the eyes of critics, rather crude) condemnation of modernity was Havel's famous argument in 'The Power of the Powerless' that even under the conditions of what he now described as 'post-totalitarianism' individuals could begin 'living in truth' if they stopped going through the ideological motions the state prescribed.[90] Havel's example of a greengrocer who puts out a sign saying 'Workers of the world, unite!' without any real conviction became one of the most powerful symbols for the hollowness of the regimes – and the cynical complicity of their subjects – in Central and Eastern Europe. By the same token, however, Havel had shown that despite the apparent 'auto-totality' of the system, the regimes were in fact extremely fragile. Like Yessenin-Volpin, he insisted that citizens absolutely had to stop lying – and that, at the same time, the regime should be treated as if it were not lying (even if everyone assumed that it was). Again, truth-telling was a high moral ideal, but it was also part of a savvy political strategy. As leading Polish dissident Jan Josef Lipski emphasized, truth-telling:

> also had a pragmatic basis and justification, to a greater extent even than the principle of renouncing violence and hatred: in a struggle with authorities who had especially compromised themselves when it came to telling the truth, it was better to renounce falsehood completely and gain confidence in this manner than to lay oneself open to the possibility that every departure from the truth could be blown up by the mass media.[91]

Havel was to take antipolitics to an extreme which would alienate more traditional liberal democrats. In his view, restoration of parliamentary democracy was to be merely a first step which had to be followed by an existential revolution and the 'restoration of the order of being'. Rather than copying existing models in the West, the goal was a 'post-democracy' (characterized, among other things, by the absence of political parties).

Not everyone subscribed to antipolitics; unlike human rights, this concept remained contested throughout the 1980s. An alternative more alert to the need for institution building was what Václav Benda had termed 'the parallel polis'. This polis would be created within a fledgling civil society; it would be made of institutions with very concrete purposes parallel to those of the state: workers' defence committees, most prominently the Komitet Obrony Robotników (KOR) in Poland, underground trade unions, 'flying universities', organizations supporting the poor (a provocation, of course, in socialist countries where poverty was supposed to have been eliminated), also counter-cultural groups, and, in the 1980s, they were joined by social movements dealing with the horrendous environmental consequences of state socialism. Organizations like KOR crucially paved the way for the alliance between intellectuals and workers: the workers saw intellectuals defend their rights, which diffused lingering suspicions about the intelligentsia. This was an essential part of the strategy not to let the opposition once again be divided and conquered by the state. A Gramscian might have said that this alliance was the real thing: an emerging hegemony.

Demands for 'truth-telling' and 'truth-living' against a background of high European philosophy were thus complemented by the self-consciously limited, practical pursuits of an ever proliferating number of civic associations. Benda summarized the strategy by saying that 'we join forces in creating, slowly but surely, parallel structures that are capable, to a limited degree at least, of supplementing the generally beneficial and necessary functions that are missing in the existing structures, and where possible, to use those structures, to humanize them'.[92]

Unavoidably, opposition movements also reflected long-standing splits and cleavages in different countries' political cultures. Hungary, for instance, saw the emergence of an opposition divided between 'democrat-urbanists' and 'populist-nationalists', mirroring the old divide between 'shallow' Hungarians (supposedly all to be found in Budapest) and the 'deep' ones of the country-side.[93] In such circumstances, it was all the more important that intellectual figures could be found whose ideas integrated different groups. In Hungary, Bibó – or rather the memory of Bibó – performed such a function: he had been positively feared by the nomenklatura as a 'model' of fearless public conduct.[94] What mattered beyond the example of personal courage was that the man sometimes described as 'Central Europe's Political Therapist' and 'the most tolerant Hungarian' had identified distinctive regional and national traditions which at the same time could be construed as national *and* democratic.[95] In particular, a fusion of nationalism and liberalism could be translated into the concrete demand for popular sovereignty and territorial independence.

Meta-revolutions and the End of Leninism

In the end, the Soviet Union and its satellites were afflicted with 'the disintegration of civil order, the breakdown of social discipline, the debility of leaders, and the alienation of citizens' – in short, the very ills which the Trilateral Commission had diagnosed for the West. 'Developed socialism' under Leonid Brezhnev and his immediate successors had meant stagnation, corruption and the increasing feudalization of society. Above all, it led to a comprehensive loss of confidence among the leadership. A similar sense of demoralization had spread in the satellite countries. In such a situation, dissidents could have an enormous impact by deploying legal positivism as a weapon: they could demonstrate that 'state socialism' rested on a vast confidence trick of elites claiming: 'we, the governors, pretend to deliver'; and the population acquiescing, 'we, the governed, pretend that the state is legitimate'.

The fact that the regime simply was not legitimate also proved the undoing of Mikhail Gorbachev, the best last hope for reforming the Soviet Union. Theoretically, there was little new in what the Soviet leader was trying to do. Gorbachev's close adviser Gennady Gerasimov, when asked in 1987 what constituted the difference between Gorbachev's programme and the Prague Spring, replied: 'Nineteen years.' In fact, Gorbachev had been a roommate of Zdeněk Mlynář when both had been studying at Moscow State University in the 1950s. Many of the reformers who came to be known as 'the Gorbachev boys' had been junior Soviet bureaucrats in Prague in the late 1960s.

It was plain for all to see in the early 1980s that Brezhnev's ideal of the 'stability of cadres' – directed against Khrushchev's disruptive 'democratization' – had effectively led to the senility of cadres.[96] The Communist Party had long ceased to be a charismatic impersonal force: it inspired no devotion, other than as an instrument to private enrichment; its power was thus based as much on personal dependencies as on impersonal organization. Gorbachev wanted modernization, but modernization would have to involve more freedom, which in turn might come to undermine the very foundations of the Leninist state. The Soviet leader therefore saw himself placed in a paradoxical situation: the position of general secretary had accumulated enormous centralized power, which could be used to force through decentralization and to create possibilities for more participation. But that process might erode the very power needed to complete reform.

Initially, Gorbachev, often echoing Khrushchev's 'democratization' rhetoric, attempted to use some of the political instruments from the past which had fallen into disuse – the soviets in particular. He tried hard to drag along what he called 'this colossus of conservatism . . . this dirty, mean dog' – by which he meant his very own Communist Party.[97] When the dog dug himself in, Gorbachev changed tactics. The general secretary attempted to shift his power base from party to state, though to some degree he had to construct a state truly separate from the party to begin with. For instance, a new Supreme Soviet was established, independent of the CP. He strenuously attempted to disentangle and eventually dismantle the highly problematic dual power structure (Lenin's 'flexible amalgamation') which had characterized the Soviet

Union since the 1920s. Symbolic gestures were also to underline that real change was under way: Bukharin was readmitted to the party in 1988. A year later, *The Gulag Archipelago* could finally be published.

In the end, however, the inner contradictions that had afflicted revisionism everywhere – in particular the impossibility of combining democracy and a 'leading role' for the Communist Party – also scuppered Gorbachev's projects of 'openness' and 'restructuring'. The party disappeared as a power base, but the new state – to the extent that it could be successfully constructed at all – would not necessarily serve as a framework for what Gorbachev envisaged as a 'socialist market economy'.

The precise causes of what in some countries was simply called 'the changes' varied. What they all had in common, though, was a curious absence: the fact that the end of the old regimes was neither triggered nor followed by revolutions conforming to the templates of the French and Russian ones. This fact crucially contributed to the success of the dissidents: the regimes looked for signs of another 1956, missing the fact that change did not take a violent, insurrectionist form; that form had played itself out by 1968, in both East and West. Nonetheless, when the changes came, they came quickly, and they spread from country to country, just as the Bolsheviks had once hoped spontaneous revolution would. As soon as people ceased to be afraid – and, in particular, as soon as it became clear that the Soviet Union would not venture out for another 1956 or 1968 – what had appeared as totalitarian sovereignty simply collapsed. The intuition of Lefort and other theorists was vindicated: in the end, what had appeared as totalitarian, undivided power, while seeming to stretch across all of society, was actually very fragile. At the same time, the carefully constructed parallel polis prevented the collapse of state power from turning into political chaos.

Václav Havel claimed in his New Year's address after his election as Czechoslovak president in December 1989, 'People, your government has returned to you,' invoking Marta Kubišová's iconic 1968 pop song which had in turn invoked T. G. Masaryk's inaugural 1918 address – which had in turn invoked Comenius, the seventeenth-century philosopher of education often celebrated as a kind of symbol of the Czech nation.[98] But 'the people' as *one* unified, collective, self-determining subject was neither visible nor, for the most part, invoked in 1989. Mass rallies and demonstrations played a vital role, but even more important were the 'round tables', civic networks and forums which negotiated with the old regimes. These were about people, not 'the people' – sovereignty was effectively regained, but not invoked or represented for some revolutionary-political or nation-building project, as had been the case in 1789 and 1917 (and in many minor revolutions). The revolutions of 1989 were self-consciously self-limiting and pluralist, united only by their opposition to the old regimes – revolutions against the Revolution, as the political theorist Andrew Arato put it, or indeed, just as Volpin had hoped, meta-revolutions. They did not want to draw a black-and-white picture of past and present, allowing many servants of the former regimes to save face. Grey is beautiful, as Michnik once said.

What did the people – or, rather, what did people – seek to do with the power that had been returned to them? For the most part, they sought to create liberal democracies. But not just any liberal democracy. It was a type of liberal democracy recognizable as the constellation of institutions that had evolved in post-1945 Western Europe.[99] The Central and Eastern Europeans also turned to free markets, and, at least for a while, enthusiastically endorsed Hayek. However, many soon abandoned libertarian blueprints; they implicitly agreed with Oakeshott that a plan to resist all planning was still a rationalist politics insufficiently attentive to local conditions.

Ironically, while Margaret Thatcher had insisted that 'There Is No Alternative' when it came to pushing her free-market policies, this was not true in Western Europe – but 'TINA' *was* true in Central and Eastern Europe, as far as West European templates of democracy went. Nowhere did the non-Communist left have any countervailing vision on offer; and it was not so obviously a sign of condescension when Habermas called the events of 1989 'catching-up revolutions', insisting that they had taken 'their methods and standards entirely from the familiar repertoire of the modern age' (a sentiment echoed by Furet, who claimed that 'with all the fuss and noise, not a single new idea has come out of Eastern Europe').[100]

True, only rarely were institutions imported wholesale (such as the German Constitutional Court in Hungary); usually there was tinkering to adapt to local circumstances. But clearly none of the more concrete institutional ideals of the dissidents survived. This was true in particular for ideas of self-management which had failed to gain any lasting institutional expression so many times before in the twentieth century. Still under 'goulash Communism' Konrád had asserted that 'when there is parliamentary democracy but no self-administration, the political class alone occupies the stage'. After 1989 there was little self-administration, and the proponents of antipolitics found it difficult to adapt to humdrum political life, if they did not retreat from it altogether. But it did not follow that politicians or dissidents-turned-politicians alone occupied the stage; rather – and for better or for worse – it was now also populated with the actors who had been central to the West European post-war settlements, such as constitutional court judges and Brussels bureaucrats.

By 1991 it was clear that the Soviet Union itself could not house the various constituent nations, let alone be the political form for a 'Soviet people' (which had been declared a fait accompli in the 1977 constitution and in which Gorbachev still believed). 'Restructuring' made things fall apart completely, and there was no way of putting them together again. At the very end, Gorbachev was for a few days president of a state that had already dissolved into its constituent states and peoples. The disappearance of the Soviet Union was the penultimate act in the great, bloody post-war decolonization drama and appeared as yet another confirmation that if democracy emerged at all in twentieth-century Europe, it did so within political forms mostly recognizable as nation-states – which was not to say that every nation-state would turn out to be a democracy.

However, the *ultimate* act in the century-long European drama – or, rather, tragedy – of exterminations, expulsions and exchanges (of populations, that is) was the Yugoslav wars of the 1990s. At their end seemed to stand the triumph of Curzon's fateful principle, the 'unmixing of peoples'. The demise of Yugoslavia also spelt the conclusive end of the once most admired experiment in worker self-administration. It had never really functioned as advertised, and after the 1960s self-management essentially became a rather undemocratic form of 'self-government' for the different nations united in Yugoslavia. As we have seen, the ideal of self-administration, or 'collective autonomy', kept appearing in many different circumstances: the Austro-Marxist Max Adler had called it 'the dearest concept in the hearts and spirits of the revolutionary proletariat'; the British pluralists espoused it; the Hungarian revolutionaries of 1956 practised it; the French Second Left of the 1970s tried theoretically to revive it. Guy Debord still thought it the best bet for overcoming the society of the spectacle. After 1989 it virtually disappeared as an ideal, and arguably it belongs to what Hannah Arendt once called the 'lost treasures' of political history and political thought.

A Late Liberal Triumph?

In retrospect it can easily seem that the 1980s were a decade of renewed confidence and optimism – in both Europe and the West as a whole – leading right up to Francis Fukuyama's 1989 thesis about the 'end of history'. For a while, it might have seemed that history had come to a close with the Oakeshottian strong state standing above a society of libertarian (and share-owning) adventurers: a form of antipolitics in its own way, as there was supposed to be no ongoing negotiation between groups in society and the state, that is to say, the humdrum politics of liberal democracy. But once the utopian energies of Thatcherism had dissipated, the European picture still recognizably featured the contours of the post-war constitutional settlement (including the welfare state, in either a Christian Democratic or Social Democratic version).

The apparent triumph of the Western European way, as it was extended further east throughout the 1990s, did not alleviate all of the anxieties that would increasingly plague the continent as a whole. When stable democracies had eventually emerged in Western Europe, this had happened under very specific historical circumstances: countries were highly constrained internationally, not too ethnically diverse inside and able to rely on durable systems of mass and people's parties. But now Europe was no longer so constrained internationally. Mass parties were weakening everywhere and parliaments – already enfeebled as part of the post-war constitutional settlement – became even less influential. Bureaucratic, procedural legitimacy had increasingly come under suspicion after 1968; states were no longer obviously the right instruments for improvement to be adopted by decent men, in the way Tawney had claimed in 1946. Despite many hopeful predictions by West European conservatives, Christian Democracy did not flower in Central and Eastern Europe after 1989; where it did, as in Hungary, the bloom was over by the mid-1990s.

The very foundations of post-war democracy might be undermined, then, making some observers nostalgic for what they saw as the genuine mass democracy of the 1950s and 1960s – in contrast with the supposed 'post-democratic' condition after 1989.[101] Yet such nostalgia forgets that 1968 had also been triggered by a crisis in representation and that European democracies could never legitimately go back to an age before new identity claims – whether of women, gays or ethnic minorities – had been voiced. They could also not in any obvious or attractive sense go back to an age when stability had been based on supposedly unquestionable moral foundations which limited human autonomy – as was the case with Maritain's personalism, for instance.

There was something else that seemed hard, if not impossible, to reverse: 1989 or, at the latest, the end of the Yugoslav wars, appeared to spell the conclusive triumph of the nation-state – albeit a relatively heterogeneous nation-state. The de facto triumph of Curzon's principle of 'unmixing peoples' made Europe, and the EU in particular, a group of states significantly more homogeneous than the political associations covering Europe at the beginning of the twentieth century. The European Union is the most important and most successful institutional innovation since the emergence of the democratic welfare state. But the way it celebrates itself as a paragon of diversity, even as a kind of global beacon for 'multicultural values' such as tolerance and mutual recognition, ignores the darker pasts that partly made European nation-states what they are today.

After its triumph, the political form of the nation-state finally found its philosophers: David Miller in Britain, for instance, and Pierre Manent in France.[102] Not by chance, perhaps, did they start defending the idea of nation-states just as European societies were becoming more diverse again internally, and as the EU appeared to move towards yet closer integration. The latter apparently diminished further an already tamed kind of national sovereignty. And it relied more on a shared culture of consensus and compromise among political leaders and bureaucrats than on democratic elections. Partly because of its steady expansion and the fact that it seemed to be held together by a benevolent transnational bureaucracy, observers began to describe the present-day European Union as an 'empire'. But this could be no more than a metaphor, if one compares the Union to either the continental or the colonial empires that dominated the political landscape at the beginning of the twentieth century. The fact is that empire has never returned as a legitimate political form in Europe. And the German and Italian philosophers of *Grossraum* and *spazio vitale* respectively were its last theorists.

Fukuyama's 'End of History', whatever else one thinks of it, hit a nerve. It was by no means the naive liberal triumphalism which it has been caricatured as so often in retrospect. Fukuyama, after all, did not predict the end of all conflict and violence; rather, he asserted that there was, in the long run, no attractive alternative way of life or means of organizing human collectives that could rival liberal democracy.[103] His theory had a distinctly European twist: he argued that the world was going to go the way of post-Hitler – that is, 'post-ideological' and therefore 'post-historical' – Western Europe; he also held that there would in all likelihood be a ' "Common-Marketization" of international relations'.[104]

Fukuyama was not afraid of asserting what the postmodernists had allegedly discredited: a 'grand narrative'. His story could at first sight seem like a fancy (and credulous) restatement of modernization theory. But not for nothing had Fukuyama been a student of the American political philosopher Alan Bloom, who had in turn been influenced by the French Hegelian (and Russian émigré) Alexandre Kojève (who, as we saw in Chapter 3, had identified one of the basic contradictions of the Third Reich). Just as on that drizzly June morning in 1978 the ghost of Dostoevsky appeared to be standing behind Solzhenitsyn at Harvard, the erstwhile Alexander Kojevnikoff was looming behind the State Department official's theses on the philosophy of history.

Why? Because Fukuyama's account was suffused with the very cultural pessimism that had animated Bloom: might liberal democracies in the end be populated by Nietzschean 'last men', that is, docile, self-satisfied, mediocre, utterly unheroic philistines – thus falling far short of what human beings could be? As Fukuyama put it: 'the end of history will be a very sad time . . . In the post-historical period there will be neither art nor philosophy, just the perpetual caretaking of the museum of human history.' The Weberian spectre of specialists without spirit busying themselves in the steely casing had reappeared once more. But the idea that politics (in particular the activity of collective political subjects) could somehow generate meaning to counter this trend had been thoroughly discredited – in both East and West.

Nineteen-eighty-nine was an *annus mirabilis*. But it was also the year of the Tiananmen Square massacre and, in a sense, the beginning of a Chinese form of market-driven Communism that would not obviously be destroyed by the kinds of inner contradictions that had characterized Gorbachev's revisionism. More problematic still for those eager to tell a story of the final burial of Leninism after Russia had turned to wild capitalism, in Beijing a vanguard party ruled and ruled (and confirmed the Weberian point that capitalism had an affinity only with bureaucracy and not with democracy).

Nineteen-eighty-nine was also the year of the fatwa against Salman Rushdie. And it was the year of an altogether different peaceful transition against the odds: that of the Iranian regime, after the death of its charismatic leader Ayatollah Khomeini. Were there, then, perhaps challenges to liberal democracy left, or could one confidently assert with Fukuyama that 'our task is not to answer exhaustively the challenges to liberalism promoted by every crackpot messiah around the world, but only those that are embodied in important social or political forces and movements, and which are therefore part of world history'?[105] The questions were already there at the end of what Karl-Dietrich Bracher, the German liberal antitotalitarian, had called 'the age of ideologies'.

Certainly, there is no end of ideology, as long as there are human beings to contest the way they create and recreate their arrangements for tolerably living together. But *that* particular age of ideologies is over. The great nineteenth-century 'isms' played themselves out in the twentieth century; one telling sign that they cannot be and are not being revived *in toto* or even with some marginal adjustments is our very use of political language: the prefixes 'neo' and 'post' proliferate; new concepts seem to be a rarity. Even today's more or less authoritarian regimes in Moscow and in Beijing are curiously subdued, if not entirely mute, when it comes to justifying their practices with one form or another of ideology production.[106]

Does this indicate an impoverishment, perhaps even the depletion, of the political imagination? The comforting answer that suggests itself is of course that it is a sign of pragmatism: it's not that political thought is no longer responsive to real political problems; there is simply less pressure to locate one's proposals in a grand ideological scheme – in particular, but not only, the tradition of Marxism. Contrary to an almost universally accepted cliché,

1989 did not mean the end of broadly speaking Marxist theorizing – especially for those eager to learn or relearn Lukács' lesson that Marxism was a method, not a dogma. But de facto it spelled the end of Marxism as a global language of opposition, a lingua franca of protest which could be understood among Western Marxists as much as Eastern revisionists, among Cold War liberals (especially the many converts from Marxism) as much as the intellectual elites of post-colonial states. This was partly because questions that, as we saw, had once been relevant for Marxists everywhere – what to do about peasants, how to bring culture to 'the masses' – in Europe simply ceased to be questions.

All this is not the same as saying that Marxism as a theory had been entirely disproved by the end of the Soviet Union – in fact, it might be as plausible or implausible to say that Marxism had already been disproved by the beginnings of the Soviet Union and its failure to erect a 'commune state' on the model of the Paris Commune. It is simply an empirical point that a shared political language went into steep and probably irreversible decline. Neither postmodernism nor self-critical forms of liberalism were able to take its place.

All this is not to be triumphalist about a particular political model. It is true that the post-war constitutional settlement helped to consolidate the victory that Britain and the United States had won over fascism and proved superior to state socialism in the East – including its conception of 'people's democracy' which sought to compete with Western understandings of popular political participation. But only victors' history could overlook that what emerged as dominant in Europe was a particular kind of liberal democracy – one that fell far short of many democratic ideals which had been formulated in the course of the twentieth century.

It is not for the historian of political thought to say how secure this settlement will be in the future. It is for the historian, however, to say that many of its intellectual foundations have become eroded or almost entirely forgotten. Few Europeans today would know what to make of the term 'Christian personalism', even if not long ago a European with truly global influence – John Paul II – was among its adherents. It is also for the historian to remind contemporaries that the post-war settlement survived two major ideological challenges – '68 and neoliberalism – though both had deep effects on European society. While the story we have followed has often shown Europeans to lose their nerve, the durability and flexibility of the post-war way of doing politics might well furnish Europeans with some (no doubt also chastened) sense of confidence as to past achievement and future possibility.

It is, on the other hand, for the political philosopher to say that no single master idea or value – whether stability or autonomy or something else – will furnish European democracies with certainty about their future. Thus the last word belongs to a member of the non-Communist left: totalitarianism, as Claude Lefort had long argued, constitutes an attempt to have certainty once and for all. Democracy, on the other hand, is institutionalized uncertainty.

Notes

Introduction

1. Quoted in Eric Hobsbawm, *The Age of Extremes: The Short Twentieth Century 1914–1991* (London: Abacus, 1995), 1.
2. Czesław Miłosz, *The Captive Mind*, trans. Jane Zielonko (1953; New York: Vintage, 1990), 3.
3. The classic account is Karl Dietrich Bracher, *Zeit der Ideologien: Eine Geschichte politischen Denkens im 20. Jahrhundert* (Stuttgart: Deutsche Verlags-Anstalt, 1982).
4. Giovanni Gentile, 'The Philosophic Basis of Fascism', in *Foreign Affairs*, vol. 6 (1927/8), 290–304; here 301.
5. My perspective here is indebted to the work of Michael Freeden and Pierre Rosanvallon.
6. In fact, a proper understanding of just why certain ideas had such power in the past is to render them less dangerous in the present, even if we might find ourselves initially more disturbed by an account that does not dismiss past beliefs immediately as pathological.
7. To be sure, it is virtually impossible to prove, let alone quantify, that ever elusive thing called 'influence' in the history of ideas – and yet thinking about influence one way or another seems the only way to proceed, unless we want simply to collapse the history of political thought into the history of academic philosophical debate, or want to assume that political institutions evolve solely by way of 'thought-less' pragmatism or power struggles, instead of being themselves in some sense solidified political thought. As Alasdair MacIntyre once put it: 'there ought not to be two histories, one of political and moral action and one of political and moral theorizing, because there were not two pasts, one populated only by actions, the other only by theories. Every action is the bearer and expression of more or less theory-laden beliefs and concepts; every piece of theorizing and every expression of belief is a political and moral action.' See Alasdair MacIntyre, *After Virtue: A Study in Moral Theory*, 2nd edn (London: Duckworth, 2004), 61.
8. F. A. Hayek, 'The Intellectuals and Socialism', in *University of Chicago Law Review*, vol. 16 (1949), 417–33; here 417.
9. A focus on institutions is not necessarily state-centric: parties and councils (as sites of worker self-management, for instance, and more broadly as explicitly anti-statist institutions) are undoubtedly also political institutions. Moreover, such a history of institutions does not have to turn into a kind of *Siegerwissenschaft*, that is, a history of the victors: frustrated institutional proposals, or institutions that clearly failed as institutions, must be given their due, where they illuminate a larger set of political challenges and responses.
10. Michael Oakeshott, *The Social and Political Doctrines of Contemporary Europe*, with a foreword by Ernest Barker (Cambridge: Cambridge University Press, 1939), xi.
11. Gentile, 'The Philosophic Basis of Fascism', 302.

12. I am indebted here to David D. Roberts, *The Totalitarian Experiment in Twentieth-Century Europe: Understanding the Poverty of Great Politics* (New York: Routledge, 2006).
13. Hans Kelsen, 'Foundations of Democracy', in *Ethics*, vol. 66 (1955), 1–101; here 1.
14. Quoted in Peter Hennessy, *Having it So Good: Britain in the Fifties* (London: Allen Lane, 2006), 26.
15. Quoted by David Marquand, *Britain since 1918: The Strange Career of British Democracy* (London: Weidenfeld & Nicolson, 2008), 283.

Chapter 1: The Molten Mass

 1. These were the three 'pure' types of legitimacy (although there is evidence that Weber might have considered a fourth type, democratic legitimacy, where charisma was not authoritatively imposed by the charismatic person, but where the people endowed a leader with charisma from below, so to speak, through election). In theory, these types excluded each other: charisma was anti-traditional, for instance. But in practice, as Weber always underlined, they could appear in manifold combinations, especially if charisma had become 'routinized' and part of the everyday operations of institutions (such as the church, where offices conferred charisma on the office-holder, rather than the other way around). See especially the early texts on charisma in *Max Weber-Gesamtausgabe* I:22:4, ed. Edith Hanke, in collaboration with Thomas Kroll (Tübingen: Mohr Siebeck, 2005).
 2. Max Weber, 'Politik als Beruf', in *Max Weber-Gesamtausgabe* I:17, ed. Wolfgang J. Mommsen and Wolfgang Schluchter, in collaboration with Birgitt Morgenbrod (Tübingen: Mohr Siebeck, 1992), 157–252; here 157.
 3. Stefan Zweig, *The World of Yesterday: An Autobiography* (1942; Lincoln: University of Nebraska Press, 1964), literally *Weltvertrauen*.
 4. James Sheehan, *Where Have All the Soldiers Gone?: The Transformation of Modern Europe* (New York: Houghton Mifflin, 2008).
 5. Quoted by Marc Stears, *Progressives, Pluralists, and the Problems of the State: Ideologies of Reform in the United States and Britain, 1909–1926* (Oxford: Oxford University Press, 2002), 2.
 6. Felix Somary, *Erinnerungen eines politischen Meteorologen* (Munich: Matthes & Seitz, 1994), 97.
 7. A. J. P. Taylor, *English History 1914–1945* (Oxford: Oxford University Press, 1992), 1.
 8. John Maynard Keynes, *The Economic Consequences of the Peace* (New York: Harcourt, Brace & Howe, 1920), 12.
 9. For the Europe-wide liberal discourse on preconditions for participation or 'capacity' (a concept closely associated with Guizot), see Alan Kahan, *Liberalism in Nineteenth-Century Europe: The Political Culture of Limited Suffrage* (New York: Palgrave, 2003).
10. Charles S. Maier, 'Political Crisis and Partial Modernization: The Outcomes in Germany, Austria, Hungary, and Italy after World War I', in Charles L. Bertrand (ed.), *Revolutionary Situations in Europe, 1917–1922: Germany, Italy, Austria-Hungary* (Montreal: Interuniversity Centre for European Studies, 1977), 119–39.
11. Quoted in Sheri Berman, *The Primacy of Politics: Social Democracy and the Making of Europe's Twentieth Century* (New York: Cambridge University Press, 2006), 53.
12. Jürgen Osterhammel, *Die Verwandlung der Welt: Eine Geschichte des 19. Jahrhunderts* (Munich: Beck, 2009), 849.
13. A belief also based on sheer numbers: in 1914 there were proportionally more Europeans in the world than ever before or after.
14. Paul Valéry, 'The European', in Paul Valéry, *History and Politics*, trans. Denise Folliot and Jackson Matthews (Princeton, NJ: Princeton University Press, 1962), 307–23; here 323.
15. William James, *The Varieties of Religious Experience: A Study in Human Nature* (1902; New York: Modern Library, 2002), 3.
16. Leonard Woolf, *Beginning Again: An Autobiography of the Years 1911 to 1918* (New York: Harcourt, Brace & World, 1964), 36.
17. I owe this point to Ivan Krastev. On Russian–German parallels in this respect: Gerd Koenen, *Der Russland-Komplex: Die Deutschen und der Osten 1900–1945* (Munich: Beck, 2005), 15–16.

18. Charles S. Maier, *Among Empires: American Ascendancy and its Predecessors* (Cambridge, Mass.: Harvard University Press, 2006), 5.

19. One reason for the difference between democratizing colonial empires and authoritarian continental empires was structural: the former could have more democracy or constitutionalism in the centre without affecting the colonies; such a form of apartheid was not feasible for contiguous empires. See Ronald Grigor Suny, 'The Empire Strikes Out: Imperial Russia, "National" Identity, and Theories of Empire', in Ronald Grigor Suny and Terry Martin (eds), *A State of Nations: Empires and Nation-Making in the Age of Lenin and Stalin* (New York: Oxford University Press, 2001), 23–66.

20. Tomáš Masaryk, *The New Europe – the Slav Standpoint*, ed. W. Preston Warren and William B. Weist (1918; Lewisburg, Pa.: Bucknell University Press, 1972), 47.

21. J. M. Roberts, *Twentieth Century: A History of the World from 1901 to the Present* (London: Allen Lane, 1999), 9. In terms of two (in theory mutually exclusive) Weberian categories: monarchy combined tradition and hereditary as well as institutionalized charisma in generating legitimacy. The more autocratic types tended towards the former, the modern, self-publicizing ones towards the latter.

22. Arno J. Mayer, *The Persistence of the Old Regime: Europe to the Great War* (New York: Pantheon, 1981), 153.

23. Walter Bagehot, *The English Constitution*, ed. Paul Smith (1865; Cambridge: Cambridge University Press, 2001), 34.

24. For the following I draw on Hermann Heller, 'Der monarchische Ideenkreis', in Hermann Heller, *Die politischen Ideenkreise der Gegenwart* (Breslau: Hirt, 1926), 22–47.

25. Francis Oakley, *Kingship: The Politics of Enchantment* (Cambridge, Mass.: Blackwell, 2006), 135.

26. Wolfgang Reinhard, *Geschichte der Staatsgewalt* (Munich: C. H. Beck, 1999), 429–30.

27. David Cannadine, 'The Context, Performance and Meaning of Ritual: The British Monarchy and the "Invention of Tradition", ca. 1820–1977', in Eric Hobsbawm and Terence Ranger (eds), *The Invention of Tradition* (Cambridge: Cambridge University Press, 1983), 101–64.

28. Quoted in *ibid.*, 122.

29. *Ibid.*, 116.

30. Roberts, *Twentieth Century*, 161.

31. *Ibid.*, 163.

32. Gert Maak, *In Europe* (London: Vintage, 2008), 169 and Mayer, *Persistence*, 146.

33. Richard Pipes, *Russian Conservatism and its Critics: A Study in Political Culture* (New Haven, Conn.: Yale University Press, 2007), 167.

34. Robert Musil, *Der Mann ohne Eigenschaften*, ed. Adolf Frisé (Reinbek: Rowohlt, 2002), 35: 'Der Staat, der sich selbst irgendwie nur noch mitmachte'.

35. Koenen, *Der Russland-Komplex*, 132–3.

36. The obvious counter-example is Albert of Belgium, who became a hero for staying in the country and leading his army in resisting the Germans.

37. Harold James, *Europe Reborn* (Harlow: Pearson Longman, 2003), 57.

38. Hannah Arendt observed that 'since the end of the First World War we almost automatically expect that no government, and no state or form of government, will be strong enough to survive a defeat in war'.

39. But it was also much more mundane authority figures whose claims stood exposed as hollow, such as the fervently nationalist (and thoroughly hypocritical) schoolteacher in Remarque's *All Quiet on the Western Front*.

40. G. D. H. and Margaret Cole, *The Intelligent Man's Review of Europe Today* (New York: Alfred A. Knopf, 1934), 385.

41. Taylor, *English History*, 2.

42. Daniel T. Rodgers, *Atlantic Crossings: Social Politics in a Progressive Age* (Cambridge, Mass.: Harvard University Press, 1998), 281.

43. Quoted by Henry Pachter, *The Fall and Rise of Europe: A Political, Social, and Cultural History of the Twentieth Century* (Newton Abbot: David & Charles, 1975), 91.

44. José Ortega y Gasset, *The Revolt of the Masses*, anonymous trans. (1930; New York: Norton, 1957), 11–12.
45. Anti-liberals, however, also specifically tended to associate technology with liberalism. Witness the Romanian writer Mircea Eliade announcing in 1927, 'we wish to see a triumph of those values that do not come from political economy, from technology, or from parliamentarism'. Quoted in Marta Petreu, *An Infamous Past: E. M. Cioran and the Rise of Fascism in Romania*, trans. Bogdan Alea (Chicago: Ivan R. Dee, 2005), 4–5.
46. Quoted in *ibid.*, 6.
47. 'The Problem of Small Nations and States, the Federation of Small Nations (1918)', in Zdenka and Jan Munzer (eds), *We Were and We Shall Be: The Czechoslovak Spirit though the Centuries* (New York: Frederick Ungar, 1941), 152–8; here 153.
48. Eric Hobsbawm, *Age of Extremes: The Short Twentieth Century, 1914–1991* (London: Abacus, 1995), 34.
49. Quoted in Marianne Weber, *Max Weber: Ein Lebensbild* (1926; Heidelberg: L. Schneider, 1950), 673.
50. Nadezhda Mandelstam, *Hope against Hope: A Memoir*, trans. Max Hayward (1970; New York: Modern Library, 1999), 98.
51. Quoted in Mark Mazower, *Dark Continent: Europe's Twentieth Century* (London: Allen Lane, 1998), 43.
52. Zwi Batscha, *Eine Philosophie der Demokratie: Thomas G. Masaryks Begründung der neuzeitlichen Demokratie* (Frankfurt/Main: Suhrkamp, 1994).
53. Eric D. Weitz, 'From the Vienna to the Paris System: International Politics and the Entangled Histories of Human Rights, Forced Deportations, and Civilizing Missions', in *American Historical Review*, vol. 113 (2008), 1313–43.
54. There was generally a great deal of copying, appropriation and also misappropriation of constitutions and state practices across borders after 1919. The Romanian constitution, for instance, was modelled on the French, while the Albanian constitution took the American one as its template (although there were usually modifications: the Albanian president was conveniently to have unlimited powers).
55. Quoted in Bernard Lewis, *The Emergence of Modern Turkey* (New York: Oxford University Press, 1968), 268; see also Paul Dumont, 'The Origins of Kemalist Ideology', in Jacob M. Landau, *Atatürk and the Modernization of Turkey* (Leiden: Brill, 1984), 25–44.
56. Quoted in Udo Steinbach, *Die Türkei im 20. Jahrhundert* (Bergisch-Gladbach: Lübbe, 1996), 126 and 128.
57. As, appropriately enough, the inscription on the Atatürk museum claims: 'sovereignty resides unconditionally and without reservations in the nation'.
58. I am indebted to Harold James on this point.
59. John Maynard Keynes, *A Revision of the Treaty: Being a Sequel to The Economic Consequences of the Peace* (New York: Harcourt Brace, 1922), 14.
60. John Maynard Keynes, *The Economic Consequences of the Peace* (New York: Harcourt, Brace & Howe, 1920), 297.
61. Quoted by Hartmut Kaelble, *Europäer über Europa: Die Entstehung des europäischen Selbstverständnisses im 19. und 20. Jahrhundert* (Frankfurt/Main: Campus, 2001), 140.
62. Karel Čapek, *Talks with T. G. Masaryk*, trans. Dora Round, ed. Michael Henry Heim (1935/1938; North Haven, Conn.: Catbird, 1995), 232.
63. Paul Valéry, 'The Crisis of the Mind', in Valéry, *History*, 23–36; here 23.
64. Ernst Jünger, *The Storm of Steel* (London: Chatto & Windus, 1929), 235.
65. Ernst Jünger, *Copse 125: A Chronicle from the Trench Warfare of 1918*, trans. Basil Creighton (London: Chatto & Windus, 1930), 21.
66. Weber used the expression *Legitimitätsglaube* – a 'belief' or even 'faith' in legitimacy.
67. Max Weber, 'Die Protestantische Ethik und der Geist des Kapitalismus', in *Gesammelte Aufsätze zur Religionssoziologie* I (1920; Tübingen: Mohr Siebeck, 1988), 17–206; here 110–11. Of course one could *never* be entirely sure that success meant salvation; the proper Calvinist could *never* fully resolve, let alone entirely release, his tremendous inner tension.
68. Calvinists were not the only carriers of 'ascetic Protestantism': Weber also included Baptist sects, the Puritans and the Methodists.

69. Weber, 'Ethik', 35–6.
70. *Ibid.*, 203.
71. *Ibid. Beruf* poses particular challenges for translation. For the Calvinists, it was undoubtedly a calling; they enjoyed an inner connection to their work duties. Aspects of this sense survive in 'professional', but when Weber speaks about the fate of modern *Berufsmenschentum* – which includes almost all of us – he means to say that we are, unless we are very special or very lucky, forced to take on a 'job', with predetermined duties, and to undergo a disciplining that reshapes the inner life, rather than derives from it.
72. Max Weber, 'Wissenschaft als Beruf', in *Max Weber-Gesamtausgabe* I:17, 71–111; here 100.
73. Lawrence Scaff, *Fleeing the Iron Cage: Culture, Politics, and Modernity in the Thought of Max Weber* (Berkeley: University of California Press, 1989).
74. *Ibid.*
75. Weber, 'Wissenschaft', 109–10.
76. And, strictly speaking, 'culture' *was* the interaction between 'soul' and 'form'.
77. Musil, *Mann ohne Eigenschaften*, 32.
78. As Weber put it: 'Es gibt nichts in der Welt, keine Maschinerie der Welt, die so präzise arbeitet, wie diese Menschenmaschine es tut – und dazu noch: so billig!'
79. Weber, *Max Weber*, 626.
80. Chris Thornhill, *Political Theory in Modern Germany* (Cambridge: Polity, 2000), 18–54.
81. This (long-overlooked) aspect of Weber's thought has been brought out most forcefully by Wilhelm Hennis, *Max Weber: Essays in Reconstruction*, trans. Keith Tribe (London: Allen & Unwin, 1988).
82. Apart from the Russians, only the Serb parliamentary socialist party voted against the war effort. In effect, that meant two people.
83. Roberts, *Totalitarian Experiment*, 116–30.
84. Nikolai Chernyshevsky, *What is to be Done? From Tales about New People*, trans. Michael B. Katz (1863; Ithaca, NY: Cornell University Press, 1989).
85. Fëdor Dan quoted in Robert Service, *Lenin: A Biography* (Cambridge, Mass.: Harvard University Press, 2000), 195.
86. V. I. Lenin, ' "Left-Wing" Communism – An Infantile Disorder', in Robert C. Tucker (ed.), *The Lenin Anthology* (New York: W. W. Norton, 1975), 550–618; here 554.
87. V. I. Lenin, 'What is to be Done? Burning Questions of our Movement', in *ibid.*, 2–114; here 15.
88. Eric Hobsbawm, *Interesting Times: A Twentieth-Century Life* (London: Allen Lane, 2002), 133.
89. Quoted in David Priestland, *The Red Flag: A History of Communism* (New York: Grove Press, 2009), 77.
90. Kenneth Jowitt, *New World Disorder: The Leninist Extinction* (Berkeley: University of California Press, 1992). The following draws on Jowitt's work.
91. The concept of collective or institutional charisma might seem peculiar at first sight. But Weber's initial inspiration for his theory of charisma had actually been a book about a 'charismatic organization', Rudolf Sohm's account in *Kirchenrecht* of the early Christians. They were fully devoted as a group, but lacked anything like permanent offices – hence they were *not* a church.
92. Raphael Samuel, *The Lost World of British Communism* (London: Verso, 2006), 58. In Weber's terminology, they would be a sect, rather than a church, where charisma attached to offices and did not depend on the individual devotion of office-holders.
93. Robert C. Tucker, 'Introduction', in Tucker (ed.), *Lenin Anthology*, xxv–lxiv; here xlv–xlvi.
94. Leszek Kolakowski, *Main Currents of Marxism*, trans. P. S. Falla (1976; New York: W. W. Norton, 2005), 733.
95. In the same vein, he insisted that truth and partiality went together – contrary to what bourgeois thought might suggest.
96. Quoted in Tucker, 'Introduction', lx.
97. V. I. Lenin, *The State and Revolution*, trans. Robert Service (1918; London: Penguin, 1992), 45.

98. *Ibid.*, 73–4.
99. *Ibid.*, 44.
100. David Priestland, 'Soviet Democracy, 1917–91', in *European History Quarterly*, vol. 32 (2002), 111–30; here 114–15.
101. Priestland, *Red Flag*, 93.
102. *Ibid.*
103. Quoted in *ibid.*, 96.
104. Leon Trotsky, *Terrorism and Communism: A Reply to Karl Kautsky* (1920; Ann Arbor: University of Michigan Press, 1961), 58.
105. *Ibid.*, 63
106. Leon Trotsky, 'Our Political Tasks', in Robert V. Daniels (ed.), *A Documentary History of Communism: From Lenin to Gorbachev* (Hanover, NH: University Press of New England, 1993), 16–17; here 16.
107. Steven Kotkin, *Magnetic Mountain: Stalinism as a Civilization* (Berkeley: University of California Press, 1997), 293.
108. *Ibid.*, 293–4. Officially, it was to provide 'the leading core of all organizations of the working people, both public and state'.
109. Manfred Hildermeier, *Geschichte der Sowjetunion 1917–1991: Entstehung und Niedergang des ersten sozialistischen Staates* (Munich: C. H. Beck, 1998), 133.
110. Priestland, 'Soviet Democracy', 116.
111. V. I. Lenin, 'Oblomov Still Lives – on Mayakovsky', in *Not by Politics Alone . . . – the Other Lenin*, ed. and intr. by Tamara Deutscher (London: Allen & Unwin, 1973), 187.
112. Kolakowski, *Main Currents*, 767.
113. Max Weber 'Sozialismus', in *Max Weber-Gesamtausgabe* I:15: *Zur Politik im Weltkrieg – Schriften und Reden 1914–1918*, ed. Wolfgang Mommsen, in collaboration with Gangolf Hübinger (Tübingen: Mohr Siebeck, 1984), 599–633; here 621.
114. For the following see Somary, *Erinnerungen*, 178–80.
115. Harry Liebersohn, *Fate and Utopia in German Sociology, 1870–1923* (Cambridge, Mass.: MIT Press, 1988), 82 and 96.
116. Letter to Robert Michels, 4 August 1908, in *Max Weber-Gesamtausgabe* II:5, ed. M. Rainer Lepsius and Wolfgang J. Mommsen, in collaboration with Birgit Rudhard and Manfred Schön (Tübingen: Mohr Siebeck, 1990), 615.
117. Still, a contradiction remained between the axiom that the masses were politically infantile and the demand that they were to provide feedback for politicians, and even become a check on them.
118. Weber, 'Politik', 237–8.
119. *Ibid.*, 250.
120. Thornhill, *Political Theory*.
121. Richard Bellamy, *Liberalism and Modern Society: An Historical Argument* (Cambridge: Polity, 1992), 211–16.
122. Weber, *Max Weber*, 681.
123. Joachim Radkau, *Max Weber: Die Leidenschaft des Denkens* (Munich: Hanser, 2005), 779–81. Weber always held it particularly against Eisner that he had published secret documents from the summer of 1914, which appeared to prove the Allies right that Germany had largely caused the war.
124. Quoted by Charles S. Maier, *Recasting Bourgeois Europe* (Princeton, NJ: Princeton University Press, 1988), 57.
125. Radkau, *Max Weber*, 738.
126. Keynes, *Revision*, 14.
127. Maier, *Recasting*.
128. Carl Schmitt, *The Crisis of Parliamentary Democracy*, trans. Ellen Kennedy (1923; Cambridge, Mass.: MIT Press, 1988), 6.
129. *Ibid.*, 7.
130. The Rt Hon. Lord Hewart of Bury, *The New Despotism* (London: Ernest Benn, 1929), 14.

Chapter 2: Interwar Experiments: Making Peoples, Remaking Souls

1. Paul Ricoeur, *Critique and Conviction: Conversations with François Azouvi and Marc de Launay*, trans. Kathleen Blamey (Cambridge: Polity, 1998), 13.
2. Karel Čapek, *Talks with T. G. Masaryk*, trans. Dora Round, ed. Michael Henry Heim (1935/8; North Haven, Conn.: Catbird, 1995), 247.
3. Margaret Cole, *The Life of G. D. H. Cole* (New York: St Martin's, 1971), 62.
4. Ricardo Bavaj, 'Otto Kirchheimers Parlamentarismuskritik in der Weimarer Republik', in *Vierteljahrshefte für Zeitgeschichte*, vol. 55 (2007), 33–51.
5. J. N. Figgis, *Antichrist, and other Sermons*: (London: Longmans, Green and Co., 1913) 226.
6. David Runciman, *Pluralism and the Personality of the State* (Cambridge: Cambridge University Press, 1997), 37.
7. *Ibid.*, 84. What the *Kulturkampf* had been for Germany, the legal cases of the Scottish Free Church and of W. V. Osborne turned out to be for Britain: in the former, the House of Lords forbade the Scottish Free Church to merge with the United Presbyterians, even though an overwhelming majority in both churches were in favour. Osborne was a branch secretary of the Railway Servants Union who rejected the union's demand to pay a contribution to the Labour Party (he won, which led the Court of Appeal and the House of Lords to ask for more state involvement in making groups and associations define their goals clearly). Both cases raised profound questions about the nature of groups – did they have their own life, goals and 'spirit' independent of individual members? – but they also showed the state trying to regulate the lives of associations.
8. Ernest Barker, 'The Discredited State', in *Political Quarterly*, no. 5 (1915), 101–21; here 106.
9. *Ibid.*, 108.
10. Issac Kramnick and Barry Sheerman, *Harold Laski: A Life on the Left* (New York: Allen Lane, 1993), 93.
11. Andrew Vincent, *Theories of the State* (Oxford: Blackwell, 1987), 184.
12. Kramnick and Sheerman, *Laski*, 136.
13. G. D. H. Cole, *Guild Socialism Restated* (1920; London: L. Parsons, 1921), 32.
14. Harold Laski, *The Foundations of Sovereignty and Other Essays* (New York: Harcourt, Brace & Company, 1921), 70.
15. Cole, *Guild Socialism*, 33–4.
16. *Ibid.*, 12–13.
17. T. R. Powell quoted in Stears, *Progressives*, 176.
18. Carl Schmitt, *The Concept of the Political*, trans. George Schwab (1932; Chicago: University of Chicago Press, 1996), 44–5.
19. As Margaret Cole put it: ' "Direct action" and the dreams of the syndicalists wilted and died in that May. Not until the troubles of 1968 did the strike as a political weapon again make an appearance'. Cole, *Life*, 54.
20. Laski quoted by Julia Stapleton, *Englishness and the Study of Politics: The Social and Political Thought of Ernest Barker* (New York: Cambridge University Press, 1994), 5.
21. Quoted by Kramnick and Sheerman, *Laski*, 156.
22. Cole, *Life*, 58.
23. Quoted by Dick Geary, 'The Second International: Socialism and Social Democracy', in Terence Ball and Richard Bellamy (eds), *The Cambridge History of Twentieth-Century Political Thought* (Cambridge: Cambridge University Press, 2003), 219–38; here 224.
24. Eduard Bernstein, *The Preconditions of Socialism*, trans. Henry Tudor (Cambridge: Cambridge University Press, 1993), 142.
25. *Ibid.*, 148.
26. Karl Liebknecht quoted in Geoff Eley, *Forging Democracy: The History of the Left in Europe, 1850–2000* (New York: Oxford University Press, 2002), 88.
27. Much of the following is based on Helmut Gruber, *Red Vienna: Experiment in Working-Class Culture, 1919–1934* (New York: Oxford University Press, 1991), Anson Rabinbach (ed.), *The Austrian Socialist Experiment: Social Democracy and Austromarxism, 1918–1934* (Boulder, Colo.: Westview Press, 1985), and Martin Kitchen, *The Coming of Austrian Fascism* (London: Croom Helm, 1980).

28. Quoted by Tom Bottomore, 'Introduction', in Tom Bottomore and Patrick Goode (eds), *Austro-Marxism* (Oxford: Clarendon, 1978), 1–44; here 13.
29. Otto Bauer, *Die Nationalitätenfrage und die Sozialdemokratie* (Vienna: Ignaz Brand, 1907), 92.
30. *Ibid.*, 105.
31. Kolakowski, *Main Currents*, 550–1.
32. Eley, *Forging*, 213.
33. *Ibid.*, 212–15.
34. Victor Serge, *Memoirs of a Revolutionary* (New York: Oxford University Press, 1963), 189.
35. *Ibid.*
36. Quoted in Giuseppe Fiori, *Antonio Gramsci: Life of a Revolutionary*, trans. Tom Nairn (1965; London: Verso, 1990), 70.
37. Antonio Gramsci, 'Workers' Democracy', in Antonio Gramsci, *Pre-Prison Writings*, ed. Richard Bellamy, trans. Virginia Cox (Cambridge: Cambridge University Press, 1994), 96–100.
38. I am indebted here to the work of Darrow Schecter, in particular his chapter on council Communism in *Radical Theories* (Manchester: Manchester University Press, 1994).
39. James Joll, *Gramsci* (London: Penguin, 1978), 39.
40. Maier, 'Political Crisis'.
41. Joll, *Gramsci*, 56.
42. *Ibid.*, 71.
43. *Ibid.*, 91–3.
44. Quoted in Joseph Buttigieg, 'Introduction', in Antonio Gramsci, *Prison Notebooks*, vol. 1 (New York: Columbia University Press, 1992), 19.
45. Antonio Gramsci, 'Socialism and Culture', in Gramsci, *Pre-Prison Writings*, 10.
46. Peter Ghosh, 'Gramscian Hegemony: An Absolutely Historicist Approach', in *History of European Ideas*, vol. 27 (2001), 1–43.
47. *Selections from the Prison Notebooks of Antonio Gramsci*, ed. and trans. Quintin Hoare and Geoffrey Nowell Smith (1971; London: Lawrence & Wishart, 1996), 333.
48. Ghosh, 'Gramscian Hegemony'.
49. Gramsci, *Prison Notebooks*, 238.
50. Serge, *Memoirs*, 186.
51. Quoted in Fiori, *Gramsci*, 230.
52. Berman, *Primacy*, 152–3.
53. Quoted in *ibid.*, 157.
54. Sheri Berman, *The Social Democratic Moment: Ideas and Politics in the Making of Interwar Europe* (Cambridge, Mass.: Harvard University Press, 1998), 49.
55. Mary Hilson, 'Scandinavia', in Robert Gerwarth (ed.), *Twisted Paths: Europe 1914–1945* (Oxford: Oxford University Press, 2007), 8–32; here 25.
56. Timothy Tilton, *The Political Theory of Swedish Social Democracy: Through the Welfare State to Socialism* (New York: Oxford University Press, 1990), 128.
57. Quoted by Berman, *Social Democratic Moment*, 53. Laski was called a 'chastened pluralist' by W. Y. Elliott, *The Pragmatic Revolt in Politics* (New York: Macmillan, 1928), 10.
58. Tilton, *Political Theory*, 41.
59. Donald Sassoon, *One Hundred Years of Socialism: The West European Left in the Twentieth Century* (New York: New Press, 1996), 44.
60. Franz-Xaver Kaufmann, *Varianten des Wohlfahrtsstaats: Der deutsche Sozialstaat im internationalen Vergleich* (Frankfurt/Main: Suhrkamp, 2003), 175.
61. Margaret Cole, 'Introduction', in Margaret Cole and Charles Smith (eds), *Democratic Sweden: A Volume of Studies Prepared by Members of the New Fabian Research Bureau* (London: Routledge, 1938), 1–7; here 2.
62. Kaufmann, *Varianten*, 161–70.
63. Cole, 'Introduction', 3. Cole also pointed out that 'opinion in Sweden seems to be remarkably homogeneous' on politics, and that Henri de Man's proposals for a 'social-ized sector' had already been realized there.
64. Berman, *Social Democratic Moment*, 46.
65. Koenen, *Der Russland-Komplex*, 228.

66. Alberto Spektorowski and Elisabet Mizrachi, 'Eugenics and the Welfare State in Sweden: The Politics of Social Margins and the Idea of a Productive Society', in *Journal of Contemporary History*, vol. 39 (2004), 333–52.

67. *Ibid.*

68. A continuity in some biopolitical concerns between the democratic welfare state and the fascist *Volksstaat* is not the same as identity between them. On this important point see Edward Ross Dickinson, 'Biopolitics, Fascism, Democracy: Some Reflections on our Discourse about "Modernity" ', in *Central European History*, vol. 37 (2004), 1–48.

69. The following account of Lukács' life is mostly based on Arpad Kadarkay, *Georg Lukács: Life, Thought, and Politics* (Cambridge, Mass.: Blackwell, 1991), Georg Lukács, *Record of a Life: An Autobiographical Sketch*, ed. Istvan Eörsi, trans Rodney Livingstone (London: Verso, 1983), and Michael Löwy, *Pour une sociologie des intellectuels révolutionnaires: L'evolution politique de Lukacs 1909–1929* (Paris: PUF, 1976).

70. Georg Lukács, *The Theory of the Novel*, trans. Anna Bostock (Cambridge, Mass.: MIT Press, 1971), 11.

71. Lukács, *Record*, 63.

72. 'Speech at the Young Workers' Congress', in Georg Lukács, *Tactics and Ethics: Political Essays, 1919–1929* (New York: Harper & Row, 1972), 39–40; here 40.

73. Arno J. Mayer, *Politics and Diplomacy of Peacemaking: Containment and Counterrevolution at Versailles, 1918–1919* (New York: Knopf, 1967), 591.

74. Quoted in Kadarkay, *Lukács*, 222.

75. *Ibid.*, 265.

76. Max Weber to Lukács, in *Georg Lukács: Selected Correspondence 1902–1920*, ed. and trans. Judith Marcus and Zoltán Tarr (New York: Columbia University Press, 1986), 281–2.

77. Kadarkay, *Lukács*, 270.

78. For the following: Georg Lukács, *History and Class Consciousness: Studies in Marxist Dialectics*, trans. Rodney Livingstone (1923; Cambridge, Mass.: MIT Press, 1999).

79. The actual argument was significantly more subtle and relied on the distinction between the empirical consciousness of the proletariat and what Lukács called the 'imputed' consciousness of the proletariat, or between subjective and objective possibility.

80. Lukács, *History*, 315. This contrasted markedly with other statements such as: 'The Communist Party must be the primary incarnation of the realm of freedom; above all, the spirit of comradeliness, of true solidarity, and of self-sacrifice must govern everything it does.'

81. Quoted by Kadarkay, *Lukács*, 280.

82. Michael Löwy, 'Lukács and Stalinism', in *New Left Review*, no. 91 (1975), 25–41.

83. Archie Brown, *The Rise and Fall of Communism* (London: Bodley Head, 2009), 169.

84. At least according to Victor Serge, *Memoirs*, 191–2.

85. Kadarkay, *Lukács*, 364.

86. 'Erbschaft aus Dekadenz? Ein Gespräch mit Iring Fetscher und Georg Lukács', in Werner Traub and Harald Wieser (eds), *Gespräche mit Ernst Bloch* (Frankfurt/Main: Suhrkamp, 1975), 28–40; here 32.

87. *Ibid.* Their relations cooled considerably over time, not so much because of politics directly as because of the relationship between art and politics. Lukács, the great advocate of realism, attacked expressionism as having paved the way for fascism; and Bloch, for his whole life, was nothing if not an expressionist.

88. Michael Löwy, *Georg Lukács: From Romanticism to Bolshevism* (London: New Left Books, 1979), 93.

89. Quoted by Éva Karádi, 'Ernst Bloch und Georg Lukács im Max Weber-Kreis', in Wolfgang J. Mommsen and Wolfgang Schwentker (eds), *Max Weber und seine Zeitgenossen* (Göttingen: Vandenhoek & Ruprecht, 1988), 682–702; here 687.

90. Around this time, Bloch also published his first major book, *The Spirit of Utopia*, which was less analysis than an expressionist, even mystical ranting against the culture of machines. He contrasted his utopian philosophy with the gradual reformism of the Social Democrats. Utopia was to be opposed to any merely materialistic promises, and consisted instead in a kind of deification of man. The censor in the Bavarian War Ministry let this all pass, claiming that he could see no link to practical politics whatsoever.

91. Ernst Bloch, *Tübinger Einleitung in die Philosophie* (Frankfurt/Main: Suhrkamp, 1977), 224.
92. After the Second World War Bloch taught in East Germany for a while, but was forced to retire and harassed about his unorthodox Marxism. He eventually left for West Germany, but not without having confronted state officials and philosophers again and again with Lenin's words that 'intelligent idealism is closer to intelligent materialism than is stupid materialism'. When Bloch left the GDR in 1961, he carried a single book with him: an Agatha Christie mystery.
93. James, *Europe*, 168.
94. Simon Sebag Montefiore, *Stalin: The Court of the Red Tsar* (New York: Knopf, 2004), 6.
95. Tzvetan Todorov, *Hope and Memory: Lessons from the Twentieth Century*, trans. David Bellos (Princeton, NJ: Princeton University Press, 2003), 84. However, as Harold James has observed, the opposite held at the level of international relations: the Soviet Union was relatively calculable in its choice of friends and enemies, whereas Hitler's racism only partially informed his foreign policy. See James, *Europe*, 178.
96. Quoted in Erik van Ree, *The Political Thought of Joseph Stalin: A Study in Twentieth-Century Revolutionary Patriotism* (New York: Routledge, 2002), 2.
97. Hannah Arendt, 'The Eggs Speak Up', in Hannah Arendt, *Essays in Understanding, 1930-1954: Formation, Exile, and Totalitarianism*, ed. Jerome Kohn (New York: Schocken, 1994), 270-84; here 275.
98. Georg Lukács, 'Privatbrief über Stalinismus: Brief an Albert Carocci', in *Forum*, nos 115-16 (July/August 1963), 335-7, and 'Stalin ist noch nicht tot', in *Forum*, no. 117 (September 1963), 407-11.
99. Piers Brendon, *Dark Valley: A Panorama of the 1930s* (London: Pimlico, 2001), 196.
100. Yoram Gorlizki and Hans Mommsen, 'The Political (Dis)Orders of Stalinism and National Socialism', in Michael Geyer and Sheila Fitzpatrick (eds), *Beyond Totalitarianism: Stalinism and Nazism Compared* (New York: Cambridge University Press, 2009), 41-86; here 85.
101. Gerd Koenen, *Utopie der Säuberung: Was war der Kommunismus?* (Frankfurt/Main: Fischer, 2000), 147.
102. This point is most forcefully argued in Martin Malia, *The Soviet Tragedy: A History of Socialism in Russia, 1917-1991* (New York: Free Press, 1994).
103. Lenin, ' "Left-Wing" Communism', 551.
104. Quoted in Brendon, *Dark Valley*, 202.
105. Quoted in *ibid.*, 204.
106. *Ibid.*, 202 and 213.
107. As one party official put it, 'Karl Marx, our dear dead party leader, wrote that peasants are potatoes in a sack. We have got you in our sack.' Quoted in *ibid.*, 214.
108. Jan Philip Reemtsma, *Vertrauen und Gewalt: Versuch über eine besondere Konstellation der Moderne* (Hamburg: Hamburger Edition, 2008), 378, and Jörg Baberowski, *Der rote Terror: Die Geschichte des Stalinismus* (Munich: Deutsche Verlags-Anstalt, 2003).
109. This contrasted markedly with the Nazi secret police: the Gestapo was after the truth; the Soviet secret police was after confessions.
110. Georg Lukács, 'Die neue Verfassung der UdSSR und das Problem der Persönlichkeit', in *Deutsche Blätter*, vol. 6, no. 9 (1936), 50-3; here 52.
111. Karl Schlögel, *Terror und Traum: Moskau 1937* (Munich: Hanser, 2008), 600-1.
112. Quoted by Ree, *Political Thought*, 131.
113. Lukács, *History*, 337.
114. I. Stalin, *Bolshevism: Some Questions Answered* (London: Communist Party of Great Britain, 1926), 12-13.
115. Schlögel, *Terror*, 250-3.
116. Stalin, *Bolshevism*, 10.
117. As Bukharin himself had put it in 1923: 'Proletarian compulsion in all its forms, beginning with executions by shooting and ending with the compulsory labor obligation, is – however paradoxical this might sound – the means for producing a Communist

humanity from the human material of the capitalist epoch.' Quoted by Daniel Beer, *Renovating Russia* (Ithaca, NY: Cornell University Press, 2008), 23.

118. Vadim Volkov, 'The Concept of Kul'turnost': Notes on the Stalinist Civilizing Process', in Sheila Fitzpatrick (ed.), *Stalinism: New Directions* (New York: Routledge, 2000), 210–30.

119. Ronald Grigor Suny, 'Stalin and his Stalinism: Power and Authority in the Soviet Union, 1930–1953', in Ian Kershaw and Moshe Lewin (eds), *Stalinism and Nazism: Dictatorships in Comparison* (New York: Cambridge University Press, 1997), 26–52.

120. Quoted in *ibid.*, 39.

121. Quoted in Ree, *Political Thought*, 136.

122. Quoted in Roy A. Medvedev, 'New Pages from the Political Biography of Stalin', in Robert C. Tucker (ed.), *Stalinism: Essays in Historical Interpretation* (New Brunswick, NJ: Transaction, 1999), 199–235; here 208.

123. Jochen Hellbeck, 'With Hegel to Salvation: Bukharin's Other Trial', in *Representations*, no. 107 (2009), 56–90; here 74.

124. Ree, *Political Thought*, 275.

125. Schlögel, *Terror*, 28

126. *Ibid.*, 601–2.

127. Eugenia Semyonova Ginzburg, *Journey into the Whirlwind*, trans. Paul Stevenson and Max Hayward (1967; New York: Harcourt Brace Jovanovich, 1975), 227.

128. Mandelstam, *Hope*, 96.

129. Hellbeck, 'With Hegel', 79.

130. Put differently: Stalin's will triumphed much more than Hitler's ever did, but there could not have been a Soviet movie resembling *Triumph of the Will*.

131. Milovan Djilas, *Conversations with Stalin*, trans. Michael B. Petrovich (New York: Harcourt, Brace & World, 1962), 57.

132. This observation was first made by Slavoj Žižek.

133. Ree, *Political Thought*, 81.

134. Simone de Beauvoir, *Force of Circumstance*, trans. Richard Howard (1963; London: Penguin, 1987), 15.

135. Martin Sabrow, 'Das Charisma des Kommunismus', at http://www.zzf-pdm.de/Portals/_Rainbow/Documents/Sabrow/sabrow_charisma.pdf (last accessed 7 August 2009).

136. Vladimir Tismaneanu, *Stalinism for All Seasons: A Political History of Romanian Communism* (Berkeley: University of California Press, 2003), 187.

137. Quoted in Dagros Petrescu, ' "Communist Legacies in the "New Europe". History, Ethnicity, and the Creation of a "Socialist" Nation in Romania, 1945–1989', in Konrad H. Jarausch and Thomas Lindenberger (eds), *Conflicted Memories: Europeanizing Contemporary Histories* (New York: Berghahn Books, 2007), 37–54; here 45.

138. The boulevard leading up to it, Ceaușescu insisted, had to be exactly one metre longer than the Champs-Elysées.

139. Claude Lefort, *Un Homme en trop: Réflexions sur 'L'Archipel du Goulag'* (Paris: Seuil, 1976), especially 57–89.

Chapter 3: Fascist Subjects: The Total State and *Volksgemeinschaft*

1. A. J. P. Taylor, *The Origins of the Second World War* (New York: Atheneum, 1962), 69.

2. Dino Grandi quoted in Emilio Gentile, 'Mussolini's Charisma', in *Modern Italy*, vol. 3 (1998), 219–35; here 227.

3. Emil Ludwig, *Talks with Mussolini*, trans. Eden and Cedar Paul (Boston: Little, Brown, 1933), 162.

4. Quoted in Richard Vinen, *A History in Fragments: Europe in the Twentieth Century* (New York: Da Capo, 2001), 133. The very word fascism is derived not from a recognizable political concept or the name of a politician or a philosopher, for that matter, but from an object carried around by Romans 2,000 years ago: an axe encased in a bundle. The *fascio* was originally a symbol of authority and unity; later it turned into a metaphor for a closely knit band of people.

5. Joachim Fest, *Hitler: Eine Biographie* (Berlin: Ullstein, 2004), 613.

6. What he was above all, though, was the type that Weber thought typical of democracy: a demagogue, or, put more nicely, a political publicist and journalist. Hitler talked (and, less so, wrote) his way to power. Mussolini initially trained as a high school teacher in French and was a journalist before becoming party leader; as Duce, he was still, above all, a wordsmith (though, unlike Hitler, he took his administrative responsibilities seriously as well).

7. Aldo Bertelè quoted in Robert O. Paxton, *The Anatomy of Fascism* (London: Allen Lane, 2004), 16. The notion that acts, not arguments, confirm theories was widespread at all levels of the National Socialist hierarchy. See Michael Wildt's account of the staff of the Reichssicherheitshauptamt, *Generation des Unbedingten: Das Führungskorps des Reichssicherheitshauptamtes* (Hamburg: Hamburger Edition, 2002).

8. Quoted in Karl Dietrich Bracher, *The German Dictatorship: The Origins, Structure, and Effects of National Socialism*, trans. Jean Steinberg (New York: Holt, Rinehart & Winston, 1970), 10.

9. Quoted by Michael Freund, *Georges Sorel: Der revolutionäre Konservativismus* (Frankfurt/Main: Vittorio Klostermann, 1932), 8.

10. Quoted in *ibid.*, 7.

11. Quoted by Helmut Berding, *Rationalismus und Mythos: Geschichtsauffassung und politische Theorie bei Georges Sorel* (Munich: Oldenbourg, 1969), 7.

12. Georges Sorel, *Reflections on Violence*, trans. T. E. Hulme (1915; New York: Peter Smith, 1941), 3–4.

13. *Ibid.*, 3 and 5.

14. See Jeremy R. Jennings, *Georges Sorel: The Character and Development of his Thought* (Basingstoke: Macmillan, 1985).

15. Freund, *Georges Sorel*, 13.

16. *Ibid.*, 14.

17. This point is brought out most forcefully in Isaiah Berlin, 'Georges Sorel', in Isaiah Berlin, *Against the Current: Essays in the History of Ideas* (Oxford: Clarendon, 1981), 296–332.

18. Letter to Robert Michels, 12 May 1909, in *Max Weber-Gesamtausgabe* II:6, ed. M. Rainer Lepsius and Wolfgang J. Mommsen, in collaboration with Birgit Rudhard and Manfred Schön (Tübingen: Mohr Siebeck, 1994), 125. See also Weber's remarks on syndicalists in 'Der Sozialismus' and 'Politik als Beruf'.

19. Sorel, *Reflections*, 172.

20. *Ibid.*, 15.

21. Sorel sharply contrasted myths with utopias. Utopias were 'intellectual products', while myths were 'identical with the convictions of a group, being the expressions of these convictions in the language of movement'. He pointed out that 'whilst contemporary myths lead men to prepare themselves for a combat which will destroy the existing state of things, the effect of Utopias has always been to direct men's minds towards reforms which can be brought about by patching up the existing system'. *Ibid.*, 33.

22. *Ibid.*, 37.

23. *Ibid.*, 86.

24. *Ibid.*, 144.

25. *Ibid.*, 91.

26. *Ibid.*, 99.

27. Zeev Sternhell, with Mario Sznajder and Maia Asheri, *The Birth of Fascist Ideology: From Cultural Rebellion to Political Revolution*, trans. David Maisel (Princeton, NJ: Princeton University Press, 1994).

28. Mark Antliff, *Avant-garde Fascism: The Mobilization of Myth, Art, and Culture in France, 1909–1939* (Durham, NC: Duke University Press, 2007).

29. Carl Schmitt, 'Die politische Theorie des Mythus', in Carl Schmitt, *Positionen und Begriffe im Kampf mit Weimar – Genf – Versailles* (1940; Berlin: Duncker & Humblot, 1988), 9–18; here 11.

30. *Ibid.*, 15 and 17.

31. *Ibid.*, 16 and 17.
32. Quoted in Vinen, *A History in Fragments*, 136.
33. François Furet, *Le Passé d'une illusion: Essai sur l'idée communiste au XXe siècle* (Paris: Robert Laffont, 1995), 197–8.
34. Lest there be any doubt that they meant it (and foreshadowed Fascism): in 1909 Marinetti, asked in an interview if war did not constitute 'a return to a barbaric age', declared: 'Yes, but it's a question of health, which takes precedence over everything else. Is not the life of nations, when all's said and done, just like that of the individual who only rids himself of infections and excess of blood by having recourse to the bathtub and to bloodletting?' 'Futurism: An Interview with Mr. Marinetti in *Comoedia*', in *F. T. Marinetti: Critical Writings*, ed. Günter Berghaus, trans. Doug Thompson (New York: Farrar, Straus & Giroux, 2006), 18–21; here 19.
35. 'In This Futurist Year', in *ibid.*, 231–7; here 235. This text appeared several times between November 1914 and the end of the war.
36. In particular, Marinetti blamed pasta for inducing 'fiacchezza, pessimismo, inattività nostalgica e neutralismo'. Quoted in Vinen, *A History*, 135.
37. Jeffrey Herf, *Reactionary Modernism: Technology, Culture, and Politics in Weimar and the Third Reich* (New York: Cambridge University Press, 1984), 2; see also Roger Griffin, *Fascism and Modernism: The Sense of a Beginning under Mussolini and Hitler* (New York: Palgrave, 2007).
38. Keynes himself abhorred the Nazis from the very beginning. But after 1945 libertarian critics of Keynesianism were trying to tar the 'Middle Way' of state intervention in the economy with 'fascism' – sometimes successfully, as in Italy.
39. Donald Sassoon, *Mussolini and the Rise of Fascism* (London: HarperPress, 2007), 13.
40. Ilse Staff, 'Der faschistische Korporativstaat und die ihn bestimmenden Ideologien', in Aldo Mazzacane *et al.* (eds), *Korporativismus in den südeuropäischen Diktaturen* (Frankfurt/Main: Vittorio Klostermann, 2005), 91–127.
41. Quoted by Luciano Canfora, *Democracy in Europe: A History of an Ideology*, trans. Simon Jones (Malden, Mass.: Blackwell, 2006), 159.
42. A fact recognized at the time: conservative Harvard professor W. Y. Elliott observed that 'the ideology of Fascism contains a very queer potpourri of a sort of Machiavellian Pragmatism, Gentilean Idealism, Sorelian myth-making and violence, and even the functionalism of the Guild Socialists and Syndicalists of Italy'. See Elliott, *Pragmatic Revolt*, 10.
43. Confusingly, Spann actually called his holism (and national particularism) 'universalism'. See Othmar Spann, *Der wahre Staat: Vorlesungen über Abbruch und Neubau der Gesellschaft* (1921; Graz: Akademische Druck- u. Verlagsanstalt, 1972).
44. Gerard Mozetič, 'Outsiders and True Believers: Austrian Sociologists Respond to Fascism', in Stephen Turner and Dirk Käsler (eds), *Sociology Responds to Fascism* (New York: Routledge, 1992), 14–41.
45. Benito Mussolini, *My Rise and Fall* (1928/48; New York: Da Capo Press, 1998), 274.
46. Quoted in A. James Gregor, *Mussolini's Intellectuals: Fascist Social and Political Thought* (Princeton, NJ: Princeton University Press, 2006), 128.
47. Quoted in *ibid.*, 129.
48. See also his *Memoirs of the Twentieth Century*, trans. Anthony G. Costantini (Amsterdam: Rodopi, 2000), 37–46.
49. See Wolfgang Schivelbusch, *Three New Deals: Reflections on Roosevelt's America, Mussolini's Italy, and Hitler's Germany, 1933–1939* (New York: Metropolitan, 2006).
50. Giovanni Gentile, 'Il mio liberalismo', in Giovanni Gentile, *Che cosa è il fascismo? Discorsi e polemiche* (Florence: Vallechi, 1925), 119–22. This essay had originally appeared in 1923.
51. A. James Gregor, *Giovanni Gentile: Philosopher of Fascism* (New Brunswick, NJ: Transaction, 2001), 30–1.
52. Richard Bellamy, *Modern Italian Social Theory: Ideology and Politics from Pareto to the Present* (Cambridge: Polity, 1987), 109.
53. *Ibid.*, 58.

54. M. E. Moss, *Mussolini's Fascist Philosopher: Giovanni Gentile Reconsidered* (New York: Peter Lang, 2004).
55. Quoted in Gregor, *Gentile*, 34.
56. Quoted in *ibid.*, 59.
57. Quoted in Reinhard Mehring, *Carl Schmitt: Aufstieg und Fall* (Munich: C. H. Beck, 2009), 370.
58. Quoted in Gregor, *Gentile*, 63.
59. Gentile, 'The Philosophic Basis', 302–3. See also the 1917 'Futurist Democracy': 'We can . . . safely entrust every right to do and undo to number, to quantity, to the mass, since, in our case, number, quantity, and mass will not be, as they are in Germany and Russia, number, quantity, and mass of mediocre, inept or feckless beings', in *Marinetti*, 300–3; here 301.
60. Before being transformed yet again into a seemingly value-neutral social-scientific term to describe a particular kind of regime in the 1950s . . .
61. Quoted by Ruth Ben-Ghiat, *Fascist Modernities: Italy, 1922–1945* (Berkeley: University of California Press, 2001), 4.
62. R. J. B. Bosworth, 'Italy', in Gerwarth (ed.), *Twisted Paths*, 161–83; here 170–1.
63. Paul Baxa, 'Capturing the Fascist Moment: Hitler's Visit to Italy in 1938 and the Radicalization of Fascist Italy', in *Journal of Contemporary History*, vol. 42 (2007), 227–42, and Fest, *Hitler*, 787.
64. Paolo Pombeni, 'The Roots of the Italian Political Crisis: A View from History, 1918, 1945, 1989, and After', in Carl Levy and Mark Roseman (eds), *Three Postwar Eras in Comparison: Western Europe, 1918–1945–1989* (New York: Palgrave, 2002), 276–96.
65. Bosworth, 'Italy', 177.
66. Quoted in Sassoon, *Mussolini*, 11.
67. Alessandra Tarquini, *Il Gentile dei fascisti: gentiliani e antigentiliani nel regime fascista* (Bologna: Il Mulino, 2009).
68. Horthy was under intense pressure from the Entente to do so. The monarch was officially dethroned in 1921.
69. António Costa Pinto, *Salazar's Dictatorship and European Fascism: Problems of Interpretation* (New York: Columbia University Press, 1995).
70. Paul Hanebrink, *In Defense of Christian Hungary: Religion, Nationalism, and Antisemitism, 1890–1944* (Ithaca, NY: Cornell University Press, 2006), 165.
71. Gerhard Besier, *Das Europa der Diktaturen* (Munich: DVA, 2006), 126–7.
72. Quoted in Mazower, *Dark Continent*, 27.
73. In the 1960s Salazar would still declare: 'The formula which seems best and which will perhaps be the formula of the future, is that Government should legislate, in consultative collaboration with the Corporative Chambers, possibly with the assistance of a Council of legal experts'; he also affirmed 'there is no greater blessing for a nation, I think, than the stability of a good government'. See *Salazar Says . . .* (Lisbon: S.P.N., 1963), 27 and 26.
74. Literally 'Dilettantische Seifenblasen'. See Weber, 'Wahlrecht und Demokratie in Deutschland', in *Max Weber-Gesamtausgabe* I:15, ed. Wolfgang Mommsen in collaboration with Gangolf Hübinger (Tübingen: Mohr Siebeck, 1984), 347–96; here 355–63.
75. Mozetič, 'Outsiders'.
76. Besier, *Das Europa*, 280.
77. Ivan T. Berend, *Decades of Crisis: Central and Eastern Europe before World War II* (Berkeley: University of California Press, 1998), 305.
78. *Ibid.*, 304.
79. The self-flagellating nature of Vichy propaganda is brilliantly exposed in Claude Chabrol's *L'Oeil de Vichy*.
80. James, *Europe*, 205.
81. Quoted by Marc Olivier Baruch, 'Charisma and Hybrid Legitimacy in Pétain's *Etat français* (1940–44)', in António Costa Pinto, Roger Eatwell and Stein Ugelvik Larsen

(eds), *Charisma and Fascism in Interwar Europe* (London: Routledge, 2007), 77–86; here 80.

82. Sigmund Neumann, *Permanent Revolution: The Total State in a World at War* (New York: Harper, 1942), 230.

83. To be sure, Nazi Germany and Fascist Italy did not go to their ends entirely in parallel. The Nazis really had completely to self-destruct, whereas in Italy traditional institutions retained some power (and the army was largely loyal to the king). Yet a categorical difference remains between these two regimes and the authoritarian ones. See MacGregor Knox, *Common Destiny: Dictatorship, Foreign Policy, and War in Fascist Italy and Nazi Germany* (New York: Cambridge University Press, 2000).

84. An interesting in-between case is Franco, who handed power over to a monarch.

85. Emilio Gentile, *The Sacralization of Politics in Fascist Italy*, trans. Keith Botsford (Cambridge, Mass.: Harvard University Press, 1996). The designation 'political religion' captures important aspects of fascism, as does the definition of fascism as 'a populist, palingenetic form of ultra-nationalism'; the former is associated with the Italian scholar Emilio Gentile, the latter with Roger Griffin, who accepts most of Gentile's approach to fascism, including the political religion paradigm. However, as my discussion in the main text should make clear, both are too unspecific in some respects, while also failing to capture the fascist belief in the value of struggle as such. 'Ultra-nationalism' is still too harmless for the fascist conceptions of collective bodies which always shaded into racism; while 'palingenetic' applies to many (quite possibly all) other political movements. A further problem is that work on political religion often – though not necessarily – comes with highly questionable social and normative assumptions concerning the supposed anomie and longing for meaning in secularized societies. I should like to stress that my somewhat sceptical view of the political religion paradigm is not rooted in the fact that men and women under fascism might in many cases not have experienced at all what Gentile calls the 'anthropological revolution' promoted by fascist ideologues. As with the concept of totalitarianism, it is important to distinguish the aspirations of movements and the reality of life under realized regimes: as long as it is clear that the conceptual work concerns the former, the fact that *es eigentlich ganz anders gewesen* as lived experience cannot be a decisive objection. For Griffin's approach, see *The Nature of Fascism* (London: Pinter, 1991).

86. Alfred Baeumler, *Bildung und Gemeinschaft* (Berlin: Junker & Dünnhaupt, 1942).

87. However, there were also many Nazi thinkers who advocated a particular Nazi Christianity. See Richard Steigmann-Gall, *The Holy Reich: Nazi Conceptions of Christianity, 1919–1945* (New York: Cambridge University Press, 2003).

88. Hitler himself admitted that he had read only small parts of it. Ernst Piper, *Alfred Rosenberg: Hitlers Chefideologe* (Munich: Karl Blessing, 2005), 186.

89. Quoted by Roberto Esposito, *Bíos: Biopolitics and Philosophy*, trans. Timothy Campbell (Minneapolis: University of Minnesota Press, 2008), 142.

90. In baptisms, now renamed *Namensweihen*, the following lines were supposed to be spoken: 'Wir glauben an das Volk, des Blutes Träger / Und an den Führer, den uns Gott bestimmt' (We believe in the Volk, the carrier of blood / and in the Führer who was given to us by God). See Peter Longerich, *Heinrich Himmler* (Berlin: Siedler, 2008), 299.

91. Quoted in Michael Burleigh, *The Third Reich: A New History* (London: Pan, 2001), 13.

92. Wolfgang Schieder, *Faschistische Diktaturen: Studien zu Italien und Deutschland* (Göttingen: Wallstein, 2008), 17.

93. Ben-Ghiat, *Fascist Modernities*, 17–9.

94. *Ibid.*, 5.

95. Quoted by Ben-Ghiat, *Fascist Modernities*, 19.

96. Robert S. C. Gordon, 'Race', in R. J. B. Bosworth (ed.), *The Oxford Handbook of Fascism* (New York: Oxford University Press, 2009), 296–316.

97. Quoted by Esposito, *Bíos*, 112.

98. Is this sufficient as a specificity of fascism and as a common denominator of the Italian and the German regimes? Yes, because no other major ideology shared that sense of

the value of struggle as such. Of course, the proletariat was a collective body engaged in struggle as well, but that struggle had an end-point and nothing was really lost once struggle could be left behind.

99. Rosenberg's spiritual racism best exemplifies this – never quite resolved – contradiction between political will and biological determinism. Of course, one could argue that the Germans losing the war had revealed them as not the race Hitler thought they were, which would explain why he essentially wanted the German people to perish altogether in 1945.

100. See the brilliant chapter by Peter Fritzsche and Jochen Hellbeck, 'The New Man in Stalinist Russia and Nazi Germany', in Geyer and Fitzpatrick (eds), *Beyond*, 302–41; here 303, 314 and 339.

101. Claudia Koonz, *The Nazi Conscience* (Cambridge, Mass.: Harvard University Press, 2003).

102. Michael Wildt, *Volksgemeinschaft als Selbstermächtigung: Gewalt gegen Juden in der deutschen Provinz 1919 bis 1939* (Hamburg: Hamburger Edition, 2007).

103. Michael Stolleis, 'Gemeinschaft und Volksgemeinschaft: Zur juristischen Terminologie im Nationalsozialismus', in *Vierteljahrshefte für Zeitgeschichte*, vol. 20 (1972), 16–38.

104. Reemtsma, *Vetrauen und Gewalt*, 392.

105. Mehring, *Schmitt*, 367.

106. Quoted in Gregor, *Mussolini's Intellectuals*, 119.

107. Carl Schmitt, *Constitutional Theory*, trans. Jeffrey Seitzer (1927; Durham, NC: Duke University Press, 2008).

108. Reinhard Höhn, *Frankreichs Demokratie und ihr geistiger Zusammenbruch* (Darmstadt: L. C. Wittich, 1940).

109. Alfred Baeumler, *Alfred Rosenberg und der Mythus des 20. Jahrhunderts* (Munich: Hoheneichen, 1943), 19.

110. Quoted in Fest, *Hitler*, 595.

111. Gentile, 'Mussolini's Charisma', 230–1.

112. *Ibid.*, 227. This is true, at any rate, of the period after the Night of the Long Knives.

113. Fest, *Hitler*, 597.

114. Wildt, *Generation*, 13.

115. Stolleis, 'Gemeinschaft'.

116. Carl Schmitt, *Staat, Bewegung, Volk: Die Dreigliederung der politischen Einheit* (Hamburg: Hanseatische Verlagsanstalt, 1935).

117. Quoted in Gorlizki and Mommsen, 'The Political (Dis)Orders', 54.

118. This was a radicalization of the medieval theory of the king's two bodies; see Ernst H. Kantorowicz, *The King's Two Bodies: A Study in Medieval Political Theology* (Princeton, NJ: Princeton University Press, 1997).

119. Ernst Fraenkel, *The Dual State: A Contribution to the Theory of Dictatorship*, trans. E. A. Shils, in collaboration with Edith Lowenstein and Klaus Knorr (New York: Oxford University Press, 1941).

120. The phrase was coined by the civil servant Werner Willikens and became central to Ian Kershaw's interpretation of Hitler's role in a seemingly self-radicalizing regime. See Ian Kershaw, *Hitler*, 2 vols (New York: W. W. Norton, 2000 and 2001).

121. Gorlizki and Mommsen, 'Political (Dis)Orders', 56.

122. Franz Neumann, *Behemoth: The Structure and Practice of National Socialism* (London: Left Book Club Edition, 1942), 383.

123. Mehring, *Schmitt*, 340.

124. Hannah Arendt, *The Origins of Totalitarianism* (New York: Harcourt, 1976), 459.

125. Christopher R. Browning and Lewis H. Siegelbaum, 'Frameworks of Social Engineering: Stalinist Schema of Identification and the Nazi Volksgemeinschaft', in Geyer and Fitzpatrick (eds), *Beyond*, 231–65; here 262.

126. Gorlizki and Mommsen, 'Political (Dis)Orders', 64.

127. *Ibid.*, 82.

128. Dan Diner, *Weltordnungen: Über Geschichte und Wirkung von Recht und Macht* (Frankfurt/Main: Fischer, 1993).

129. Hitler's definition of the state simply read: 'the state has nothing at all to do with any definite economic conception of development. It is not a collection of economic contracting parties in a definite delimited living space for the fulfillment of economic tasks, but the organization of a community of physically and psychologically similar living beings for the better facilitation of the maintenance of their species and the achievement of the aim which has been allotted to this species by Providence. This and nothing else is the aim and meaning of a state.' *Mein Kampf*, trans. Ralph Mannheim (London: Pimlico, 2001), 137.
130. Quoted in Davide Rodogno, *Fascism's European Empire: Italian Occupation during the Second World War*, trans. Adrian Belton (New York: Cambridge University Press, 2006), 59.
131. Richard Overy, *The Dictators: Hitler's Germany and Stalin's Russia* (London: Penguin, 2004), 574–7.
132. Quoted in Piper, *Rosenberg*, 598.
133. Hannah Arendt, 'The Seeds of a Fascist International', in Arendt, *Essays*, 140–50; here 144. This essay had first appeared in 1945.
134. Alexandre Kojève, 'Outline of a Doctrine of French Policy', in *Policy Review*, no. 123 (2004), 3–40 (translation modified).
135. Browning and Siegelbaum, 'Frameworks', 261.
136. Quoted in Kershaw, *Hitler*, vol. 1, 125.
137. Gunnar Heinsohn, *Warum Auschwitz?* (Hamburg: Rowohlt, 1995) and Roberts, *Totalitarian Experiment*.
138. Quoted in Overy, *Dictators*, 589.
139. Quoted by Fest, *Hitler*, 1046.
140. Thomas Mann, 'Schicksal und Aufgabe', in *Gesammelte Werke*, vol. 12 (Frankfurt/Main: Fischer, 1960), 918–39. One may well question the use of medical metaphors in coming to terms with fascism (Croce calling Fascism a 'moral illness' is another notable instance), not only because they naturalize political phenomena, but because they might remain caught in the very language which they aim to oppose.

Chapter 4: Reconstruction Thought: Self-Disciplined Democracies, 'People's Democracies'

1. Richard Bessel and Dirk Schumann, 'Violence, Normality, and the Construction of Postwar Europe', in Richard Bessel and Dirk Schumann (eds), *Life after Death: Approaches to a Cultural and Social History of Europe during the 1940s and 1950s* (New York: Cambridge University Press, 2003), 1–14; here 1.
2. *Ibid.*
3. Quoted in *ibid.*
4. Hannah Arendt, 'Nightmare and Flight', in Arendt, *Essays*, 133–5; here 134.
5. Friedrich Meinecke, *Die deutsche Katastrophe: Betrachtungen und Erinnerungen* (Wiesbaden: Eberhard Brockhaus, 1946), 21.
6. Arendt, *Origins*, 317.
7. Paul Nolte, *Die Ordnung der deutschen Gesellschaft* (Munich: C. H. Beck, 2000), 305.
8. Beauvoir, *Force*, 162 and 47.
9. Charles S. Maier, 'The Two Postwar Eras and the Conditions for Stability in Twentieth-Century Western Europe', in *American Historical Review*, vol. 86 (1981), 327–52.
10. Tony Judt, *Postwar: A History of Europe since 1945* (New York: Penguin, 2005).
11. For this point see also Marcel Gauchet, *L'Avènement de la démocratie* (Paris: Gallimard, 2007).
12. Paolo Pombeni, 'The Ideology of Christian Democracy', in *Journal of Political Ideologies*, vol. 5 (2000), 289–300; here 299.
13. Martin Conway, 'The Rise and Fall of Western Europe's Democratic Age, 1945–1973', in *Contemporary European History*, 13 (2004), 67–88; here 81.

14. This generalization needs to be relativized with regard to France: there the 'welfare state' – if that expression is appropriate at all – emerged in a more incremental fashion from traditions of mutualism, solidarism, Catholic social doctrine, but also pro-natalist campaigns. In other words, there was no great moment of foundation and rationalization. Pierre Laroque, who established *sécurité sociale* in 1945, was hardly a 'French Beveridge', but rather a technocrat who had to make crucial concessions in his institutional designs not to socialists but to Christian Democrats. See Paul V. Dutton, *Origins of the French Welfare State: The Struggle for Social Reform in France 1914–1945* (New York: Cambridge University Press, 2002), and Philip Nord, *France's New Deal: From the Thirties to the Postwar Era* (Princeton, NJ: Princeton University Press, 2010). In another sense, however, this generalization needs to be relativized for all Western European countries: from a longer-term perspective, socialism *was* the ultimate cause of the post-war welfare states – without its threat, there would have been no Christian Democracy in the first place.

15. There were also, however, some leading Labour figures who understood themselves as Christian Democrats. See, above all, Stafford Cripps, *Towards Christian Democracy* (New York: Philosophical Library, 1946).

16. Conway, 'The Rise', 76–7.

17. R. H. S. Crossman, 'Towards a Philosophy of Socialism', in R. H. S. Crossman (ed.), *New Fabian Essays* (London: Turnstile Press, 1952), 1–32; here 16.

18. Judt, *Postwar*, 76–7.

19. José Harris, 'Political Thought and the State', in S. J. D. Green and R. C. Whiting (eds), *The Boundaries of the State in Modern Britain* (Cambridge: Cambridge University Press, 2002), 15–28; here 23.

20. R. H. S. Crossman, 'Introduction', in Crossman (ed.), *New Fabian Essays*, ix–xiv; here xi.

21. Crossman, 'Towards', 28.

22. José Harris, *William Beveridge: A Biography* (Oxford: Oxford University Press, 1997), 452.

23. Crossman, 'Towards', 3.

24. This and the following are largely based on Stathis Kalyvas, *The Rise of Christian Democracy in Europe* (Ithaca, NJ: Cornell University Press, 1996).

25. As Antonio Gramsci observed, 'it is no longer the Church that determines the battle-field and weapons; it has instead to accept the terrain imposed on it by the adversaries'.

26. John Pollard, 'Italy', in Tom Buchanan and Martin Conway (eds), *Political Catholicism in Europe, 1918–1965* (Oxford: Oxford University Press, 1996), 69–96.

27. Quoted in Samuel Moyn, 'Personalism, Community, and the Origins of Human Rights', in Stefan-Ludwig Hoffmann (ed.), *Human Rights in the Twentieth Century* (New York: Cambridge University Press, 2010), 86–106; here 89.

28. Quoted in *ibid.*, 94. The personalists have been taken to task for these affinities by Tony Judt, *Past Imperfect: French Intellectuals, 1944–1956* (Berkeley: University of California Press, 1992), and John Hellman, *The Knight-Monks of Vichy France: Uriage, 1940–1945* (Montreal: McGill-Queen's University Press, 1997); for a subtle and sympathetic, but not uncritical, contemporary appreciation of personalism: Paul Ricoeur, 'Une Philosophie personaliste', in *Esprit*, vol. 18 (1950), 860–87.

29. Don Luigi Sturzo, 'Has Fascism Ended with Mussolini?', in *Review of Politics*, vol. 7 (1945), 306–15; here 309.

30. My account is based mainly on Bernard Doering, *Jacques Maritain and the French Catholic Intellectuals* (Notre Dame, Ind.: University of Notre Dame Press, 1983), and Jean-Luc Barré, *Jacques et Raïssa Maritain – les mendiants du ciel – biographies croisées* (Paris: Stock, 1995).

31. One of his earliest works from the time was translated into Italian by G. Battista Montini, later known as Pope Paul VI.

32. Jacques Maritain, *Réflexions sur l'Amérique* (Paris: Arthème Fayard, 1958).

33. Jacques Maritain, *Christianity and Democracy* (1944; New York: Scribner, 1950), 37.

34. Jacques Maritain, 'The Concept of Sovereignty', in *American Political Science Review*, vol. 44 (1950), 343–57; here 343–4.

35. Carl Schmitt, *Glossarium: Aufzeichnungen der Jahre 1947–1951* (Berlin: Duncker & Humblot, 1991), 267; Aurel Kolnai, 'The Synthesis of Christ and Anti-Christ', in *Integrity*, vol. 5 (1951), 40–5; here 41.

36. Christian Heidrich, *Leszek Kolakowski: Zwischen Skepsis und Mystik* (Frankfurt/Main: Neue Kritik, 1995), 73.

37. Paolo Pombeni, *Il gruppo dossettiano e la fondazione della democrazia italiana (1938–1948)* (Bologna: Il Mulino, 1979), 51–5.

38. Quoted in Paolo Pombeni, 'Anti-Liberalism and the Liberal Legacy in Postwar European Constitutionalism: Considerations on Some Case Studies', in *European Journal of Political Theory*, vol. 7 (2008), 31–44; here 36.

39. Carlo Masala, 'Born for Government: The Democrazia Cristiana in Italy', in Michael Gehler and Wolfram Kaiser (eds), *Christian Democracy in Europe since 1945*, vol. 2 (London: Routledge, 2004), 101–17; here 104.

40. *Ibid.*, 107.

41. See Paolo Pombeni, 'Individuo/persona nella Costituzione italiana. Il contributo del dossettismo', in *Parole Chiave*, nos 10/11 (1996), 197–218. The left of the DC also managed to have their version of the first article of the constitution passed: the personalist-sounding 'Italy is a democratic Republic founded upon work' prevailed over the 'Italy is a democratic republic of workers' proposed by Communist leader Palmiro Togliatti. See Canfora, *Democracy*, 182–4.

42. The name MRP also suggested the novelty of Christian Democracy in French history: it was explicitly republican, but also understood itself as a broader movement rather than a mere party. Critics, however, claimed that MRP really stood for 'Machine pour Ramasser les Pétainistes'. See Michael Burleigh, *Sacred Causes: The Clash of Religion and Politics, from the Great War to the War on Terror* (New York: HarperCollins, 2007), 288–90.

43. Peter Pulzer, 'Nationalism and Internationalism in European Christian Democracy', in Michael Gehler, Wolfram Kaiser and Helmut Wohnout (eds), *Christdemokratie im Europa im 20. Jahrhundert* (Vienna: Böhlau, 2001), 60–73; here 72.

44. Quoted by Paul Ginsborg, *A History of Contemporary Italy, 1943–1980* (London: Penguin, 1990), 76–7.

45. Pulzer, 'Nationalism', 62.

46. Advocates of a more direct approach to European unity had immediately after the war called for a European constitutional assembly to draft a federalist European constitution. But almost all these advocates – many of whom had emerged from the resistance – had been quickly sidelined after 1945.

47. Quoted in Judt, *Postwar*, 275.

48. Quoted in Paolo Acanfora, 'Myths and the Political Use of Religion in Christian Democratic Culture', in *Journal of Modern Italian Studies*, vol. 12 (2007), 307–38; here 326.

49. Jürgen Habermas, *Autonomy and Solidarity: Interviews with Jürgen Habermas*, ed. Peter Dews (London: Verso, 1992), 79.

50. Hugh Clegg, *Industrial Democracy and Nationalization* (Oxford: Blackwell, 1951), 22.

51. Robert Skidelsky, *John Maynard Keynes: The Economist as Savior, 1920–1937* (New York: Penguin, 1992), 228.

52. Herbert Tingsten, 'Stability and Vitality in Swedish Democracy', in *Political Quarterly*, vol. 26 (1955), 140–51; here 147.

53. Quoted in James, *Europe*, 245.

54. Gabriele Metzler, *Konzeptionen politischen Handelns von Adenauer bis Brandt: Politische Planung in der pluralistischen Gesellschaft* (Paderborn: F. Schöningh, 2005), 83.

55. Skidelsky, *Keynes*, 223.

56. Marquand, *Britain*, 147.

57. For the foregoing quotations see Stapleton, *Englishness*, 167–70.

58. Quoted in Conway, 'The Rise', 69.

59. Ernst Forsthoff, *Der Staat der Industriegesellschaft* (Munich: C. H. Beck, 1971), 164.

60. Dominic Sandbrook, *White Heat: A History of Britain in the Swinging Sixties* (London: Little, Brown, 2006), 4.

61. See Nolte, *Die Ordnung,* and Metzler, *Konzeptionen,* 37.
62. Burleigh, *Sacred Causes,* 304.
63. See Theo Öhlinger, 'The Genesis of the Austrian Model of Constitutional Review of Legislation', in *Ratio Juris,* vol. 16 (2003), 206–22.
64. Hans Kelsen, 'Wer soll der Hüter der Verfassung sein?', in *Die Justiz,* vol. 6 (1931), 576–628.
65. Christian Bommarius, *Das Grundgesetz: Eine Biographie* (Berlin: Rowohlt, 2009), 219–26.
66. Karl Loewenstein, 'Militant Democracy and Fundamental Rights I', in *American Political Science Review,* vol. 31 (1937), 417–32.
67. *Ibid.,* 424.
68. Karl Loewenstein, 'Militant Democracy and Fundamental Rights II', in *American Political Science Review,* vol. 31 (1937), 638–58; here 647.
69. *Ibid.,* 656–7.
70. Ginsborg, *History,* 142.
71. I am grateful to Giovanni Cappoccia on this point.
72. As is clearly and with much evidence argued in Peter Lindseth, 'The Paradox of Parliamentary Supremacy: Delegation, Democracy, and Dictatorship in Germany and France, 1920–1950s', in *Yale Law Journal,* vol. 113 (2004), 1341–415.
73. As early as 1936 Karl Loewenstein – the inventor of militant democracy – had observed: 'A fundamental transformation of legislative technique has accompanied the new method of legislation inasmuch as the differences between statute law and executory ordinance were almost completely obliterated. The government decrees usually contain only a proclamation of policy, in the broadest outlines, while details are regulated by unlimited delegation of powers to ministers, boards, commissioners, or subordinated authorities . . .' See 'Law in the Third Reich', in *Yale Law Journal,* vol. 45 (1936), 779–815; here 788.
74. Karl Loewenstein, *Max Weber's Political Ideas in the Perspective of our Time,* trans. Richard and Clara Winston (Amherst: University of Massachusetts Press, 1966), 48.
75. Kelsen, 'Foundations of Democracy'.
76. Isaiah Berlin, 'European Unity and its Vicissitudes', in Isaiah Berlin, *The Crooked Timber of Humanity: Chapters in the History of Ideas* (London: John Murray, 1990), 175–206; here 202.
77. Lindseth, 'The Paradox'.
78. Andrew Moravcsik, 'The Origins of Human Rights Regimes: Democratic Delegation in Postwar Europe', in *International Organization,* vol. 54 (2000), 217–52.
79. C. A. R. Crosland, *Socialism Now* (London: Cape, 1974), 65–6.
80. The account of Hayek's life is mostly based on Alan Ebenstein, *Friedrich Hayek: A Biography* (Chicago: University of Chicago Press, 2003), and Hans-Jörg Hennecke, *Friedrich August von Hayek: Die Tradition der Freiheit* (Düsseldorf: Verlag Wirtschaft und Finanzen, 2000).
81. Quoted in Ebenstein, *Hayek,* 313. This statement is from 1984, but sums up what Hayek always thought wrong with socialism.
82. Quoted in *ibid.,* 130.
83. R. H. Tawney, 'We Mean Freedom', in *Review of Politics,* vol. 8 (1946), 223–39; here 233.
84. Quoted in Ebenstein, *Hayek,* 137–8.
85. *Ibid.,* 138.
86. R. M. Hartwell, *A History of the Mont Pèlerin Society* (Indianapolis: Liberty Fund, 1995), xiii.
87. The other major exception was Italy's president Luigi Einaudi.
88. Hennecke, *Hayek,* 267.
89. Alexander Rüstow, 'Paläoliberalismus, Kommunismus und Neoliberalismus', in Franz Greiss and Fritz W. Meyer (eds), *Wirtschaft, Gesellschaft und Kultur: Festgabe für Alfred Müller-Armack* (Berlin: Duncker & Humblot, 1961), 61–70.
90. Alexander Rüstow, *Das Versagen des Wirtschaftsliberalismus,* 2nd edn (Düsseldorf: Küpper, 1950), 91.
91. Philip Manow, 'Ordoliberalismus als ökonomische Ordnungstheologie', in *Leviathan,* vol. 29 (2001), 179–98.
92. Hennecke, *Hayek,* 210.

93. The Netherlands extended the Convention to Surinam and the Netherlands Antilles, at a time when major Dutch possessions had already been lost. Denmark extended it to Greenland in 1953.

94. A. W. Brian Simpson, *Human Rights and the End of Empire: Britain and the Genesis of the European Convention* (New York: Oxford University Press, 2004).

95. John Springhall, *Decolonization since 1945: The Collapse of European Overseas Empires* (New York: Palgrave, 2001), 21.

96. *Ibid.*, 22.

97. Quoted in Ronald Hyam, *Britain's Declining Empire: The Road to Decolonisation, 1918–1968* (Cambridge: Cambridge University Press, 2006), 14.

98. Quoted in Springhall, *Decolonization*, 29.

99. Observers within the Third Reich had already noted the revealing use of colonialist language – such as *Konzentrationslager* and *Strafexpedition* – by Hitler and his henchmen. See, above all, Victor Klemperer, *LTI – Lingua Tertii Imperii: A Philologist's Notebook*, trans. Martin Brady (London: Continuum, 2006).

100. Aimé Césaire, *Discourse on Colonialism* (New York: Monthly Review Press, 1970), 15.

101. Jean-Paul Sartre, 'Preface', in Frantz Fanon, *The Wretched of the Earth*, trans. Richard Philcox (1961; New York: Grove, 2004), xliii–lxii; here lv (translation modified).

102. *Ibid.*, xlix.

103. His speech to that effect can be seen in the later part of Marcel Ophüls' *The Sorrow and the Pity*.

104. Edgar Morin, *Penser l'Europe* (Paris: Gallimard, 1987), 140–7.

105. As the Hungarian intellectual Gáspár Miklós Tamás was to put it: 'It is true that the Communist party dictatorship was brought to the small East European countries by the victorious troops of Stalin, but we should admit that we were ready for it.' The notion of 'people's democracy' designated a transitional stage between bourgeois democracy and fully socialist democracy. In theory, it was to be characterized by 'the rule of the toiling people'; beyond this, the concept became highly contested, the main question being: could there be independent roads to socialism, or did everyone have to approximate the model of the USSR?

106. Zdeněk Mlynář, *Nightfrost in Prague: The End of Humane Socialism*, trans. Paul Wilson (New York: Karz, 1980), 1–2.

107. Árpád von Klimó, *Ungarn seit 1945* (Göttingen: Vandenhoeck & Ruprecht, 2006), 63.

108. Quoted in Kadarkay, *Lukács*, 385.

109. 'Speech by N. S. Khrushchev on the Stalin Cult delivered Feb. 25, 1956, at a closed session of the 20th Congress of the Soviet Communist Party', in *Khrushchev Speaks: Selected Speeches, Articles, and Press Conferences, 1949–1961*, ed. Thomas P. Whitney (Ann Arbor: University of Michigan Press, 1963), 207–65; here 220 and 208. The revelations were a profound shock: people in Khrushchev's audience fainted; at other times they are said to have laughed hysterically. The West would send little balloons with copies of the speech attached across the Iron Curtain.

110. Robert Service, *A History of Twentieth-Century Russia* (Cambridge, Mass.: Harvard University Press, 1997), 331–55.

111. Priestland, 'Soviet Democracy', 121–3.

112. Moshe Lewin, 'Bureaucracy and the Stalinist State', in Kershaw and Lewin (eds), *Stalinism*, 53–74.

113. Todorov, *Hope and Memory*, 44.

114. Isaiah Berlin, *The Soviet Mind: Russian Culture under Communism*, ed. Henry Hardy (Washington, DC: Brookings, 2004), 120.

115. David Pryce-Jones, 'Remembering Milovan Djilas', in *New Criterion*, vol. 18 (October 1999), 4–9.

116. Vladimir Tismaneanu, *Reinventing Politics* (New York: Free Press, 1992), 46–7.

117. *Ibid.*, 48–9.

118. Milovan Djilas, *The New Class: An Analysis of the Communist System* (London: Thames & Hudson, 1957), 35.

119. *Ibid.*, 36.

120. Quoted by Grzegorz Ekiert, *The State against Society: Political Crises and their Aftermath in East Central Europe* (Princeton, NJ: Princeton University Press, 1996), 61.

121. Ferenc Fehér and Agnes Heller, *Hungary 1956 Revisited: The Message of a Revolution – a Quarter of a Century After* (London: Allen & Unwin, 1983), 95.

122. *Ibid.*, 17.

123. 'Report from Anastas Mikoyan and Mikhail Suslov in Budapest to the CPSU CC, October 27, 1956', in Csaba Békés et al. (eds), *The 1956 Hungarian Revolution: A History in Documents* (Budapest: CEU Press, 2002), 251–2; here 251.

124. Lukács, *Record of a Life*, 128.

125. Istvan Bibó, 'The Hungarian Revolution of 1956: Scandal and Hope', in *Democracy, Revolution, Self-Determination: Selected Writings*, ed. Károly Nagy, trans. András Boros-Kazai (New York: Columbia University Press, 1991), 331–54; here 337.

126. Quoted in Fehér and Heller, *Hungary*, 136.

127. *Ibid.*, 103–4.

128. János Kornai, *By Force of Thought: Irregular Memoirs of an Intellectual Journey* (Cambridge, Mass.: MIT Press, 2006), 101.

129. François Fejtö, *1956, Budapest, l'insurrection: La première révolution anti-totalitaire* (Brussels: Complexe, 2006), 176.

130. Tismaneanu, *Reinventing*, 70.

131. Fehér and Heller, *Hungary*, 89.

132. Quoted in Robert Service, *Comrades! A World History of Communism* (Cambridge, Mass.: Harvard University Press, 2007), 382.

133. Fehér and Heller, *Hungary*, ix.

134. Fejtö, *1956*, 172.

135. János Kornai, *The Dilemmas of a Socialist Economy: The Hungarian Experience* (Dublin: Economic and Social Research Institute, 1979), 9.

136. Beauvoir, *Force*, 211–12.

137. Vladimir Kusin, *The Intellectual Origins of the Prague Spring: The Development of Reformist Ideas in Czechoslovakia, 1956–1967* (New York: Cambridge University Press, 1971).

138. Quoted in James H. Satterwhite, 'Introduction', in Karel Kosík, *The Crisis of Modernity: Essays and Observations from the 1968 Era*, ed. James H. Satterwhite (Lanham, Md.: Rowman & Littlefield, 1995), 1–11; here 4.

139. Jan Pauer, *Prag 1968: Der Einmarsch des Warschauer Paktes* (Bremen: Edition Temmen, 1995).

140. Kieran Williams, *The Prague Spring and its Aftermath* (Cambridge: Cambridge University Press, 1997), 10.

141. *Ibid.*, 3.

142. *Ibid.*, 15.

143. *Ibid.*, 18.

144. 'The CPCz CC Action Program, April 1968', in *The Prague Spring 1968*, ed. Jaromír Navrátil et al. (Budapest: CEU Press, 1998), 92–5; here 92.

145. *Ibid.*, 27, and Fehér and Heller, *Hungary*, 109. Others began to demand a proper constitutional court, while plans were also made to create democracy through workers' councils – which led Kosík to warn that 'radical democracy' and worker representation were actually two different things. See Kosík, 'A Word of Caution on Workers' Councils', in Kosík, *Crisis*, 209–10.

146. Ekiert, *State*, 123.

147. Mikhail Gorbachev and Zdeněk Mlynář, *Conversations with Gorbachev: On Perestroika, the Prague Spring, and the Crossroads of Socialism*, trans. George Shriver (New York: Columbia University Press, 2002), 40.

148. Ota Šik, *Argumente für den Dritten Weg* (Hamburg: Hoffmann & Campe, 1973).

149. Kornai, *Dilemmas*, 18.

150. Milan Kundera, *The Joke*, trans. Michael Henry Heim (New York: Harper & Row, 1982), x.

151. Leszek Kolakowski, 'My Correct Views on Everything: A Rejoinder to Edward Thompson's "Open Letter to Leszek Kolakowski" ', in *Socialist Register* (1974), 1–20; here 20.
152. Tismaneanu, *Reinventing*, 114.
153. Michael Newman, *Ralph Miliband and the Politics of the New Left* (London: Merlin Press, 2002), 146 and 143.
154. Quoted in Tismaneanu, *Reinventing*, 72.
155. Quoted in Jacques Rupnik, *The Other Europe* (London: Weidenfeld & Nicolson, 1988), 256–7.
156. Quoted in Gale Stokes, *The Walls Came Tumbling Down: The Collapse of Communism in Eastern Europe* (New York: Oxford University Press, 1993), 12, and Barbara J. Falk, *The Dilemmas of Dissidence in East-Central Europe: Citizen Intellectuals and Philosopher Kings* (Budapest: CEU Press, 2003), 209.
157. Kołakowski is said to have replied to this claim: 'Ah, yes, the advantages of Albania over Sweden are self-evident.'

Chapter 5: The New Time of Contestation: Towards a Fatherless Society

1. Thomas Hecken, *1968: Von Texten und Theorien aus einer Zeit euphorischer Kritik* (Bielefeld: transcript, 2008), 135–48. In this costume drama, different people dressed up as, for example, Lenin or Robespierre. But Aron always appeared as Tocqueville.
2. Sunil Khilnani, *Arguing Revolution: The Intellectual Left in Postwar France* (New Haven, Conn.: Yale University Press 1993), 122.
3. The cunning of reason seemed to have ensured that anti-Americanism, which at the time appeared to be a distinctive feature of the Western European '68, turned out to be the supreme means of promoting Americanization.
4. Dutschke quoted by Gérard Sandoz, 'Etre révolutionnaire', in Rudi Dutschke, *Ecrits politiques (1967–1968)* (Paris: Christian Bourgois, 1968), 31.
5. It is important to emphasize that until about 1970 the widely desired 'revolution in consciousness' was certainly not to be brought about with violence. At the beginning, 'guerilla' only meant a 'refusal and sabotage guerilla', in Dutschke's phrase.
6. Ginsborg, *History*, 299.
7. Gino Martinoli, *L'università come impresa* (Florence: La Nuova Italia, 1967).
8. 'On the Poverty of Student Life: Considered in its Economic, Political, Psychological, Sexual and Especially Intellectual Aspects, with a Modest Proposal for its Remedy', in *Situationist International Anthology*, ed. and trans. Ken Knabb (Berkeley, Calif.: Bureau of Public Secrets, 1981), 319–37; here 319 and 321.
9. Hervé Hamon and Patrick Rotman, *Génération: Les années de rêve* (Paris: Seuil, 1987), 400–1.
10. Quoted in Sassoon, *One Hundred*, 384.
11. De Gaulle's resolve was apparently strengthened by Massu telling him: 'Vous êtes dans la merde, il faut y rester encore.'
12. Ginsborg, *History*, 306.
13. Ingrid Gilcher-Holtey, *1968: Eine Zeitreise* (Frankfurt/Main: Suhrkamp, 2008), 83.
14. On this point see also Hecken, *1968*.
15. Robert Lumley, '1968/1989: Social Movements in Italy Reconsidered', in Levy and Roseman (eds), *Three Postwar Eras*, 199–215; here 201.
16. Gerd Koenen, 'Der transzendental Obdachlose – Hans-Jürgen Krahl', in *Zeitschrift für Ideengeschichte*, vol. 2 (2008), 5–22.
17. Lukács, *Record*, 173. For Dutschke's extensive engagement with Lukács, see his *Versuch, Lenin auf die Füße zu stellen: Über den halbasiatischen und westeuropäischen Weg zum Sozialismus. Lenin, Lukács und die Dritte Internationale* (Berlin: Wagenbach, 1974).

18. Rudi Dutschke, 'Besuch bei Georg Lukács', in *Geschichte ist machbar: Texte über das herrschende Falsche und die Radikalität des Friedens*, ed. Jürgen Miermeister (Berlin: Wagenbach, 1980), 43–4.

19. Gilcher-Holtey, *1968*, 142.

20. Andy Merrifield, *Guy Debord* (London: Reaktion Books, 2005). The emblematic novel about consumer capitalism and the obsession with 'things' in the 1960s was Georges Perec's *Things: A Story of the Sixties*.

21. Quoted in *ibid.*, 28. There was in the end nothing very playful or spontaneous about the way Debord and some of his allies approached the proposed 'revolution in everyday life'. Debord had assiduously read Machiavelli and had thought hard about an overall almost military strategy of how to 'take over the world'. The Situationist International itself turned out to be intensely sectarian: exclusions were frequent, and members' lives were to be tightly regulated; in particular, they were not supposed to have any kind of private family existence.

22. Another major method of the Situationists was *détournement* – the refunctionalization of, for instance, art and advertisements, by painting over them with subversive messages.

23. Quoted in Andrew Hussey, *The Game of War* (London: Cape, 2001), 219.

24. Guy Debord, *The Society of the Spectacle*, trans. Donald Nicholson-Smith (1967; New York: Zed Books, 1999), 12.

25. *Ibid.*, 13.

26. *Ibid.*, 18.

27. *Ibid.*, 19.

28. *Ibid.*, 20.

29. *Ibid.*, 86–7.

30. Christophe Bourseiller, *Vie et mort de Guy Debord, 1931–1994* (Paris: Plon, 1999), 217.

31. Merrifield, *Debord*, 10.

32. He was already dying of an alcohol-related illness which was apparently causing himgreat pain. See *ibid.*, 8.

33. Frank Böckelmann, 'Anfänge: Situationisten, Subversive und ihre Vorgänger', in Frank Böckelmann, *Die Emanzipation ins Leere: Beiträge zur Gesinnungsgeschichte 1960–2000* (Berlin: Philo, 2000), 21–43; here 26–7.

34. *Ibid.*, 41.

35. Ulrich Chaussy, *Die drei Leben des Rudi Dutschke: Eine Biographie* (Zurich: Pendo, 1999), 44–53.

36. Frank Böckelmann and Herbert Nagel (eds), *Subversive Aktion: Der Sinn der Organisation ist ihr Scheitern* (Frankfurt/Main: Verlag Neue Kritik, 1976).

37. It is telling that Dutschke did not join the famous Berlin Kommune 1, but instead sought to create a 'Wissenschaftskommune'. The Kommune leader Kunzelmann in turn famously declared: 'Was geht mich Vietnam an – ich habe Orgasmusschwierigkeiten'. Hecken, *1968*, 117.

38. Barbara Görres Agnoli, *Johannes Agnoli: Eine biografische Skizze* (Hamburg: Konkret Literatur Verlag, 2004).

39. Johannes Agnoli and Peter Brückner, *Die Transformation der Demokratie* (Frankfurt/Main: Europäische Verlagsanstalt, 1968), 10.

40. *Ibid.*, 17.

41. *Ibid.*, 26.

42. *Ibid.*, 11.

43. *Ibid.*, 18 and 21.

44. *Ibid.*, 16.

45. *Ibid.*, 154.

46. Hannah Arendt, *The Human Condition* (Chicago: University of Chicago Press, 1998), 322.

47. Hervé Bourges (ed.), *The French Student Revolt: The Leaders Speak*, trans. B. R. Brewster (New York: Hill & Wang, 1968), 43.

48. Herbert Marcuse, *Soviet Marxism: A Critical Analysis* (New York: Columbia University Press, 1958), 1. See also Tim B. Müller, 'Die gelehrten Krieger und die Rockefeller-

Revolution: Intellektuelle zwischen Geheimdienst, Neuer Linker und dem Entwurf einer neuen Ideengeschichte', in *Geschichte und Gesellschaft*, vol. 33 (2007), 198–227.

49. Michael Horowitz, 'Portrait of the Marxist as an Old Trouper', in *Playboy*, September 1970. The issue also featured an interview with Peter Fonda and a 'loving look at the no-bra look'.

50. Herbert Marcuse, *Konterrevolution und Revolte* (Frankfurt/Main: Suhrkamp, 1973), 9.

51. Herbert Marcuse, *One-Dimensional Man: Studies in the Ideology of Advanced Industrial Society* (1964; Boston: Beacon Press, 1966), 57.

52. *Ibid.*, 52.

53. *Ibid.*, 256–7.

54. Herbert Marcuse, 'The Problem of Violence and the Radical Opposition', in Herbert Marcuse, *The New Left and the 1960s* [Collected Papers of Herbert Marcuse, vol. 3], ed. Douglas Kellner (New York: Routledge, 2005), 56–75; here 64.

55. Herbert Marcuse, *Nachgelassene Schriften*, vol. 4: *Die Studentenbewegung und ihre Folgen*, ed. Peter-Erwin Jansen (Springe: zu Klampen, 2004), 105.

56. See the correspondence with Leo Löwenthal quoted in *ibid.*, 185–6.

57. Marcuse, *Nachgelassene Schriften*, 132.

58. Quoted by Peter-Erwin Jansen, 'Vorwort', in *ibid.*, 7–14; here 10.

59. Marcuse, 'The Problem of Violence', 57.

60. *Ibid.*, 108–10.

61. Marcuse, *Konterrevolution*, 12.

62. *Ibid.*, 139.

63. This was a point that did not escape Marcuse's left-wing critics at the time – see for instance Claus Offe, 'Technik und Eindimensionalität: Eine Version der Technokratiethese?', in Jürgen Habermas (ed.), *Antworten auf Herbert Marcuse* (Frankfurt/Main: Suhrkamp, 1968), 73–88.

64. Tobias Abse, 'Italy: A New Agenda', in Perry Anderson and Patrick Camiller (eds), *Mapping the West European Left* (London: Verso, 1994), 189–232; here 189.

65. Gerd-Rainer Horn, *The Spirit of '68: Rebellion in Western Europe and North America, 1956–1976* (New York: Oxford University Press, 2007), 111.

66. Antonio Negri, *Du retour: abécédaire autobiographique* (Paris: Calman-Lévy, 2002).

67. Donatella Della Porta, *Social Movements, Political Violence, and the State: A Comparative Analysis of Italy and Germany* (New York: Cambridge University Press, 1995).

68. Richard Drake, *The Revolutionary Mystique and Terrorism in Contemporary Italy* (Bloomington: Indiana University Press, 1989), 40.

69. *Ibid.*, 46.

70. Newman, *Miliband*, 144–5.

71. *Ibid.*, 92.

72. Ginsborg, *History*, 315.

73. Butz Peters, *Tödlicher Irrtum: Die Geschichte der RAF* (Berlin: Argon, 2004), 72.

74. *Ibid.*, 268.

75. *Ibid.*, 272.

76. At the risk of repeating clichés about Italy: there was also what Neal Ascherson called the 'sinister frivolity of Italian urban terrorism' – style mattered, in a way that it didn't for the earnest Germans, who remained earnest even at their most romantic. See, for instance, Giorgio, *Memoirs of an Italian Terrorist*, trans. Antony Shuggar (New York: Carroll & Graf, 2003).

77. Henner Hess, 'Italien: Die ambivalente Revolte', in *Angriff auf das Herz des Staates: Soziale Entwicklung und Terrorismus*, vol. 2 (Frankfurt/Main: Suhrkamp, 1988), 9–166; here 53–9.

78. For the Italian reception of Schmitt – and the *Marxisti Schmittiani* in particular – see Ilse Staff, *Staatsdenken im Italien des 20. Jahrhunderts: Ein Beitrag zur Carl Schmitt-Rezeption* (Baden-Baden: Nomos, 1991), and my own *A Dangerous Mind: Carl Schmitt in Post-war European Thought* (London, 2003), 177–80.

79. Eley, *Forging Democracy*, 409.

80. Santiago Carrillo, *Eurocomunismo y estado* (Barcelona: Editorial Crítica, 1977).
81. Ginsborg, *History*, 304.
82. Quoted in *ibid.*, 307.
83. Görres, *Agnoli*. Supposedly Dutschke once wondered about the enormous revolutionary impact if all housewives went on strike, but never followed up on this thought.
84. Some student leaders responded that the women could always engage in a 'Lysistrata boycott'. After all, it was all about bringing the war home – but home could also mean the bedroom. See Gilcher-Holtey, *1968*.
85. For the incident (and its implications) see Sidney Tarrow, *Democracy and Disorder: Protest and Politics in Italy, 1965–1975* (Oxford: Clarendon, 1989), 325–48.
86. Sheila Rowbotham, *Women's Liberation and the New Politics*, Spokesman Pamphlet, no. 17 (n.d.), 29.
87. *Ibid.*, 29.
88. Beauvoir, *Force*, 202.
89. Perry Anderson, Ronald Fraser, Quintin Hoare and Simone de Beauvoir, *Conversations with Jean-Paul Sartre* (Calcutta: Seagull Books, 2006), 75.
90. Ginsborg, *History*, 368–9.
91. Quoted by Robert Lumley, *States of Emergency: The Cultures of Revolt in Italy from 1968 to 1978* (London: Verso, 1990), 2.

Chapter 6: Antipolitics, and the Sense of an Ending

1. Quoted in Jens Hacke, *Philosophie der Bürgerlichkeit: Die liberalkonservative Begründung der Bundesrepublik* (Göttingen: Vandenhoeck & Ruprecht, 2006), 105.
2. *Solzhenitsyn at Harvard*, ed. Ronald Berman (Washington, DC: Ethics and Public Policy Center), 5.
3. Michel Crozier, Samuel P. Huntington and Joji Watanuki, *The Crisis of Democracy: Report on the Governability of Democracies to the Trilateral Commission* (New York: New York University Press, 1975), 2.
4. *Ibid.*, 6.
5. *Ibid.*, 7.
6. Thornhill, *Political Theory*, 174.
7. Helmut Schelsky, *Die Arbeit tun die anderen: Klassenkampf und Priesterherrschaft der Intellektuellen* (Opladen: Westdeutscher Verlag, 1975).
8. Niklas Luhmann, 'The "State" of the Political System', in *Essays on Self-Reference* (New York: Columbia University Press, 1990), 165–74.
9. See the direct confrontation in Jürgen Habermas and Niklas Luhmann, *Theorie der Gesellschaft oder Sozialtechnologie* (Frankfurt/Main: Suhrkamp, 1971).
10. Perry Anderson, 'A New Germany?', in *New Left Review*, second series, no. 57 (May/June 2009), 5–40; here 26.
11. Jürgen Habermas, *Between Facts and Norms* (1992; Cambridge, Mass.: MIT Press, 1996).
12. Michel Rocard claimed in retrospect that the PSU had picked up the slogan *autogestion* from the CFDT in the chemical industries in 1965 or 1966. But *autogestion* had already been used in newly independent Algeria.
13. Pierre Rosanvallon, *L'Âge de l'autogestion, ou la politique au poste de commandement* (Paris: Seuil, 1976), 7–8.
14. *Ibid.*, 15.
15. Pierre Grémion, *Modernisation et progressisme: fin d'une époque 1968–1981* (Paris: Editions Esprit, 2005).
16. The following draws on Michael Scott Christofferson, *French Intellectuals against the Left: France's Antitotalitarian Moment* (New York: Berghahn, 2004).
17. Quoted in *ibid.*, 96.
18. Quoted in *ibid.*, 186.
19. Raymond Aron, 'Pour le progrès: après la chute des idoles', in *Commentaire*, vol. 1 (1978), 233–43.
20. Quoted in Christofferson, *French Intellectuals*, 105–6.

21. Antitotalitarianism was not just revived anti-Communism or a loss of faith in any vision of violent revolutionary action: as Tony Judt has pointed out, it undermined a whole left-wing narrative about the twentieth century, as 'the traditional "progressive" insistence on treating attacks on Communism as implicit threats to *all* socially-ameliorative goals – i.e. the claim that Communism, Socialism, Social Democracy, nationalization, central planning and progressive social engineering were part of a common political project – began to work against itself'. See *Postwar*, 561.

22. Quoted by Eric Paras, *Foucault 2.0: Beyond Power and Knowledge* (New York: Other Press, 2006), 85.

23. Michel Foucault, ' "Die Folter, das ist die Vernunft" ', in *Literaturmagazin*, no. 8 (December 1977), 60–8; here 67. To be sure, this can look like a glib generalization: not every theorist of revolution was either invested in Marxism or willing to latch on to what might have seemed to be new forms of revolutionary action (such as the Iranian Revolution). The idiosyncratic Cornelius Castoriadis would be a good example, although arguably his stress on 'autonomy' and the 'self-institution of society' proved popular precisely because it could be fused with the political languages of the post-'68 social movements. See 'L'Exigence révolutionnaire (entretien avec Olivier Mongin, Paul Thibaud et Pierre Rosanvallon enregistré le 6 juillet 1976)', in *Esprit* (February 1977), 201–30.

24. Samuel Moyn, *The Last Utopia: Human Rights in History* (Cambridge, Mass.: Harvard University Press, 2010).

25. Sartre died in 1980 and with him disappeared a certain model of the universal intellectual who can speak on anything, based purely on his moral stature. Aron, the liberal sceptic, the sometimes pedantic-seeming academic and, above all, the anti-Sartre, enjoyed a late and gratifying moment of recognition when his *Mémoires* appeared in 1982. What at least two generations of French intellectuals had taken as an unquestionable moral-political maxim – that it was better to be wrong with Sartre than right with Aron – seemed to have been abandoned on the Left Bank.

26. Marcel Gauchet, 'Les Droits de l'homme ne sont pas une politique', in *Le Débat*, no. 3 (1980), 3–21.

27. Ralf Dahrendorf, 'Am Ende des sozialdemokratischen Konsensus? Zur Frage der Legitimität der politischen Macht in der Gegenwart', in *Lebenschancen: Anläufe zur sozialen und politischen Theorie* (Frankfurt/Main: Suhrkamp, 1979), 147–66.

28. André Gorz, *Farewell to the Working Class* (1980; London: Pluto Press, 1997), 3.

29. What, then, was to be done more concretely, one may be left to wonder. Gorz called for 'a constitutive act which, aware of its free subjectivity, asserts itself as an absolute end in itself within each individual'. Only the non-class of non-workers, according to Gorz, was capable of such an act, 'for it embodies what lies beyond productivism: the rejection of the accumulation ethic and the dissolution of all classes'. Gorz, seemingly the failed novelist, published another book that was not political theory in 2006: a letter addressed to Dorine, his wife of fifty-eight years (who had been portrayed in a rather unflattering way in *The Traitor* and who was painfully dying from an incurable disease), and which begins: 'You're 82 years old. You've shrunk six centimetres, you only weigh 45 kilos yet you're still beautiful, graceful and desirable.' In September 2007, Gorz and his wife committed suicide together. *Lettre à D.: histoire d'un amour* might well be the most moving text penned by any twentieth-century European political thinker.

30. As Rudolf Bahro put it, environmentalism was like a new 'magnetic field' – it thus changed the direction and position of existing parties (although Bahro drew exactly the opposite conclusion from his metaphor: he argued that 'it is difficult to absorb this into the existing party political system, and so the ecology movement has in fact turned into an alternative type of party'). See Rudolf Bahro, *From Red to Green: Interviews with New Left Review*, trans. Gus Fagan and Richard Hurst (London: Verso, 1984), 130.

31. E. P. Thompson and Dan Smith (eds), *Protest and Survive* (New York: Monthly Press, 1981).

32. Bahro, *From Red*, 138.

33. *Ibid.*, 146.

34. Rudolf Bahro, 'Who Can Stop the Apocalypse? Or the Task, Substance and Strategy of the Social Movements', in *Praxis International*, vol. 2, no. 3 (1982), 255–67; here 255.
35. Jürgen Habermas, 'Die Krise des Wohlfahrtsstaates und die Erschöpfung utopischer Energien', in *Die neue Unübersichtlichkeit* (Frankfurt/Main: Suhrkamp, 1985), 141–63; Dahrendorf, *Lebenschancen*.
36. Quoted in Mark Bevir, ' "A Kind of Radicality": The Avant-Garde Legacy in Postmodern Ethics', in Mark Bevir, Jill Hargis and Sara Rushing (eds), *Histories of Postmodernism* (New York: Routledge, 2007), 131–48; here 131.
37. The following is mostly based on David Macey, *Michel Foucault* (London: Reaktion, 2004).
38. Foucault also wrote apropos one of Sartre's major philosophical works: 'The critique of dialectical reason is the magnificent and pathetic effort of a man of the nineteenth century to think the twentieth. In this sense, Sartre is the last Hegelian, and I would even say the last Marxist.' And just in case anyone had missed the implications: 'Marxism resides in the thought of the nineteenth century like a fish in water: which is to say, anywhere else it stops breathing.'
39. 'Truth and Power', in *Michel Foucault: Power*, trans. Robert Hurley and others (New York: New Press, 2000), 111–33; here 126.
40. It had been coined by Lucien Goldmann, Lukács' most distinguished follower in France.
41. The broader contours of the (strange) transition from revolution to human rights via Maoism are traced in Julian Bourg, *From Revolution to Ethics: May 1968 and Contemporary French Thought* (Montreal: McGill-Queen's University Press, 2007), and Richard Wolin, *The Wind from the East: French Intellectuals, the Cultural Revolution, and the Legacy of the 1960s* (Princeton, NJ: Princeton University Press, 2010).
42. Michel Foucault, *La Naissance de la biopolitique: cours au Collège de France, 1978–1979* (Paris: Gallimard, 2004).
43. As Foucault himself wrote, with typical over-generalization and flourish: 'If genocide is indeed the dream of modern power, this is not because of the recent return to the ancient right to kill; it is because power is situated and exercised at the level of life, the species, the race, and the large-scale phenomena of the population.'
44. 'Truth and Power', 122.
45. *Ibid.*, 120.
46. 'À quoi rêvent les Iraniens?', in *Dits et Ecrits, 1954–1988*, vol. 2 (Paris: Gallimard, 2001), 688–94; here 694.
47. Foucault occupied a minibus carrying medical supplies and printing equipment to Warsaw. Riding with him were the actress Simone Signoret and Bernard Kouchner, founder of Médecins sans Frontières. They were singing Piaf chansons all the way, and Foucault knew all the words (but was tone-deaf . . .). Macey, *Foucault*, 139.
48. 'La Grande Colère des faits', in *Dits*, 277–81.
49. Michel Foucault, *'Society Must Be defended': Lectures at the Collège de France, 1975–1976*, ed. Mauro Bertani and Alessandro Fontana, trans. David Macey (New York: Picador, 2003), 40. In the late 1970s and 1980s he seemed to have rediscovered the individual – despite all previous strictures about the subject – and began to investigate (and in a sense prescribe) what he called the 'care of the self'. He now spoke of 'the constitution of oneself as the laborer of the beauty of one's own life'.
50. ' "Die Folter, das ist die Vernunft" ', 65.
51. Habermas – arguably with the generosity of the philosophical victor – could much later admit that 'there can be no doubt concerning the healthy influence that postmodernism has had for contemporary debates. The critique of a form of reason that attributes a teleological design to history as a whole is just as convincing as the critiques of the ridiculous pretension of eliminating all social alienation.' See Jürgen Habermas, *The Postnational Constellation*, trans. Max Pensky (Cambridge: Polity, 2001), 146.
52. Quoted in Hennecke, *Hayek*, 223.
53. Marquand, *Britain*, 258.
54. It is important to realize that Hayek – even though habitually lumped together with Milton Friedman – was no monetarist.

55. F. A. Hayek, *The Road to Serfdom* (1944; London: Routledge, 2001), 73.

56. F. A. Hayek, *Law, Legislation and Liberty: The Political Order of a Free People* (Chicago: University of Chicago Press, 1981), 113.

57. His ideas also influenced dissidents east of the Iron Curtain: 'liberalism' came to be identified with Hayek much more than with, for instance, the American liberal philosopher John Rawls; in fact, Hayek turned into an iconic figure for intellectuals such as Václav Klaus, who was to emerge as a Czech prime minister and eventually as Czech president after the end of state socialism.

58. The account of Oakeshott's career is mostly based on Paul Franco, *Michael Oakeshott: An Introduction* (New Haven, Conn.: Yale University Press, 2004).

59. Bernard Susser, *The Grammar of Modern Ideology* (London: Routledge, 1988), 174.

60. Michael Oakeshott, 'Rationalism in Politics', in *Rationalism in Politics and Other Essays* (1962; Indianapolis: Liberty Press, 1991), 5–42; here 11.

61. As Ralph Miliband wrote to a Marxist correspondent during the student 'troubles' at the LSE, 'sophisticated Oakeshottimus is a fairly thin crust; when it cracks, as it did here, a rather ugly visceral sort of conservatism emerges'. Newman, *Miliband*, 151.

62. Michael Oakeshott, *On Human Conduct* (1975; Oxford: Clarendon, 2003), 201.

63. *Ibid.*, 277 and 308.

64. http://www.michael-oakeshott-association.com/pdfs/mo_letters_popper.pdf (last accessed 16 August 2010).

65. Robert Devigne, *Recasting Conservatism: Oakeshott, Strauss, and the Response to Postmodernism* (New Haven, Conn.: Yale University Press, 1994).

66. Joseph's infamous Edgbaston speech cost him any chance of gaining the leadership of the Conservative Party.

67. F. A. Hayek, 'Postscript: Why I Am Not a Conservative', in *The Constitution of Liberty* (1960; London: Routledge, 2003), 397–411; here 398.

68. Interestingly, however, the American version of libertarianism was also at the same time more popular (or perhaps populist) and more philosophically grounded. Only in America was there a ten-part television series on 'Free to Choose' by Milton Friedman; only in America did libertarian novels like those of Ayn Rand become bestsellers; and only in America could there be a viable trade in Mises t-shirts. But it was also more systematically developed philosophically: Robert Nozick's 1974 *Anarchy, State, and Utopia* was a libertarian answer to John Rawls' Social Democratic *Theory of Justice* which argued from first principles – and which found no equivalent in Europe.

69. *Reversing the Trend: A Critical Re-appraisal of Conservative Economic and Social Policies – Seven Speeches by the Rt. Hon. Sir Keith Joseph Bt. MP* (Chichester: Barry Rose, 1975), 55 and 56.

70. Dahrendorf, *Lebenschancen*, 150.

71. Admonishing the regimes to act according to their own laws had occurred to comrades and citizens before. An example of someone prominent in our narrative is Lukács, who in a number of personal letters to Kádár in 1971, shortly before his death, asked the leader – addressing him with the informal 'you' and without mincing his words – properly to charge and try the young Maoist (sic!) dissidents Miklós Haraszti and György Dalos, who were being held in prison at the time. He charged that in upholding socialist legality Kádár's honour was at stake. See Lukács Archivum, Budapest, letters to Kádár of 15 February, 22 February and 26 February 1971 (859/6–859/8).

72. Benjamin Nathans, 'The Dictatorship of Reason: Aleksand Vol'Pin and the Idea of Rights under "Developed Socialism"', in *Slavic Review*, vol. 66 (2007), 630–63.

73. *Ibid.*, 649.

74. Ludmilla Alexeyeva, *Soviet Dissent: Contemporary Movements for National, Religious, and Human Rights*, trans. Carol Pearce and John Glad (Middletown, Conn.: Wesleyan University Press, 1985), 275.

75. Nathans, 'The Dictatorship', 635.

76. Quoted in Tismaneanu, *Reinventing*, 8.

77. Priestland, *Red Flag*, 448–9.

78. Václav Benda, 'The Parallel "*Polis*"', in H. Gordon Skilling and Paul Wilson (eds), *Civic Freedom in Central Europe: Voices from Czechoslovakia* (London: Macmillan, 1991), 35–41; here 35.

79. *New York Times*, 14 April 1977.

80. Judt, *Postwar*, 567.

81. Quoted in Noel O'Sullivan, *European Political Thought since 1945* (London: Palgrave, 2004), 167–8.

82. Bracher, *Zeit der Ideologien*. See also Jean-François Revel, *La Tentation totalitaire* (Paris: Robert Laffont, 1976).

83. Jonathan Schell quoted in Falk, *Dilemmas*, 179.

84. Jan Patočka, *Plato and Europe*, trans. Peter Lom (Stanford Calif.: Stanford University Press, 2002).

85. Quoted in Martin Palouš, 'International Law and the Construction, Liberation, and Final Deconstruction of Czechoslovakia', in *Law and Moral Action in World Politics*, ed. Cecelia Lynch and Michael Loriaux (Minneapolis, MN: University of Minnesota Press, 2000), 232–52; here 245.

86. Aviezer Tucker, *Philosophy and Politics of Czech Dissidence from Patočka to Havel* (Pittsburgh, Pa.: University of Pittsburgh Press, 2000), 135.

87. A claim echoed by Solzhenitsyn who held that 'this is the essence of the crisis: the split in the world is less terrifying than the similarity of the disease afflicting its main societies'. *Solzhenitsyn at Harvard*, 19.

88. Quoted in Falk, *Dilemmas*, 229.

89. György Konrád, *Antipolitics: An Essay*, trans. Richard E. Allen (San Diego, Calif.: Harcourt, Brace, Jovanovich, 1984), 92.

90. Václav Havel, 'The Power of the Powerless', in John Keane (ed.), *The Power of the Powerless: Citizens against the State in Central-Eastern Europe* (New York: M. E. Sharpe, 1985), 23–96.

91. Quoted by Tismaneanu, *Reinventing*, 123.

92. Benda, 'The Parallel "*Polis*"', 36.

93. Ignác Romsics, *Hungary in the Twentieth Century*, trans. Tim Wilkinson (Budapest: Corvina, 1999), 415.

94. Falk, *Dilemmas*, 137.

95. The expression is Sandor Szilagyi's, quoted in Falk, *Dilemmas*, 261.

96. Hildermeier, *Geschichte*, 1021.

97. Maak, *In Europe*, 747.

98. Jiří Přibáň, *Dissidents of Law: On the 1989 Velvet Revolutions, Legitimations, Fictions of Legality and Contemporary Version of the Social Contract* (Aldershot: Ashgate, 2002), 40–1.

99. Which is not to say that the post-war constitutionalist ethos could immediately be reproduced.

100. Jürgen Habermas, 'What Does Socialism Mean Today? The Rectifying Revolution and the Need for New Thinking on the Left', in *New Left Review*, no. 183 (September–October 1990), 3–22; here 7; Furet quoted by Ralf Dahrendorf, *Reflections on the Revolution in Europe* (New York: Times Books, 1990), 27.

101. Colin Crouch, *Post-Democracy* (Cambridge: Polity, 1994).

102. David Miller, *On Nationality* (Oxford: Oxford University Press, 1995), and Pierre Manent, *La Raison des nations* (Paris: Gallimard, 2006).

103. Francis Fukuyama, 'The End of History?', in *National Interest*, no. 16 (Summer 1989), 3–18.

104. *Ibid.*, 18.

105. *Ibid.*, 9.

106. I am indebted to Pierre Rosanvallon on this point.

Index

Action Française 99, 136
Adenauer, Konrad 145–6, 146–7, 156, 180, 193
  and European integration, 141, 142
Adler, Max 237
Adorno, Theodor W. 189
Agnoli, Johannes 183–5, 198, 201
Agrarianism 20–1
Alexeyeva, Ludmilla 228
Allende, Salvador 196
Althusser, Louis 176
Amendola, Giovanni 107
Americanization 25, 173, 191
Amis, Kingsley 174
Anarchism 51, 52, 151
  and May '68, 172, 175, 177, 182
  and Paris Commune, 37, 55
  and terrorism, 194
Anderson, Perry 176, 198, 206
Anti-Communism 6, 141, 208
Anti-fascism 169, 193
Anti-Semitism 108, 113–16, 122–3, 172, 228–9
Antitotalitarianism 124, 130
  and May '68, 197, 206–10, 230–2
Aragon, Louis 145, 174, 185
Arato, Andrew 236
Arendt, Hannah 79–80, 84, 85, 120, 122, 237
  on Hungarian uprising of 1956, 163
  on imperialism, 156
  on post-war Europe, 126, 150, 185–6
Aristocracy 12, 14–16, 18, 127
Aron, Raymond 145, 172, 187, 197, 208–9
Astor, Nancy (Lady) 20
Atatürk, Kemal 23–4, 109, 110

Attlee, Clement 131, 221
Austro-Marxism 56–60, 200

Baader, Andreas 194
Bagehot, Walter 15, 16
Bahro, Rudolf 212–13, 231
Barker, Ernest 52, 54, 145
Baudrillard, Jean 214
Bauer, Otto 56–60, 64, 71–2
Beauvoir, Simone de 89, 199–200, 211
Benda, Václav 229–30, 232–3
Benedict XV 134
Berlin, Isaiah 1, 148, 160, 163
Berlinguer, Enrico 196
Bernstein, Eduard 55–6, 65, 72, 96
Bevan, Nye 5
Beveridge, William 131, 132, 138
Bibó, István 125, 163–4, 202, 233
Bidault, Georges 139, 156
Bismarck, Otto von 51, 101
Bloch, Ernst 68, 70, 75–8
  and Lenin, 77
Bloom, Alan 239
Bosworth, R. J. 107
Bourguiba, Habib 216
Bracher, Karl Dietrich 230, 240
Branting, Hjalmar 65
Brezhnev, Leonid 165, 168, 229, 233–4
Bruck, Arthur Moeller van den 113
Bukharin, Nikolai 80, 81, 86, 87–88, 162
  rehabilitation of, 235
Bulgakov, Mikhail 79
Bureaucracy 120, 148, 185, 186, 205, 238
  and French Second Left, 206–7
  Lenin on, 36–40
  and monarchy, 15, 17
  and neoliberalism, 227

Bureaucracy (*cont.*)
  in the Soviet Union, 36–40, 159–61,
    169–70
  Stalinism and, 78–81
  Weber's view of, 26–7, 30–2, 40–2,
    46, 110, 119
  see also Self-management

Callaghan, James 203
Cannadine, David 16
Castoriadis, Cornelius 160, 206, 214
Catholicism 103, 108–12, 113, 130, 132–41
Carol II (king of Romania) 111
Carrillo, Santiago 196
Césaire, Aimé 156
Ceaușescu, Elena 90
Ceaușescu, Nicolae 89–90
Charter 77 229–31
Chernyshevsky, Nikolai 33, 194
Chesterton, G. K. 54
Christian Democracy 5–6, 130,
    132–42, 183, 220
  decline of, 237–8
Christianity 97, 109–12, 128–9
  and neoliberalism, 153, 225
Churchill, Winston 2, 123, 152, 155
Ciano, Galeazzo 121
Cioran, Emile 21
Clegg, Hugh 143
Cohn-Bendit, Daniel 173, 175, 182,
    186, 189
Cole, G. D. H. 18, 52–4, 66, 103, 144
Cole, Margaret 18, 50, 54, 66–7
Colonialism *see* Imperialism
Comenius 235
Comte, Auguste 23
Corporatism 133, 135, 167, 191
  and fascism, 103–4, 110
Corradini, Enrico 100, 105
Croce, Benedetto 94, 106
Crosland, Tony 150
Crossman, Dick 131, 132
Crozier, Michel 204
Curcio, Roberto 195
Curzon, Lord 22, 237, 238

Dahrendorf, Ralf 210, 213, 226
Daniel, Yuli 228
Debord, Guy 179–83, 237
Djilas, Milovan 88, 160–1, 230
Dollfuss, Engelbert 59, 111
Doriot, Jacques 157
Dossetti, Giuseppe 138, 140
Dubček, Alexander 165–8
Duras, Marguerite 171
Dutschke, Rudi 174–8, 182

Eco, Umberto 200
Eisner, Kurt 8, 41, 44–5
Engels, Friedrich, 37, 55, 73, 156, 194
Ensslin, Gudrun 193
Environmentalism 182, 205, 212
Erhard, Ludwig 139, 153, 217
Eurocommunism 197
European integration 5, 141–2, 148–9, 157,
    238–9
Existentialism 127, 215–16

Fabianism 54, 131–2, 153
Fanon, Frantz 156–7
Fascism 91–124, 197
  and capitalism, 127, 184, 194
  and democracy, 4, 106–7, 116–18
  as diagnosed by Bloch, 77
  Italian Fascism compared to German
    National Socialism, 107–8, 112–13,
    117, 121–2
  May '68 as, 172, 183
  and religion, 6, 113–14
  supposedly problem-solving capacity
    of, 2, 101–5
  as a threat to the Soviet Union, 86
Fellini, Federico 107, 141
Feminism 102, 182, 198–200, 205, 212
Fisher, Antony 153
Fraenkel, Ernst 119
Franz Josef (Emperor) 17
Figgis, J. N. 51
Forsthoff, Ernst 145, 185, 187
Foucault, Michel 202, 203, 209,
    215–20, 225
Franco, Francisco 111, 112, 135, 136, 140
Frankfurt School 176, 186–90, 205–6
Friedman, Milton 203
Freud, Sigmund 187
Fukuyama, Francis 203, 237, 239–40
Furet, François 209, 236
Futurism 91, 101–2

Gasperi, Alcide De 134, 139, 140,
    141–2, 146
Gauchet, Marcel 209
Gaulle, Charles De 122, 137, 146, 149,
    207–8
  and May '68 173, 175–6, 183
Gaullism 140, 196, 200–20, 207
Geismar, Alain 178, 186
Gellner, Ernest 172
Gentile, Giovanni 2, 4, 105–8, 111, 116, 129
  comparison with ideologies of
    National Socialism, 118, 119
George V 17, 18
Gerasimov, Gennady 234

Gide, André 82
Gierke, Otto von 51
Ginzburg, Evgenia 87, 159
Giolitti, Giovanni 12
Glucksmann, André 171, 208, 209, 219
Godard, Jean-Luc 181, 182
Goebbels, Joseph 93
Gökay, Fahrettin Kerim 24
Gonella, Guido 141
Gorbachev, Mikhail 165, 168, 234–5,
     237, 240
Gorky, Maxim 82
Görres, Barbara 198
Gorz, André 211–12
Gramsci, Antonio 49, 60–5, 81, 105, 167, 233
     and post-1945 Italian Communism,
          190–1, 196, 210
     and Sorel, 94
Guareschi, Giovanni 191
Guild socialism 52–3, 103, 144

Habermas, Jürgen 143, 173, 203, 230
     and democracy, 205–6
     and postmodernism, 213–14, 219–20
     on 1989 revolutions, 236
Halévy, Daniel 97, 100
Hall, Stuart 200
Hansson, Per Albin 49, 65–6, 68
Václav Havel 170, 202, 231–2, 235
Hayek, Friedrich von 6, 27, 150–4, 203, 217
     and conservatism, 226
     and post-1989 Central and Eastern
          Europe, 236
     and resurgence of neoliberalism,
          220–2, 226–7
     on second-hand dealers in ideas, 3,
          152–3
Hegel, Hegelianism 76, 106, 118, 208,
     224, 239
Heidegger, Martin 186, 214, 231
Hess, Rudolf 91
Heuss, Theodor 146
Hewart, Gordon 47–8, 148
Hilferding, Rudolf 57–8
Himmler, Heinrich 107, 113–14
Hitler, Adolf 103, 107, 156
     and Nazism as a philosophy, 91, 92–3,
          113–14
     personality cult of, 88, 113
     relationship to the state, 119, 120
     view of liberal democracy, 116–17
Hindenburg, Paul von 117
Hobsbawm, Eric 22, 34, 172
Höhn, Reinhard 118
Holocaust 126
Honigsheim, Paul 76

Horthy, Miklós 109, 112
Horvath, Ödon von 22
Huizinga, Johan 179
Huntington, Samuel 204
Husserl, Edmund 231

Imperialism 13–14, 16–17, 21, 189, 239
     and decolonization, 154–7
     fascist forms of, 120–3

Jacobinism 35, 63
James, William 13, 21, 51
John Paul II 241
Joseph, Keith 221, 225, 226
Judt, Tony 230
Jünger, Ernst 25–6, 102

Kádár, János 164–5, 170
Kadritzke, Ulf 172
Kaganovich, Lazar 79
Karl I (Emperor) 109
Karleby, Nils 66
Kautsky, Karl 55
Kelsen, Hans 4, 58, 146–7, 148, 171
Kerensky, Alexander 32, 33
Kessler, Harry Count 24
Keynes, John Maynard 11, 125, 138,
     141, 144
     as critic of Wilson, 24, 46–7
     debate with Hayek, 150–2
Keynesianism 102, 212, 221
Kirchheimer, Otto 50, 139
Kis, János 229
Kissinger, Henry 227
Kjellén, Rudolf 65
Khomeini, Ayatollah 240
Khrushchev, Nikita 2, 79, 166, 169–70, 234
     and de-Stalinization, 159, 161
Kojève, Alexandre 122, 239
Kołakowski, Leszek 137, 169
Kolnai, Aurel 137
Konrád, György 231–2, 236
Kornai, János 164–5, 168
Koselleck, Reinhart 126
Kosík, Karel 167–8, 231
Kubišová, Marta 235
Kun, Béla 70–1, 162
Kundera, Milan 168–9
Kunzelmann, Dieter 182

Lammenais, Félicité Robert de 132
La Pira, Giorgio 138
Lask, Emil 76
Laski, Harold 7, 52–5, 60, 184, 196
Lawrence, D. H. 223
Lawson, Nigel 226

League of Nations 21, 46
Le Bon, Gustave 27
Lefort, Claude 206, 209, 214
    and totalitarianism, 90, 235, 242
Lenin, Vladimir Illyich 32–40, 49, 51,
    82, 171
    as model for Gramsci, 62–3
    on Austro-Marxism 59
    as seen by Schmitt, 99–100
    and Sorel, 94
    on Stalin, 80
    see also: Lukács, and Lenin; Bloch,
        and Lenin
Leninism 129, 165–6, 169, 186, 194, 216
    discrediting of, 178, 192, 203, 216, 240
    Miłosz on, 159
    and Situationism, 182
Leo XIII 133
Lévy, Bernard-Henri 208
Lewis, Wyndham 94
Lloyd George, David 7, 25, 103
Liberalism 129–30, 150
    and democracy, 11–12, 20
    discrediting of 2, 5, 18, 26, 129
    And Fascism, 105
    Foucault's conception of, 217
    nineteenth-century versions, 9–13,
        177, 207, 221
Libertarianism 172, 182, 189, 197, 207
    and Oakeshott, 237
Lindsay, A. D. 1, 3
Lipski, Jan Josef 232
Loewenstein, Karl 147, 148
Lübbe, Hermann 213
Ludendorff, Erich von 17, 18
Luhmann, Niklas 200, 204–6, 218
Lukács, Georg 68–75, 85, 158, 170
    and Bloch, 76–7
    and Hungarian uprising of 1956,
        162–3, 167
    and Lenin, 33, 70, 72–4
    and May '68, 178, 179
    and Sorel, 94
    and Stalinism, 80, 83
Luther, Martin 136
Luxemburg, Rosa 56
Lyotard, Jean-François 214

Maeztu, Ramiro de 103
Malraux, André 173
Man, Henri de 102
Mandelstam, Nadezhda 22, 87
Mandelstam, Osip 87
Manent, Pierre 238
Mann, Thomas 69, 71, 102
Mannheim, Karl 49

Mao 194
Maoism 178–9, 190, 208, 216
Marchais, Georges 208
Marcuse, Herbert 177, 186–90, 192, 193,
    197, 201
    and Gorz, 211
Marighella, Carlos 194
Marinetti, F. T. 101
Maritain, Jacques 135–8, 140, 238
Marshall, T. H. 131
Marx, Karl 37, 55, 73, 90, 94, 194
    impact in France, 95–6
    on peasantry, 82
Marxism 56, 57, 69, 240–1
    difficulties with environmentalism
        and feminism, 211–12
    Foucault's criticism of, 215–16
    and May '68, 176, 180–2, 187–92
    orthodox, 35, 55–6
    revisions of 65–6, 72–4, 96–9, 230
Marxism-Leninism 193–4
Masaryk, Tomáš 14, 25, 50, 56, 235
    and democracy, 21, 22
Massu, Jacques 176
Maurras, Charles 18, 136
Mazzini, Giuseppe 106
Meinecke, Friedrich 126–7
Meinhof, Ulrike 193–5
Michels, Robert 183
Michnik, Adam 170, 229–30, 236
Mikoyan, Anastas 162
Miller, David 238
Miliband, Ralph 169, 192–3
Mills, C. Wright 173, 178, 200
Miłosz, Czesław 2, 159
Mises, Ludwig von 220–1, 227
Missoffe, François 175
Mitterrand, François 196, 208, 210
Mlynář, Zdeněk 158, 166–8, 170, 229, 234
Monarchy 14–18, 41, 107–8, 117
Monnet, Jean 142, 144
Montaigne, Michel de 224
Morin, Edgar 157
Moro, Aldo 196
Mosley, Oswald 102
Mounier, Emmanuel 134, 136
Musil, Robert 17, 31
Müller-Sturmheim, Emil 25
Mussolini, Benito 50–1, 78, 91, 117, 121
    coming to power of, 102–3
    contrast with technocratic
        dictators, 109
    on Fascist doctrine, 92, 94,
        100–1, 105–8
    and Gramsci, 64
    and racism, 114

Myrdal, Alva 67
Myrdal, Gunnar 67, 221

Nagy, Imre 161–4, 169, 229
Nationalism 21, 47, 160, 164
    Austro-Marxist theory of, 56–7, 88
    and Fascism, 99–101, 105–7, 121–2
    Gramsci on 64
    in Romania, 89
    and Stalin, 88
    as political philosophy, 238–9
    in Turkey, 23–4
National Self-Determination 21–4, 46,
    57, 128
National Socialism
    compared to Stalinism, 79, 80–1,
    88–9, 90, 92, 115, 117, 118, 120
    see also Fascism
Naumann, Friedrich 20, 47
Negri, Antonio 190–2, 196
Negt, Oskar 186
Nell-Breuning, Oswald von 139
Neoconservatism 213–14, 220
Neoliberalism 6, 153–4, 210–11, 220–2
Nenning, Günter 56
Neumann, Franz 45, 91, 117, 119–20, 123
Neumann, Sigmund 112
New Deal 104
Nicholas II 13, 16, 17, 32
Nietzsche, Friedrich 100, 214, 239

Oakeshott, Michael 3, 222–7, 236, 237
Ortega y Gasset, José 20, 24, 126
Orwell, George 155
Oumansoff, Raïssa 135
Owen, Wilfred 25

Pacifism 182, 210, 212–13, 230
Panzieri, Raniero 191
Pareto, Vilfredo 7, 184
Parliamentarism 11–12, 19
    critiques of, 47–8, 183–5, 197
    Lenin on, 36
    weakening of, 148–9, 238
Parsons, Talcott 204–5
Pasolini, Pier Paolo 198
Patočka, Jan 231
Peace movement see Pacifism
Péguy, Charles 95
Personalism 134–8, 140, 154, 238, 241
Pétain, Philippe 111–12
Piłsudski, Józef 111
Pius XI 135
Pluralism 109, 133, 140, 145, 183–5
    English, 50–4, 237
Popper, Karl 153, 224–5

Postmodernism 211, 214–20, 239
Poststructuralism 214–20
Preuss, Hugo 47, 148

Rákosi, Mátyás 75
Rathenau, Walther 10
Ramm, Rudolph 114
Renner, Karl 19, 56
Resistance 127–8, 143, 160
Ricoeur, Paul 50
Rocard, Michel 210
Rocco, Alfredo 105
Röpke, Alexander 153–4, 225
Rosanvallon, Pierre 207
Rosenberg, Alfred 113–14, 116
Rousseau, Jean-Jacques 136
Rowbotham, Sheila 199
Rushdie, Salman 240
Rüstow, Wilhelm 153–4, 225

Sagnier, Marc 207
Salazar, António 109–12, 135, 140
Samuel, Raphael, 34
Sander, Helke 198
Sartre, Jean-Paul 125, 127, 140, 156–7,
    209, 211
    conflicts with Foucault, 215, 218, 219
    and feminism, 199–200
Schelsky, Helmut 145, 205
Schleyer, Hans-Martin 195
Schmidt, Helmut 195
Schmitt, Carl 98, 99–100, 106, 137
    as critic of parliamentarianism, 27,
    47, 177
    as critic of pluralism, 53
    debate with Kelsen, 146
    influence in post-war Italy, 196
    and Nazi jurisprudence, 116, 118–19,
    121, 129
Schuman, Robert 141, 156
Schumpeter, Joseph 40, 149–50
Secularism 6, 23
Self-management 66, 143, 177–8, 207
    Gorz's criticism of, 212
    Gramsci on, 61–2
    in socialist Central and Eastern Europe,
    160, 162–4, 166, 170, 236, 237
Serge, Victor 1, 59, 60, 64, 75
Šik, Ota 165, 168
Simmel, Georg 30–1, 69, 75, 76, 96
Sinyavsky, Andrei 228
Situationism 178, 179–83, 198, 214, 217
Social Democracy 5, 54–60, 130, 183, 207
    Foucault and, 215
    late twentieth-century decline of, 203,
    210–14, 220–6

Solzhenitsyn, Alexander 90, 159, 203,
    208–9, 235
Somary, Felix 10, 24, 40
Sombart, Werner 67
Sorel, Georges 94–100, 103, 114, 142,
    156, 185
Spaemann, Robert 203
Spann, Othmar 103–4, 111
Spirito, Ugo 104
Stahl, Friedrich von 18
Stalin 39, 78, 115, 118, 148, 166
    and Foucault, 215
    Lukács on, 75, 80, 83, 84
    and post-1945 Central and Eastern
        Europe, 157–60
    and the state, 38
    see also Stalinism
Stalinism 78–90, 157–8, 209
    and French Communist Party, 208
    and de-Stalinization, 159–60
    See also National Socialism, compared
        to Stalinism
Stamboliski, Alexander 20–1
Sternhell, Zeev 99
Strauß, Franz Josef 141
Structuralism 216, 220
Sturzo, Luigi 134, 135, 140
Sukarno 155
Suslov, Mikhail 162

Tawney, R. H. 125, 152, 219, 238
Taylor, A. J. P. 10, 18
Terrorism 192–6, 203
Thatcher, Margaret 6, 202, 221–2,
    225–7, 237
Thomism 137
Thompson, Edward 212
Tingsten, Herbert 125, 144
Titmuss, Richard 131
Tito, Josip Broz 160–1
Tocqueville, Alexis de 1, 224
Todorov, Tzvetan 79, 83, 117, 160
Toller, Ernst 45
Togliatti, Palmiro 60, 190–1
Totalitarianism 79, 151, 192, 235, 242
    Hannah Arendt on, 126, 150
    and Christian Democracy, 139
    and the French and Russian
        Revolutions, 209
    Italian Fascist state as a form of,
        106–8
    Stalinism as, 90
Tronti, Mario 191–2
Trotsky, Leon 38, 80, 115, 171
    on Austro-Marxism 59

Valéry, Paul 7, 13, 25, 48
Vaneigem, Raoul 179–80
Verschuer, Otmar von 113
Vichy regime 111–12, 134–5, 157
Vico, Giambattista 30, 73, 96, 184
Victoria (Queen) 14, 15
Vittorio Emanuele III 107, 108, 121
Volksgemeinschaft 5, 115–16, 122, 128

Watanuki, Joji 204
Webb, Beatrice 54
Weber, Max 96, 99, 117, 129
    and Bloch, 76–7
    and bureaucracy, 26–7, 30–2,
        40–2, 46, 110, 119
    and capitalism, 27–9
    on corporatism, 110
    and democracy, 9, 41–2, 47, 146,
        202, 240
    and German politics, 7–8, 40–1,
        44–6, 148
    and legitimacy, 8–9, 14, 18, 24, 26, 34,
        42, 81, 159
    and liberalism in the democratic age,
        44, 48
    and Lukács, 69–70, 72
    and nation-states, 141
    and political ethics, 42–4, 97, 182,
        197, 205
    and the Russian Revolution and
        Marxism, 32, 38, 40, 46, 78
    and the state, 7, 26–7, 32, 149–50,
        217
    and systems theory, 204–6
    and value pluralism, 29–30, 44
    on war, 31–2
    on Woodrow Wilson, 21–2
    see also Bureaucracy
Welfare state 131–2, 144, 187, 224, 237
Wilhelm II 17, 41
Wilson, Harold 144, 145
Wilson, Woodrow 21, 23, 24
Witte, Sergei 13
Wolff, K. D. 175
Women's suffrage 11, 19–20
    see also Feminism
Woolf, Leonard 13

Yessenin-Volpin, Alexander 227–8, 229,
    230, 232, 236

Zhdanov, Andrei 193
Zinoviev, Grigory 74, 82
Zog (King of Albania) 18
Zweig, Stefan 9–10

Acknowledgements

THIS BOOK was conceived many years ago. For initial discussions I am grateful to the late John Burrow, who encouraged me to lecture on twentieth-century European political thought at Oxford, and to Peter Ghosh, who critically followed the lectures and who, in correspondence much later on, raised the bar on how to write responsibly about Weber (or, for that matter, how to write any kind of intellectual history). Andy Rabinbach at Princeton also proved an inspiration. Tony Judt and Mark Lilla provided very helpful and encouraging comments on how to conceptualize what seemed an essentially undo-able project which, I kept insisting, had to be done. In retrospect, I am amazed – and humbled – by their confidence that a fresh PhD could make good his promise to write a history from 'a perspective beyond the Cold War', as I then rather presumptuously put it.

Robert Baldock at Yale University Press proved gracious and patient, and fortunately understood that writing a short book might take much more time than writing a long one.

I am very grateful to the following for reading and reacting to individual sections of the book: David Abraham, Norman Birnbaum, Edyta Bojanowska, Patrick Gavigan, Peter Ghosh, Lionel Gossman, István Hegedűs, Dick Howard, Ellen Kennedy, Erika A. Kiss, Michal Kopeček, Melissa Lane, Walter Laqueur, Mark Lilla, Peter Lindseth, Andy Moravcsik, Samuel Moyn, Heidrun Müller, Philip Nord, Alan Patten, Jennifer Pitts, Paolo Pombeni, Jonas Pontusson, Olivier Remaud, Martin Rühl, Johan Tralau and Balazs Trencsényi. The remaining mistakes (and I fear in a book of this scope there must be many) are mine; credit for saving me from making even more goes to those who generously gave their time and shared their expertise.

I am also grateful to the staff at the Lukács Archivum in Budapest and to Erika A. Kiss for invaluable help with making sense of some of Lukács' correspondence. Thanks also to the staff at the Oakeshott archive at the LSE and to the tireless librarians in Princeton, who managed to find even the most obscure materials and delivered them promptly.

My greatest scholarly debt resulting from an enterprise like this, though, is to the authors of the many monographs and also the more synthetic works on which I have drawn. One's own assessments of such debts tend to be incomplete and can be deceptive, but I trust it will be obvious to many readers of the preceding pages that I have learnt much from the writings of Tony Judt, Mark Mazower, Peter Lindseth and Martin Conway. I also benefited from teaching a course on twentieth-century European history at Princeton with Harold James, Phil Nord and Ezra Suleiman – and facing the challenge of how to interest teenagers in a period (and a world of political passions) that might appear about as close to them as the Middle Ages.

A number of institutions provided intellectual homes while I worked on the manuscript: All Souls College, Oxford; the Center for European Studies, Harvard University (where Charles Maier and Pierre Hassner pushed me to clarify my ideas); the Collegium Budapest and Central European University, Budapest, where Balazs Trencsényi helped a non-Hungarian to make sense of national and regional political *Kulturkämpfe*, past and present; and, in particular, the Politics Department at Princeton, which proved wonderfully supportive (and where conversations with Andy Moravcsik taught me much about the EU). Special thanks to Timothy Garton Ash for giving me a base at the European Studies Centre at St Antony's College, Oxford, at a difficult moment of transition.

Some sections in the Introduction use material from my 'The Triumph of What (If Anything)? Rethinking Political Ideologies and Political Institutions in Twentieth-Century Europe', in *Journal of Political Ideologies*, vol. 14 (2009); some parts of Chapter 4 repeat what I have said in 'Making Muslim Democracies', in *Boston Review* (November/December 2010); sections of Chapter 5 draw on my book *A Dangerous Mind: Carl Schmitt Post-War European Thought* (London: Yale University Press, 2003), on my '1968 as Event, Milieu and Ideology', in *Journal of Political Ideologies*, vol. 7 (2002), and on 'What Did They Think They Were Doing? The Political Thought of the West European '68', in Vladimir Tismaneanu (ed.), *Promises of 1968: Crisis, Illusion, and Utopia* (Budapest: Central European University Press, 2010). Some parts of Chapter 6 overlap with 'The Cold War and the Intellectual History of the Late Twentieth Century', in *The Cambridge History of the Cold War*, Vol. 3, ed. Melvyn P. Leffler and Odd Arne Westad (New York, Cambridge University Press, 2009). I am grateful for permissions to use the material here. Every effort has been made to trace copyright holders and any failure to cite them will be corrected in future editions.

André and Mark arrived during the writing of this book; Sophie soon after. They made it seem much less important in so many ways but also more urgent in others. They are citizens of what is already clearly discernible as a different kind of democratic age, an age when in all likelihood democracy will be contested in novel ways and will face unforeseen dangers. Will there remain any 'historical lessons' to be learnt from the story told here? I hope so. But, in any case, may the three of them be at least as lucky as the Western Europeans were – by and large – after '45.

Finally, the most important word of thanks to Erika, who for ten years accompanied the writing of this book with close, critical readings, spirited conversations and strong opinions, tireless attempts to make me understand what the history on the other side of the Iron Curtain really felt like – and with constant reminders of what a great fortune it is to share a family life and the life of the mind. The book is dedicated to her, with love.